Heinemann Business Studies

for AS Level

David Browne

Mick Baross

Wendy Davies

Rob Dransfield

Dave Needham

Heinemann Educational Publishers,
Halley Court, Jordan Hill, Oxford OX2 8EJ
A division of Reed Educational & Professional Publishing Ltd

Heinemann is a registered trademark of Reed Educational & Professional Publishing Limited

OXFORD MELBOURNE AUCKLAND JOHANNESBURG BLANTYRE GABORONE
IBADAN PORTSMOUTH NH (USA) CHICAGO

First published 2001
2004 2003 2002 2001
10 9 8 7 6 5 4 3 2 1

A catalogue record for this book is available from the British Library on request.

ISBN 0 435 45325 4

Typeset by 𝍍 Tek Art, Croydon, Surrey

Printed and bound in Great Britain by The Bath Press Ltd., Bath

Tel: 01865 888058

Website: www.heinemann.co.uk

CONTENTS

INTRODUCTION

In this book we have set out to provide you with the essential knowledge required by AS students in Business Studies. In writing it we recognised the importance of setting business in the context of an Internet world.

The Internet has transformed the structure of the global, national and local business world. The millennium marked a watershed in the way that business is conducted. The term 'the new economy' has been coined to identify the way in which a whole swathe of new Internet-based companies have developed. The 'old economy', as represented by firms that have been around for some time, is now alert to the need to embrace the new economy, and all major firms are rushing to develop an Internet presence. Indeed, large established companies have the most to gain from embracing new technologies which will enable them to cut their costs and to develop much closer links with individual customers.

This book therefore has been written to bring you right up to date with the realities of this new business world. The book consists of key sections to match national specification for the AS level. Each section contains a number of short, discrete chapters which will enable you to build the essential knowledge and understanding required for success in your examinations. Applied case studies are used to help you to think your way through the subject matter and to develop an enquiry-based approach to the subject. The 'Truth is stranger than fiction' section at the end of each chapter is designed to add a light-hearted touch to study. Throughout this text, you will find lots of questions that will test your knowledge and understanding. Not all of these questions are at AS level standard, but they will help you to internalise your learning and apply it to AS questions.

We believe that students and tutors will find this to be the most up-to-date coverage of contemporary Business Studies.

ACKNOWLEDGEMENTS

The authors would like to thank Margaret Berriman, our publisher over many years, Anna Fabrizio, Susan Ross and Andrew Nash. Thanks also go to Paul Plumridge and Anne Griffin for providing some useful material on Japanese management techniques. We are also grateful to the library staff at Nottingham Trent University.

The authors and publishers would like to thank the following individuals and organisations for permission to reproduce photographs and other copyright material:

pp. 14, 77 Press Association; p. 17 Dyson (left); pp. 17 (right), 50, 183 Roger Scruton; p. 25 British School of Motoring; p. 79 Popperfoto; p. 94 Co-operative Bank; p. 128 Courtesy of Richer Sounds; p. 134 Blue Circle Cement; p. 180 Courtesy of Volkswagen; p. 181 Rex Features/Crispen Rodwell; p. 184 Advertising Archives; p. 192 *General Studies Review*; p. 206 Selfridges; p. 209 Tony Stone; p. 212 Colorsport; p. 214 Photodisc; p. 218 John Walmsley; p. 225 Courtesy of Jaguar; pp. 342–347 Edexcel.

Every effort has been made to contact copyright holders of material published in this book. We would be glad to hear from unacknowledged sources at the first opportunity.

THE EXAMINER SPEAKS TO THE CANDIDATE

This section is addressed to the candidate taking the AS level examinations, but teachers also may find it of some relevance.

Both AS and Advanced GCE Business Studies examinations will be assessed by means of a 'Levels of Response' marking scheme. There are four Levels to be tested. Starting with the highest they are:

- **evaluation**
- **analysis**
- **application**
- **knowledge**.

It is not enough for you to show knowledge of areas of Business Studies theory, relevant legislation or recent and contemporary events in the business world. Your *knowledge must be applied* to the situations depicted in the examination paper, whether a case study, a data response question or a coursework or assignment topic. Most examination questions will require even more than this. You will be expected to analyse or evaluate in order to be rewarded at Levels 3 or 4.

At AS level, roughly 20 per cent of the marks in each paper will be awarded for analysis and 20 per cent for evaluation, leaving 30 per cent for application and 30 per cent for knowledge. For the full Advanced GCE, these proportions will be reversed for the three higher level units. Table 1 shows the percentage of marks allocated to each level.

Table 1 Percentage of marks allocated to each Level at AS level and the full GCE Advanced level

Level	AS level	Advanced level (full GCE)
1 Knowledge	30%	20%
2 Application	30%	20%
3 Analysis	20%	30%
4 Evaluation	20%	30%

The clue to the type of response required is given in the question set. For example a question seeking a Level 4 response will contain a keyword such as **evaluate**, **assess**, **justify**, or **recommend**. A response at Level 3 will be required if the question contains the word **analyse**.

Suppose a question is set in an examination on Unit 1 which, after presenting either some data on a situation in an imaginary business or an extract from a journal or newspaper, asks you to:

> Evaluate the ways in which Company X could improve motivation among its assembly line workers. **(10 marks)**

The mark scheme would outline some relevant points which candidates could make and would then contain guidelines as follows:

If the candidate only:

- shows knowledge of relevant motivational theory. **Level 1**
1–3 marks

But if the candidate:

- applies knowledge in the context of the data provided. **Level 2**
4–6 marks

However, if the candidate:

- analyses the information in the context of the data provided, but does not present a convincing conclusion, or the arguments may not be balanced. **Level 3**
7–8 marks

For the candidate who:

- evaluates the information in the context of the data provided and presents a conclusion which is justified. **Level 4**
9–10 marks

Thus, while evaluation is required for this question, candidates who do not provide it will still be rewarded at the highest level they achieve in their answer.

So, just what *is* required to reach the highest level?

Evaluation

Evaluation can be achieved by displaying any of the following skills which are appropriate to the question set:

1 **Assessment** or **appraisal** of the **validity** and **relevance** of the information given in the data or case study, or of information collected in researching a coursework title or assignment. In other words, is the source reliable, authoritative, or likely to be biased? For example, all articles in journals and newspapers are likely to be written from a certain 'angle' or be attempting to prove a point. Opinions of management and employees may differ. Why is this? Who presents the stronger case?

2   A discussion of both sides of a problem leading to a **conclusion**, which is reasoned and appears **justified** by the candidate's earlier discussion. For example, in the question about motivation posed above, a Level 4 answer would consider various methods and their relevance, consider factors like cost, time and expertise available, and present a conclusion or **recommendation** to the firm.

3   A recognition of the **limits or inadequacy of the data provided** and **a reasoned suggestion for additional information required** in order to give a more authoritative answer. In giving a 'reasoned suggestion' you would have to state not only what data is required, but *what use you would make of it*. For example, to state that 'I would want to see the firm's profit and loss account' may be relevant, but would only earn the highest marks if valid reasons were stated for needing this information and it was clear how the information in this document would be used. In the question about motivation presented above, you might suggest that a profile of the workforce or detailed job descriptions or an investigation of management style would help to assess the problem more accurately (assuming this information was not given by the examiner in the data relating to the question).

4   Some questions, notably in Unit 2 on the subject of marketing, might require you to **recommend a strategy**. A strategy requires that you show **links** between all the policies recommended and **prioritise** them by explaining why one factor or idea or problem is either the **most important** or should be **tackled first**.

5   Perhaps one of the most sophisticated evaluative skills is the **two-link argument**. For example, the **short-run** and **long-run effects** of a recommendation could be compared and contrasted, or a policy could be seen to produce advantages and disadvantages, so that a difficult choice would have to be made or a less than perfect solution be found (see Unit 1 for the concept of 'satisficing'). You may be understandably keen to present an 'answer', but often there is no simple answer to the fiendish problem posed by the (fiendish?) examiner, and a recognition of this, after suitable discussion, is perfectly acceptable. A **balanced** discussion is needed before a conclusion or recommendation is provided. A one-sided presentation is rarely evaluative, if only because examiners do not often set questions to which there is a straightforward and clear solution.

Analysis

Some questions might only be seeking analysis as the highest level of response required. For example, the question given above about motivation might have appeared as:

> Analyse the possible consequences of poor motivation of the workforce of Company X.

However, questions seeking a Level 4 response will still carry rewards for candidates who produce an analytical response, but do not manage to evaluate, as the mark scheme quoted earlier illustrates.

Analysis can be achieved by displaying any of the following skills which are appropriate to the question set:

1 Discussion of possible **causes and/or consequences** of the situation described in the data given in the examination paper. For example, with reference to the question stated above, poor motivation can lead to poor performance, unsatisfactory products, customer complaints, higher costs of quality control, absenteeism or a high rate of labour turnover.

2 Suggestions concerning the **advantages and/or disadvantages** of a course of action could be made. For example, offering employees a chance of promotion or more responsibility might result in better-quality work and a more enthusiastic attitude.

3 The above are example of the **one-link argument**. Perhaps immediate consequences might be identified, but not long-term ones or balancing points.

4 **Suggesting new data are needed** would be classed as analytical if the response were not made wholly clear or if there was no explanation of how these data would help to solve the problem. For example, to state that a firm's profit and loss statement would be needed so that the financial performance in the last year could be examined would be *analytical*. To specify the ratios which could be applied (see Unit 3) in order to assess specific areas of the firm's performance and suggest reasons for this performance would be *evaluative*.

5 To **break down into component parts** is an analytical skill. The different items of a marketing mix (see Unit 2) that are relevant to a specific problem could be identified, but the evaluative skill of linking and prioritising might not be displayed.

You may like to return to this section after studying the contents of each of the three units and before tackling the specimen questions provided at the end of each unit. (These questions are of an AS level type, but are not taken from actual papers that have been set.)

Remember at all times that, in order to achieve an answer at Level 3 or Level 4, you must bring some of *your own thinking* to your answer and produce something which is *not simply taken from the data* provided in the question or a standard textbook answer. Of course, you must display basic knowledge and understanding of the data as well. Analysis and evaluation cannot be displayed in a vacuum. It must be built upon knowledge and application of that knowledge to the data.

1 BUSINESS STRUCTURES, OBJECTIVES AND EXTERNAL INFLUENCES

INTRODUCTION   There are all sorts of **businesses** – small ones, medium-sized ones and large ones; businesses owned by one or two people, and those owned by thousands of shareholders; businesses that make things and others that sell things; businesses that are just starting out and ones that have been in existence for hundreds of years.

This unit will introduce you to:
1   the structure of business and business objectives
2   the external influences and constraints on business which affect the achievement of objectives
3   the internal organisation of business, with specific reference to the motivation of employees.

By the end of the unit you should be able to:
1   understand, interpret and analyse data relating to structures and objectives
2   analyse and evaluate data referring to external influences on business
3   assess appropriate strategies for the organisation and motivation of employees in a business organisation.

SECTION A *The structure of business*

INTRODUCTION   You need to understand the general pattern or structure of business activity in this country. In the UK in the 21st century, most businesses are small, but it is the big businesses that produce most of the goods that we consume – companies like Cadbury-Schweppes making food and drink, Unilever producing a range of household consumer goods ranging from margarine to soap powder, and BP and Shell producing a range of chemicals including petroleum.

A major change to the structure of business is that today the **service sector** of the economy is far more important than manufacturing in terms of the value of its output – services like insurance, banking, and leisure.

In the UK today most of the goods and services that we enjoy are provided by **private sector** businesses – ones owned by private citizens rather than the government. These private sector businesses seek to make a **profit** for their **shareholders** or other individuals who own them. However, businesses don't just seek to make a profit. They may have other objectives such as to be the firm that sells the most in the **market**, or even in come cases to provide a service to the community, as for example with the Co-operative Bank.

In the private sector of the economy businesses can take many forms, ranging from the sole trader (one-person business), such as a plumber or window cleaner, to the massive transnational corporation, like Coca-Cola or Heinz, which have operations and sell their products in nearly every country.

In the early 21st century we live in a business world of intense **competition** between rival companies. The structure of this competition varies from industry to industry, and between products. However, it is true to say that whenever firms are making sizeable profits then this will soon come to the attention of competitors who will quickly set up rival operations. Large corporations usually have the financial resources which enable them to quickly buy up existing firms which produce profitable goods and services.

Having a good understanding of the structure of business in this country will provide you with a firm foundation for the key units in your business course.

Critical thinking

In May 1999, the president of the Confederation of British Industry (CBI) referred to the state of businesses in the UK as the **champagne glass economy**. He described a situation in which company life is divided into five stages. First came the infant phase, when companies were starting up; second, the youth phase, when they may remain small and successful but also have the potential to develop into large national or global organisations; third was middle age, when there was fierce competition; fourth was the mid-life crisis, when companies merged and reorganised to

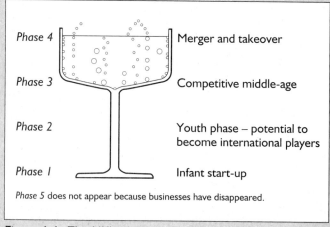

Figure 1.1 *The UK's champagne glass economy*

take each other over; and fifth, which might be reached if the outcome of the fourth was unsatisfactory, was decline and death (see Figure 1.1).

He argued that Britain had plenty of companies in stage one and a good number in stages three and four. Most of those in stage five had been swept away in the 1980s. But the problem was the lack of companies in stage two. We do not build our small businesses into world-class players, he reflected.

A few British companies have leapt to world-class status in the past few years, but not many. With the exception of the telecommunications company Vodaphone Airtouch, most companies, even those with the latest technology, have remained quite small.

One of the main explanations for the lack of British businesses at the youth phase compared with the USA, where there are plenty, is cultural. In the USA a higher proportion of people than in the UK are determined to start up and then grow businesses by putting a lot of time and effort into them. In the UK many people set up a business in order to gain independence and to earn the money to enable them to do what they really want to do. They prefer to have balanced, well-rounded lives rather than to work night and day to create a business empire.

WHAT DO YOU THINK?

1 Do you think that people in the UK who set up their own businesses are more interested in earning a living than in creating a business empire?
2 If this were true, is it a good or a bad thing?
3 If Britain does have a 'champagne glass economy' with few businesses at stage two, what problems is this likely to create for the UK economy in the longer term?

Chapter 1 *The structure of business*

Most advanced industrial societies such as the UK, Japan, France, Germany and the USA have experienced a number of waves of development (see Figure 1.2).

Before the Industrial Revolution of the nineteenth century, people relied on agricultural activities for a livelihood. Some people settled on farms while others roamed with their flocks.

Eventually, **agriculture** became productive enough to allow specialists to be released from farming work to set up as traders and shopkeepers, as well as specialist manufacturers of items such as shoes, clothes, etc. As people became richer they were able to purchase clothes and household items on a larger scale, so that there was enough demand to encourage the development of factory production – hence the arrival of the industrial society.

The development of factories and machines was the dominant influence in the industrial age. Large numbers of people worked in factories, and their work was often dominated by

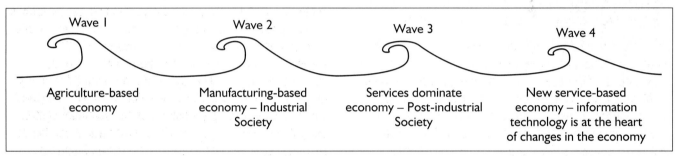

Wave 1	Wave 2	Wave 3	Wave 4
Agriculture-based economy	Manufacturing-based economy – Industrial Society	Services dominate economy – Post-industrial Society	New service-based economy – information technology is at the heart of changes in the economy

Figure 1.2 Waves of development

CASE STUDY: THE TRANSFORMATION OF 'BIG BLUE'

IBM, or 'Big Blue' as it was affectionately known, was one of the major success stories of the latter part of the twentieth century, and the USA's major computer company until Microsoft began to dominate the market.

For many years, the emphasis at IBM was on producing computers and the software that helped businesses large and small to run.

However, right at the end of the twentieth century, IBM realised that increasingly communications were going to be dominated by Internet links. The company already had a strong presence in this field producing networks which help the Internet to run effectively and in creating links with the Internet. It therefore put a substantial part of its resources (as much as 50 per cent) into new activities which involved providing the know-how and equipment to enable other companies to develop their electronic business (e-business), that is, helping these businesses to develop web sites and a range of other links with customers and suppliers using the Internet. Banks and retailers are therefore using the expertise, know-how and equipment provided by IBM to develop their new forms of e-business and e-commerce (buying and selling through the Internet).

QUESTIONS FOR DISCUSSION

1 How can IBM be said to have provided a link between the industrial, service and new service economies?

2 Why do you think IBM has put so much of its resources into helping other businesses to operate successfully in the new service economy?

Table 1.1 The structure of Ghana's economy

	Percentage of GDP			
	1976	**1986**	**1996**	**2006***
Agriculture	50.6	47.8	44.4	40.0
Industry	19.2	17.2	16.6	16.0
Manufacturing	13.1	11.1	9.4	8.0
Services	30.2	35.1	38.9	44.0

*estimate

Source: *World Bank Report*

Table 1.2 Growth in each sector of Ghana's economy

	Percentage			
	1976	**1986**	**1996**	**2006***
Agriculture	1.0	2.4	4.0	4.0
Industry	−5.8	4.6	4.2	4.0
Manufacturing	−6.1	2.9	3.0	3.5
Services	1.5	6.6	6.5	7.0

* estimate

Source: *World Bank Report*

the needs of the machines that they had to work with (for example, the speed with which they had to work).

The UK in the nineteenth century was one of the world's great manufacturers. In the twentieth century we saw the increasing growth of services. Whereas **manufacturing** is concerned with the production of physical products such as shoes, foodstuffs, furniture, etc., **services** are concerned with providing 'intangible' benefits (things that you can't physically touch or see) to businesses and to people. Services to businesses include the rovision of insurance and finance. Services to people include having your hair cut, or being able to watch a film at the cinema, as well as the postal service and insurance. As working hours fell during the twentieth century people began increasingly to purchase services associated with leisure, for example a visit to a local l eisure centre or golf club.

However, perhaps the biggest transformation in the economy has come in the past few years with the rise of the **Internet**, and other revolutionary changes in **information and communications technology (ICT)**. The ICT revolution has reduced costs for most (if not all) manufacturers, while at the same time creating a service revolution, for example telephone banking and home delivery shopping using the Internet.

We can see the transformation of society through waves of development by considering the recent history of industrialisation in Ghana, West Africa. To understand this, we need to look at the structure of the country's economy through its **gross domestic product (GDP)** and the growth in each sector of Ghana's economy (see Tables 1.1 and 1.2). (GDP is a measure of the total value of output in a country in a given year.)

Tables 1.1 and 1.2 show that the economy does not grow in smooth patterns (for example, you can see the impact of a recession/downturn in economic activity in 1976). However, it does show the growing importance of the services sector, such that by 1996 it accounted for nearly 40 per cent of the value of production in the economy and was rapidly replacing agriculture as the dominant sector. The rate of growth of the services sector was much faster than the rate of growth in manufacturing and industry.

In the UK today production is dominated by the services sector of the economy, which accounts for almost 70 per cent of the value of production and continues to grow in importance. This trend is a reflection of changing patterns of consumption in advanced modern economies. Table 1.3 shows the change in weekly household expenditure in Britain between 1957 and 1996 and clearly shows the change in household buying as a percentage of income away from agricultural and industrial products towards the consumption of services.

The primary, secondary and tertiary sectors

Production is usually classified under the following three headings:

- The **primary sector** is concerned with taking out 'the gifts of nature', that is, extracting natural resources.
- The **secondary sector** is concerned with constructing and making things.
- The **tertiary (services) sector** is made up of two parts:
  - commercial services involving trading activity
  - direct services to people.

Table 1.3 Weekly household expenditure, 1957 and 1996

| | 1957 | | | 1996 | |
Item	Amount spent per week (£)	Percentage of total income	Item	Amount spent per week (£)	Percentage of total income
Food	£4.77	33.0	Food and non-alcoholic drinks	£55.10	18.0
Clothing and footwear	£1.45	10.0	Leisure goods and services	£49.10	16.0
Services	£1.25	8.7	Housing	£49.10	16.0
Housing	£1.24	8.7	Transport	£48.70	15.7
Transport and vehicles	£1.16	8.0	Household goods and services	£43.10	14.0
Durable household goods	£1.09	7.6	Clothing and footwear	£18.30	6.0
Other goods	£1.04	7.6	Fuel and power	£13.30	4.3
Fuel, light and power	£0.87	6.0	Alcoholic drinks	£12.40	4.0
Tobacco	£0.87	6.0	Personal goods and services	£11.60	3.8
Alcoholic drinks	£0.46	3.2	Tobacco	£6.10	2.0
Pocket money to children	£0.07	0.5	Miscellaneous	£2.20	0.7
Total:	**£14.27**			**£309.10**	

Source: *Family Expenditure Survey*

Table 1.4 Occupations by sector

| Primary | Secondary | Tertiary | |
		Commercial services	Direct services
Oil drilling	Oil refining	Petrol retailing	Hairdressing
Farming	Food processing	Food transportation	Police
Coal mining	Building work	Wholesaling	Chiropody
Forestry	Brewing	Business insurance	Household insurance

Table 1.4 illustrates some examples of occupations that would fit into each category. You should add to this list.

The economy is made up of a number of component parts or 'sectors'. **Sectors** may be defined widely to include groups of industries (for example the energy industries) or narrowly drawn to identify parts of industries (for example solar panel supply), depending on the purpose in making the definition.

In addition to the primary, secondary and tertiary sectors, the following are also important:

- The **goods sector** is the primary and secondary sectors combined.
- The **production sector** (production industries) includes the secondary sector together with mining and quarrying from the primary sector. The term **industry** is widely used to mean this sector, and an index (measure) of industrial production is drawn up on this basis.

The secondary sector includes the following sub-classifications (in the UK):

- metals, minerals and mineral products
- chemicals and artificial fibres
- engineering
- food, drink and tobacco
- textiles, footwear, clothing and leather goods
- building
- civil engineering.

The tertiary sector is subdivided into:

- retailing
- distribution
- hotels and catering
- banking and finance
- post and telecommunications
- public administration
- education
- health services.

The truth is stranger than fiction

In the 1950s and 1960s the pop music industry was born in this country at a time when the textiles industry was still a significant employer. Today, 'Cool Britannia', that is, pop music, films and videos, contributes more to the UK economy and employs more people than the remnants of our textiles industry. This trend is representative of the significant restructuring of the UK economy.

Chapter 2 *The mixed economy*

In the UK we have a **mixed economy**. The mixture is made up of economic decisions taken by the government and decisions taken by private citizens and private organisations (see Figure 1.3).

The UK economy lies somewhere between two extremes – a **completely planned economy**, where all economic decisions are made by the government, and a **completely free enterprise economy**, where there is no government interference in the decisions made by private citizens and organisations (see Figure 1.4).

In this book one of the key themes will be the way in which the balance of decision making is continually switching between 'a little more private decision making, or a little bit more government decision making'.

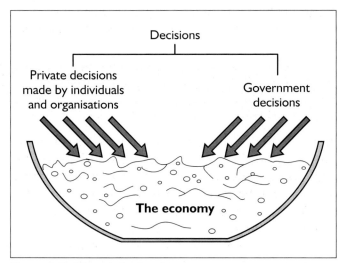

Figure 1.3 *The mixing bowl economy*

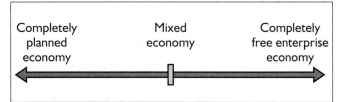

Figure 1.4 *Types of economy*

WHAT DO YOU THINK?
In mid-2000 the Labour government was still pressing ahead with plans to hand over air traffic control, from being a government-run service, to being a service run by private firms. Who do you think should be responsible for air traffic control? Why?

Economic systems

All societies must develop a system for dealing with three interrelated problems:

- **What will be produced?** For example, should we produce more military goods or non-military goods; should we spend more money on education?
- **How will it be produced?** For example, will goods be produced in the private sector or by government (the public sector); will goods be produced using lots of machinery, or with lots of labour?
- **For whom will it be produced?** For example, will goods be produced for the most needy or those with the most money; will profits go to employees or to shareholders?

The systems which developed to deal with these problems in the twentieth century were:

- The **planned system**, characteristic (in the past) of eastern European economies (such as the former Soviet Union and Poland), China, North Korea and other parts of South-East Asia such as North Vietnam. These systems were most in evidence from the 1950s until the late 1980s. They stemmed from the communist ideas of Karl Marx and others. Writing in the nineteenth century, Marx had argued that society would only work to serve the needs of all people if it was based on communist principles, that is, a state based on equality where there would be no master or slave, no factory owner or wage slave.

- The **free enterprise system**, with very little government interference in the economy, characterised by economies such as Hong Kong, Taiwan, and Mauritius. The free enterprise system is controlled by the market, that is, a free arrangement involving trade between buyers and sellers. Prices determine what is bought and sold. Consumers are able to signal their preferences to producers and sellers of goods by bidding with their money for the items that they want produced. Producers therefore simply serve the needs of the consumer.

- **Mixed economies**, covering most of the economies of the world in the twentieth century, including the USA, the countries of the European Union, Japan, South Korea, etc. A mixed economy combines central planning (that is, the role of government in decision making) with free enterprise (through the existence of a self-regulating market place).

CASE STUDY: MAKING PLANS IN A CENTRALLY PLANNED ECONOMY

In the former Soviet Union state planners created five-year plans for the whole economy. The five-year plan would set out which industries were to be given priority, and the quantity of resources that would be allocated to each industry – for example so much coal would be produced for the steel industry, so much steel would go into bridge production, etc. At one stage planning took place in a large aircraft hangar. The planners moved tokens around on a diagram which showed resources being moved from one industry to another.

It was the Soviet leader Stalin who originally introduced the policy of centralisation. During the 1920s and 1930s, Stalin rapidly expanded industrial production and brought most firms under state ownership. He also introduced a system of 'collectivised' farming. Land owned by better-off peasants was confiscated and turned into large holdings owned by the state or collectives of peasants so that eventually 99 per cent of all land was collectively or state owned.

At first, the system was successful in industrialising the Soviet Union, providing full employment and boosting food production. In the long term, however, it stifled enterprise because all decisions were taken centrally. Bureaucrats began to build their own empires and lose touch with the needs of consumers.

QUESTIONS FOR DISCUSSION

1 What do you see as being the main merits of central planning?
2 Do you think that central planning would be suitable for running the economy of the UK?
3 What would be the main drawbacks to a system of central planning?

CASE STUDY: THE FALL OF COMMUNISM

Slavenka Draculic, the Yugoslavian writer, in her book *Forward to the Past*, tells how she finally realised that there was no future for communism. She believes that communism foundered in a soggy mire of scratchy brown lavatory paper. She describes the coarse, dark sheets of *Golub* she used in her childhood; then the soft, pink rolls eventually achieved by 'socialism with a human face' of the 1970s; then the day in 1985, when she stood with her 17-year-old daughter in a chemist's shop, arguing bitterly because the recent price rises meant that they had had to go back to *Golub*. Her daughter refused point blank to adopt this symbol of poverty and Draculic knew then that it was all over:

'This was how the Communists lost: when the first free elections came in May 1990, the entire younger generation voted against *Golub*, against shortages, deprivation, double standards and false promises.'

The collapse of communist regimes in eastern Europe in the early 1990s had, according to historians, many complex causes.

In looking for political causes, they point out that Mikhail Gorbachev, who became leader of the Soviet Communist Party in 1985, allowed criticism of the state after 50 years of repression. The process of *glasnost* (openness) made the workings of the government less secretive. This allowed new political parties to set themselves up. New nationalist groups, such as those in the Baltic republics, began to demand independence. *Glasnost* spread through eastern Europe like wildfire.

However, perhaps the most important factor behind the fall of communism has been the failure of the economic system. Communist parties failed to achieve one of their central objectives – to improve living standards.

Decisions, problems, choices and resources

Economic decisions are ones which are concerned with solving the main **economic problems** of society: that is, making **choices** about how **scarce resources** should be used.

An example of a scarce resource is metal. In a planned economy the government would decide what to do with the metal which is available in a society, for example how much of it should go into making weapons, how much into creating factory machinery, how much into motor cars, etc. In a free enterprise economy it would be business organisations that would decide what to do with the metal available. Profitable enterprises would be able to buy up metal and use it to make the sorts of goods that consumers were prepared to pay for, such as washing machines, frames and components, metal furniture, car bodies and so on. In a mixed economy some of the decisions would be made by the government, for example a National Health Service purchase of a body scanner, and some of the decisions would be made by private firms, such as the purchase by a firm of metal and other raw materials to make exercise bikes for health-conscious customers.

In any society, resources are scarce relative to the number of uses to which they can be put. A **resource** is a means of support and is any part of our environment which helps to support us and improve our well-being. Examples are food to satisfy our need for nourishment and the pleasure of eating; fibres that go into producing clothes which cover our nakedness, give us warmth and help us to make fashion statements; metals that go into a thousand and one household appliances, etc.

There are two main types of resources:

- **physical or natural resources** – such as oil, climate, water, minerals, forests and fisheries
- **human resources** – people and their various skills.

If we were to take stock of the world's existing bundle of resources we would find that there are severe limitations to its ability to meet our infinite wants.

Scarce resources can be broken down into:

- **land** – includes all natural resources
- **labour** – includes all physical and mental effort
- **capital** – includes machinery and other items that go into furthering production
- **enterprise** – the art of combining the other three factors in the production process.

These four production resources are termed the **factors of production**.

Major points of difference

Table 1.5 summarises the main differences between a centrally planned economy and a free enterprise economy.

Table 1.5 The differences between centrally planned and free enterprise economies

Centrally planned economy	Free enterprise economy
Central control of economic choices	Individual consumers and business decision makers make individual choices
Driving force behind economic activity is the mutual benefits for members of society	Driving force behind economic activity is self-interest
Planning is the decision making mechanism	The price system is the decision making mechanism
State ownership	Private ownership
State monopoly	Competition

In a mixed economy you will find elements of both the left- and the right-hand columns of Table 1.5 mixed together. An economy that wants to move away from central planning will increasingly move towards the characteristics shown in the right-hand column.

The truth is stranger than fiction

The centrally planned system in eastern Europe led to all sorts of anomalies. One of its major benefits was that everyone had a job of sorts to do, and was provided with basics such as bread. However, resources were not always used in the most efficient way. For example, the UK Chancellor of the Exchequer Norman Lamont reported that during a visit to Kiev in 1991 he had seen a Kazakh woman selling water melons on a street corner. She had flown thousands of miles to Kiev using subsidised state transport. Clearly, the price which she was charging for her melons was nowhere near the cost of getting them to the market.

Chapter 3 *Public and private sectors*

One way to classify organisations is whether they operate in the private or the public sector of the economy.

The **private sector** is made up of organisations that are owned and run by one or more private individuals or other groups. The sector includes organisations such as your local newsagent, baker and dentist as well as much larger organisations such as the food retailer Iceland.com, Boots the chemists, NatWest Bank and oil producer Shell (see Figure 1.5).

The **public sector** is made up of organisations which are owned and run by national or local government. The sector includes organisations such as the BBC, the Bank of England, the Department of Social Security and most hospitals, libraries and schools.

Today, many types of organisation are found in both the private and public sectors, for example *some* hospitals and schools are privately owned and are paid for by the payment of fees and other charges, whereas *most* schools and hospitals receive much of their funding from central government.

In the private sector of the economy the objective of making **profits** is a major business motivation. In the public sector it is also important because if the government and its agents are to use public money well, then they will need to show a suitable rate of return on money invested. There should be no resources wasted in either the public or the private sectors.

The private sector

The importance of profit in the private sector

A 'good private sector business' must display all of the following characteristics:

- It makes a profit by supplying products or services that people want to buy.
- It contributes to its own and the community's long-term prosperity by making the best possible use of resources.
- It minimises waste of every kind and where possible promotes the use of recycling.
- It respects the environment, locally, nationally and globally.
- It sets performance standards for its suppliers – and helps in their achievement.
- It offers its employees worthwhile career prospects, professional training, job satisfaction and a safe working environment.
- It expects the best from its employees and rewards them accordingly.
- It acts at all times as a good citizen, aware of its influence on the rest of society, including the local communities nearby its factories and offices.

A private sector company therefore has responsibilities which extend well beyond its own purely commercial ambitions. However, it should organise itself in such a way that it can meet all its responsibilities and still make a profit.

Unless it does, it cannot afford to modernise itself, install new technologies, or take commercial risks with, say, new product ranges. Nor can it continue to fulfil its social responsibilities. Nor can it justify the investment of its owners – private individuals or institutions such as pension funds and insurance companies – who need to seek the best possible long-term return on their resources.

In a free competitive market, and in all but the shortest term, profit is the measure of how good a private sector business is, how well run and how effectively it meets its responsibilities. Unless it makes a profit, a business has no reason to exist and its assets, most particularly the energies and skills of its staff, will be better employed elsewhere.

Figure 1.5 Well-known private sector organisations

Not-for-profit organisations

While most businesses in the private sector place a heavy emphasis on profit, there are others which are set up for charitable purposes (and therefore operate on a not-for-profit basis). However, most **charities** today are run on well-organised business lines, with salaried officials and clear targets and goals.

In the UK many large and small charities receive donations which they then use for the purposes of the particular charity.

CASE STUDY: NOT FOR PROFIT . . . OXFAM GB

Oxfam GB is a charity whose trustees are legally responsible under the Charities Acts for all the organisation's activities. Oxfam GB is also incorporated as a registered limited company and must comply with the requirements of the Companies Act 1985.

Oxfam's structure

The Council

Oxfam's trustees form the Council, which is the governing body of Oxfam, and meets approximately seven times a year. Trustees, who are all unpaid volunteers, are responsible in law for everything Oxfam does.

These responsibilities are:

- to ensure that Oxfam abides by its charitable aims and constitution, and operates within the law
- to be accountable ultimately for the overall management of Oxfam
- to ensure that income and assets are used to help Oxfam's beneficiaries, and that its finances are properly and effectively managed and monitored
- to set policy and objectives, and to ensure the monitoring of their implementation and evaluation of the results
- to preserve Oxfam's good name and reputation.

There are between ten and twelve members of the Council. Trustees serve on the Council for three years with the possibility of a second consecutive three-year term of office, extendible up to nine years in the case of honorary officers.

Oxfam's Association

The Association can have up to 32 members. It is made up of all the current trustees, plus around 20 other members. The Association has powers to remove and replace trustees in the event of a major failure or default on the part of the Council.

The Assembly

The Assembly is a body of Oxfam people who facilitate informed debate and exchange of views between the various interests and voices within Oxfam on issues of strategic or corporate importance. The Assembly actively encourages a growing involvement in Oxfam debates by volunteers, staff, partners, advisers, and Friends of Oxfam. It has about 140 members, including all Association members and therefore all trustees. The Assembly has no decision making powers, but enables decision makers to hear a wide range of views on policy issues.

Staff and volunteers

There are approximately 23,000 Oxfam volunteers in Great Britain, in roles throughout the organisation. About 1,300 staff are employed by Oxfam in Great Britain, including staff with UK citizenship on contracts overseas. Of this number, about 700 staff are based at Oxfam House in Oxford. There are about 1,500 locally recruited staff working overseas.

QUESTIONS FOR DISCUSSION

1 In what ways is a charity like Oxfam similar to a private sector company?
2 How is Oxfam different from a private sector company?
3 What evidence is provided in the case study that Oxfam is concerned to meet the requirements of a number of interested groups (rather than shareholders in the case of a company)?

Charities are normally set up to meet a defined need, or to provide help to a specific section of the community. Many UK charities such as Oxfam and War Child collect money to be spent on projects overseas. The donations received by the charity constitute its income. The amount of income remaining after the charity has paid its running costs can be used for charitable purposes. Charities therefore need to operate in a businesslike way if they are going to make best use of their resources.

Voluntary organisations also set out to serve people rather than to make profits – their volunteers are unpaid.

The public sector

In the nineteenth century the **government** played only a very limited part in running business organisations and its activities were restricted to specific state activities, for example the establishment of the Post Office and, of course, running certain military concerns such as the Royal Docks.

However, during the twentieth century the hand of government became more widespread. In particular the two world wars saw the government take over an increasing number of essential industries which were seen as 'the commanding heights' of the economy. After World War II the country elected a Labour government and increasingly industries were **nationalised**, that is, taken over by the government, for example coal, steel and the railways. The 1960s and 1970s saw considerable parts of major industries being taken over by the government.

However, the election of a Conservative government in 1979 saw a complete turnaround in this policy. From 1979 the emphasis was on **privatisation**, with industries being

CASE STUDY: LEADING THINKER

Margaret Thatcher (Figure 1.6) was one of the leading advocates of reducing the role of the public sector and encouraging the private sector. One of her most famous speeches included the following statement:

'Too many people have been given to understand that if they have a problem it's the government's job to cope with it … They're casting their problem on society. And, you know, there is no such thing as society. There are individual men and women, and there are families. And no government can do anything except through people, and people must look to themselves first. It's our duty to look after ourselves and then, also, to look after our neighbour. People have got the entitlements too much in mind, without the obligations. There's no such thing as entitlement, unless someone has first met an obligation.'

Figure 1.6 Margaret Thatcher, Conservative prime minister 1979–90, with her husband, Dennis

QUESTIONS FOR DISCUSSION

1 What do you think Margaret Thatcher was saying about the role of the public and private sectors in the economy?
2 Do you agree with her?

3 What are the implications for the role that:
   a) the government
   b) individuals and organisations
   play in the economy?

returned to private shareholders. Indeed, Britain was to lead the world in this sphere, increasingly to be copied by other countries. An extension of this movement was the privatisation of state industries as former communist countries in eastern Europe turned to the market system in the late 1980s and the 1990s. The Labour government elected in 1997 has continued with this commitment to creating a competitive market, although it believes in seeking to make sure that social provision is still made for the weak and needy (that is, it believes in the **social market**).

There are three major elements of public sector involvement in industry:

- Direct state participation in industry through public corporations known as the nationalised industries and other Crown corporations. Not many of these are left today. The best known example is the BBC, which is regarded by many as the world's premier broadcasting body. It is funded by a licence fee paid by everyone with a television set. The BBC's Charter gives the Corporation a responsibility to represent the diversity of modern society and to provide a channel for bringing the nation together for key occasions, such as the FA Cup Final.
- Industries in which there is public-sector involvement together with private investment, for example the government held a 39 per cent share in the oil producer BP from before the Second World War until the late 1980s when the shares were sold to the public.
- Industries in which there is a public sector involvement at local government level rather than at the level of national government.

A fourth group that can be identified is businesses that receive support from the government to establish new activities, such as research and development or product development in a particular field.

Privatisation

Since 1979 when Margaret Thatcher's Conservative government first came to power, the most significant feature of public sector/private sector relations has been the wide scale privatisation of industries (see Figure 1.7).

In addition, privatisations have included the sale of council houses, the contracting out of local-authority controlled services such as street cleaning, and the introduction of private prisons.

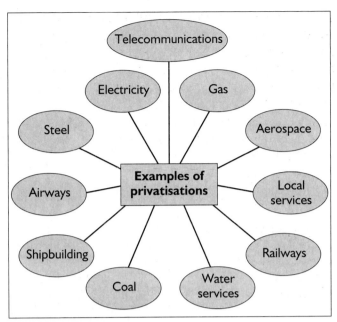

Figure 1.7 The privatised industries

Reasons for privatisation

Those in favour of privatisation have argued the following:

- State-run firms are not efficient because they do not have any real competition and do not risk going bankrupt, because the government will always pay off their debts.
- In a modern society as many people as possible should have shares in business. The idea is that everyone – not just the very rich – should become shareholders; people have therefore been encouraged to buy, in some cases, just a few hundred pounds' worth of shares in enterprises like British Telecom.
- Many public corporations were top heavy and slow to react in today's market place. People in these corporations had secure jobs because the state would pay for any losses they made. They could therefore carry high levels of inefficiency for a number of years. Employees did not feel obliged to provide a high-quality service for people. The corporations were therefore product orientated rather than consumer orientated.

The case against privatisation

Those against privatisation have argued the following:

- Competition can be harmful in areas where standards need to be maintained, such as the National Health Service. Competition can lead to 'cutting corners' and to the deterioration of safety standards, for example in maintaining track and signalling systems on the railways.

- It is a nonsense to sell to the public shares in industries that are already owned by the people. Instead of an industry being owned by all citizens, it then became the property of shareholders.

Regulating the privatised industries

In order to maintain some government influence in the newly privatised industries, official **regulators** were created to set up and maintain a framework of requirements in which the privatised industries would operate, for example OFWAT (in the water industry) and OFGAS (in the gas industry). The regulator, for example, creates formulas which limit the ability of privatised industries to raise prices, and also creates standards for quality performance such as the delivery of services to households, water quality, etc. So privatised industries operate in a competitive environment which encourages them to increase efficiency while at the same time they have to make sure that they do not allow standards to drop in a way that is harmful to the interests of the public.

The truth is stranger than fiction

When train services were run by British Rail, a UK public corporation, there were endless jokes about the inefficiency of the state-run industry. It was said that trains rarely if ever ran on time and that other aspects left a lot to be desired, from surly railway porters to 'cardboard-tasting' sandwiches served in the buffet cars.

However, in terms of efficiency the privatised rail services also appear to be failing. In 1999 record levels of complaints were made to the regulators about late services. In late 1999 Railtrack, which is responsible for maintaining track and other physical capital of the railway system, had to spend £2 million trimming station platform edges by a few millimetres because additional equipment on new sliding-door trains to be used on routes in south-east England had made the trains wider! Twenty stations were affected including Dover and Hastings.

Chapter 4 Role of entrepreneurs

Governments in recent years have all stressed the importance of **enterprise** in the economy. **Entrepreneurs** are people who take risks and bring together the various ingredients that are required to ensure business success.

Today, many of the modern products that we are able to enjoy stem from the drive and enterprise of particular individuals. Below are some examples (see Figure 1.8).

The vacuum cleaner, 1902

Engineer Hubert Cecil Booth's first British vacuum cleaner was a rather unwieldy machine – almost one and a half metres high, one and a half metres long and over a metre wide – and cost £350. Painted bright red and driven by a five-horsepower piston engine, it was carried through the streets of London on a horse-drawn cart which was parked outside the building to be cleaned. The hoses were taken into the building by operators wearing white drill suits. It was not long before portable machines were developed and it became a social occasion to invite friends round for a cup of tea and to watch the carpet being vacuumed! Because very few homes at that time had electricity, the early portable machines had to be hand operated by two people: one maid pumped the bellows to create the suction and a second operated the cleaning tool.

Figure 1.8 The best things since sliced bread! Mars and the Dyson Dual-Cyclone

The paper cup, 1908

At the start of the twentieth century, petrol stations and public buildings in the USA offered free water from a shared tin cup. Harvard University drop-out Hugh Moore thought it was unhygienic and with a friend, Lawrence Luellan, invented a water cooler that came with disposable cups. Fears of passing germs led to shared drinking cups being banned in some towns in the USA, leading to a ready market for the 'public cup', later called the Dixie cup.

Sliced bread, 1928

Sliced bread holds a particularly important place in the development of new ideas for consumer products leading to the saying, 'The best thing since sliced bread'. In 1928 Otto Frederick Rohwedder's sliced-bread machine went on the market leading to a bread revolution. Otto had been told in 1915 that he had only a year to live, and then lost everything in a fire in 1922. So his first pre-sliced wrapped bread, sold in a bakery at Battle Creek in Michigan, USA, really was a wonder loaf. By 1933 about 80 per cent of all bread was sliced and wrapped.

The Mars Bar, 1932

The first Mars Bar was first sold for two old pennies (1p) in 1932. Forrest E. Mars, the son of a US confectioner, brought his recipe to Britain and began producing the bars at a rented factory in Slough, Berkshire. The hand-made bar with layers of nougat, caramel and milk chocolate was an immediate success. It was such a valuable energy source that it was distributed to the armed forces during World War II. When rationing ended, the bar was heavily promoted with the slogan, 'A Mars a day helps you work, rest and play'. Today, Mars makes 3 million bars a day.

The shopping trolley, 1937

If shoppers have only a basket to carry goods in, there is a limit to how much they can buy. So, in 1937, Sylvan Goldman, manager of Oklahoma City's Humpty Dumpty supermarket, decided to boost trade by putting an extra-large shopping basket on wheels. It doubled his trade.

The ring-pull, 1962

The Iron City Brewery Company of Pittsburgh, Pennsylvania, changed the face of casual drinking in 1962. It developed a can with a pre-scored keyhole in the top which was peeled back by pulling an attached ring. The public quickly took to the new invention and in 1964 beer sales shot up by 1.5 billion cans.

The hover mower, 1963

A Swedish inventor, Karl Dahlman, dreamed of a lawnmower that needed no wheels and floated on a cushion of air. In 1963, inspired by the hovercraft developed by Briton Christopher Cockerell, he produced his first hover-mower – the Flymo (the flying mower). The company became part of the electrical goods manufacturer Electrolux six years later, and the Flymo now accounts for half of the mower market in Britain.

The baby buggy, 1965

The Maclaren baby buggy was the great leap forward from the pram. Former test pilot and retired aeronautical engineer Owen Finlay Maclaren, who designed the undercarriage of the Spitfire, took out a patent in 1965. The design brought a new lightness to baby carriages with an aluminium frame of 3 kg and a folding mechanism that made the buggy collapse as easily as an umbrella.

The calculator, 1972

The first calculator that was actually pocket sized (9.5 mm by 140 mm) was the Sinclair Executive. Invented by Clive Sinclair in 1972, it was far more successful than his later battery-operated C5 car.

Post-It note, 1981

American research chemist Spencer Silver was working for the 3M Corporation trying to produce the strongest glue in history when, in 1970, he spectacularly failed by inventing a glue that wouldn't stick permanently to anything. It was 11 years before a colleague, Arthur Fry, found a use for it. Every Sunday he marked his hymn book at church with slips of paper that promptly fell out when he opened the book. A gummed slip that could be removed with leaving a mark was the perfect answer.

Where do business ideas come from?

Most people at some time or another think about setting up an enterprise of their own. You will hear people say things like: 'Someone could make a fortune out of selling such and such' or 'If I had some money, I could make a business out of making this or that'. Entrepreneurs like Dahlman, Mars, Sinclair and Maclaren had the courage to put their ideas into practice.

Where does the idea to set up an enterprise like Mars or Maclaren come from? Some people copy ideas that they have seen somewhere else (such as selling flowers at a busy railway station). Other people spot a gap in the market – 'Nobody round here runs a mobile disco service!' Others turn a hobby into a business – 'I always enjoy making wooden toys!' Other businesses start from brilliant new inventions such as Post-Its, hover mowers, vacuum cleaners, etc. These are just some of the ways in which people come up with business ideas.

However, there is more to being entrepreneurial than simply coming up with a good idea. The entrepreneur will turn a good idea into an actual proposition that works. For every successful entrepreneur there are millions of dreamers who never progressed beyond the 'ideas' stage of a new project. The entrepreneur will make things happen and is often referred to as a 'mover and shaker'. To be entrepreneurial therefore you usually have to be very hard working, and have the commitment and confidence to marshal people and other resources behind a plan of action. Indeed many entrepreneurs will poach someone else's good idea and put it into practice!

Entrepreneurs are prepared to take **risks** (see Figure 1.9). In life there are some people who are inclined to take risks (it is a natural part of their personality). Others are 'risk averse' (reluctant to take risks).

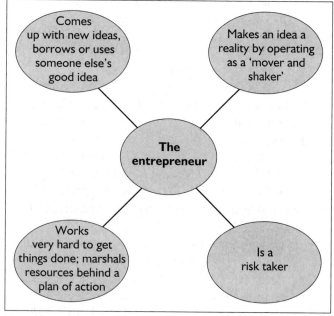

Figure 1.9 What makes an entrepreneur

Enterprise as a factor of production

The four factors of production may be explained as follows:

- The term **land** refers to all natural resources, for example farmland, water, coal, etc. The reward to the landowner is termed rent.
- **Labour** refers to all the physical and mental contributions of an employee. So it is more than just the physical effort of digging coal, or making car parts. It also includes the mental effort of an accountant or the services and skill provided by a hairdresser. The reward for labour is wages.
- **Capital** includes all those items that go into producing other things, for example a machine to manufacture products, the tools that contribute to this process, and so on. Machines, tools and buildings are all examples of

CASE STUDY: A CENTURY OF ASPIRIN, 1899–1999

- Ancient Egyptians took an infusion of dried myrtle leaves to treat muscle pain, while Hippocrates, the father of modern medicine, prescribed willow bark tea for the pain of childbirth. The active ingredient of both these remedies is salicylic acid – aspirin's active ingredient.
- In Britain in 1758 the Reverend Edward Stone chewed a twig of white willow to ease pain and fever. He was so impressed with its effect that he wrote to the Royal Society in 1763 to alert the members to its benefits.
- In 1835 the German chemist Karl Jakob Lowig found a second source of salicylic acid in meadow sweet, a wild flower plant that grows on riverbanks.
- By 1853 salicylic acid was successfully being synthesised in the laboratory, enabling mass production for the first time. But while it was effective in reducing fever and relieving pain, its side-effects were unpleasant – severe irritation of the mouth, oesophagus and stomach.
- Felix Hoffmann, a young graduate working for the German pharmaceuticals company Bayer, had a severely arthritic father who couldn't take salicylic acid because of the side-effects. He asked his son to create a milder alternative, and in 1897 Felix invented acetyl salicylic acid (ASA), a new formulation that was more gentle.
- After initial experiments proved unsuccessful the head of Bayer's testing lab decided to suspend temporarily further development work on the drug while they proceeded with what appeared to be more promising opportunities – in this case the development of heroin. However, work was later resumed with ASA

and in January 1899 it was given its brand name Aspirin.
- Hoffman did not profit from the drug. However, Heinrich Dreser, the head of Bayer's lab who had postponed the testing, earned a vast fortune in royalties from the drug that he had been reluctant to develop.
- Initially sold to doctors and hospitals rather than the public, aspirin was an instant success, and was the first 'scientific' medicine to be mass marketed. It was the first major pharmaceuticals product to be sold as a tablet instead of a powder.
- Today, we consume 100 billion aspirin tablets worldwide a year. Aspirin is used to prevent heart attacks and strokes, and is under investigation in the management of bowel cancer, thromboses, dementia, the formation of cataracts, and blindness in diabetics. It has been estimated that aspirin could save more than 110,000 lives each year by helping combat cardiovascular disease.

QUESTIONS FOR DISCUSSION

1 The properties of salicylic acid have been known for a long time. How and when did entrepreneurial approaches come into play, thereby enabling the product to be mass marketed?
2 Being entrepreneurial involves taking risks. Was this the case with the development of aspirin?
3 Is it the individuals that come up with the new ideas, or the organisations that put those ideas into practice that are the real entrepreneurs?

physical capital. In order to purchase these items you would need money capital, and you reward people who lend you money by paying them interest.

Enterprise is the factor that brings the four factors of production together to produce a good in order to make profits. Forrest Mars set up his plant in Slough on a large vacant site employing local labour. Entrepreneurs like Mars put their own risk capital into a business. They take a risk, because the business might fail – the entrepreneur might make no profit, and indeed lose the capital injected into the business to pay off business debts. Shareholders in a company play an entrepreneurial role – they risk their capital when they assist the firm in which they have invested to make business ventures.

In recent years we have become aware of a new type of entrepreneur working in the most dynamic part of the new economy – the Internet whiz kid. The **Internet** has been a fertile ground for young people with novel ideas creating new businesses. Of course, many of these businesses will fail or have already failed, but there is still plenty of room for dynamic new ideas which are carefully thought through and planned in detail.

The following series of first steps might prove helpful to someone thinking of setting up a business using the Internet:

- Research your market and decide how your customers will pay.
- Design your website and decide how you will fulfil your orders.
- Choose a reliable Internet service provider (ISP).
- Seek legal and tax advice before going 'live'.
- Include your website address on all printed materials and on your business answer phone.

The truth is stranger than fiction

When the Americans entered World War II they seized not only the right to aspirin, but also Bayer's New York factory and its name. These were sold to US drugs firm Sterling Products for US$5 million. But the company couldn't decipher the German instructions for making aspirin, nor work out how to operate the factory. In 1919 it had to seek advice from the Germans and do a deal on international rights in return.

Chapter 5 Legal forms of business

Businesses take many legal forms – sole traders, partnerships, companies, mutuals and franchises, as well as charity organisations; and in the public sector, public corporations and municipal enterprises.

In the private sector, the most important legal distinction in business is between companies and other forms of organisation.

A **company** is an organisation which is recognised in law as being different from its owners. If you wanted to take a company to court, it is the company rather than the individual owners that you would take action against. This is because shareholders in companies are protected in law by **limited liability**.

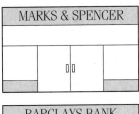
MARKS & SPENCER

has limited liability ...

... whereas a window cleaner most likely does not.

BARCLAYS BANK

has limited liability ...

... whereas a small hairdressing business probably does not.

In simple terms, limited liability means that shareholders in a company can only lose up to the value of their shareholding should the company go **bankrupt** – they cannot be sued further than this to meet the company's debts. This means that the houses and personal possessions of shareholders do not have to be sold off should the company in which they own shares fail.

This fact is made clear to people dealing with companies, for example suppliers. A **private limited company** will have **Ltd** following its name; a **public limited company** will have the initials **plc**.

Limited liability was created in the nineteenth century to enable the economy to take off. It encourages investors to buy shares in large companies; without limited liability they would be a lot more reluctant to do so (because of what they might lose).

Who runs companies?

A company is run by a **board of directors** who make the major decisions. The shareholders choose the directors. Often they are able to replace directors by voting them off the company board. The **managing director** is the senior manager in a company (see Figure 1.10).

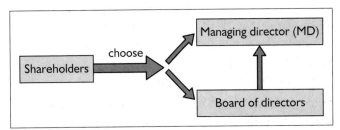

Figure 1.10 Structure of a company

There are two types of companies:

- **Private companies** tend to be smaller companies (although not always – Mars, for example, is a private limited company). Sometimes they are family companies, with a number of family members on the board of directors. The shares of private companies cannot be bought and sold without the permission of other directors. They are therefore not traded on the stock exchange.
- **Public companies**, in contrast, have their shares traded on the **stock exchange**. The minimum capital requirement of a public company is £50,000 (there is no minimum for a private company). The danger of creating a public company is that the owners can quickly lose control of it if someone else, or some other company, buys a majority (51 per cent plus) shareholding.

Gaining company status

There are a number of steps to be taken to gain company status (that is, to be **incorporated** – recognising the company as a corporate body in law) so that the company can sue or be sued in its own right.

A company must be registered with the **Registrar of Companies**. Like most registration processes this involves filling in some paperwork. Two documents need to be completed:

- A **Memorandum of Association** governs the legal relationships between the company and the outside world. Included in this document are:

- the name of the company
- the objectives of the company
- the fact that the company has limited liability
- the amount of capital that the company is authorised to sell in shares.
- **Articles of Association** set out the internal management of the company. For example:
  - the rights of shareholders
  - when shareholders' meetings will take place
  - the role of directors in managing the company.

A company is a popular form of business organisation because:

- shareholders are protected by limited liability
- it is separate in law from the individuals that own it
- it is able to raise capital by selling shares – borrowing money is also easier when a company is recognised.

Setting up a company in the new economy

Setting up a company is an exciting prospect in the early twenty-first century. Recently, there have been a host of start-up businesses, often associated with the Internet.

Setting up a new company starts with a good idea. It makes sense for a young entrepreneur with a good business idea to go ahead with it straight away before someone else thinks of it. Of course, the world wide web (the Internet) is a high-risk medium, just as any new business set-up is, but if you have guts, determination and a truly good business proposition, there is no reason why you shouldn't succeed where others have failed.

To help a business to succeed you need first to identify a genuine need. It makes sense to find a **niche** in the market that involves selling unusual or one-off items or offering an online service for the first time.

Once a young business is able to establish that the idea is going to be a success, then it makes sense to expand, and this is where company status will come in helpful. For example, one of the major stories of early 2000 was the launch of Lastminute.com on the stock exchange. Lastminute.com is based on the idea of meeting people's last-minute needs for holidays, theatre tickets, travel, etc.

The new Internet companies need to raise capital by selling shares in order to expand their businesses, for example to pay a large number of administrative staff to key in lots of information to their Internet sites.

In late 1999 and early 2000 many investors were willing to take the risk of buying into new Internet companies like Lastminute.com because they anticipated that these companies could make large profits in the year to come. Very few of the 'dotcom' companies that people were investing in were making profits – it was the potential that they had to make profits that excited potential shareholders.

However, by mid-2000 some of the gloss had worn off the dotcoms as shareholders realised that their money was being ploughed into companies that in the short and medium term would yield very low returns on shares.

Financing, control and decision making in a company

Companies raise capital by selling **shares**. They are also able to borrow money from banks and other institutions in the form of **loans**. Companies can also sell debentures to raise finance. A **debenture** is a piece of paper which states that an investor has put money into a company and is entitled to a given interest rate each year. While debenture holders mostly receive their reward before shareholders, they do not have the same rights (for example to vote for a company's board of directors). Debenture holders (unlike shareholders) are not part owners of the company they invest in.

In a private limited company, shareholders own the company, and as directors will have control over the company, making the major decisions.

In a public company, however, ownership and control are in some ways divorced.

The shareholders own the company, but the directors usually employ professional managers to run the company. These managers are paid by the company, and the security of their jobs depends on their ability to make suitable profits for shareholders.

Shareholders can remove the board of directors at the **annual general meeting** of the company. However, day-to-day control is in the hands of the paid managers.

Sole traders and partnerships

Sole traders and **partnerships** are common in forms of business where not much capital is required. Sole traders include small shops, web page designers, graphic artists, window cleaners, etc.

Sole traders work for themselves, and thus have a certain amount of freedom to make decisions. However, by having to do everything themselves they may find themselves too tied to their business, for example the farmer or hairdresser who can't afford the time to take a holiday.

Partnerships are a way of getting around the problems of the one-person business. The partners can share the workload, and the profits, while pooling their skills in the business. Partnerships are usually set up in law by registering a **Deed of Partnership** with a solicitor. The actions of partners are laid down in the Deed, as is the way in which the profits of the business will be shared.

Sole traders and partners do not have limited liability.

Finance, control and decision making in sole traders and partnerships

A major weakness of the sole trader and partnership is the lack of capital in contrast with a company. Sole traders and partners cannot sell shares. Their capital is limited to owner's savings, borrowing from banks and other borrowing, and grants from the government and other bodies. The control and decision making in a sole trader business is carried out by the one person. Partnerships are controlled by the partners, although a senior partner may steer decision making.

Other forms of business organisation

Franchises are discussed in Chapter 6.

The **mutual** is a form of business organisation in the UK which is widely respected. Mutuals are owned by their members; they do not have shareholders and they do not seek to make profits. Building societies are usually mutuals and there are also mutual life assurance companies. The idea of a mutual is that it serves the joint interest of members, for example in the early days of building societies people would club together to build houses.

In the 1990s and early 2000s, in an era in which people sought to further their own interests rather than to club

---

CASE STUDY: WWW.CUSACKBOOKS.COM

Cusackbooks.com is a good example of a sole trader business. Elaine Cusack, the owner of the business, is a 30-year-old entrepreneur with a love of books. At the start of 1999 she set up her own cyber-bookstore specialising in out-of-print, TV-related titles – anything from *Andy Pandy* to *Z-cars*. Her business, which is currently based in her Greenwich flat, is taking off quickly. Customers for her personalised book search service include traditional bookshops as well as TV fans from as far afield as Canada and Japan. By 2002 Elaine expects to have opened up a central London bookstore.

In terms of start-up costs, Elaine Cusack's initial kitty was just £4,000, of which £3,500 was a loan from the Prince's Youth Business Trust and £1,500 was a bank loan. Added to this she had £500 worth of stock.

It is relatively simple and cheap to have a website designed for you – as little as £500. However, the quality of the website is very important – it must be clearly designed to meet customer needs and requirements.

QUESTIONS FOR DISCUSSION

1 Who owns and controls cusackbooks.com?
2 Why might cusackbooks.com benefit from forming a partnership?
3 Why might cusackbooks.com become a company?
4 What would be the dangers to cusackbooks.com of becoming a company?

together, many mutuals have been converted to public companies, for example Abbey National and Halifax, both former building societies. The members of these mutual societies were asked to vote for or against becoming a public company. They were offered substantial cash or share incentives to vote to go public. In most cases the members voted in favour, often so that they could gain a windfall of several thousand pounds. Some mutuals do still exist but they find it hard to compete with the big public companies in the field of banking and insurance. Mutuals receive their finance from the contributions of members and are managed by a professional board of managers.

Co-operatives are another form of business organisation which owe their history to a bygone age. They were often set up to prevent exploitation of poor workers. The co-operators would club together to pool money so that they could jointly buy goods for resale (retail co-operatives), or to provide a service which all could benefit from (for example the co-operative funeral, insurance and banking services).

Co-operators contributed money into a central pool. The co-operative would then buy goods and customers would share in the success of the co-operative in the form of low prices, or stamps in accordance with how much they spent in the co-operative. The co-operatives continue to exist today, and in recent years they have sought to win loyalty through the ethical way they carry out business, for example by buying only from sources where there is no exploitation of workers, and in the case of the Co-op Bank by investing only in ethical companies.

Not-for-profit organisations

Not-for-profit organisations include charities and voluntary societies. A **charity** is an organisation that seeks to meet charitable objectives and which has limited liability status. It raises funds largely through donations, although it will also carry out commercial activities, for example selling produce. A charity will have paid managers, and possibly some paid workers. In contrast, a **voluntary society** is based purely on volunteer work.

Charities include pressure groups like Friends of the Earth, and other organisations which while creating pressure for change also focus heavily on meeting needs of the less fortunate, for example Oxfam and Save the Children Fund.

Not-for-profit organisations have increasingly been run in a professional way in recent years. They recognise the importance of using resources well to meet their objectives.

The truth is stranger than fiction

Internet electrical sales in the UK will account for 5 per cent of all UK retail sales by 2005, it is estimated, representing a £12.5 billion market. By 2010 this could be 13 per cent of the market as digital television takes off.

This should revolutionise the sale of electrical goods in this country. In mid-2000 the market was still dominated by Dixons and Comet who together had over 40 per cent of the market. However, this is likely to change as new companies such as Helpful.co.uk, Jungle.com and Buy.com enter the market. More and more firms will be selling electrical goods through the Internet, enabling them to drive down prices. Interestingly, the first chief executive of Helpful.co.uk, Eddie Styring, was a former Dixons and Comet director.

Chapter 6 *Franchises*

A **franchise** is a 'business marriage' between an existing, proven business and a newcomer. The newcomer (the **franchisee**) buys permission to copy the business idea of the established company (the **franchisor**).

Franchising is a very important way of organising business in the private sector and looks set to grow. In the USA, which leads UK business development in many ways, more than 50 per cent of all retail sales take place through franchising organisations. In the UK the figure lies somewhere between 10 per cent and 20 per cent.

The reason why franchising is likely to be the way forward for many organisations is because of the flexibility involved in the arrangement. The franchisor effectively hands over a lot of responsibility, organisation and effort to the individual or groups of individuals taking out the franchise.

For example, BSM franchises its name and approach to training, giving a particular franchisee the exclusive right to trade as a driving instructor under the BSM name in a particular location. The franchisee commits his or her capital and effort. BSM provides the trading name and

Figure 1.11 A BSM franchised car

management experience, and will supply the car, as well as providing national advertising (see Figure 1.11). The franchisee buys a licence to copy the franchisor's business system. In return, he or she promises to pay the franchisor a percentage of sales.

CASE STUDY: COCA-COLA BOTTLING FRANCHISES

It is not surprising that most of the world's leading bottling companies have become Coca-Cola franchisees. By participating in the franchise arrangement they are able to bottle and sell to retailers the classic Coca-Cola drink, and trade using one of the most famous brand images in the world today. The classic Coca-Cola drink consists of water and a concentrate made of sugar, caramel (which gives it its colour), phosphoric acid (which gives it its tartness), caffeine (a mild stimulant also found in coffee and tea), and natural flavourings. The proportions of the ingredients in Coca-Cola concentrate are a closely guarded trade secret, though all ingredients comply with the health laws of the countries where it is made and sold.

The exact combination of these flavourings is known mysteriously as 'Seven-X'. The formula lies locked in a bank vault in Atlanta. It is said that only three people on the present staff have seen it.

The Coca-Cola brand image is widely recognised throughout the world and has become the symbol of global marketing.

The Coca-Cola franchisee therefore has access to one of the most highly desired products and one of the most successful marketing operations in the world.

The franchise business is strictly controlled by Coca-Cola. The company ships syrup or concentrate to the bottling plants. The franchisees mix it with sugar and local water, and carbonate it. The water is purified to the highest standards using equipment specified by Coca-Cola. Samples are taken regularly for chemical analysis, and Coca-Cola staff make frequent spot checks to ensure that plants are maintaining the company's standards of cleanliness and quality. Coca-Cola provides its franchisees with the most up-to-date ▶

technology available. Franchisees are happy to pay for this 'state of the art' equipment because they need it to meet the company's exacting standards.

Each bottler or canner supplies Coca-Cola and other company products to the retail trade (see Figure 1.12). Outlets are supermarkets, sweetshops, restaurants, off-licences, pubs and bars. These outlets often sell Coca-Cola from vending machines and coolers which the franchisees must supply and service.

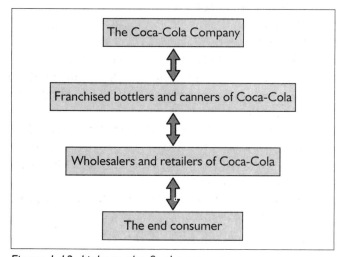

Figure 1.12 Links to the final consumer

There is a clear division of responsibility between Coca-Cola and its franchisees, as shown in Table 1.6.

Bottling plants for Coca-Cola are, with few exceptions, owned and operated by independent business people (franchisees) native to the countries in which they are located. By contract to The Coca-Cola Company or its local subsidiaries, franchisees are authorised to bottle and sell Coca-Cola and other soft drinks within certain territorial boundaries and to meet set standards which ensure the quality and uniformity of the product.

The independent bottler provides the required capital investment for land, buildings, machinery and equipment, lorries, bottles and cases.

Table 1.6 Division of responsibility between The Coca-Cola Company and its franchisees

Responsibility of Coca-Cola	Responsibility of franchisees
Owner of the trade mark	Management of sales
Supplier of syrups and key ingredients	Management of manufacturing
Responsibility for global marketing and advertising to consumers	Management of distribution

The company not only supplies the bottler with syrup or concentrate and beverage bases, but also actively engages in management guidance to help ensure the profitable growth of the bottler's business, enhancing the value of the franchise. Management advice will cover all sorts of topics such as product quality control, marketing, advertising, financial and personnel training.

Advertising for Coca-Cola around the world projects a uniform brand image, to promote a strong consumer appeal for this successful product. Uniformity in advertising also establishes the image of the product in each country.

QUESTIONS FOR DISCUSSION

1 Why do you think that The Coca-Cola Company operates a franchised bottling arrangement rather than controlling all stages of operations directly itself?
2 What are the benefits to Coca-Cola of this franchising arrangement?
3 What are the benefits to the franchisees?
4 What risks does Coca-Cola take in operating such an arrangement? How can these risks be minimised?

The franchisee needs to work hard, put in long hours and use a lot of initiative to get the business started and to develop it. In 1999 there were almost 1,000 franchise opportunities in the UK. The *UK Franchise Directory* lists and describes all established franchise opportunities in the UK. The *Franchise Magazine* provides up-to-date information about franchising. (Both of these publications are available for reference at all JobCentres. Copies can be obtained from: The Franchise Development Service Ltd, Castle House, Castle Meadow, Norwich NR2 1PJ.)

Franchising is common in the fast-food industry – examples include Spud-U-Like and Pizza Hut. Other examples are Dyno-Rod in the plumbing business, Tumbletots, The Body Shop and Prontaprint.

Moshe Gersenhaber, who set up one of the UK's most successful franchises, the printing business Kall Kwik, believes that at the heart of a successful franchise is the set of relationships that develop between the franchisor and the franchisee. The most important part of this relationship is that of 'partnership'. Essentially, the franchisor brings to the partnership his or her dreams and skills, which are then combined with the business system, expertise and experience of the franchisor.

Successful franchising is all about people and therefore favours individuals who are people oriented and who enjoy ongoing contact in a give and take relationship. The successful franchisor will be one who shows a keen interest in the welfare of the franchisees. The franchisees will therefore feel that they are 'in business for themselves but not by themselves'.

It is the franchisors who provide a proven and tested method of going about business – they provide a good valued-added concept. It is then up to the franchisee to create a first-rate service which will generate a flow of repeat business.

Prospective franchisees should audit their own personal qualities before they consider setting up. This audit should include considering the following:

- **Attitude to hard work**. Franchising has no room for those who are workshy.
- **Dedication**. Taking out a franchise is a long-term commitment.
- **Work enjoyment**. Franchising offers lots of opportunities for work satisfaction and for fun for those who are outgoing and enjoy meeting and working with other people.
- **Rewards**. Franchisees need to recognise that rewards from setting up are not immediate. These take time to arrive and need to be worked for. However, when they materialise they are substantial.
- **Being positive**. There is no substitute for a positive 'can do anything' attitude.

The truth is stranger than fiction

In the USA many of McDonald's operations are run on a franchise basis. McDonald's provides the equipment and training for the franchisees. It has even set up its own McDonald's University where students can graduate with a degree in hamburgerology!

Chapter 7 *Activities of business*

A business combines human, physical and financial resources in order to produce a good or service to sell to consumers – usually in a competitive market.

- **Human resources** are the organisation's people.
- **Physical resources** are the machines, equipment, tools, materials, etc. that the organisation uses in the production process.
- **Financial resources** consist of the financial capital and cash resources that the organisation employs to purchase long-term assets such as machinery and buildings, and uses for short-term purposes such as paying next week's wages or purchasing raw materials and supplies.

Managing operations

Organisations depend upon the skills of their **operations managers** (in manufacturing these are often referred to as **production managers**). They need to be able to organise operations to produce products that satisfy consumers. It is often said that production is at the 'sharp end' of business activity. What this means is that if production does not produce the right goods at the right time, then the organisation will fail. **Targets** have to be met and standards kept up.

Production management involves managing the organisation's resources such as machinery and manpower. Timetables and schedules will need to be set out to show how these resources will be used in production. Figure 1.13 shows the management process required to transform **inputs** into finished **outputs**.

A useful distinction can be made between transforming resources and transformed resources:

- Managers, employees, machinery and equipment are an organisation's transforming resources.
- The transformed resources are the materials and information which they process.

Operations management is looked at in more detail in the sections on operational efficiency and quality (see Unit 2, Section E).

Marketing activities

Without a good product a company will struggle. To find out what makes a good product the company will need to engage in marketing activities.

Marketing is defined as 'the management process involved in identifying, anticipating and satisfying consumer requirements profitably'.

If you want to find out what constitutes a good product you will need to carry out extensive **market research** to find out what your potential consumers want. Being market focused therefore involves listening to consumers. Marketing activity and production activity should be seen as being bound up together (see Figure 1.14).

The most successful companies today set out to find what their customers want and then seek to provide the sorts of product benefits that are most sought after.

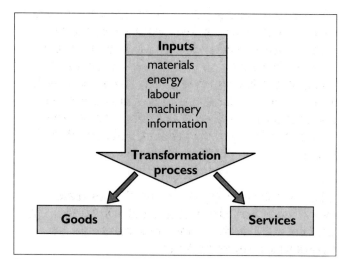

Figure 1.13 *Transformation of inputs into outputs*

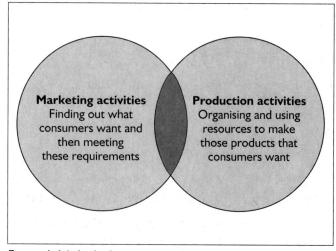

Figure 1.14 *Links between marketing and production*

A remarkable new record appeared on the shelves of music shops in the UK in 1979. There was nothing extraordinary about the singer or the song: Jonathan King reviving a 1930s standard 'The Sun Has Got His Hat On'.

The disc itself was the unusual thing. Called a 'flexi-disc', it was the latest technological innovation in the ailing British music industry. Made of flimsy, bendy vinyl – as opposed to the usual, brittle sort – it was so light it could blow away in a breeze. It sold for just 33p, a third of the price of a normal vinyl single. The flexi-disc was cheaper and quicker to produce and, because of its lightness, far easier to distribute and store than its conventional counterpart.

Jonathan King believed it could herald a boom in record sales, and provide the spark needed to revitalise an industry where sales were falling. He felt that the flexi-disc revolution could be as significant as the arrival of the paperback book. He argued that this was just what the pocket-money market, the 12- to 15-year-olds, was crying out for – a disc that would give them change from 50p could soon bring them back into the record shops. Unfortunately, very little research was carried out with 12- to 15-year-olds, who had reservations about the quality of sound on the new discs. The large record companies felt the same – they did not want to be associated with an inferior-sounding product.

A year later the 'nu-disc' was invented – a cross between an album and a single, with eight minutes of music on each side, selling for only £1.25. But this, too, made little impact.

It was, of course, the compact disc (CD) – more, not less, expensive than earlier products – which finally revolutionised the music industry in the early 1980s.

The latest innovation is 'digital distribution'. Consumers will soon be able to download music from the record companies' websites on to their home computers, thus bypassing retail outlets altogether.

QUESTIONS FOR DISCUSSION

1 How does the 'flexi-disc' provide an example of a lack of integration between the production and marketing activities of a business?
2 What were the major weaknesses of the 'flexi-disc' concept which led to its lack of success?
3 Why, in contrast, do you think that the compact disc was so successful? (Your answer should relate to the relationship between the production and the marketing activities of an organisation.)

Marketing activities are dealt with in greater detail in Unit 2.

Financial activities of a business

The effective business needs to bring together production, marketing and financial activities in a coordinated way.

Any well-run organisation must keep a detailed scrutiny of the financial side of its operations. Not only must the organisation give the best value for money for every pound that it spends, it must also make sure that it is always able to more than cover its **expenditures** through **revenues**.

Organisations must maintain accurate and detailed financial records and this is particularly important in the management of all activities – marketing, production, etc.

All companies, whatever their size or type, have to spend money in order to earn it. The spending money comes from a variety of sources, but one source dominates, the customer, hence the importance of making sure that a company organises its marketing and production activities in an effective way (see Table 1.7). Unless the company is to remain for ever in debt, money from the customer must eventually pay back money obtained from other sources.

A firm may obtain money in the form of **bank loans** (which can be long term or short term), and **credit** from suppliers (which is short term). Some companies own **assets** which they let out for rent.

Table 1.7 Organisation of a company's activities

Marketing activity	Production activity	Financial activity
Anticipate and identify consumer requirements and meet them	Produce the goods and services that consumers require	Manage financial flows that support marketing and production activity and keep detailed records of financial activity

A company spends its money in three main ways: on **operating costs** (day-to-day running), on **capital costs** (expenditures on major long-term items such as machinery) and on **dividends** to its shareholders (the owners). It also has to pay **taxes**.

Failure is a constant threat. Success is never guaranteed. There is always risk. But risk can have a positive impact. In fact, it can be an essential ingredient in the running of a successful business. Without risk, there can be no innovation, no new products, no improved methods of working, no progress. However, risk must be managed and contained (that is, companies should not risk more than they can afford to lose). Otherwise the business will fail.

The risk that can most easily be managed and contained is poor **cash flow** caused by late payment of bills. Poor cash flow means that the company doesn't have the ready money to pay its own suppliers on time. As a result, it may lose the discounts that are often offered for prompt payment. Suppliers can refuse to accept any more orders. They may even take legal proceedings against the company. Finally, the company may be forced into receivership and closure. Poor cash flow is the cause of nearly one-third of all business failures in the UK.

Financial activity is looked at in greater detail in Unit 3.

Human activity

Another important resource for the organisation, which it must manage effectively, is its human activity. A useful distinction can be made between a 'machine company' which tends to behave like a machine and a 'person company' which operates in a people-focused way.

A 'machine' company aims at the maximisation of profit through the most efficient conversion of raw materials into sellable products and services. Its assets – property, equipment and personnel – are deployed in the way that best meets this aim.

However, it is a fact that companies rarely behave like machines. They tend to behave like people. They want to be liked. They develop a personality which transcends the particular products and services they produce and sell. Above all, they want to survive.

A company that treats its people as individuals is likely to win the loyalty and commitment of its employees.

Loyalty in a sense can be bought. The 'machine' company that pays the best wages and salaries can expect its employees to continue working for its best interests. But in times of difficulty when wages and salaries fall, so does the loyalty, and the company suffers.

The 'person' company is better placed. Even in prosperity, it will tend to do better than the 'machine' company. People are not machines; they generally prefer to work in a person company.

This point is more important now than ever. For instance, many people, particularly those starting off their careers in business, will refuse to join companies whose treatment of the environment is thought morally unacceptable, even though it may be legally permissible. (Managing people in organisations is dealt with in greater detail in the section on motivation in business in Unit 1, Chapter 29.)

Of course, the company that treats its people well is most likely to be successful. Its people will want to do well for the company. They will want to serve customers, and create the right sort of image for the company. They will help to produce the right sorts of quality products, and they will create the financial systems that will enable the company to be a success.

It should be clear therefore that the principal activities of a business are mutually intertwined – marketing activities, people activities, financial activities and production activities all support each other and are interlinked.

The truth is stranger than fiction

The Gillette Mach 3 razor was heralded by the New Yorker magazine as 'the billion dollar blade'. This was based on a conservative estimate of how much it had cost over seven years to turn the prototype into the production-line model: $750 million (£440 million) to design and build machines for the factories, $300 million on the marketing that is expected to establish Mach 3 as the most popular razor in the world. Not included in the calculation was the $200 million that Gillette spends each year on research and development. The whole project involved extensive marketing, production and financial planning, and careful coordination between the many experts from across the company involved in the project.

Chapter 8 *Competitive influences*

Business activities and structures are influenced by the level of competition that they face. For example, in 2000 we witnessed high levels of **competition** between firms in many business sectors as they responded to the dotcom revolution. Businesses are able to communicate with their customers using the Internet at a low cost by creating organisational websites.

New businesses have been able to enter markets and gain global prominence for their brands very quickly. The Internet certainly enables new and still relatively small companies to achieve a global brand recognition that up to now would have taken years of effort. Two examples are the Internet bookseller Amazon and the Internet search engine Yahoo!

Competition is very important in business. The dictionary provides us with some useful definitions of competition:

'A contest in which a winner is chosen from among two or more entrants.'

'The opposition offered by competitors.'

The implication is that if the **market** for daily newspapers in the UK is about 15 million, then each individual newspaper publisher will not be able to sell 15 million copies. In fact, in May 2000, the national daily newspaper market was divided as shown in Table 1.8.

Of course, the nature of a market, like that for daily papers, is that it is divided up into a number of **segments** – for which rivals compete – for example while the tabloids such as the *Daily Star*, *The Sun* and *The Mirror* compete in one segment, broadsheets like *The Independent*, the *Guardian*, and *The Times* compete in another segment.

The tabloids are said to be in **direct** competition with each other and **indirect** competition with the broadsheets.

In the summer of 2000 all of the daily newspapers were worried about a new form of competition in their industry. A new paper had been launched called *Metro* – a free paper which was being read in increasing numbers by commuters on the London underground and which was going nationwide. Research carried out by *The Mirror* showed that their sales were being hit by the *Metro* effect in London. By June 2000 Metro was distributing 750,000 papers per day.

How do newspapers compete? They compete in a number of ways including price. For example, they compete to have:

Table 1.8 Sales of daily newspapers, May 2000

Daily newspapers	Daily sales
The Sun	3,497,563
Daily Mail	2,371,421
The Mirror	2,274,324
Daily Express	1,096,862
Daily Telegraph	1,035,615
The Times	723,689
Daily Star	608,288
The Financial Times	461,498
Guardian	397,704
The Independent	225,372
The Scotsman	94,290

Source: *The Independent*, Statistics Division

Tabloid newspapers compete by trying to have the most exciting stories and be the best value for money

- the best stories
- the widest range of topics
- the best sports reports
- the most attractive layouts
- the most interesting pictures
- the most up-to-date and juicy gossip

and to be the best value for money, etc.

WHAT DO YOU THINK?

How do the following organisations compete in the market place? List the factors they compete over.

a) Fast-food restaurants.
b) Political parties.
c) Mobile discotheques.

Being competitive

The well-known US business writer Michael Porter suggests that there are two major ways to be competitive:

- **Low costs.** In a competitive market it is often helpful to be the producer that produces at the lowest cost. The low-cost producer is best placed to charge lower prices than rivals. Alternatively, the low-cost producer can charge a medium or higher price and potentially make larger profits than rivals. Low costs can be achieved through producing and selling very large quantities of products. Companies like Coca-Cola and soap-powder manufacturers like Unilever are able to produce individual items at very little cost because they literally produce millions of units. They will have lower costs than their rivals by winning a bigger share of the market than them.
- **Differentiation.** This involves making your product 'better' than that of rivals while at the same time making sure that the product is bought by customers. A Parker pen is different from other pens: as well as being distinctive, it is a little more expensive. It is a success because enough people are prepared to buy the product because of its high quality.

The influence of competition

Competition is a major influence on business. For example, some businesses are most likely to be competitive if they are small, such as sole traders or partnerships. A corner shop catering for a small local community may be competitive by building close relationships with people, for example by buying in goods that meet their personal orders. In contrast, a supermarket may only be competitive by being a public company with a lot of share capital so that it can operate on a national (or international) scale, providing a large variety of goods at relatively low prices.

Firms which sell to mass markets need to have the production capacity to sell large quantities of their goods or services. Organisations such as Coca-Cola, Unilever, Shell or BP could only compete as a public company which is able to raise large sums of capital through the stock exchange.

Competition also affects the activities of business. In a highly competitive market a strong emphasis will be placed on competition. The competitive firm needs to know exactly what consumers want in order to meet their needs. For example, daily newspapers need to carry out research into the sorts of supplements and articles that their readers are most likely to read.

Competitive firms will only compete successfully if they are able to employ top-quality people, use the best possible machinery and equipment, organise production efficiently and have access to finance at a competitive rate of interest.

Levels of competition

There are a number of levels of competition (see Figure 1.15).

Figure 1.15 Levels of competition

Complete market power would exist if there was only one firm dominating the market.

In the real world successful **monopolies** don't last for very long, because high profits encourage new firms to enter the market. A monopolist will sometimes try to create barriers to prevent new firms from entering the market, for example by agreeing with retailers only to stock the monopolist's products.

In any town you will find a number of service stations (selling petrol, newspapers, confectionery, soft drinks, fresh milk and a range of household goods). These service stations are in close competition with large supermarkets (although the service stations are usually open for longer hours).

Service stations need to be highly competitive, particularly in relation to price, because by law prices have to be advertised on hoardings outside the service area. Passing motorists can quickly compare prices. Service stations are typically located on the major roads leading into a town in order to pick up the most passing trade.

In contrast, motorway service stations have much less competition because they may be many miles from the nearest competitor. Typically, therefore the price of buying petrol and other goods will be much higher at a motorway service station than within a town. The service station is able to exert monopoly powers while the town service station operates in a strongly competitive market (see Figure 1.16).

However, the costs of operating a motorway service station may be higher than a town service station because the owners of the motorway sites on which the service stations are based are able to charge higher rents because of the 'superior' location.

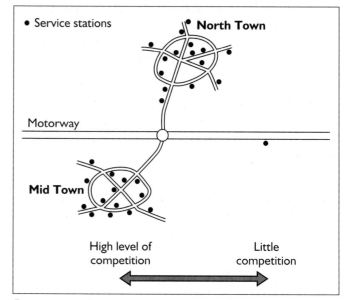

Figure 1.16 Competition faced by service stations

QUESTIONS FOR DISCUSSION

1 What other markets can you think of where part of the market is highly competitive, while other parts of the market are dominated by monopoly producers?
2 Why is it that motorway service stations tend to be dominated by the large petrol retailers, whereas smaller firms are able to operate within town areas?
3 Why is marketing important in enabling service stations to compete?

However, the monopolist that seeks to prevent competition in the UK will fall foul of the government which, through the Competition Commission, will seek to break up that monopoly.

A good example of a large-scale monopoly was Standard Oil in the early years of the twentieth century. Owned by John D. Rockefeller, it sought to buy up all competing oil companies to create a monopoly. The US government and law courts eventually stepped in and broke up Standard Oil into a number of smaller companies.

History repeated itself in recent years when Bill Gates's company Microsoft was deemed by the US courts to have

restricted access to the Internet. The courts ruled that Microsoft should be broken into two.

Competition between small firms

Competition between small firms can be very intense. This is likely to be the case in the following situations:

- Where it is relatively easy for a small firm to enter an industry. This would be the case if there are no barriers to entry into the market (for example you don't need to have a patent to produce a product) and where the cost of setting up is not very high (for example the low cost of creating a company website for an Internet trader).

- Where the goods or services that are produced or sold by the small firm are highly similar, for example rival record shops in a small town.
- Where consumers 'shop around', and are therefore familiar with the different products and prices of competitors.

In these situations there may be considerable rivalry between firms over prices and other aspects of the offer made to consumers – similar products, similar packaging, similar service, etc.

However, simply because firms are small does not mean that the market is highly competitive. Small firms will seek to develop a **niche market** (part of the market which is different from other parts of the market) and to differentiate their product from those of rivals. For example, a hairdresser may be able to differentiate (and thus charge higher prices) by offering better hair stylists, more fashionable cuts, better personal service, a trendier image, etc.

Competition between large firms

Some large firms have considerable monopoly powers. Indeed, this is one of the reasons why firms grow and buy up competitors. They seek to reduce or eliminate competition. However, whenever large firms make high profits this will attract competitors into their industry.

People often make the mistake of assuming that the existence of a few large firms in a market indicates monopoly powers and monopoly profits. However, the reality is that situations with only a few competitors can be intensely competitive. This is particularly true when the largest firms have similar market shares and are wrestling with each other to dominate the market. For example, today one of the biggest battles is in the supermarket industry. In the late 1990s Tesco overtook Sainsbury's as the market leader, but Sainsbury's has continued to fight back. In 1999 Asda was taken over by US giant Wal-Mart, leading to further intense rivalry.

Where a large firm does have monopoly powers it is able to:

- charge prices which are higher than would exist in a more competitive environment

CASE STUDY: ENTERING PROFITABLE INDUSTRIES

Richard Branson's Virgin provides a good example of a company that has spotted profitable opportunities and taken advantage of them. Virgin identifies markets which are dominated by just a few large firms that are making high levels of profits. Virgin then enters these markets by investing heavily and aggressively in order to win customer interest.

An example of a market that Virgin has entered is that of contraceptives. In the contraceptive market, Virgin spotted the fact that the market was dominated largely by a single producer – the London Rubber Company, producing brands like Durex. During the 1990s global markets have opened up as never before, including the Chinese, Indian and eastern European markets. Virgin recognised the potential to sell literally billions of contraceptives on a global scale. The company therefore invested considerable amounts of capital to create a new product 'Mates' which

could be sold not only in the UK but across the globe.

Virgin also recognised that British Airways was exploiting a monopoly position and that, with the worldwide move to open up international airways to more competition, there would be scope for a major new British airline offering good-quality, low-cost deals to a variety of locations. Virgin Airways was born.

QUESTIONS FOR DISCUSSION

1 Why do you think that Virgin targeted markets which were dominated by existing monopolists?
2 Why does a company need to be a substantial public company like Virgin before it can take on the large companies in other industries?
3 Can you think of other examples where Virgin moved into new industries? How successful were these Virgin ventures?

- make profits which are higher than in a competitive market

- use its profits to continue to gain advantages over rivals, for example through research and production and marketing improvements.

The truth is stranger than fiction

Over the years Virgin has had a long-standing battle with British Airways (BA) in which Virgin has claimed that BA sought to protect its own position by preventing a competitive environment from developing.

Since 1990 Richard Branson has been fighting against what he believes to be a 'dirty tricks' campaign which had been waged by BA. He has used the courts consistently to get back at his rival:

1991 – Virgin accuses BA of poaching its passengers, hacking into its computers, hiring private investigators and feeding anti-Virgin stories to the media. Branson writes to BA calling for the allegations to be investigated so it can be confirmed that the rival airline is not behind any anti-Virgin campaign. Sir Colin Marshall, then BA's chief executive, replies that there is no foundation in the allegations, and BA's weekly staff newspaper suggests that Virgin has invented the claim. It is this newspaper article that Branson seizes on to provide the basis of his libel claim against BA. BA then also sues, alleging libel by Branson. But Virgin emerges triumphant from the high court hearing. BA is forced to admit there was some foundation for the Virgin chief's dirty tricks allegations and apologises unreservedly. It also has to pay £510,000 in libel damages to Branson and Virgin, and pay legal costs of about £3 million.

1993 – Virgin lodges a $1 billion lawsuit in a New York court seeking compensation for the 'dirty tricks'.

1994 – Virgin wins a separate, long-running battle with BA over maintenance of its aircraft in the late 1980s. BA agrees to pay £2.65 million compensation, after Virgin says BA had kept Virgin aircraft grounded, with one airliner being out of action for three weeks during a busy summer period.

1998 – Branson attacks the proposed alliance between BA and American Airlines which he says will dominate transatlantic routes and be anti-competitive.

1999 – A US court throws out the $1 billion lawsuit. Branson rejects calls from a triumphant Robert Ayling, BA's then chief executive, for his company and Virgin finally to bury the hatchet after almost a decade of heated courtroom battles.

February 2000 – On the same side, but still working separately in public, Branson and Ayling lobby successfully against liberalisation of routes to the US that would allow rivals to enter the market.

June 2000 – Branson and Rod Eddington, the new BA boss, meet to bury the hatchet.

SECTION B *Business objectives and stakeholders*

INTRODUCTION   Every business needs to have a clear sense of direction. *Without* a clear sense of direction it is impossible to know and to communicate what the business is seeking to achieve. Without clear **objectives** it is impossible to measure **performance** and to outline ways of improving the business.

In establishing objectives for a business it is necessary to take into consideration the various **stakeholder** groupings who have a stake in the way the business is run. These stakeholder interests will vary – employees will seek good wages and conditions, shareholders will want a good return on their investment, suppliers will want to be paid on time and to receive regular contracts, the local community will want to make sure that business activities are in harmony with the needs of local people, and so on. It is not surprising, therefore, that there will often be conflicts between the interests of the various stakeholder groupings. The wise company will seek to reconcile differences of interest and to create clear objectives which are of mutual benefit to all stakeholders.

Traditionally, making a **profit** has been a key objective of most business organisations in the private sector. Today, businesses seek to make a profit but they have to make sure that they operate in an **ethical** way, and that they serve the interests of their consumers.

Once objectives have been established for an organisation, it is essential that these are communicated clearly so that everyone pulls in the desired direction.

In a fast-changing business world it is essential that business organisations create objectives and a **strategy** (long-term plan) which enable them to embrace the latest technologies, and which enable them to be flexible. In the early part of the 21st century we have seen many new ventures involving **e-commerce** and the start-up of many dotcom ventures. The success of these businesses depends in some measure on whether they are clear about their objectives and of the advantages they can gain from new forms of electronic trading, and have therefore created a clear strategy to take them forward. Some businesses that have embraced the new technologies have been very successful because they have thought carefully about how e-commerce can help them to gain competitive advantages. Others have rushed into e-commerce with no clear objectives, strategy or understanding of how they can benefit from the new environment in which they are operating. It is the businesses with the clearest objectives that are most likely to be successful.

Critical thinking

In 2000 Kingfisher plc, the retail group which includes B&Q and Woolworth's, unveiled its e-commerce strategy. It forecast online sales of £1.5 billion by 2004 and profitability within three years.

The group estimated that by 2004 online spending in key European markets in its sector could be £11 billion or 5 per cent of the total market.

Sir Geoff Mulcahy, Kingfisher chief executive, dismissed the threat of dotcom start-ups. He said: 'The established rules of business are not abolished when you go online. Simply being online is not enough. You need strong brands and a clear retail proposition.'

The group set up an e-Kingfisher division in March 2000 and launched a health and beauty Internet portal in conjunction with Freeserve, combining content from Kingfisher's Superdrug format and from ThinkNatural, a natural health Internet company in which Kingfisher has a stake. The portal offers an online pharmacy service.

Kingfisher has also registered the domain name Trade.co.uk, to form the basis of an Internet portal aimed at small builders. It is also creating a 'home portal' with content from its main sectors such as DIY, electrical and general merchandise, plus new areas such as furniture.

Source: Kingfisher press release, June 2000

WHAT DO YOU THINK?

1 Why is it so important for Kingfisher that its e-commerce strategy is profitable? Who does the business need to be profitable for?
2 What is the key objective of moving into e-commerce?
3 Why might going online be 'not enough' in terms of developing a successful business?
4 Why is Kingfisher registering new domain names?

Chapter 9 *The nature, role and importance of objectives*

Modern organisations need to have a clear sense of their **objectives**. An objective is something that an individual or organisation sets out to achieve. The mountaineer sets out with the objective of reaching the top of the mountain; the student sets out with the objective of gaining an A grade pass; the multinational company sets out to have the biggest global market share in its main lines of production.

For example, the objectives of a supermarket chain might include:

- becoming the market leader in the national market
- developing a global presence by moving into overseas markets
- meeting customer needs and requirements each and every time.

The objectives of a charity providing sheltered accommodation to homeless people might include:

- using donations and resources as effectively as possible
- meeting the needs of the maximum number of homeless people
- providing a safe and secure environment for clients.

Having objectives gives a clear focus and direction to work towards. Objectives can be written down and communicated to other people to create a shared sense of purpose.

Starting out with clear objectives makes it possible to measure performance and to take corrective action should an individual or organisation fail to make progress towards meeting objectives.

One of the biggest causes of friction in business life stems from a lack of clear objectives. Objectives may be expressed in a vague way so that there is no clear sense of purpose. Alternatively, there may be a conflict of objectives – working towards the achievement of a particular objective may work against another objective being met.

Wherever possible, therefore, it is important to establish **specific objectives**. Many objectives can be expressed in numbers, for example output in a particular period of time, levels of profit, the number of consumer complaints, etc.

Characteristics of effective objectives

Effective objectives should have the following characteristics:

- They should be **specific**. Specific objectives make it possible to be precise about what the organisation is trying to achieve. A specific objective is clear and precise. It gives direction, and it is then possible to check that the direction has been followed. For example, Tesco has set itself the objective of being the UK's number one supermarket chain and has succeeded in this objective. SkyDigital set itself the short-term objective of reaching 200,000 homes by the end of 1999 and has set itself the long-term objective of reaching 10 million homes by 2005.
- They should be easily **understood**. Objectives usually need to be communicated to lots of people. They should therefore be presented in clear and easy-to-understand language where there is no ambiguity. For example, a Tesco's sales objective which is to create satisfied customers who see Tesco as their number one choice is easy to understand and to turn into practical actions. In contrast, a sales objective which demands that sales staff should increase their sales in a particular period lacks clarity – the sales staff may be able initially to persuade people to buy goods, but if customers are not content they may return goods or fail to make repeat orders.
- They should be **widely communicated**. Today, most organisations involve a considerable amount of democracy, and responsibility for decision making is widely spread within the organisation. Serious problems may occur if key objectives are not communicated widely to everyone concerned. Communication of objectives can take place through a variety of channels such as team briefings (where team members are informed about what is happening in the organisation), and particularly through training courses, as well as through company newsletters, notice boards, etc.
- They should be **challenging** and not too easy to achieve. Objectives can help to raise people's sights and standards, but ones that are too easy to achieve will serve to lower expectations and standards.
- They should be **attainable**. Objectives should not be so difficult to achieve that people give up and get disgruntled about the unrealistic nature of the objectives.
- Wherever possible they should be **measurable**. Quantifiable objectives are very helpful for measuring performance. If an organisation has an objective of winning 50 per cent of the market by 2005, then it can

measure its performance against this objective. It becomes possible to check performance regularly and where possible to make alterations and adjustments to improve performance.

Leading thinkers – Peter Drucker

Peter Drucker is most widely associated with the idea of **management by objectives** (MbO) which he first set out in his book *The Practice of Management* in 1954.

Peter Drucker wanted to find out how best to manage a business to make sure that profits are made and that the enterprise is successful over time. He felt that business objectives help management to explain, predict and control activities. The business should establish a number of objectives in a small number of general statements. These statements can then be tested in the light of business experience, and it becomes possible to predict performance. The soundness of decisions can be examined while they are being made, rather than by looking back on what has happened. Performance in the future can be improved in the light of previous and current experience.

Management, according to Drucker, is the job of organising resources to achieve required performance.

Drucker listed eight areas in which performance objectives need to be set out. They are:

*   market standing
*   innovation
*   productivity
*   physical and financial resources
*   profitability
*   manager performance and development
*   worker performance and attitude
*   public responsibility.

The driving objective of a business

'What drives a particular business?' is a frequently asked question. For example, is it driven by a desire to maximise profits at all costs, to serve customers, or to dominate the market? Let us examine a few of these **driving objectives**.

Profit maximisation

One of the leading business writers of the twentieth century, Milton Friedman, argued that the business of business is business. What he meant by this is that the primary objective of a business is to make a profit so that the business can flourish. The reality is that most businesses have to give a

high priority to profit making. Without profits a business is unable to do all the things that it wants to do – spend money on research and innovation, improve conditions for employees, make contributions to the community, etc.

Few if any businesses go all out to **maximise profits** at the expense of other goals. The business that was 'hell bent' on profit maximisation would quickly lose friends and customer support, and this would work against profit making. Most businesses therefore give a strong emphasis to profitability but they combine this with other considerations.

Creating shareholder value

Most public companies have to place a strong priority on providing a good return to their shareholders who are the owners of the company. Shareholders generally buy shares because they expect a suitable rate of return on their shares. If their shares perform badly they can quite easily switch to buying shares in another company. Most large public companies therefore place a strong emphasis on the objective of **providing 'shareholder value'**.

Dominating the market

Gaining a large market share is an important business objective. The firm that dominates a market has considerable power relative to competitors. By producing larger quantities than rivals it becomes possible to reduce costs per unit, for example by operating with lower distribution and advertising costs per unit sold. The US writer Michael Porter expresses this relationship in the following simple way: 'If you can gain the lion's share of the market the profits will follow'. In recent years we have seen this emphasis on **winning market share** in many industries, for example in the supermarket wars between Tesco and Sainsbury's, and in digital television where business tycoon Rupert Murdoch has been determined to make sure that SkyDigital dominates the market.

Survival

Peter Drucker has argued that the principal objective of a business is **survival**. Many business writers have borrowed from Charles Darwin's theory of evolution to show how the process of survival works in the business sphere. Organisations must continually adapt and change in order to cope with changes in the environment in which they operate. Often change has to be wide scale if an organisation is to survive. For example, a number of companies producing heavy industrial chemicals in recent years have sold off the high-pollution creating parts of their businesses to focus on consumer goods chemicals which are more environmentally friendly.

Customer satisfaction

Today, many businesses realise that their success is based on satisfying customers. If they can achieve this, then they are best placed to dominate the market, to make profits, to create shareholder value, to survive, etc. The prime objective of the business therefore becomes the provision of customer service in order to **grow more contented customers**.

Growth

Many businesses pursue **growth** as their main objective. Business people argue that firms must grow in order to survive. Failure to grow might result in a loss of competitiveness, a fall in demand and eventual closure. In some large companies the salaries earned by managers may depend on the size of the business. Thus their objective may be to make the business as large as possible. Controlling a large business concern might also give individuals satisfaction from the power at their command. Increased sales also mean reduced sales for competitors, which in the long term can be seen as being consistent with a policy of profit maximisation.

Prestige

For some, the image and name of a company may be very important. The company may spend a lot of money on public relations so that it is well thought of. This policy is not inconsistent with that of long-term profit maximisation.

Projecting an **image** of quality can be seen as being important for the morale of shareholders, customers and

CASE STUDY: WAL-MART IN THE UK

In June 1999 the world's largest retailer, the US-based Wal-Mart, succeeded in taking over the UK supermarket chain Asda. Wal-Mart is promising to deliver the American dream to British families – high service and the lowest possible prices for groceries, clothes, electrical goods and computers.

Wal-Mart's philosophy – that the customer is king and staff must be motivated to serve them by a culture of praise and rewards – could revolutionise retailing patterns in the UK.

The company slogan is: 'Who is most important? The customer.' Its central belief is 'aggressive hospitality'. As shoppers enter the 3,600 Wal-Mart stores across the USA and in eight other countries they are welcomed by 'people greeters'.

At the checkouts, customers' goods are packed for them and carried to their cars. Employees are known as associates and share in the annual profits.

Wal-Mart's founder Sam Walton, an Oklahoma farmer's son, borrowed £15,000 to open his first small country store in Arkansas in 1945. He died in 1992, one of the world's richest men with a personal fortune of more than £8 billion, and employing nearly a million people.

'Mister Sam', as he was known, once described his homespun approach to selling as a 'whistle while you work' philosophy.

Staff pledge to make eye-contact with customers and offer to help anyone within ten feet of them. Shopping is often enlivened by employees bursting into the Wal-Mart company cheer, and every morning they must sing the company song.

However, the down-to-earth philosophy of the company is matched by the latest high-tech techniques.

When Walton set out to spread his empire abroad, he pledged: 'We'll lower the cost of living for everyone, not just in America, but we'll give the world an opportunity to see what it's like to save and have a better lifestyle, a better life for all.'

QUESTIONS FOR DISCUSSION

1 What are the principal driving objectives of Wal-Mart?
2 What aspects of Wal-Mart's activities are likely to enable profit maximisation, market leadership, growth, survival, public service and customer satisfaction?

employees. Shareholders and customers are likely to withdraw their support for a company when they feel that its practice and performance are substandard. The loyalty of employees will be tested if they feel that the practices of their company are 'slightly shady' or slipshod.

Public service

Many organisations in the public sector and those which run on a charitable or voluntary basis will make **public service** a key objective. The emphasis will be on providing a suitable level of service to everyone who needs it rather than just to those who can afford it. For example, the government may provide a postal and ferry service to remote islands, where the service could not be justified on commercial grounds. A charity may seek to provide health services to individuals who could not possibly afford to pay for them out of private means.

What determines the objectives of the organisation?

Business objectives should not be viewed simply from a **managerial perspective**. Many business structures are based on a coalition of interested groups. A business may include a number of **internal groups** whose interests might be widely different, for example employees, managers and shareholders. At the same time **external interests** will include consumers, governments, pressure groups and other producers. It is inevitable that the creation of objectives will involve a balance of interests. Establishing business objectives will therefore involve a compromise between interested parties whose interests may conflict.

Other factors which may influence the objectives of an organisation include:

- the size of the business – larger firms may be more inclined to seek profit maximisation and market leadership
- the age of the business – new and mature businesses may be more concerned with survival than ones going through a dynamic phase of growth
- the state of the economy – in a period of boom organisations may go for growth, high profits, market share, etc.; in a recession they may be content simply to survive
- whether a business is in the public or private sectors
- whether the business is a charity or voluntary organisation, etc.

The truth is stranger than fiction

In his book <u>Management: Tasks, Responsibilities and Practices</u> (1973), Peter Drucker wrote:

'A manager, in the first place, sets objectives. He determines what the objectives should be. He determines what the goals in each area of the business should be. He decides what has to be done to reach these objectives. He makes the objectives effective by communicating them to the people whose performance is needed to attain them.'

In recent years a number of management writers have been critical of this approach. They feel that in the modern dynamic world of business it is important to be more flexible. Working with too tight objectives may prevent an organisation from responding to new challenges. Managers therefore need to build the skills to respond creatively to emerging situations rather than be held in a straightjacket of objectives. What do you think?

Chapter 10 *The hierarchy of objectives*

Organisations set out their objectives in a **hierarchical** way. The most important objectives will be those that concern the whole of the organisation, followed by objectives that affect major parts of the organisation, and then objectives which concern smaller units, teams and, finally, individuals.

Objectives are important in giving clarity to the purpose that the organisation is working towards. Having established a clear purpose it then becomes possible to make sure that all of the parts of an organisation are pulling in the same direction.

Figure 1.17 Organisational objectives

Figure 1.17 identifies the three major sets of organisational objectives.

What is a mission?

A **mission** describes the purpose of an organisation; it outlines the organisation's reason for being. Specifically, it answers the following questions:

- What business are we in? What do we do?
- Who do we do it for?
- What products will we provide?
- Where will we conduct our business?
- How will we conduct our business?
- What do we aim to provide?

Why a mission?

A mission is usually set out in a brief **statement** which defines the existing scope and boundaries of a business so it can remain focused. It provides overall direction. A mission is often referred to as a generalised aim of an organisation rather than as a specific objective. This is because the mission defines the overall purpose of the organisation rather than specific detail.

CASE STUDY: THE MISSION STATEMENT OF THE STANDARD LIFE ASSURANCE COMPANY

'We are one of the world's leading mutual life assurance companies and operate in the UK, Canada, Republic of Ireland and Spain. We provide our customers with a range of financial products and services.

'We aim to provide quality products, a level of financial security and performance, and a quality of service which fully meet the needs of our customers, while at all times maintaining the financial strength of the Company.

'For specific markets, products and services, we will expand our business if such expansion would be in the long term interests of our policyholders.'

Source: Standard Life Assurance Company

QUESTIONS FOR DISCUSSION

1 What does Standard Life's mission statement say about the following?
   a) What business is it in? What does it do?
   b) Who does it do it for?
   c) What products does it provide?
   d) Where does it conduct its business?
   e) How does it conduct its business?
   f) What does it aim to provide?
2 How useful do you find Standard Life's mission statement to be in defining the objective of the organisation?
3 Who would benefit from Standard Life's mission statement? How?

For example, Newcastle United Plc set out its mission in the following way:

> 'The business of Newcastle United is football – our aim is to play attractive football, to win trophies, to satisfy our supporters and shareholders and to continually improve our position as a top European club.'

While many organisations use the term mission, there are many others who refer to their main aim or general objectives as a values statement, or in some other way. For example, soap-powder manufacturer Unilever refers to a corporate purpose:

> 'Our purpose in Unilever is to meet the everyday needs of people everywhere – to anticipate the aspirations of our consumers and customers and to respond creatively and competitively with branded products and services which raise the quality of life.'

What is a strategy?

A **strategy** is an overall plan, with clearly defined objectives, that provides a clear sense of direction and assists decision making within an organisation. A strategy covers the medium to long period, that is, three to five years.

What are strategic objectives?

Strategic objectives are the objectives which are set for the whole organisation, have long-term implications and involve major uses of resources. The strategic objectives will typically be created at a senior managerial level (hopefully, after consultation with other lower levels).

Strategic objectives will set out the direction that the organisation is to take. Having established these, it then becomes possible to focus all the activities and efforts of the organisation into meeting them.

For example, in the late 1990s Standard Life, recognising that it was working in a competitive service market, set out its central strategic objective as creating 'customer satisfaction'. Standard Life was then able to create a number of strategies – a marketing strategy, a financial strategy, and a development strategy – which would enable it to ensure customer satisfaction.

What are operations?

Operations are the processes and methods through which an organisation uses its resources to produce something or to provide a service. For example, in a factory, operations are the processes used to turn raw materials and other inputs into finished products.

Every organisation will have its operations – handling financial transactions in a bank, stocking shelves and serving customers in a supermarket, processing documents in an office, etc. Operations are thus the day-to-day activities of an organisation which are concerned with getting things done.

What are operational objectives?

Operational objectives give direction to operations. Once an organisation is clear about its operational objectives, then it becomes possible to design the processes that make it possible to work in the desired direction.

Clearly, operational objectives need to fit tightly with strategic objectives. For example, if an organisation has the strategic objective of creating customer satisfaction, it will need to set out a series of operational objectives that further this, and which will then enable it to design processes such as handling customer enquiries, face-to-face interactions with customers, etc. that directly create customer satisfaction.

Figure 1.18 shows a more detailed hierarchy of objectives and which areas of the organisation might be responsible for establishing these objectives.

The mission, corporate level and divisional objectives of a large organisation are likely to be created by senior managers. Where the organisation is divided into a series of divisions it is important that they work in the same general direction, rather

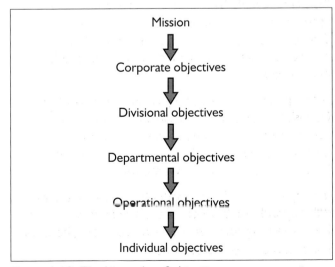

Figure 1.18 The hierarchy of objectives

than having divisions pulling in different directions.

Individual divisions may then be subdivided into different departments. Departmental objectives will need to fit with corporate objectives, through divisional objectives.

Each major operation within a department will then need to have clear operational objectives which fit with operational objectives, which fit divisional objectives and so on.

Finally, it should be possible to create individual objectives for the people that carry out the organisation's processes. Ideally, each employee will be aware of the organisation's mission and will have a clear understanding of how his or her individual efforts fit into the objectives of the whole organisation.

The relationship between strategic and operational levels

What then is more important to the organisation: *strategic-level decision making* or *decision making at an operational level*? This is by no means clear. On the surface it would appear that strategy is most important because it concerns the big decisions, which involve sorting out a lot of complex information into clear plans, and which are usually made by senior managers. However, the operational level lies at the heart of the organisation and its success. In the past operational-level employees in an organisation often played down their importance by saying 'I'm just the oily rag in the engine room'. However, without the oily rag the engine of an organisation often seizes up. Today, this is truer than ever. In modern service organisations many of the key operations concern interpersonal relationships between an organisation's employees and its customers. The intelligent organisation clarifies a set of operational objectives for employees (often working in teams) to work to. These employees are often given considerable responsibility to make decisions for themselves and to decide how best they can meet operational objectives.

Problems with objectives

There is a real danger in being too prescriptive in establishing objectives. Some people feel that **management by objectives** (**MbO**) is not helpful because it creates static objectives. In a world of change this may restrict the sort of flexibility that is required in a dynamic organisation that constantly needs to re-invent itself and to re-invent the strategies and operations that it is concerned with.

The truth is stranger than fiction

In the 1980s a Japanese motor-cycle manufacturer set itself the mission statement: 'We will crush, squash, slaughter Yamaha!'

Chapter 11 *The role and importance of profits*

The main aim of most business organisations in the private sector is to make a profit. Indeed, one of the first questions someone interested in business will ask about an organisation is 'How profitable is it?' The profitability of the company acts as a broad indicator of the health of the organisation.

CASE STUDY: PROFITS SLUMP BY 70 PER CENT AT AILING MFI

MFI, the struggling furniture retailer and manufacturer, reported £25 million pre-tax losses for 1998–9, a slump of 70 per cent on the previous year.

The group posted pre-tax profits before exceptionals of £17.2 million for the year to 24 April 1999 against £56.9 million the previous year.

Exceptional charges stood at £42 million, mainly as a result of the restructuring of its UK retail operations. At the same time a number of key executives at MFI announced that they would be resigning.

The poor results, described as 'tragic' by analysts, came after a series of profit warnings and weak performance in the out-of-town household goods sector.

It seems difficult to guess where MFI will turn next. An attempt to move upmarket into the mid-higher range, a switch to smaller formats on the high street and even a change of name have all been mooted as possible remedies to strengthen the ailing brand.

Shares which have more than halved since March 1998 fell 12.5 per cent to close at 38.5p each and analysts remained unimpressed, pointing to disappointing current trading figures with sales of product lines down 12 per cent in ten weeks.

QUESTIONS FOR DISCUSSION

1 Why do you think profits had fallen so badly in the year leading up to 24 April 1999?
2 What does the fall in profits tell you about the health of the company at the time?
3 Why do you think that the share price of MFI had fallen?
4 Why might it be difficult to turn MFI's profits round?
5 What do you think is meant by 'exceptional charges'? How did these affect profits?
6 What has happened to MFI since 1999?

CASE STUDY: M&S REVEALS SEVERE SALES SLUMP AT AGM

Marks & Spencer, the high street fashion and food chain, added another chapter to its troubled recent history in July 1999 when it revealed a slump in sales over the previous trading quarter. Britain's premier retailer told shareholders at the annual general meeting that tough trading conditions and increased competition had caused a sharp year-on-year fall in sales. At the same time Marks & Spencer announced that it was closing six stores in Germany and France.

QUESTIONS FOR DISCUSSION

1 How would the fall in sales be likely to have affected profits?

2 How else might M&S have experienced a fall in profits apart from a fall in turnover?

In June 2000 Tesco announced its profit figures showing continued growth in sales and profits:

Five-year record	1996	1997	1998	1999	2000
Turnover (£ billion)	12.1	13.9	16.5	17.2	18.8
Pre-tax profits (£ million)	675	750	760	842	933

Source: Tesco

The Tesco group is adding as much retail space in 2000 as Sainsbury's, Asda and Safeway put together. Through Tesco Direct, Tesco was the world's biggest Internet grocer.

QUESTIONS FOR DISCUSSION

1 Is there likely to be any relationship between growth of turnover and growth of profits?
2 Why do you think Tesco was expanding both its retail space and its online presence?

Measuring profit

In simple terms the **profit** of a business can be measured by deducting the **expenses** which a business incurs from the **revenues** that it receives from the total value of sales (turnover).

Profit can be measured by:

Profit = Total revenue – Total cost.

The most important way of presenting profit by a business is in the form of profit after tax, because this is what is available for use by the business.

Profit can be put to various uses (referred to as the allocation of profit), including:

* payments to shareholders in the form of **dividends**, for example Tesco's dividends per share rose from 3.20 pence in 1996 to 4.48 pence in 2000
* **reinvestment** into the business to purchase capital items such as premises and machinery.

What can a company do with its profits?

A business can do a number of things with its profits including the following:

* **Retain the profits** within the business. The profit can then be used to fund expansion or to buy new machinery and equipment, or kept in reserve against a rainy day. The profits could also be used to pay off some of the business's accumulated debts.
* **Distribute the profit** among the owners of the business, for example the shareholders in a company. The return to shareholders is called the dividend. When shareholders receive a healthy dividend they will have confidence in the way that the business is being managed and run and will not be inclined to sell their shares – which might lead to a fall in share prices (and the potential for a possible takeover by another company).
* **Distribute the profit to employees** as a bonus.
* **Use part of the profit to pay off taxes**, for example taxes on profit.

The Coca-Cola Company, the world's leading soft drinks manufacturer, is a good example of a major organisation that ploughs a large amount of its profits back into the business.

At the end of the twentieth century Coca-Cola was ploughing 60 per cent of its profits back into the business in order to finance expansion. Indeed, the company used a substantial amount of profit to buy back shares from shareholders so that less profit would have to be taken out of the company in paying dividends. Coca-Cola realises that to stay ahead of the competition it must plough money into better plant and equipment, better marketing and advertising and so on.

The importance of profit

Profit is very important to business for the following reasons:

* Profits help to measure the success of a business. Profit comparisons can be made between one business and another.

- Profits provide funds for investment in new fixed assets.
- Healthy profits will attract new investors to invest in the company because of the possibility of making healthy rewards.
- Profit is the source of more than 60 per cent of all the finance used to help companies to grow – without profit firms would stagnate.

Satisficing

H. A. Simon suggested that businesses will often seek to 'satisfice' rather than to maximise profits. By **satisficing** he meant generating sufficient profits to satisfy the shareholders of a company, which would not necessarily involve producing at the profit-maximising output, or going all out to maximise returns on capital.

This situation can arise when the managers of a company are different from the owners. Providing that the managers can produce sufficient profits to keep the shareholders satisfied, then a proportion of the profits can be diverted to provide more perks for managers and larger departments. Satisficing policies are most likely to be associated with industries where there is only a limited degree of competition. It is fairly common in many organisations ranging from schools to oil companies. Managers will readily produce long lists of achievements which do not always relate to a profit margin at the bottom line. In large organisations it is often fairly easy to produce sets of financial statistics which are difficult for the layperson to interpret (although where large blocks of shares are owned by financial institutions such as pension and insurance companies, this will be more difficult).

In a study into 728 UK firms the researcher Shipley showed that only 15.9 per cent of the sample could be regarded as all-out profit maximisers. The implication was that the vast proportion of firms place at least some emphasis on satisficing (see Table 1.9).

Table 1.9 The tendency not to profit-maximise

Questionnaire	Percentage of 728 firms
1 Does your firm try to achieve:	
a) maximum profits	47.7
b) satisfactory profits?	52.3
2 Compared to your firm's other leading objectives, is the achievement of a target profit regarded as being	
a) of little importance	2.1
b) fairly important	12.9
c) very important	58.9
d) of overriding importance?	26.1
Those responding with **1**a and **2**d	15.9

The truth is stranger than fiction

In June 2000 C&A, the clothing retailer, announced that it would be closing down all of its UK stores with the loss of up to 4,800 jobs. The company had been in decline for a number of years. In 1996 it controlled 4.4 per cent of the UK retailing clothing market, but by June 2000 this had fallen to 1.9 per cent. The company made a loss in the UK of £250 million between 1995 and 2000.

Price deflation (falling prices due to competition) exacerbated by the growth in Internet shopping, combined with flat demand and high fixed costs, such as shop rents and labour, helped to wipe out profits.

Chapter 12 *Wealth creation and adding value*

Adding value to products is one of the most important business activities. It is a process which requires considerable imagination and skill and is at the heart of wealth creation in organisations and nations.

Let's look at some well-known examples.

Coca-Cola is probably the world's best-known soft drink. In essence, it consists of water, sugar, caramel and a secret ingredient which makes it unique. However, what really adds value to the product is the famous Coca-Cola **logo**, which is an icon of modern consumerism (see Figure 1.19).

The Coca-Cola logo adds billions of pounds to the value of the brand. Every day millions of consumers across the globe look for the Coca-Cola brand (which is instantly recognisable) because they know that it is 'the real thing'.

In the case of Coca-Cola, then, it is the **branding** and the **advertising** that adds most value to the product.

Figure 1.19 Coca-Cola is the most widely known global catchphrase after OK!

Love Hearts is a well-known brand of confectionery (see Figure 1.20). Children in particular enjoy eating Love Hearts, but what makes this brand distinctive is the little messages that are written on them – 'Kiss me quick', 'Bad boy' and so on. Whoever came up with the idea of writing the messages on the sweets created the mechanism through which much of the value was added to Love Hearts.

Soap-powder manufacturers constantly seek to be able to promote that added extra ingredient or feature to their product which will give them a competitive advantage over rival brands.

Figure 1.20 The messages on Love Hearts adds value to this brand of confectionery

Adding value is thus a highly creative business and one in which organisations are willing to invest considerable resources – time, energy, money, etc.

Modern consumers are constantly in pursuit of something new and different, and so producers continually seek ways to give it to them, for example ring pulls on drinks cans, envelopes that can be sealed without licking them, car windows that can be lowered and raised by pressing a button, and colourful packaging on many goods. In a fast changing society it is almost certain that you will have recently used a good which is better, more gimmicky and more advanced than similar goods which were available until recently.

The process of adding value is simply concerned with making goods and services more desirable so that consumers will be prepared to pay more for them. There are all sorts of ways of adding value to products including the following:

- **Changing the product** by adding a little extra to it, such as building in safety features and other design features into cars. For example, James Dyson revolutionised vacuum cleaners by creating a more efficient twin-cyclone machine.
- **Changing the promotion** of the product by bringing the product to the attention of the public in a more appealing way, for example through catchy advertising and sales promotion. For example, an advert for Levi jeans showing a young model, Nick Kamen, stripping down to his boxer shorts in a laundrette added millions

of sales to the product overnight.

- **Changing the availability** of the product by getting the product to people when they want it and where they want it. For example, modern multi-screen cinemas have proved a great hit with parents who are able to drive to the cinema and be out in two hours having watched a film in comfort without any delays or hassles in between.

- **Changing customer service**. Today, one of the most important ways of adding value to products is through customer service. Many companies realise that in a service-focused economy the relationships that employees can build with customers are at a premium. The intelligent organisation will therefore place a strong emphasis on maximising service to customers, whether it be in answering the telephone quickly, carrying out after-sales service, or simply serving a customer in a shop or restaurant.

Value may be added at every stage of production. A simple example is the jam manufacturer converting relatively inexpensive strawberries into more expensive strawberry jam. The difference between the cost of the strawberries and other materials and the price of the finished strawberry jam is the wealth which he or she has created. Figure 1.21 shows the simple stages involved.

At stage 1 strawberries are cultivated on a farm. At stage 2 the strawberries are processed into jam. At stage 3 they are bottled in the factory. At each stage value is added (and, of course, further value is added in the processes of advertising, branding and selling the finished jam).

Consider the following:

- The strawberry farmer buys £100,000 worth of young plants from a plant nursery which eventually grow into £500,000 worth of strawberries.

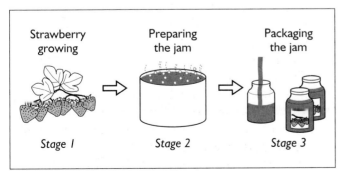

Figure 1.21 *The stages of adding value to strawberries*

Strawberry growing → Preparing the jam → Packaging the jam

Stage 1   *Stage 2*   *Stage 3*

- The £500,000 worth of strawberries is then converted into jam in a factory. The jam is now worth £1 million.

- The factory then bottles and labels the jam ready for sale to retailers for £2 million.

Table 1.10 shows how value is added at each stage of production.

Table 1.10 *The amount of value added at each stage of production*

Stages of production	Input	Output	Value added
Plant nursery	£0	£100,000	£100,000
Strawberry farm	£100,000	£500,000	£400,000
Conversion into jam	£500,000	£1,000,000	£500,000
Bottling and labelling	£1,000,000	£2,000,000	£1,000,000

You can see in Table 1.10 that the final value of the bottled strawberry jam is £2,000,000, and this value has been created to a greater or lesser extent at each stage in the chain of production:

Value added by plant nursery	=	£100,000
Value added by strawberry farm	=	£400,000
Value added in conversion to jam	=	£500,000
Value added in bottling and labelling	=	£1,000,000

Creating consumer benefits through adding value

Businesses compete with each other. They are all involved in adding value. However, if a company's rivals are more successful at adding value than the company is, then they are more likely to win sales. This is why organisations are constantly seeking ways of adding more value. For example, this trend can be seen in supermarkets which in recent years have moved into home delivery, customer loyalty cards, greeting customers on entry into stores, and many other approaches to adding value.

Benefits are advantages gained by customers from a product or service. Consumers will buy those products which give them the greatest benefit. Adding value therefore should involve creating and adding benefits which consumers want, and then producing these at an acceptable price and in an environmentally acceptable way.

In 1999 the computer manufacturer IBM launched a prototype newspaper which could replace printers, paperboys and papergirls, and newsprint.

This is the new reusable high-tech newspaper that could make inky fingers a thing of the past. The paper is based on folding electronic pages. It is designed to take account of how people handle newspapers – the way they read them, fold them and carry them.

It is made possible by foldable plastic pages coated with electronic 'ink'. In the IBM vision, readers with a subscription to a newspaper would connect to the Internet for the latest edition. Articles would be displayed on the 16 double-sided tabloid pages. When one section had been read, it could be cleared at the touch of a button, either discarding the articles or storing them in the e-paper's memory. The subscriber could then display and read the next section. Any items of particular interest could be electronically clipped and saved or e-mailed to friends.

The e-ink that coats the pages consists of microscopic balls – black on one side, white on the other – floating in individual liquid-filled pockets. When an electric current is applied, the balls rotate turning the 'ink' on or off like the dots on a computer screen.

IBM expects the first versions of its e-newspaper will be used in industries such as aircraft production, where engineers need information instantly.

QUESTIONS FOR DISCUSSION

1 What new benefits does the new e-newspaper provide? Why might these be attractive to consumers?
2 How can this new concept in newspaper production add value to newspapers?
3 Do you think that this new development will transform the newspaper industry?

The chain of production

For every product there is a **chain of production**. Some products go through many stages in the chain of production, while for others the chain is considerably shorter. For example, there are many stages in exploring, drilling, refining, storing and distributing petrol to people, whereas some farmers sell potatoes and fresh vegetables directly over the farm gate.

A crucial part of adding value successfully is the way in which each stage in the chain is linked. If we look at how a business operates we can see that it requires:

* excellent links with suppliers
* excellent links with external customers
* excellent internal links between activities inside the company.

Links with suppliers

A business needs to make sure that it gets inputs of the right quality, at the right price and at the right time. For example, a company like Tesco will insist that the goods it buys from outside sources meet very high standards. If suppliers cannot meet these standards, it will no longer buy from them.

Links with external customers

There needs to be very close liaison with customers, so that the goods can be transferred smoothly to the next stage in the chain with no hold-ups or complications. There also needs to be a very good relationship with firms later on in the chain of production, so that everybody involved works together to create maximum consumer benefits.

Links within the company

Everyone who works for a company has internal customers whom they work for. By seeing colleagues as internal customers and by seeking to ensure that these customers are satisfied, then a company will maximise its potential.

The truth is stranger than fiction

Today, environmental friendliness is one of the greatest sources of value added in the motor car industry. Once, old bangers simply rusted in peace on the scrap heap. Now, in the drive towards environmentally friendly transport, Nissan has announced the arrival of the fully recyclable car. After it has reached the end of the road, every part can be taken out and, after being sorted, processed, melted or moulded, used again to help make a new vehicle.

Chapter 13 *Stakeholders*

A **stakeholder** is someone who has an interest in the running of an organisation. His or her livelihood, well-being and peace of mind will be affected by the decisions that the organisation makes.

A good business will be aware of the 'knock-on' effects of its activities. Investment in a new factory may attract workers from outside the area and increase the local population significantly. It is not enough for the company simply to pay good wages and offer good working conditions. It will also help ensure that housing and other social facilities are in place – cooperating as necessary with the local authorities. Likewise, if a factory has to be closed, or a significant proportion of the staff made redundant (either because of a business downturn or internal inefficiencies), the company will work with others to help the displaced staff find new employment. The closing of a factory or even 'downsizing' can lead to the closure of a variety of companies supplying either the factory itself (with raw materials and services) or the workers and their families (with food, clothing, entertainment, etc.). A good business will therefore think long and hard before deciding to close and, where appropriate, will make every effort to encourage other companies to take over the site.

In short, a company has responsibilities to a range of interested parties – the people who have a 'stake' in what the company does. A company's stakeholders include not only its customers and owners, its workforce and suppliers (and their families), but also those living near its sites, as well as special interest groups and, of course, society as a whole, including society in its role as 'steward' of the environment. Balancing these responsibilities is difficult but far from impossible.

Stakeholders and the setting of objectives

1 Shareholders/owners

Shareholders and other **owners** of businesses will inevitably be interested in profits. The dividend they receive is a reward for the risk that they take in buying shares. Shareholders appoint the board of directors of a company who in turn appoint the management team (see Figure 1.22).

However, shareholders are not simply concerned with profit maximisation. Most shareholders take a pride in their

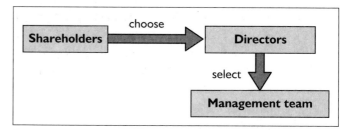

Figure 1.22 The role of shareholders

company and its reputation. Many of them will be employees or former employees. A number of shareholders will ask questions of their directors at the annual general meeting and in some cases may vote to remove certain directors from the board.

Large companies today place a strong emphasis on giving 'shareholder value' – that is, making sure that shareholders receive a good return on their investment. The company that fails to give shareholder value will find that its shareholders start to sell off their shares – share prices fall – and the company becomes prone to takeover by another business.

2 Customers

The **customer** is a powerful stakeholder in any business organisation. If customers prefer Coke to Pepsi, then this will have a direct impact on Coca-Cola's turnover and hence profits. Most modern business organisations give a very strong priority to customers and customer requirements in business decision making.

Many businesses supply goods to other businesses – their customers are those other businesses. Suppliers will need to make sure that they meet the exacting requirements of their business customers.

3 Managers

Managers do not own a company (although they may have shares). However, managers make many important decisions. Managers have to serve customers – because if they don't, sales are likely to fall. Managers must also meet the wishes of the directors if they are to keep their jobs secure. In the 1970s it was widely felt that the power of managers had risen relative to that of shareholders. This is no longer the case – shareholders are far more aware of their rights than in the past. In particular, large blocks of company shares are held by financial institutions and these institutional shareholders put a lot of pressure on company managers to perform.

Managers will develop plans for organisations, often with a long-term view to making the company profitable. At times they will resent shareholders who tend to want their dividends now, making it difficult for managers to plough money into long-term investments.

4 Employees

We have long since moved beyond the days when the organisation simply saw **employees** as a resource to be manipulated. The scientific managers of the early twentieth century looked to ways to increase the efficiency of labour by reducing the time taken to carry out operations and by eliminating unnecessary movements around the workplace. However, it did not take long to appreciate that this sort of treatment of labour was highly demotivating.

Today, the emphasis is on creating a 'commitment model' of work in which employees are committed to their organisations and to their work because they feel cared for and because they see that the organisation is seeking to help individuals with personal development. When employees are valued in this way they are moving towards being genuine stakeholders.

A stakeholder view of the employee involves giving the employee responsibility for making decisions at work and gives the employee a real voice. Employees' concerns about the way that the business runs are listened to and the employees are treated as a genuine partner in the business.

5 Creditors

In business many trading transactions are carried out on a credit basis. **Creditors** thus have a stake in the business – they want to make sure that they are paid on time. This means that in many cases suppliers will want to know more about how a business is being run if they are to supply goods on credit. In some cases they may want to interfere directly in the way that the business manages its affairs to ensure that it is creditworthy.

CASE STUDY: THREAT TO THE LAKES PENCIL TRADE

In the autumn of 1999 it appeared that the Lake District might lose its 400-year-old pencil industry because of a planning dispute centred on the National Park's age-old struggle to balance commercial development with conservation.

Keswick's famous Cumberland Pencil Factory, which draws in 100,000 visitors a year, was at the centre of the dispute. The factory's US parent, Acco, applied in early 1999 for permission to expand, but the Lake District National Park's planning officers recommended refusal. Acco's £5 million project, including a new factory, art workshops, a museum and flats, needed to be subsidised by a new shop on the town's outskirts which could be detrimental to Keswick centre, they argued.

Acco warned that it might pull out of Keswick altogether, with the loss of 100 jobs if the application was rejected. Cumbria could ill-afford the blow, being badly short of industries other than tourism.

Despite the persuasive endeavours of Keswick town council and Allerdale borough council (both of which wanted the development approved) and a 5,000-signature petition raised by workers at the factory, National Park councillors turned down the planning request.

One member of the National Park said Acco's threat to close down the factory was 'a classic case' of a big US-based multinational 'bullying their way through the National Park for their own commercial gain while holding employees to ransom'.

The company decided to appeal against the planning decision.

QUESTIONS FOR DISCUSSION

1 Who are the major stakeholders mentioned in the case study?
2 Why do the different stakeholders have different perspectives?

6 The community

The **community** is an important stakeholder in modern business activity. Businesses need to earn a licence to operate in the way they do. In carrying out their operations they should not ride roughshod over the interests of the community.

Business activity can impact on local communities in all sorts of ways ranging from the positive – creating employment, and enhancing the reputation of a local area – to the negative – creating redundancies and pollution.

Compromising between the objectives of various stakeholders

In the 1970s some irate business people used to state that 'managers should be allowed to manage a business'. What they were worried about was the growing influence of other groups of stakeholders such as employees through the trade unions.

Today, most businesses have come to realise that the art of management is to skilfully identify and then to meet the often contrasting requirements of different groups of stakeholders.

Having a '**licence to operate**' involves meeting the requirements of a diversity of stakeholders.

Different groups of stakeholders have different levels of power and influence within the organisation. Over time, this power and influence changes. For example, in the last decade of the twentieth century we saw the increasing power and influence of consumers in many markets, coupled with an increase in community influence (often supported by strong **media** campaigns – the media are undoubtedly influential stakeholders!).

Stakeholders thus have a direct impact on an organisation's objectives, and this is apparent when we read the mission statements, values statements and objectives of many organisations, which include clear consideration of a variety of stakeholders.

Typically these objectives will be concerned with:

- identifying and serving the needs of customers
- meeting the needs and aspirations of employees
- serving the community and the environment
- creating shareholder value
- meeting the needs of other stakeholder groupings.

Clearly, business organisations have moved a long way forward from the day in which they primarily served their owners.

Organisational theory today recognises the importance of taking a pluralistic rather than a unitary approach. With a **unitary frame of reference** an organisation has a single values system, and seeks to create the mechanisms that best meet the needs of this system. Many modern business thinkers now recognise that organisations operate in an environment of internal and external diversity – and it is by recognising this diversity, that is by taking a **pluralistic approach**, that organisations can best create a values system and set of objectives that best meet the needs of all of its stakeholders.

The truth is stranger than fiction

It seems that the UK's record in terms of creating a wider stakeholder perspective by taking account of the social and environmental requirements of the wider community leaves a lot to be desired. British companies are among the worst in the world when it comes to protecting the environment and tackling social issues, according to a new stock market index which appeared in September 1999.

The Dow Jones Sustainability Group Indexes (DJSGI) show that only one UK firm, the Anglo-Dutch consumer products giant Unilever, beats its sector rivals in the commitment to sustainable development.

Four of the 18 DJSGI sectors were headed by a Canadian company including the steel producer Dofasco and the electrical group Transalta. German companies also fared well, with Deutsche Telekom topping the telecommunications sector and BMW leading the car grouping.

SECTION C *Economic influences*

INTRODUCTION   Business activity takes place against a background of change in the economy. Every student of business needs to have a good grasp of **economic influences** on business.

Economic analysis gives us a good understanding of how the market works, for example in influencing the demand and supply of different products, and hence their prices in the market place. We also need to have an understanding of how the **economy** works as a whole – the factors influencing the general level of price changes, factors influencing the level of employment in the economy, factors influencing the overall level of production in the economy, etc.

This section therefore should provide you with an invaluable introduction to how the economy works, and how changes in the economy influence business.

When the economy as a whole is improving, then most businesses and most people involved with business will benefit. If firms produce more goods they will employ more people, buy more supplies from other businesses, and invest more in buying machinery and equipment. These are periods of relative **prosperity** and generally make people more optimistic.

In times when the economy is slowing down, or when there is a **slump** in business activity, then there will be negative knock-on effects for everyone. A factory that loses orders may be forced to shut down or to slow down the rate of production, and employees may be laid off. They then will have less money to spend in local shops, and so there will be a knock-on effect on more and more businesses.

In the early part of the 21st century we have a Labour government in power. However, its view on how the economy should be run is very different from that of the old Labour Party in the 20th century. Today both Labour and Conservative parties are believers in allowing the **free market** to make many of the economic decisions. Consumers like you and me vote with our spending for the products that we want to be produced. The demand that we generate for goods acts as an incentive to businesses to supply the goods which are demanded. **Government** only plays a very small part in the economy of the 21st century – for example by purchasing some goods (such as through the National Health Service), and through its taxation policies. Many people believe that after the Second World War the government became too involved in running the economy and that this often led to a waste of resources. It is unlikely that we will return to the days of high government spending of the 1970s. Indeed, a number of commentators saw the petrol station blockades in September 2000 in the UK and other European Union countries as a sign that people were less willing to pay taxes to central government.

Critical thinking

In June 2000 an unmarked truck laden with several hundred cases of Coca-Cola made its way across the border into North Korea, spearheading the capitalist invasion of the world's last Stalinist state.

North Korea was practically the only place on earth where the ultimate symbol of US capitalism did not have a presence. The company moved within 48 hours of the USA lifting trade sanctions against the country in response to the historic summit between the leaders of North and South Korea.

Not to be outdone, Coca Cola's arch-rival Pepsi said it was also planning to sell its products in North Korea.

The poor state of the North Korean economy is expected to deter most other western companies from following Coca-Cola at this stage, but McDonald's is expected to follow, if only for the advertising value.

WHAT DO YOU THINK?

1 Why do companies like Coca-Cola and Pepsi want to sell their products in North Korea?
2 In what ways would you expect business life to be different in a country like North Korea than for example in the UK?
3 Why might some western businesses be reluctant to set up in North Korea?

Chapter 14 *The roles of markets*

In a **market economy** like that of the UK, decisions about what to produce are largely made through the market place. For example, a student is able to follow a course in business at a school or college if there are enough students wanting to do the course. The students provide the course fees that make it worthwhile to the school or college to allocate tutors to that course. It is the market which determines the fact that very few schools today offer Latin and Greek at A-level, while most will provide French, mathematics and history.

The market consists of two groups – buyers and sellers. **Buyers** are seeking satisfaction mainly in the form of value for money, while **sellers** are seeking to earn a living and hope to make a profit. Because sellers have to make a living, they tend to try and sell items which sell well and more than cover the cost of bringing the item to the market place.

Because most markets are competitive the buyer tends to have the upper hand. If buyers are not happy with the offerings of a particular seller (supplier) they can switch to an alternative seller.

The forces of demand and supply

In business we use the concepts supply and demand to illustrate the relationship between buyers and sellers and to show how the market works.

Demand

The **demand** for a product is the quantity that will be bought at a particular price. More of a product will be bought at a cheaper than a higher price. For example, market research into the number of fans who would buy a football club's programmes each week revealed the information given in Table 1.11.

Table 1.11 Weekly demand for football programmes

Price of programme	Number of programmes demanded
£1.40	3,200
£1.60	2,800
£1.80	2,400
£2.00	2,000
£2.20	1,600
£2.40	1,200

The information given in Table 1.11 can be plotted on a 'demand curve' as shown in Figure 1.23.

An individual demand curve can be likened to a snapshot taken at a particular moment in time, showing how much of a product would be bought at different prices. At that point,

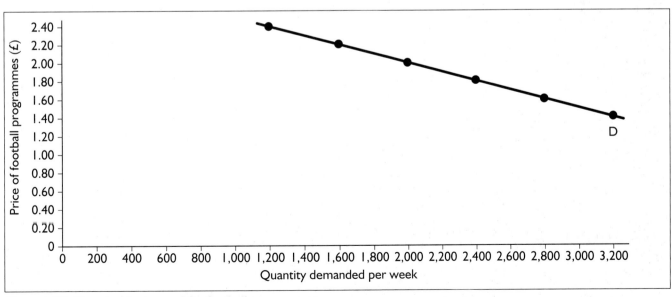

Figure 1.23 The weekly demand for football programmes

price is seen to be the only variable that can be altered which will influence the quantity purchased.

Supply

The **supply** of a product is the quantity that will be supplied at a particular price. More will be supplied to the market at higher than at lower prices (more suppliers will want to enter the market as prices rise, and existing suppliers will want to increase their quantities). The logic behind this is that as prices rise there will be more potential to cover costs and to make profits. (However, note that the cost of production may rise as output increases. For example, a commercial gardener who takes on an ever-increasing number of customers may have to buy new and expensive equipment.)

A supply schedule for football programmes for our football club may therefore look like the one shown in Table 1.12. The supply schedule can then be shown in the form of a supply curve (see Figure 1.24).

The formation of a market price

In the market place the forces of demand and supply will interact to create a **market price**. This can be illustrated by bringing together the demand and supply schedules, and then illustrating this by bringing together the supply and demand curves (see Table 1.13 and Figure 1.25). From these you can see that there is only one price at which the wishes of consumers and suppliers coincide, that is £2.00. At this price the quantity which will be bought and sold is 2,000.

Table 1.12 Supply schedule for football programmes

Price of programme	Numbers that club is willing to supply
£1.40	1,400
£1.60	1,600
£1.80	1,800
£2.00	2,000
£2.20	2,200
£2.40	2,400

Table 1.13 Demand and supply for football programmes

Price of programme	Quantity demanded	Quantity supplied
£1.40	3,200	1,400
£1.60	2,800	1,600
£1.80	2,400	1,800
£2.00	2,000	2,000
£2.20	1,600	2,200
£2.40	1,200	2,400

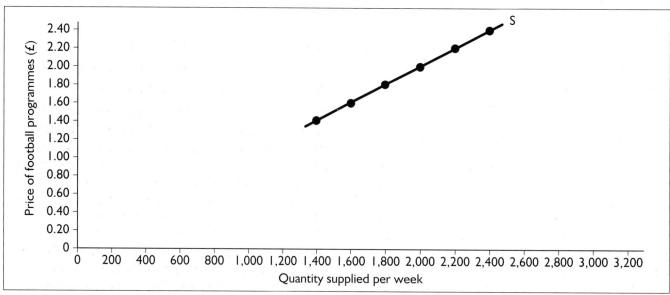

Figure 1.24 Weekly supply of programmes

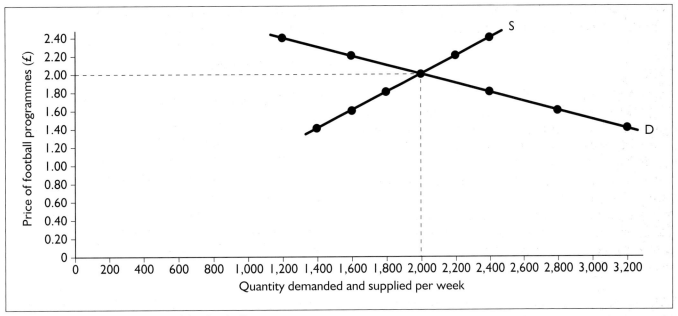

Figure 1.25 Supply and demand for football programmes

The market provides a mechanism for automatically bringing the decisions of consumers and producers into line, even though the two groups have different motives (the producer will want to sell at the highest price possible, and the consumer to purchase at the lowest price possible).

We can see how the market process of forming an **equilibrium price** comes about by considering two disequilibrium situations. If, for example, we consider a price of £2.40 it is seen that at this price the club would be willing to print more programmes each week – 2,400. However, at £2.40, fans would only be prepared to buy 1,200 programmes, leaving a surplus stock of 1,200 programmes which would go to waste (although in this case the club might be able to sell them in the future as collectors' items – it would then be left with the costs of storing unsold programmes). In reality, the club would realise that it was overpricing its programmes and would probably reduce the numbers it produced and lower prices.

Alternatively, if the price of the programmes was pitched at £1.60, fans would be prepared to buy 2,400. However, at such a low price the club would only be prepared to run off a small quantity – 1,600. There would now be a shortage of programmes – stocks would rapidly sell out on match day and there would be many frustrated fans who would be prepared to bid up the prices to get hold of the programmes. This would make it worthwhile for the club to print more and to increase prices.

The net effect is that if prices are above £2.00, too many will be printed and so forces will interact to pull prices down to £2.00. At prices below £2.00, too few will be produced and so forces will interact to push prices up to £2.00. At £2.00 prices are just right and there is no tendency to change (see Figure 1.26).

The above analysis is a simplification. In the real world markets do not always move smoothly towards equilibrium. Consumers and producers frequently lack important market information that would assist them in responding promptly to changes.

Lots of buyers and sellers

In the above example of the football programmes there were a single seller and lots of local buyers.

The market mechanism works on a more general level, bringing the wishes and actions of consumers and sellers into line. For example, in the market for Golden Delicious apples there are lots of apple growers. Many of the Golden Delicious apples sold in the UK come from abroad, and of course there are millions of individual purchasers of Golden Delicious apples, some making bulk purchases, such as hotel chains, others making small purchases, like a household of one person. The market brings the actions of all these suppliers and demanders into line to create a market price. The demand for Golden Delicious apples at a particular moment is the sum of all the decisions made by

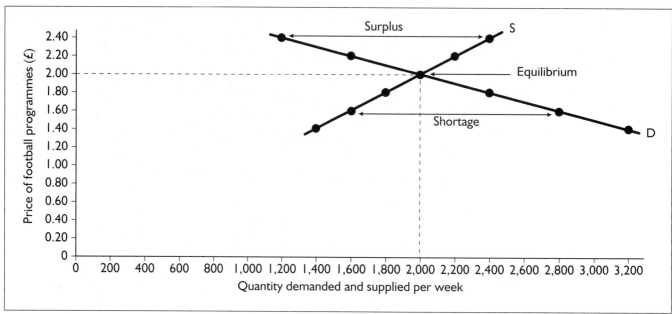

Figure 1.26 The equilibrium price

buyers, and the supply of Golden Delicious apples at that same moment is the sum of all the decisions made by suppliers – so that, for example, should many more people want to buy Golden Delicious this month this would be certain to push up the price of these apples once this signal has fed its way into the market place (which it would do very quickly, as empty shelves in supermarkets would quickly feed into increased orders from supermarket chains to apple growers).

CASE STUDY: HOW CAN NICKY CLARKE ASK £300 FOR A CUT AND BLOW-DRY?

Nicky Clarke, 41, is Britain's top celebrity hairstylist. He worked for Leonard of Mayfair and John Frieda before he set up the Nicky Clarke salon in 1991. His Mayfair salon was described by *Vogue* magazine as 'London's finest' and has a three-month waiting list. His salon styles the hair for more shows during London Fashion Week than any other salon team and he has a long list of celebrity clients.

Nicky Clarke says that the prices charged at the Nicky Clarke salon are set by the management team according to the forces of supply and demand. While the average price of getting a good haircut with a stylist in central London was about £50 (January 2000), it was much higher with Nicky Clarke. In the autumn of 1999 Nicky Clarke introduced a 'fast track' appointment system for clients who wanted their hair cut immediately (at £500). There is a long waiting list for clients wanting new appointments at £300 and regular clients are charged £200. However, even at these prices Nicky Clarke is not able to keep up with the demand. Clarke believes that the fact that clients keep coming back justifies the prices charged.

QUESTIONS FOR DISCUSSION

1 Why is Nicky Clarke able to charge the prices he does?
2 If demand increases further what might Nicky Clarke do?
3 Why do you think that clients are prepared to pay £500 for a haircut with Nicky Clarke?

The truth is stranger than fiction

The great Austrian economist Joseph Schumpeter stated the case for the market when he said that:

'Queen Elizabeth (the First) owned silk stockings. The capitalist achievement does not typically consist in providing more silk stockings for queens, but in bringing them within the reach of factory girls in return for steadily decreasing amounts of effort.'

A survey carried out by the Encyclopaedia Britannica in 1999 showed how the market had successfully led to falling prices for most products:

* A pair of Levi jeans cost £4 a century ago. Today, that would mean forking out £230, while the real shop price is £49 or less.
* A half-pound Hovis loaf was on the shelf 100 years ago at 4d (less than 2p), which is equivalent to 95p today, while the actual shop price in 1999 was 63p.

However, not everything has fallen in price:

* A top-price season ticket to watch Arsenal cost £1 in 1899, which is the equivalent of £57.50 today. However, Gunners' fans now face paying £866.50 to watch all home games.

Chapter 15 *Changes in the market place*

The market place is highly dynamic – prices frequently change in response to market forces (that is, changes in demand and supply). It is helpful to examine why these changes take place. We will therefore first examine changes in demand before going on to consider changes in supply.

Factors influencing demand

There are a number of factors which influence the demand for a product in addition to price. If one of these factors alters the conditions of demand are said to have changed. These factors include tastes, income, population, the price of substitute products and the price of complementary products.

Changes in one or a combination of these factors will cause shifts in the **demand curve**. The demand curve can shift either to the left or to the right. A shift to the left indicates that smaller quantities are wanted than before at given prices. A shift to the right indicates that larger quantities are wanted than before at given prices.

For example, if the football club that we examined in Chapter 14 suddenly got into the top three of its division it might find that the demand for its programmes increased substantially. Instead of 2,000 programmes being demanded at £2.00 it might find that 3,000 programmes were demanded – its demand curve would have shifted to the right. When the new demand curve is drawn it can be seen that a new equilibrium price is formed where the club is able to charge a higher price for its programmes (see Figure 1.27).

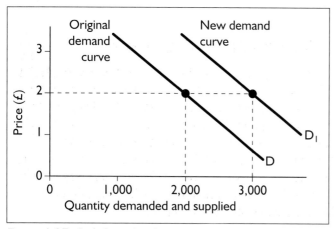

Figure 1.27 A shift in the demand curve

Tastes

As time moves on, new products become fashionable and popular while others go into decline. For example, in the 1970s platform shoes were the height of fashion; by the 1980s this was no longer so. They came back in the 1990s, and will probably disappear in the first decade of the twenty-first century to reappear again when the wheel of fashion turns again.

As time progresses, products lose popularity and the demand curve shifts to the left. For example, fewer people today eat the 'traditional English breakfast' of bacon and eggs, while many have switched to high-fibre cereals. A pronounced example of a rapid shift to the left in the demand curve for a product occurred with worries about BSE affecting beef in the 1990s.

Population

Population statistics can be very helpful for forecasting changes in demand. Demographers (people who compile population statistics) frequently make predictions about future population trends based on existing statistics. Predictions based on the size of the population in particular age groups are particularly easy to chart, because once a child has been born, he or she will become steadily older.

Populations can be classified in a number of ways including age, sex, locality, race, educational background and even by the newspaper read.

Demand forecasters will often analyse population statistics according to a cluster of relevant factors, for example Asian females in the 20–29-year-old age group living in Leicester. An increase in the relevant population will tend to move the demand curve for a product to the right (such as an increase in the number of pensioners will increase the demand for magazines targeted at the elderly, for sheltered accommodation and for off-peak holidays).

A decrease in the relevant population will tend to move the demand curve to the left.

Remember that when we look at population as a determinant of demand we are concerned with changes that take place in the numbers in the relevant section of the population.

The price of substitute products

The demand for products which have close **substitutes** will usually be influenced by the price of the substitutes.

This would be the case, for example, with different brands of petrol, tabloid newspapers, personal computers and so on.

The demand curve for a product is likely to shift to the right if a substitute product rises in price. The demand curve for a product is likely to shift to the left if a substitute product falls in price (assuming that other factors influencing demand do not alter at the same time).

The impact of a change in the price of one product on demand for another product can be calculated using **cross elasticity** of demand. This can be measured by:

$$\text{Cross elasticity of demand} = \frac{\text{Percentage change in demand for product X}}{\text{Percentage change in price of product Y}}.$$

For example, if a 5 per cent fall in the price of Coca-Cola leads to a 10 per cent fall in the demand for Pepsi we can say that the cross elasticity is equal to 2.

$$\frac{-10\%}{-5\%} = 2$$

From Pepsi's point of view it would be better to have a lower cross elasticity of demand. For example, if the 5 per cent fall in Coca-Cola's price only led to a 6 per cent fall in demand for Pepsi the cross elasticity would only be 1.2. It would be better still to have a cross elasticity of less than 1.

The price of complementary products

Some products are used together, so the demand for one is linked to the price of another. An example of this might be a textbook and its corresponding study guide, or football shirts and football shorts. If a particular textbook were to rise in price, then schools and colleges might switch to an alternative book. This would also reduce the demand for the study guides that go with the book. Cross elasticity is also relevant to **complementary products**. Here the relationship will appear as a negative number. A fall in the price of a textbook will lead to a rise in the demand for the study guide. For example:

$$\frac{\text{Quantity demanded of study guide rises by 10\%}}{\text{Fall in price of textbook of 5\%}} = \frac{+10\%}{-5\%}$$

Cross elasticity = −2.

Clearly, the higher the degree of complementarity between the two goods then the higher the negative number will be. For example, if the fall in textbook prices of 5 per cent led to an increase in demand for study guides of 20 per cent, then the cross elasticity would be −4.

Income

The more money people have, the easier it is for them to buy products. The amount of income people have to spend on goods is known as their **disposable income** and is their pay less taxes and other deductions.

Average incomes tend to rise over time and this will lead to a general increase in the level of demand for goods. The demand for individual items will, however, be related more to the changes in incomes earned by different groups such as teenagers for teenage magazines, entertainment and fashion, and pensioners for retirement homes and winter sun holidays.

The demand for most products will rise as a result of an increase in incomes for the relevant population. This will lead to a shift in the demand curve to the right.

It is helpful for a producer to know what is the relationship between demand for their product and changes in income. For most goods demand will increase with income – these are said to be normal goods. For example, as incomes rise people tend to spend more of their income on leisure activities and on personal computers and software.

We can measure the relationship between demand for a product and changes in income by using a measure known as **income elasticity of demand**.

$$\text{Income elasticity of demand} = \frac{\text{Percentage change in quantity demanded of a product}}{\text{Percentage change in income}}.$$

For example, a 2 per cent increase in incomes may lead to a 0.2 per cent increase in the demand for carpets. In this case, income elasticity would be:

$$\frac{0.2\%}{2\%} = +0.1.$$

Price elasticity of demand

The most important elasticity measure is **price elasticity of demand**, which measures how much the demand for a particular product changes as a result of a change in the price of that product. Having a knowledge of elasticity is essential to the producer. For example, it helps food manufacturer Heinz to calculate the impact of lowering the price of a can of baked beans by 1p or raising it by 1p. It informs the oil and petrol producers Shell and BP of the likely impact of altering their prices.

Price elasticity of demand is measured by the formula:

Price elasticity of demand $= \dfrac{\text{Percentage change in demand for product A}}{\text{Percentage change in price of product A}}$

If the percentage change in quantity demanded is greater than the change in price, then demand is said to be elastic.

If the percentage change in quantity demanded is less than the change in price, then demand is said to be inelastic.

For example, if a 5 per cent fall in the price of bread led to a 10 per cent increase in the demand for it, we would say that demand is elastic.

Price elasticity of demand $= \dfrac{10\%}{-5\%} = -2$.

(*Note*: price elasticity is expressed as a negative number because quantity demanded and price normally move in opposite directions to each other.)

If demand is highly elastic, then there will be considerable advantages to lowering prices – lower your prices and demand increases a lot. This helps to explain the 'pile it high and sell it cheap' attitude of many supermarkets. Low-price items may sell in huge quantities.

In contrast, some companies raise prices because they know that demand for their product is inelastic (for example, a 5 per cent increase in price leading to only a 2 per cent fall in demand). If this is the case, it may pay to charge a higher rather than a lower price for the goods – many designer items fall into this category.

Factors influencing supply

There are a number of factors which influence the supply of a product in addition to price influences. If one of these factors alters, the **conditions of supply** are said to have changed. These factors include the price of factors of production, the price of other commodities, technology, tastes of producers, etc.

Changes in one or a combination of these factors will cause shifts in the supply curve. The supply curve can shift either to the left or to the right. A shift to the left indicates that smaller quantities will be supplied than before at given prices. A shift to the right indicates that larger quantities will be supplied than before at given prices (see Figure 1.28).

Figure 1.28 shows that in the original situation a quantity of 400,000 apples a day would have been supplied at 20p. When the conditions of supply move in favour of the product (for example a good harvest), then more will be supplied at all prices, so that, for example, at 20p 900,000 Golden Delicious apples will be provided. Alternatively, if the conditions of supply move against a product (for example a rise in the cost of pesticides), fewer will be supplied at all prices, so that at 20p, for example, perhaps only 200,000 Golden Delicious apples will be supplied.

Factors which can cause these shifts in supply are outlined below.

The price of factors of production

Production is based on the combination of factor inputs in order to produce outputs.

If the cost of a factor input rises, then it will become more expensive to produce outputs. Factors of production will only be used in the long term if the value of their output is

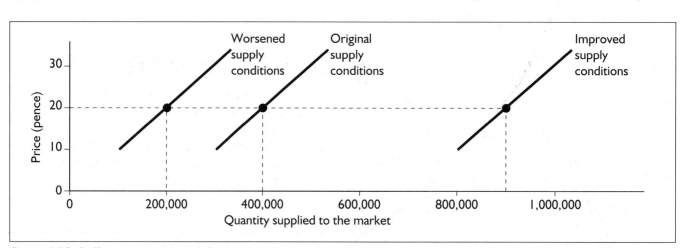

Figure 1.28 Different quantities of Golden Delicious apples supplied to the market at 20p per apple given different supply conditions

greater than their cost of hire. As factor prices rise, fewer factors will be used in production, and hence the supply of a product will fall.

For example, let us assume that an agricultural crop requires three main inputs – land, labour and chemical fertiliser. If the cost of one of these inputs (or a combination of them) were to rise, then farmers might cut back on the acreage committed to this particular crop.

Conversely, when the price of factor of production falls, then supply conditions move in favour of increased production and supply is likely to shift to the right.

The price of other commodities

In a number of areas of production it is possible to switch production from less profitable to more profitable lines. For example, many arable farmers have a certain degree of discretion over which crops to grow. A car manufacturer can choose whether to produce family cars, or smaller models. If a particular line becomes relatively more profitable, then scarce resources such as equipment, time and materials can be switched into producing it and away from producing other products. For example, a rise in the price of carrots may therefore lead to a shift to the left in the supply curve for cabbages. A fall in the price of carrots may lead to a shift to the right in the supply curve for cabbages.

CASE STUDY: RIP-OFF BRITAIN

Table 1.14 The high price of living in London (in £)

Goods	London	Paris	Berlin	New York
Apples (kilo)	1.29	0.70	0.95	0.51
Milk (litre)	0.85	0.59	0.67	0.62
Coca-Cola (can)	0.35	0.22	0.19	0.25
Premium lager (500 ml bottle)	1.15	0.35	0.45	0.78
Jeans (Levis)	50.00	39.90	41.38	21.25
Trainers (Nike)	78.00	70.00	75.86	31.23
Cinema ticket	7.50	4.90	1.38	5.31
Ford Focus	10,157.00	8,700.00	9,431.00	7,100.00
Petrol (30 litres unleaded)	21.00	20.10	16.55	9.44

Source: The Independent, 16 June 1999

In the summer of 1999 The Independent newspaper carried out a survey comparing the price of items in London, Paris, Berlin and New York and concluded that prices in the UK were a 'rip off' for consumers. Table 1.14 shows some of the differences.

The British Retail Consortium, a body representing the big retailers, explained the price differences in terms of the higher costs for British retailers in terms of higher wages and higher rents.

QUESTIONS FOR DISCUSSION

1 How would you account for the prices in London compared with those in Paris, Berlin and New York?
2 What inferences might you make from Table 1.14 about the relative levels of competition in the respective capitals?

Changes in the level of technology

An improvement in the level of technology means that more output can be produced with fewer resources. This means that the supply curve for a product will shift to the right. Modern technology based on computers and factory robots has enabled a wide range of producers to produce large outputs at lower unit costs, for example in car production, newspapers and modern breweries.

Other factors

One of the main factors influencing the supply of a number of goods and services is the weather. A number of services respond to changes in the weather, for example the appearance of umbrella sellers at the entrances to underground stations. The supply of agricultural products depends very much on changing weather conditions.

A dynamic picture

In the real world, in most markets the forces of demand and supply are changing on a regular basis – incomes change (a demand factor), while new technologies develop (a supply factor), while at the same time rival producers alter the prices of their products (influencing both demand and supply). Many markets are therefore in a constant state of flux. It is in this dynamic world that we see the importance of prices, which act as a signal to producers, encouraging them to supply more or less, and allowing consumers to make the sorts of purchasing decisions that enable them to receive the best possible value for money when choosing between alternative ways of spending their incomes.

The truth is stranger than fiction

We have already seen that many markets are highly dynamic, with frequent changes in demand and supply. In the USA economists use the term the 'hog cycle' to explain the large fluctuations that take place in the market for pigs and pig products. If the price of hogs (pigs) is high, then US farmers will rear a lot more hogs, leading to oversupply and a rapid decline in prices in the next season. When the price of hogs falls substantially, then farmers will reduce the number of pigs and switch to something else, for example turkeys. This means that in the next season there are too few hogs for the market and their prices will rise once again. The hog cycle is used to explain the wide-scale fluctuations in many agricultural and other products which take time to come onto the market.

Chapter 16 *Unemployment, inflation and economic growth*

In the previous two chapters we examined the market for individual goods and services in the economy.

It is also important to have an understanding of the **general level of demand** in the economy and the **general level of supply**.

The study of the economy as a whole is called **macroeconomics** and is concerned with issues such as:

- the general level of employment in the UK
- the rate of price increases in the economy (inflation)
- the growth of output in the economy.

All of these areas are important to businesses because:

- if employment is high, then it will be more costly to hire new labour, and existing workers will be in a strong position to push for wage rises
- if inflation is rising, this will increase costs to a business (such as the costs of raw materials)
- if the economy is growing, then people in general will have more money to spend which will be good for business.

Economic trends, economic policies, and how these affect business decision making

Economic trends are the patterns of what is happening to variables like unemployment, inflation and growth over a period of time. Perhaps the rate of inflation is increasing. Perhaps the level of growth is not as fast this year as it has been in previous years, etc.

The government uses **economic policies** to try to create favourable economic trends. The policies it uses relate to its own spending and taxation as well as changes in interest rates and some other instruments to control the economy. The sorts of favourable trends that the government tries to create are low unemployment levels, low inflation levels and sustained economic growth.

National output, national income and national expenditure

Gross domestic product (GDP) refers to the total value of the goods that are produced in a country (output) in a given period of time, for example in one year. GDP is thus a useful way of measuring the total value of the goods supplied in the economy.

Firms that produce national output will reward the various factors of production that produce the output. These rewards are in the form of incomes. So, for example:

- labour will earn wages
- shareholders and other owners will earn profits
- lenders of money will earn interest
- suppliers of land will earn rents.

If we add all these incomes together we arrive at a figure for national income:

National output = National income.

What then do the recipients of income do with their money? The answer is that they will spend it on goods and services (which, of course, have been produced by businesses). If the recipients of income spend all of what they earn, then:

National income = National expenditure.

You can therefore see that the national economy works through a circular flow of income (see Figure 1.29).

The importance of economic growth

Over time an economy needs to be able to provide its people with better living standards, so that they have more

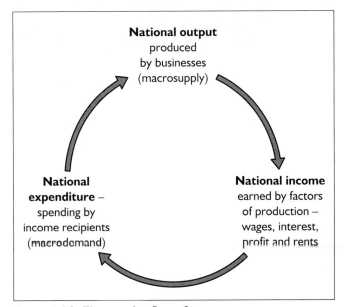

Figure 1.29 The circular flow of income

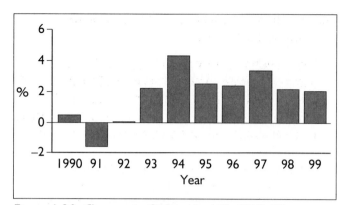

Figure 1.30 Changes in GDP in the UK, 1990–99
Source: Datastream; OECD

goods to consume, more leisure time and better environmental and other living conditions. This will only take place if there is a growth in GDP which does not threaten living conditions (for example living conditions would deteriorate with the spread of more diseases like Aids, and the creation of industrial pollution).

The nature of economic growth is that it does not take place in a steady way. The UK economy experiences periods in which the rate of growth is rising, followed by periods in which the rate of growth falls. In some periods there is even negative growth.

In Figure 1.30, which shows the changes in GDP in the UK in recent times, you can see this cyclical trend. For example, between 1992 and 1994 growth was rising at a greater rate. From 1997 to 1999 GDP was increasing, but each year at a lower rate.

The economy goes through a trade cycle of booms and slumps in economic growth (see Figure 1.31).

When the trend is one of slump, then government policies will be concerned to boost the economy (see Table 1.15).

It is obvious why a slump is undesirable – because it leads to falling living standards, and loss of jobs for some people. However, too rapid a boom is also bad for the economy. In a boom demand in the economy picks up to the extent at which demand may outstrip the ability of the economy to match the demand with supply. This leads to two undesirable effects:

• The economy 'overheats', leading to inflation.
• Some of the excess demand in the economy is met through sucking in too many imports, leading to a balance of payments problem. This means that a country is importing more than it is exporting, storing up problems for the future should the situation continue.

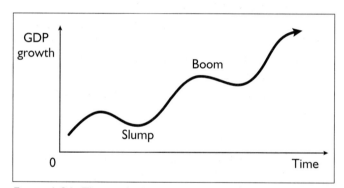

Figure 1.31 The trade cycle

Table 1.15 Government policies and impact on business in times of slump and boom

Indicators of slump	Government policies to counteract slump	Impact on business
Falling GDP Falling employment Falling prices Falling investment	Lower taxes Raise government spending Lower interest rates	Boosts spending in economy – encouraging firms to invest and to take on more employees
Indicators of boom	**Government policies to counteract boom**	**Impact on business**
Rising GDP Rising employment Rising prices Rising investment	Increase levels of taxes Lower government spending Raise interest rates	Dampens down spending in economy – discouraging firms from investing – leading to 'shake out' of labour

How then does unemployment arise?

If the real world were as simple as the model shown Table 1.15 there would be no unemployment – people would spend what they earned and this demand would encourage firms to supply more goods.

However, things are not as simple. We have seen that the economy experiences trade cycles. Unemployment resulting from the trade cycle is **cyclical unemployment**. The government can try to reduce cyclical unemployment by increasing its own spending, reducing taxes, and/or lowering interest rates in a period of slump. Business would welcome these measures, particularly tax cuts and interest rate cuts which are costs of production to the business.

A certain amount of **structural unemployment** is likely to exist in the economy, as it continually restructures. The structure of the economy is concerned with the broad structure of industry. In Chapter 1 we saw how over time the economy has restructured from being based on primary industry, to secondary industry and, finally, to a service-based (tertiary) economy. In 2000 and beyond we have seen a further restructuring of industry towards the 'new economy' based on information and communications technology.

A certain amount of **frictional unemployment** takes place in an economy as people change jobs. It is not always the case that a person is able to move straight from one job to another. Frictions in the way the market works, for example poor information about new job opportunities, lead to a time lag between leaving one job and taking on another.

The government seeks to reduce structural and frictional unemployment through a range of measures designed to enable people to find work more easily, for example the existence of JobCentres for job seekers, to provide greater contact and information between the buyers and sellers of labour services in the market. Clearly, this benefits businesses that are seeking new employees by reducing the costs of recruitment as well as access to information.

Some employees are **voluntarily unemployed** in that they are not actively seeking work. The Labour government has sought to reduce this figure by making it increasingly difficult for those avoiding work to claim state benefits.

The two current official methods of calculating UK unemployment figures are:

- The **claimant count** whereby the number of unemployed is calculated on the basis of the number of people claiming benefit (jobseeker's allowance). This is the method favoured and often used by the government. In the middle of 2000 the claimant count was just over one million.
- The **labour force survey** is conducted by the International Labour Organisation (ILO) and refers to people without a job who were available to start work in the two weeks following their interview, and had either looked for work in the four weeks prior to the interview or were waiting to start a job they had already obtained. In the middle of 2000 the figure for unemployment using this method was over one and a half million.

Since 1984 there has been a downward trend in unemployment as shown by Table 1.16, which is based on ILO figures.

Table 1.16 Unemployment, selected years 1984–2000

Year	Number of unemployed (millions)
1984	3.2
1990	2.0
1994	2.7
1995	2.5
1996	2.3
1997	2.0
1998	1.8
1999	1.6
2000	1.5

Source: International Labour Organisation

How does inflation arise?

Inflation occurs for two main reasons:

- Demand in the economy is rising more rapidly than supply. This could be because the government has printed too much money (perhaps to use for its own spending plans).
- Alternatively, it could be because the economy is already working to full capacity, so that it is very difficult to increase supply in the economy.

We can illustrate this by means of aggregate (total) supply and demand curves in the economy. At any one time the

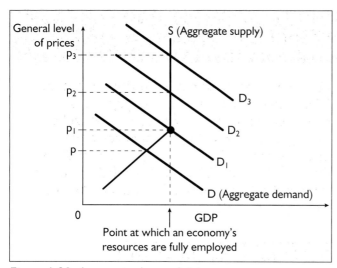

Figure 1.32 Aggregate demand rising

economy has available only so many resources. If demand increases beyond this point of full resource utilisation, then this will lead to inflation, as shown in Figure 1.32 where the general level of prices in the economy is shown on the vertical axis and GDP along the horizontal axis.

The **Retail Prices Index** (**RPI**) is used by the government to measure the rate of inflation and the change in prices over a year for the average household. It is a listing of all the prices of over 150,000 goods. The average increase in these prices over a year is the rate of inflation. Regional differences are taken into account as the same prices are collected in 180 areas and the average price is then taken for each good.

The goods which are to be included in the RPI are revised each year. This way the government is looking at the prices of the most frequently bought goods and the index is not distorted by exceptions. For example, in 1995 cabbage greens, calculators and frozen Victoria sponges were removed from the list and smoke alarms, chewing gum and replica football strips were added.

Figure 1.33 shows the trend of the RPI between 1982 and 1999.

For business, inflation is a major worry because once prices become unstable it is very difficult for businesses to make predictions about the future. Many business transactions are carried out on a credit basis. A retailer may buy goods from a manufacturer, and only pay for those goods three months later. In a period of inflation the manufacturer may lose out because by the time it is paid for the goods, the money it receives might well be worth less than it was three months earlier. In a period of rising prices, firms will seek to raise their own prices to cover rising costs, often in advance of the rise in their costs. This leads to accelerating price rises and increased levels of uncertainty.

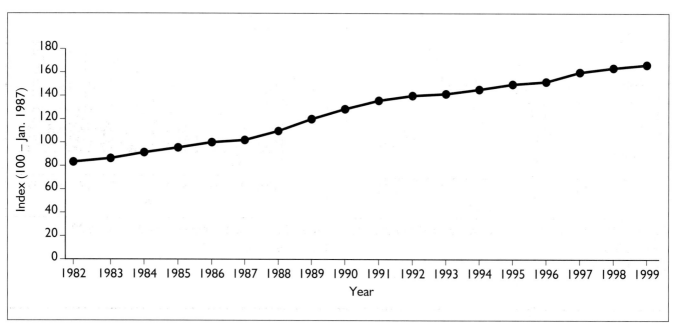

Figure 1.33 Retail Prices Index, 1982–99
Source: Office for National Statistics

Walk down a high street in the Irish Republic in the summer of 2000 and you would have seen evidence of an overheating economy. The shops were packed, and the skyline was dotted with cranes and other signs of booming construction.

This led to a major problem in the form of higher inflation. Retail prices were rising at 5.2 per cent a year – the fastest for 15 years and the highest among the eleven eurozone countries. In fact, inflation was three times the European Union's 1.7 per cent average. Ireland's unemployment rate fell to 4.6 per cent in May 2000, its lowest for 18 years. This inevitably created serious shortages of skilled workers, allowing average wages and bonuses to be bid up, adding to inflation.

Meanwhile, house prices were rising at around 20 per cent a year, as low mortgage rates combined with a strong labour market and a demographic boom. Forecasts indicate that prices might rise by up to 60 per cent by 2004. Figures 1.34 and 1.35 show the relative growth rates and inflation rates in Ireland and the UK leading up to 2000.

QUESTIONS FOR DISCUSSION

1 In what ways was the Irish economy doing well in mid-2000 according to the data?
2 What problems do the data indicate?
3 How might the Irish government have sought to deal with the overheating economy? (Note that it is not in a position to raise interest rates because these are set by the European Central Bank.)

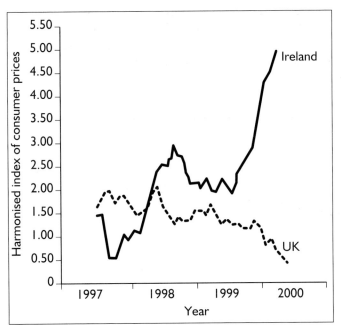

Figure 1.34 *Index of consumer prices, Ireland and the UK, 1997–2000*
Source: Datastream

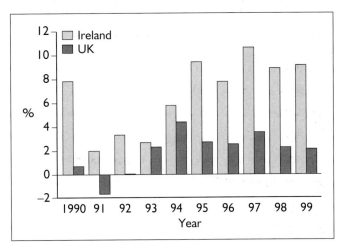

Figure 1.35 *Growth, Ireland and the UK, 1990–99*
Source: Datastream; OECD

The truth is stranger than fiction

The governments of some Latin American countries in the late twentieth century resorted to printing money to pay for their internal wars against political groups that were seeking revolution. The effect of this was to make their currencies almost worthless through hyperinflation (rampant inflation). At the same time, revolutionary groups were confiscating people's property to aid them in their armed struggle and writing promissory notes to the effect that they would return the confiscated property once the revolution was over and they were the new government. These promissory notes came to be accepted in many areas as a new means of exchange (money), because people had more confidence in the revolutionaries than in the government.

Chapter 17 Interest rates and exchange rates

Business people need to have a good understanding of how changes in interest rates and exchange rates affect their businesses. A rise in interest rates may lead to cost increases for many businesses (those that have borrowed money); changes in exchange rates can both affect business costs and the demand for a business's products.

Interest rates

The **interest rate** is the price of borrowing money. Of course, as with all prices an important determinant of interest rates is the demand and supply for money.

In a period of economic boom, people will be spending more and borrowing more, and they will demand more money, leading to an upward pressure in the price of money – the interest rate. Of course, as the interest rate rises this will help to dampen down some of the demand for money.

In Figure 1.36 you can see that the **supply of money** in the economy (notes and coins, money people have

deposited in their bank accounts and some other types of money) is fixed at a particular moment in time. As the demand for money rises from D to D_1, then the interest rate rises from IR to IR_1.

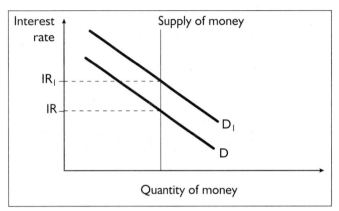

Figure 1.36 Increased spending leading to a rise in interest rates

---

CASE STUDY: FED RAISES US INTEREST RATES BY 0.5 PER CENT WITH 'MORE TO COME'

The Federal Reserve, the USA's central bank, raised interest by half a point on Wednesday 16 May 2000, emphasising fears that exceptionally strong growth could hit the US economy.

The Federal Reserve (also known as the Fed) also warned that the threat of inflation had not gone away, alerting markets to the likelihood of further increases. Throughout the 1990s the US economy had grown steadily, but by 2000 it appeared that it could not continue with the same level of increases in consumer spending without leading to inflation that could get out of control.

So, the Fed raised its interest rate from 6 to 6.5 per cent. It acted because of a future threat of inflation. 'Increases in demand have remained in excess of even the rapid pace of productivity driven gains in potential supply, exerting continued pressure on resources,' said the Fed in a statement. 'We are worried that this disparity in

the growth of demand and potential supply will continue, which could foster inflationary imbalances that would undermine the economy's outstanding performance.'

The Fed also made it clear that it did not believe that the need for tightening was over, and that its bias in the future would be towards further interest rate rises.

QUESTIONS FOR DISCUSSION

1 Why did the Federal Reserve raise interest rates?
2 How would this help to dampen inflationary pressures?
3 How might the rise in interest rates help business?
4 How might the rise in interest rates harm business?

In the UK the rate of interest at which the **Bank of England** will lend money to banks is determined by the **Monetary Policy Committee** (**MPC**), which is made up of the Chairman of the Bank of England and some independent advisers, including senior economists and financiers with a good understanding of how the economy works.

Prior to 1997, interest rates had been set by the government. One of the first things that the Labour government elected in 1997 did was to hand power for setting interest rates to the MPC.

The MPC's decisions about interest rates are determined by the state of the economy – particularly the level of inflation.

If the general level of prices in the economy is rising the MPC will be inclined to raise interest rates. Rising interest rates discourage borrowing, and hence spending in the economy.

The effect of changes in interest rates on business

The main effect of changes in interest rates on the economy is on the spending decisions of both firms and individuals:

- A rise in interest rates means an increase in the cost of credit, thus raising the cost of all financial operations (both short-term overdrafts and long-term loans and mortgages will be affected). When the cost of credit increases this is likely to reduce profits and leave firms with less ready cash. Organisations therefore become much more reluctant to borrow and will often postpone or cancel their investment plans. A rise in interest rates thus has a dampening effect on the economy. In addition, when interest rates rise this will make firms with higher gearing ratios more risky as investments. When interest rates rise – a cost of production – then firms will seek to reduce other costs.
- Changes in interest rates also have an impact on net lenders (that is, people who lend more money than they borrow). A rise in interest rates will lead to a rise in their incomes and an increase in their spending (because they are better off). A fall in interest rates will reduce their incomes (and their spending). Net lenders tend to be older people. As a result, changes in interest rates may have a major effect on firms that produce goods and services targeted at this sector.
- A rise in interest rates will also adversely affect net borrowers, for example people with large mortgages to repay, or people whose mortgage repayments are high

in proportion to their incomes. High interest rates may lead to a substantial fall in the amount of their spending with a considerable impact on the economy.

Interest rates and loans

Because small businesses are often dependent on banks and other lenders for start-up capital, they will be particularly hard hit by changes in interest rates. An increase in interest rate by one or two percentage points could completely wipe out a small business's profit margin. In a period of slump and pessimism far fewer new businesses are likely to start up, helping to dampen down the economy. Many new businesses start up on the crest of a wave of booming conditions. However, they may feel the pinch when demand conditions start to dampen down.

Exchange rates

Whenever international trade takes place, there is a need for **foreign exchange** by at least one of the parties to the transaction. The foreign exchange market is a global market providing the mechanism for the buying and selling of foreign currencies.

A country's foreign **exchange rate** is the price at which its own currency exchanges for that of others.

Every currency has many rates to reflect all traded currencies, such as the rate of sterling against the US dollar, the Japanese yen and the German deutschmark.

Why are exchange rates important for business?

Business people will tell you that when it comes to trading in international markets they are happiest in a period of stability. Most international transactions are carried out on a credit basis. If a Scottish whisky distillery sells its product to a Japanese importer, then it will need to give the importer a period of credit (usually three months) during which period the Japanese business will be able to sell the whisky in its domestic market in order to be able to make payment to the distillery.

When a business sells goods on credit it makes a sacrifice and take risks. The sacrifice is that it has invested time, effort and money in producing goods for which it is receiving nothing in the short term, that is, until payment takes place. The risks are as follows:

- There is a possibility of non-payment.

- If the payment is made in foreign currency, the value of the currency might turn out to be less than originally expected (because of poor exchange rates).

The importance of the euro

Many British businesses would like the UK to be part of the **eurozone**, that is, adopt the single European currency, the **euro** (see Figure 1.37). Since about 70 per cent of British trade takes place within the **European Union (EU)**, all the currency exchange costs of importing and exporting in the EU would be eliminated.

Linking the exchange rate to profitability

There are two ways in which exchange rates may influence business activities. First, they may affect the price of goods and services which businesses buy in international markets. Secondly, they may affect the price at which businesses sell goods and services in these markets.

Figure 1.38 shows that changes in the exchange rate may create uncertainty in both instances. For example, if a business imports goods or services, the exchange rate will influence the price of its purchases, and any changes will make pricing and costing more difficult. On the other hand,

Figure 1.37 The euro

CASE STUDY: SELLING MARKS & SPENCER UNDERWEAR TO FRANCE

During the 1990s UK high street retailer Marks & Spencer set up a chain of stores in France where its goods proved to be very popular. Marks & Spencer has always had a reputation for high quality in France. One of Marks & Spencer's best lines in the UK is underwear. Walk into any room and you can be almost certain that there will be more people wearing Marks & Spencer underwear than any other make! This trend is picking up in France.

Let us assume that in pricing its underwear lines Marks & Spencer decided to price products at a level which reflected the quality of its goods. It is here that the uncertainties of international trade may come into play.

For example, if the value of the pound rose against the French franc, as was the case in the first part of 2000, then Marks & Spencer found that its earnings increased for the same volume of goods. However,

this would only benefit Marks & Spencer if French consumers did not feel that Marks & Spencer underwear was becoming too expensive compared with rival French brands. To be successful, therefore, a company needs to have an inelastic demand for its product when the exchange rate starts to rise against foreign currencies.

Conversely, if the value of the pound had fallen against the franc, then Marks & Spencer might have found that its French earnings (when converted into sterling) were less than anticipated from the same volume of goods. Of course, one advantage of a falling pound is that UK exports become cheaper and it may be possible to sell more goods. The problem here is that if UK goods become too cheap in markets like France they may lose some of the prestige associated with a high-price, high-quality image.

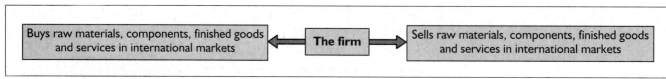

| Buys raw materials, components, finished goods and services in international markets | ⟷ | The firm | ⟶ | Sells raw materials, components, finished goods and services in international markets |

Figure 1.38 Buying and selling in international markets

if it sells goods or services abroad, changes in the exchange rate will affect the amount of foreign currency coming in and this will either earn the business more or less than it had planned. Movements in the exchange rate will thus have a distinct bearing on profit margins, as well as a business's ability to sell overseas.

The truth is stranger than fiction

While a rising pound will help you as a tourist overseas in that you will be able to get more pesetas, dollars, etc. per pound, the rise in the pound isn't always so pleasing to business. Exporters selling into competitive foreign markets are often annoyed to find that the rising pound makes their prices too high to foreigners. The solution for exporters is to make sure that they continually add value to their products so that they are seen as a necessity rather than as a luxury which can be substituted.

SECTION D *Legal, political and social influences*

<u>INTRODUCTION</u> As well as having to take account of the economic environment in which it operates a business's activity is also affected by legal, political and social influences.

Simply keeping up with changes in the **law** is a time-consuming business. Business law covers a wide range of issues including health and safety, the protection of consumers, the relationship of the business with the environment, anti-competitive practices and many more.

Political influences are also important because government has a political agenda which leads to changes being made in **economic policies** and in legal frameworks which have a particular slant. For example, the Conservative Party places a stronger emphasis on free markets than does the Labour Party, which believes that limits should be placed on the operation of markets in order to protect the socially disadvantaged. During the period 1979–97 when the Conservatives were in power, the emphasis was very much on creating a competitive business environment, for example by the privatisation of state industries, reduction in business taxes, and so on. Since 1997 the Labour government has made it clear that it supports business and enterprise while at the same time taking a less 'hands-off' approach to running the economy than the previous government.

Today, one of the major political changes for businesses is that decisions which directly affect UK businesses are increasingly being made by decision makers at European Union level, rather than just at national level by the UK government.

Social changes are also of major significance to business because of the way that they impact on demand and supply. Changes in social attitudes and behaviours such as people spending more time on leisure lead to more demand for the leisure industries. Changes in age structure such as an ageing population lead to increased demand for the types of goods and services required by older people, and so on. Other social changes, such as the change in attitudes towards women working, affect supply – by providing an increased supply of labour, women help to lower the costs of employment in some industries.

Critical thinking

At the end of June 2000 French President Jacques Chirac (Figure 1.39) threw the debate on the future of the European Union into confusion by calling for a 'pioneer group' of states to press ahead with a set of common policies ranging from economic management to defence.

His radical proposal would, in effect, push Britain on to the European sidelines until the UK government agreed to join the single currency.

The French President also called for the creation of a new 'secretariat' – bypassing the European

Figure 1.39 French President Jacques Chirac looking towards closer European union

Commission – which would coordinate the activities of the pioneer group, committed to an 'ensemble' of reinforced policies on economics, defence, security and cross-border crime.

Chirac's remarks were in response to the vision of the German Foreign Minister, Joshka Fischer, of a federal Europe, with one government and one president.

WHAT DO YOU THINK?

1 Do you think that the UK should be seeking to be part of a European Union which is directed far more from the centre with one government and president, making common decisions for the whole?

2 Why might the UK become sidelined in Europe if it doesn't agree to join the single currency?

3 Do you think that UK business might benefit from having a common European currency?

4 Why might UK business be concerned about moves to create a more centralised European Union?

5 Why might UK business be worried if the 'pioneer group' of countries, including Belgium, the Netherlands, Luxembourg, France and Germany, press ahead with common policies without the UK?

Chapter 18 *Legislation as a constraint and a framework in which business operates*

Laws both constrain (limit) what a business can or cannot do and provide a framework within which business activity is conducted. Business people must constantly examine the law, and changes in the law, in order to make sure that they are complying with its requirements.

Laws and **regulations** that affect British business are made at three levels:

- **European Union (EU) level** – increasingly, legal frameworks are being created by the EU.
- **National level** – laws are created through Acts of Parliament. Existing laws have either been created by Parliament (statute law) or are part of law because they have been around and accepted for a long time (common law).
- **Local level** – local regulations and bylaws are made by local government.

Laws made at European Union level have increasingly affected the UK since it joined the European Union in 1973. Today, the EU is made up of 15 countries, with Hungary, Poland and the Czech Republic likely to join in the near future.

In the early days the emphasis was very much on economic union in what was then known as the European Economic Community (EEC). More recently, the emphasis has been on greater political union with greater cooperation in the areas of common defence and taxation strategies.

Steps in the development of the European Union

Step 1. **The creation of a free trade area**. A free trade area is one where there are no barriers to trade such as **import tariffs**. The first EEC free trade area was created in the late 1950s but did not include the UK.

Step 2. **Creating a customs union**. A customs union is where a group of countries create a common **external tariff** imposed on countries outside the union. This was an early feature of the EEC.

Step 3. **Forming a common market**. An agreement between European Community (EC) member states in 1986 committed the countries to the creation of a **single market** by the end of 1992. The single market is one in which there are four freedoms – freedom of movement of people, freedom of movement of goods, freedom of movement of services and freedom of movement of capital (finance).

Step 4. **Economic union**. By 2000 economic union had moved further forward, and today there is a **single currency**, the euro, for most of the countries within the European Union. Interest rates within the eurozone are determined by the **European Central Bank (ECB)**, and taxes are being harmonised.

Step 5. **Political union**. Supporters of the idea of a federal Europe would like to see the creation of a United States of Europe. Currently, countries like France and Germany are pushing some way in this direction. Increasingly, social policy is being determined centrally (for example conditions of work, protection of children, etc.) in order to create common standards. However, there is still some way to go before political union is widely accepted.

WHAT DO YOU THINK?

At the heart of the debate on the European Union is whether the UK should be pushing for a deepening or a widening of the Union or both. Widening of the Union involves allowing more and more countries into the EU so that they (and we) can benefit from operating in a larger free trade market, thus involving wider economic union. Other people argue for a deepening of the union, that is, greater political ties between those within the Union so that more and more policies are determined by a single governing authority. What do you think? Deepening, widening, or both?

Types of EU legislation

Regulations and directives from the EU affect many areas of business life in the UK:

- **Regulations** are binding legally and are above the national laws of member states if any conflict arises.
- **Directives** require member states to introduce laws in their national parliaments to put into effect EU decisions. If the member does not introduce the directive the European Commission may refer the matter to the European Court of Justice, which is above national courts.

In recent years UK national and local laws have been altered and amended in many cases where they had not fitted in with EU regulations and directives.

The best way to gain an understanding of how the legal framework affects business activity is to take an example – in this case the **Working Time Directive** – bearing in mind that EU directives have to be implemented through national law.

The working time regulations enforce the European Working Time Directive which came into force in the UK on 1 October 1999.

The legislation imposes a statutory right to a maximum working week of 48 hours for many workers. However, this can be averaged out over 17 weeks, so there is room for some flexibility, but there are strict rules governing the regulation of night workers (limited to an average of eight hours in each 24-hour period) and there are changes to the hours for young workers.

Workers who want to exceed the limit can make a written agreement to do so with their employers. (The regulation also incorporates the **Annual Leave Directive** which gives all workers the right to a minimum of four weeks' paid annual leave.)

The regulations cover the majority of workers, that is, those covered by a contract of employment, and agency and temporary workers, as well as freelance workers. It does not cover the self-employed. Nor do the regulations include workers in transport, sea fishing, other work at sea and doctors in training.

Legislation such as the Working Time Directive affects businesses as follows:

- The failure of a business to comply with legislation can and often does lead to the law courts where the firm may face considerable fines as well as the resultant bad publicity.
- Businesses faced by tighter regulation of their activity will incur an increase in costs of production involved in complying with the law. For example, in the case of working time regulations they may have to employ more labour to cover shortages.
- One of the benefits of complying with the law is that a firm may gain a competitive advantage over rival organisations which are less well placed to meet the new legal requirements. For example, with the development of EU regulations covering health and safety of bakeries and other providers of food, many small bakeries had to close down because they couldn't afford the costs involved in improving their facilities. Larger, more profitable firms found themselves in a better position to comply.

To gain a better understanding of how legislation impacts on business, you should examine a current example of a change in legislation and the effect this is having on business – changes in consumer protection, health and safety, equal opportunities, environmental laws, for example – by studying a good-quality national newspaper such as *The Independent* over a period of at least a week

CASE STUDY: UNILEVER WINS EU BATTLE TO MARKET CHOLESTEROL-BUSTER

In June 2000 Unilever, the Anglo-Dutch consumer products group, won a two-year battle to be allowed to market Flora pro.activ, a cholesterol-busting margarine, in the European Union.

The company, which makes Lipton teas and Magnum ice-creams, said the EU standing committee for foodstuffs had voted in favour of authorising the product, whose key ingredients are concentrated plant extracts that are found at low levels in everyday foods.

At the time of the decision the margarine had already sold over 20 million packs in countries outside the EU including the USA, Switzerland and Brazil.

QUESTIONS FOR DISCUSSION

1 Why did Unilever have to wait for permission at EU level before selling the margarine in the UK and other member countries?

2 Why do you think that Unilever would have been more concerned about decision making at EU level than at the level of individual national governments?

The truth is stranger than fiction

When Jason Pitt was looking for a new recruit for his publishing business he decided to place the following job advertisement at his local JobCentre:

'Due to considerable growth our business to business magazine based in Walsall requires a management trainee to join our successful team. The ideal applicant will be enthusiastic and hard-working with the ability to put fresh inventive ideas into practice. Commitment and a desire to succeed are vital in a position where success will ensure earnings to match.'

However, he was not allowed to place the advertisement because he was told that it was discriminatory – the words 'enthusiastic and hard working' might be regarded as offensive to people who did not display these characteristics.

Instead, he had to place the following 'politically correct' advertisement:

'Job: Management Trainee, permanent position. You will be working in a publishing company. You will be selling the concept of client features to businesses in the Midlands that may be celebrating a new opening, anniversary, or who want to profile themselves to a wider audience. You will have A-Level English or equivalent and this position will lead to a manager's post.'

Source: reported on ITN News, 15 June 2000

Chapter 19 The state as regulator, provider of assistance and customer

In the real world no economy relies exclusively on the free market, nor can we find examples of purely planned economies. A **mixed economy** combines elements of both the free market and the planning system. Some decisions are made solely through the private sector while other decisions are made by the government.

The UK is a good example of a mixed economy; some parts of industry are owned and operated by the government but large chunks of the business world remain in private hands. The public sector is that part of the economy that is government owned. The private sector is that part of the economy that is owned by private citizens.

Throughout much of the twentieth century and into the early part of the twenty-first, **government spending** in the UK has made up a significant percentage of all spending. Figure 1.40 shows that during wartime government control of the economy, and thus spending, increases. In recent years government spending has been reduced as the government has sought to allow the market system to play a more prominent role.

Figure 1.41 shows the ways in which the activities of government, consumers and businesses are inextricably intertwined in a mixed economy. The government regulates the activities of producers and consumers, for example by setting out **health and safety standards** for the production of goods and by stipulating legal requirements

limiting the ways in which consumers can buy using **hire purchase**. Government produces goods and services which it sells direct to businesses and consumers, for example the selling of consultancy services to exporters, and the provision of goods and services by public corporations. The government also provides services to

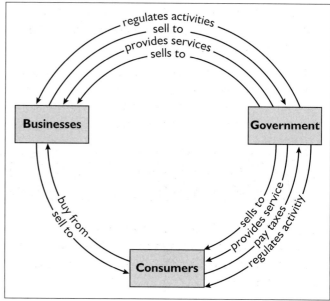

Figure 1.41 Links between business, consumers and government

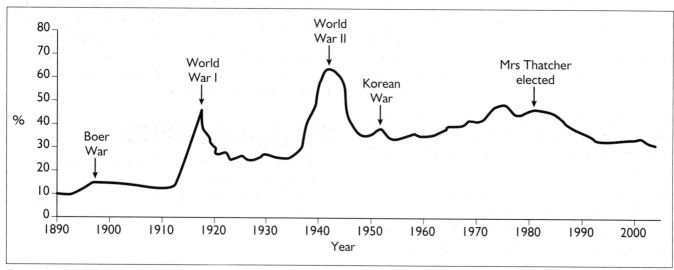

Figure 1.40 UK government spending as a percentage of all spending, 1890–2000

businesses and consumers such as the provision of street lighting and repairs to roads which are paid for indirectly by taxes. Businesses sell goods and services to the government, to other businesses and to consumers. Businesses also pay **local** and **national taxes**. Consumers buy goods and services from government and from businesses.

Regulation

In the course of time the government creates sets of rules about how businesses must operate. These rules taken together are known as **regulation**. So, for example, there are regulations covering how businesses can be set up and run, the treatment of employees in the workforce, consumer protection, competition, etc.

Sometimes it is argued that the state has taken regulation too far. By interfering too much in business activity, it limits the freedom of business to compete, and it also creates an additional administrative burden that ties up too many resources in paperwork and other administrative duties. A government that regulates heavily will also require a large civil service to administer the regulatory framework. This is costly, and the increased state costs will be passed on to business in the form of higher business taxes.

With the series of post-1979 privatisations of nationalised industries, the government created a number of official **regulatory bodies** for the new privatised industries such as OFWAT for water services and OFGAS for the gas industry. The job of these regulators was to ensure that the privatised industries didn't simply run in the interests of shareholders but also took into account the interests of other stakeholders. Regulators have subsequently imposed measures such as price increase limits on privatised firms and even asked for price cuts.

Providing assistance to business

The government provides assistance to business in a variety of ways, one of which is by providing information on

---

CASE STUDY: GOVERNMENT SUPPORT FOR RURAL POST OFFICES

At the end of June 2000 the government announced that it was to spend hundreds of millions of pounds on a rescue package for rural post offices threatened with closure.

Stephen Byers, the Trade and Industry Secretary, stated that subsidies would amount to an income guarantee to halt 'avoidable closures' of post offices. Under radical proposals, a 'Universal Bank' was to be developed to enable post offices to offer financial facilities to the 3.5 million people with no bank account. This would enable customers to have access to different high street banks through their post offices.

Account holders at the Universal Bank would be able to get cash out at any post office and use cash machines to take out money and pay bills through direct debit.

The government was forced to provide an emergency package for the network after it emerged that thousands of post offices could be threatened with closure in the next few years.

The crisis had been caused by the government's decision to switch welfare benefits from over-the-counter cash payments to electronic payments directly into people's bank account in the period 2003–5.

Announcing the proposal Stephen Byers said: 'The importance of rural post offices cannot be underestimated. Often they are the last remaining local shop, providing a vital service and also acting as a focal point of the community. In order to protect rural post offices, the government will place a formal requirement on the Post Office to maintain the rural network.'

QUESTIONS FOR DISCUSSION

1 Why is the government effectively subsidising rural post offices?
2 Do you think that this sort of subsidy activity is a good idea?

---

a range of issues from the introduction of the euro, to finding information about overseas markets, to ways of managing tax bills. In September 2000 the government launched **UKonline.gov.uk** which is a single portal providing access to all government websites. The portal is the link between the citizen (including business) and the government. Services are based on 'life episodes' – education, taxation, pensions and retirement – rather than individual government departments.

British Trade International is the joint Department of Trade and Industry/Foreign and Commonwealth Office operation which is responsible within the government for trade promotion and development. British Trade International helps businesses make the most of global trading opportunities. It supplies information from basic advice, such as for a small business which may be a first-time exporter to Dublin, to highly specific niche market (a small specialist market) information.

Within the UK, British Trade International provides dedicated market support including:

- advice/information services for initial market research
- professional help from export promoters who have widespread export experience
- information on various methods of conducting business in a specific country
- help with meeting language and cultural requirements
- assistance in bringing key contacts to the UK
- helping UK organisations market themselves overseas, including grants for visiting countries and exhibiting at international trade shows.

The government also provides direct support to business in the form of subsidies. A **subsidy** is when the government makes payment to businesses to support their activities. In recent years government subsidies have played an important part in attracting foreign companies to the UK, particularly in car production. Subsidies are provided not only by local and national government, but also by the European Union (EU) which provides subsidies for the poorer regions of the Union including parts of the UK.

Government as a customer

Because the government is the major spender of money in the UK it is a very important customer for many businesses in all sorts of industries. For example, through the National Health Service the government is a major purchaser of medicines and other medical supplies. Through defence the government is a major purchaser of defence-related products from radar systems, to tanks and aircraft. In recent years, with the scaling down of the defence industry, we have seen major reductions in employment in parts of the country where the defence industries are located.

The government must think very carefully therefore about how it alters its spending patterns because of the implications that such changes might have for business. Any reduction in government spending is likely to have a regional downward multiplier effect.

The government's central objective

The government's central economic objective is to achieve high and stable levels of growth and employment that will build a stronger economic future for Britain.

In the early 2000s the government's economic strategy is to:

- ensure economic stability as the means to achieving sustained economic growth in the long term
- to raise productivity through promoting enterprise and investment
- to increase employment opportunity, building a fairer society.

Means of government influence over the economy

In order to meet its central economic objective, the government has a number of means of influence. These include the following:

- **Monetary policy** is concerned with the money supply, rate of interest, exchange rates and credit. One of the Labour government's first steps after its election in 1997 was to make the Bank of England independent, ensuring that interest rate decisions are taken in the best long-term interests of the economy and not for short-term political considerations.
- **Fiscal policy** is concerned with ensuring that government borrowing – the difference between what the government spends and what it raises in tax revenue – is sustainable. The Labour government introduced a Code for Fiscal Stability, with strict rules to govern the public finances.
- Through its **tax raising and expenditure** roles the government has instruments to meet economic objectives. For example, the New Deal will help increase employability by giving the unemployed new opportunities.

- The government can act directly through **regulation and deregulation** – it can and does propose new laws and amendments to old ones, but it is important to remember that it is Parliament that actually makes laws. Regulation creates a framework in which organisations can operate and activities take place. Deregulation occurs when the government removes some of the controls and restrictions in order to allow economic agents greater freedom of action.
- **Control of monopoly** – UK competition law is made up of a number of Acts of Parliament, dealing with separate aspects of competition policy and consumer protection.
- **Public ownership and privatisation** – the government influences the market through its policies of public ownership and privatisation. For example, during World War II large sections of industry were taken over in order to coordinate production to meet the war effort. More recently, government has relinquished control of some major industries, including transport, gas, electricity and water, by selling shares in the companies.

Meeting the government's objective

Economic stability is essential for long-term growth and high levels of employment. The person responsible for running the nation's economy to meet this objective is the **Chancellor of the Exchequer**.

The Chancellor of the Exchequer sets the aims and objectives of the **Treasury**.

Aim

To raise the rate of sustainable growth and achieve rising prosperity through creating economic opportunities for all.

Objectives

- To maintain a stable macroeconomic framework with low inflation.
- To maintain sound public finances in accordance with the Code for Fiscal Stability.
- To improve the quality and cost effectiveness of public services.
- To increase the productivity of the economy and expand economic and employment opportunities for all, through productive investment, competition, innovation, enterprise, better regulation and increased employability.
- To promote a fair and efficient tax and benefit system with incentives to work, save and invest.
- To maintain an effective accounting and budgetary framework and promote high standards of regularity, propriety and accountability.
- To secure an efficient market in financial services and banking with fair and effective supervision.
- To arrange for cost-effective management of the government's debt and foreign currency reserves and the supply of notes and coins.
- To promote international financial stability and the UK's economic interests and ideas through international cooperation as a way of increasing global prosperity, including seeking to protect the most vulnerable groups.

The Budget

A key area of the role of the Treasury is in advising the Chancellor of the Exchequer on the government's forward financial plan, which is known as the **Budget**. This sets out the government's income and expenditure plans. Income is raised through direct and indirect taxes levied upon firms and individuals and then spent upon goods and services such as health, education, transport and defence. For example, the Budget in 1999 was used to meet the economic of objective of high and stable levels of growth and employment. Through the creation of **incentives**, it encouraged a better deal for enterprise and investment as well as the creation of economic stability as a platform for sustainable growth.

The truth is stranger than fiction
The government is the major purchaser of contraceptive sheaths in this country. Free contraceptives can be obtained in bulk from Family Planning Clinics.

Chapter 20 *The impact of changes in the political environment*

Business people have an important interest in the political environment. They know that a shift in government will influence the way in which business is treated. For much of the twentieth century, for example, many business people were wary of Labour governments. They felt that Labour tended to advance the interest of employees (particularly trade unions) at the expense of employers. They also felt that Labour tended to put too high taxes on business which added to costs.

There was also a feeling in the 1970s that Labour policies tended to lead to inflation – through too much government spending.

Many people in business looked favourably on the Conservative government that was in power between 1979 and 1997 because of the way in which it deregulated markets, privatised industry and encouraged competition, while bringing inflation under control.

Generally speaking, Conservative governments are associated with policies that favour the free market, whereas Labour is associated with greater government control of the economy.

However, following the election of a Labour government in 1997 there has been a switch in the traditional emphasis.

CASE STUDY: DEREGULATION OF THE AIRWAYS

When the airline industry took off in the 1950s, it became dominated by national carriers that enjoyed effective monopolies of flights to and from their own country.

However, things began to change in 1978 when Jimmy Carter, then US President, liberalised the North American market to allow (US-based) regional carriers to compete in their rivals' backyards.

It took another 20 years but finally, in 1997, the European Commission came up with a similarly deregulated market in the European Union (EU), allowing British Airways (now BA), for example, to compete for flights between Frankfurt and Paris.

As a result, European national airlines found their airspace invaded by competitors. This happened at the same time that national governments were reducing their state subsidies of airlines by privatising them.

In the USA the deregulation process led to increasing competition as a large number of new airlines set up so that eventually there were 30 major companies. However, because of cut-throat competition many of these collapsed or were taken over. Today, there are only six major groups.

In the EU several airlines initially agreed to create alliances with each other in the new deregulated market. Alliances typically involve members coordinating their timetables and offering tickets in the name of another airline in the same alliance. However, there are substantially greater cost savings to be gained from a full-scale merger.

It is likely therefore that we will see considerable merger activity in the EU in the near future (as long as this is allowed). BA is merging with the Dutch national carrier KLM so that the new company can use a common fleet of aircraft and jointly advertise and sell flights – leading to cost savings of as much as 10 per cent, enabling them to cut prices and be more competitive. Some commentators argue that in the competitive EU market there is only scope for three major European airlines.

Meanwhile, there seems to be no move towards an 'open skies' policy. The EU still jealously guards its own internal market, as does the USA.

QUESTIONS FOR DISCUSSION

1 What do you see as being the major benefits from deregulating the international airline market?
2 What do you see as being the major drawbacks of deregulating this market?
3 Do you think that on balance the advantages to the consumer rest with greater regulation or deregulation of the airline market?

New Labour argues that it has *modernised* relations between business and government. It sees itself as a government that supports business and enterprise. New Labour is at pains to get across the message that the UK needs to be competitive and that this is best achieved by allowing the market to operate as far as possible in the field of the economy.

Regulation and deregulation

When industry is heavily regulated, this can discourage competition. This was a key issue with the Conservative administration of 1979–97. Wherever possible it sought to deregulate industries (although the government ended up creating fresh regulations in some other areas). Examples of deregulation include the following:

- Sunday trading in England and Wales was legalised (it was already legal to trade in Scotland on a Sunday). Today, we have become accustomed to supermarkets being open on a Sunday.
- Prior to 1979 high street opticians didn't compete in the way they do today – and the issue of spectacles through the NHS was carefully controlled. Now we have far more choice about whom we buy our glasses from and, as a result, also what they look like.
- A state-run bus service, criticised for its lack of punctuality and comfort, was deregulated to allow private operators to compete for routes. Today, people have a choice on many routes. Increasingly, we are also seeing air routes (both nationally and internationally)

being opened up to competition, and there is increasing competition on the railways.

Of course, there is considerable criticism of deregulation. One of the strongest arguments relates to safety standards. The supporters of state control of industry argue that prior to privatisation and deregulation the government gave top priority to safety standards. In the new competitive environment profits, and returns to shareholders, have become more important than public safety. Some people argue that privatised concerns calculate return on investment purely in terms of profits to be made, with little consideration of the human impact of these decisions.

There now seems to be a consensus in national politics that if possible, the market rather than the state should provide goods and services.

Until recently, Labour governments believed in nationalisation and the Conservatives in privatisation. Today, all major parties accept the advantages of privatisation. Labour accepts the need for more regulation of companies previously in public ownership, but does not propose any major re-nationalisation. Indeed, the Labour Party has shown an interest in allowing the Post Office to have greater freedom to run more like a competitive private company, and in the privatisation of air traffic control.

Laissez-faire and interventionist approaches to business issues

In recent years, political debate in the UK has centred on

Table 1.17 *More or less government? The arguments in favour*

Having more government means:	Having less government means:
Greater protection for the less well-off in society (including smaller business units)	Greater freedom of choice for everyone
Greater coordination of decision making from the centre in society	Leaving the market to coordinate economic decisions
Long-term plans for industrial development involving the state as well as the private sector	Plans for industrial development left to the private sector
Using criteria to judge business decisions which go beyond profit maximisation	Making business decisions largely on the basis of profits
More taxation so that the government can spend more	Less taxation
More bureaucracy from a centralised state apparatus	Less bureaucracy
More nationalisation	More privatisation

whether there should be more or less government in our lives (see Table 1.17).

Those in favour of more government argue that the government can build an 'inclusive' society in which everyone counts – rather than just the powerful and those with the most money. They argue that the government and its representatives can make long-term structural plans for the development of society, that the state can step into deal with hardships such as unemployment and social deprivation, and that the state can protect the interests of the small entrepreneur against exploitation by the large corporation.

Those in favour of less government argue that the further we move away from the free market the more inefficient society is at allocating resources to their most efficient uses. They argue that individuals need to have an incentive to work hard and invest. Those in favour of laissez-faire (leave it alone) policies argue that when the government takes a pound out of your pocket in taxes, then it can only second-guess what you want it to spend that money on; far better for you to spend that pound for yourself. By privatising industries, they are exposed to competition and the need to become as efficient as possible.

Business people are likely to be in favour of less government where this enables their business to be more dynamic and entrepreneurial and where it is held back less by red tape and unnecessary regulation. Deregulation has enabled many businesses to set up in areas that were previously protected, for example private contract waste management and cleaning organisations taking over local government services, private bus companies, private train companies, and high street opticians.

However, there is a strong case for regulation where protection is required, for example protecting consumers against companies which have given less priority to health and safety considerations, in the pursuit of profit for shareholders.

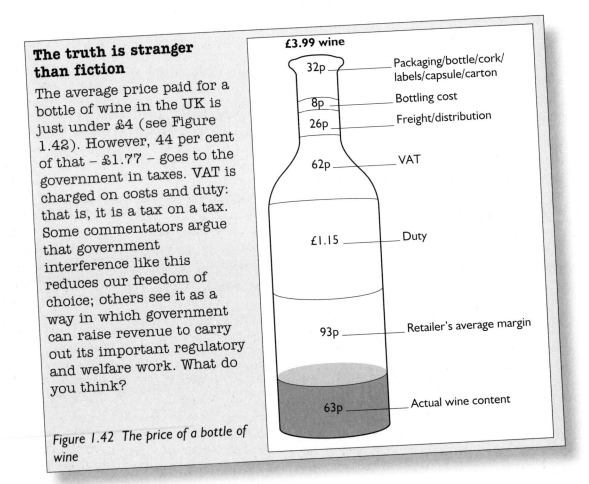

The truth is stranger than fiction

The average price paid for a bottle of wine in the UK is just under £4 (see Figure 1.42). However, 44 per cent of that – £1.77 – goes to the government in taxes. VAT is charged on costs and duty: that is, it is a tax on a tax. Some commentators argue that government interference like this reduces our freedom of choice; others see it as a way in which government can raise revenue to carry out its important regulatory and welfare work. What do you think?

£3.99 wine

32p	Packaging/bottle/cork/labels/capsule/carton
8p	Bottling cost
26p	Freight/distribution
62p	VAT
£1.15	Duty
93p	Retailer's average margin
63p	Actual wine content

Figure 1.42 The price of a bottle of wine

Chapter 21 *The impact of demographic changes*

Changes in society affect business and business decision making. Such changes include the ageing of the population (a **demographic change**) and changes in the place of women in society (a **social change**).

Businesses are affected by these changes on both the demand and the supply side:

- On the demand side, a response by business to the ageing population has been to build more homes for the elderly, to target more holidays at the elderly, etc. A response by business to the feminisation of the workplace has been a recognition by the business of the increasing buying power of the female consumer, leading to the development of an increased number of retail outlets and consumer products targeted at females, for example classic literature and publishing houses specialising in poetry.
- On the supply side, a response by business to the ageing population has been to create more jobs targeted at mature people, for example a number of DIY stores have specifically targeted older workers in their recruitment policies. A supply side response by businesses to the feminisation of labour has been to create more opportunities for flexible working and job sharing.

Demographic trends

The study of population statistics is called **demography**. Since 1801 a **population census** (survey) of the UK has been held every ten years to count the number of people in the country. Demographic studies look at the population structure and trends within it such as age distribution, family groupings, rate of growth/decline and so on.

In the UK the population has reached 60 million and is expected to peak at 63 million in 2031 before starting a slow fall. In recent years, its composition has changed. The population is ageing, with the number of people living beyond 65 increasing. The numbers of young people becoming available for work declined in the 1980s and 1990s, encouraging companies to take on older workers, such as women returners, who wish to re-enter the job market after they have raised a family. Numbers of people in dependent groups are rising, for example the number of pensioners is increasing, putting an increased burden on long-term care provision.

The crude **birth rate** is the number of births per thousand of the population in a year. This fell dramatically during the twentieth century due to:

- people waiting longer to start families
- women choosing to work rather than to stay in the home
- improved birth control – contraception when used properly is now highly efficient.

The **death rate** is the number of deaths per thousand of the population in a year. This too fell dramatically in the twentieth century because of improved housing, diet and sanitation, and because of improvements in health care through medical discoveries and the introduction of the National Health Service. This trend is likely to continue with the mapping of the human gene, providing the potential to come up with a range of new cures for life-threatening diseases.

In the UK the birth and death rates are virtually identical, leading to a static population. In such a situation shortages in the labour market can only be met by increased training of the existing workforce or through immigration.

Population structure is usually looked at in terms of sex and age. Developed countries tend to have an even sex and age structure, while less-developed ones have over half their population aged under 16.

An ageing population occurs when the average age per person is rising. A major problem of the UK's ageing population is that there are fewer people available to work and that those people who work have to support a larger and larger dependent population. The dependent population is the number of people who depend on those with jobs. The International Labour Organisation has warned that spending by the government on pensions and healthcare for the elderly will become the largest budget item for most industrialised countries during the next ten years. By 2055 in Europe, there may be one dependent to every 1.5 members of the working population.

The ageing of the population is one of the most important demographic changes facing businesses today. Clearly, there are plenty of opportunities for businesses to cater for this growing group of consumers. As the number of older people increases, it becomes increasingly worthwhile to target products at this group, many of whom have savings and spare cash to spend on holidays and leisure, luxury goods, etc.

CASE STUDY: THE BENEFIT OF IMMIGRATION TO THE UK ECONOMY

The inflows of foreigners into the UK have risen since 1992, and have reached an annual rate of 200,000 (that is, about 0.3 per cent of the UK population a year). A growing proportion of immigrants are asylum seekers, although this was actually only 3 per cent of the total inflow in 2000.

In 1997 the UK had the fifth biggest inflow of foreigners in the developed world behind the USA, Germany, Japan and Canada. Nearly a fifth of those moving to the UK were from the USA, and more than a tenth were Australian. Figure 1.43 shows immigrants to the UK by country of origin.

Economic theory outlines a number of reasons why immigration brings great benefits to an economy. Since most people are unwilling to leave their home countries, given their networks of friends and family and their love for their native land, those who do so are the ones who expect the greatest benefits for themselves. They are also the most dynamic and entrepreneurial and therefore the most likely to contribute to their host economies. If immigrants compete directly with native-born workers for jobs they can reduce wages (which would obviously be a cost for some groups later).

However, evidence suggests that immigrants fill gaps in the labour force that arise from various rigidities in the domestic economy. In the UK immigrants for the most part do either very low-wage jobs that native-born workers are unwilling to fill (especially in London, where there is a severe labour shortage); or take skilled public-sector jobs paying below-market wages, such as nursing; or fill specific high-skill gaps, in computing or financial services, for example.

Nor are immigrants a particular drain on the public purse. Few are eligible for unemployment benefit in their early years in the UK, when they are most likely to be without a job. The benefits they do receive are hardly generous. All pay indirect taxes and most pay direct taxes too. Their main cost to the state is as consumers of public services, and even on this, Treasury and Department of Social Security research suggests immigrants are more unwilling than most of us to use NHS facilities.

The empirical evidence from a number of countries suggests that economic assimilation takes, on average, about five years, although there are great disparities between different groups of immigrants. Ability to speak English on arrival seems to be one of the key reasons.

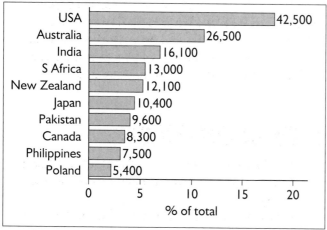

Figure 1.43 UK immigrants by country of origin, 1997
Source: OECD

QUESTIONS FOR DISCUSSION

1 How can immigration be seen as a benefit to UK business?
2 How can immigration be seen as a cost to UK business?
3 In your view, do the benefits outweigh the costs?

Social trends

Each year the government carries out a survey of **social trends** (published annually as *Social Trends*). This and other information about social and cultural changes is very important for business in making plans for the future.

Changes in social attitudes and patterns of behaviour can have a dramatic effect on business fortunes, as illustrated by the case study below.

Businesses need to examine the ways in which changes in society influence the following:

- Who has the spending power in society? There are differences in spending power in different groups in society, for example in response to the growing number of older consumers the 'grey market' has been developed in recent years.
- How social attitudes influence buying decisions. For example:
  - protests against the killing of animals for their fur has helped to curtail the fur trade in the UK
  - the rise of vegetarianism has seen a reduction in demand for some meat products
  - the development of healthy eating has changed people's attitudes to the 'traditional English breakfast' and has given rise to all sorts of 'healthy choice' menu options.
- How social attitudes influence the cost of supplying goods. For example:
  - the increasing feminisation of the workplace has helped some employers to reduce labour costs of production; other employers have responded to the feminisation of the workplace by investing in facilities which are more likely to attract female employees, such as crèche facilities or better toilet facilities
  - the increasing emphasis on environmental and ethical business practice has forced or encouraged businesses to develop a more positive environmental/ethical approach, often leading to a rise in costs as businesses invest in improved standards, for example in the area of environmental management systems.

CASE STUDY: CHANGING ATTITUDES TO THE 24-HOUR SEVEN-DAY-A-WEEK SOCIETY

Shopping centres and theme parks now count Sunday as one of the busiest days in the week, and this shows no sign of changing. However, in the early 1990s when consumers were asked their opinion whether shops should be open on Sundays, most replied 'No'.

The traditional Sunday involving a roast lunch with the family and a stroll in the park followed by a nap is largely a thing of the past.

In modern society, where many people work long hours and have little free time, it is often convenient to do things on Sunday. It seems that many people want a 24-hour society. Leisure has become a full-time industry and it seems that it has to be run according to what the customer wants.

Even Marks & Spencer, which was one of the last major high street retailers to give in to Sunday opening, would now not dream of shutting on such a busy day. In fact, Marks & Spencer started Sunday trading in many of its stores in response to customer demand. It seems that the UK is falling more and more in line with the seven-day-a-week 24-hours-a-day culture which is already a characteristic pattern in many parts of the USA.

QUESTIONS FOR DISCUSSION

1 How have businesses responded to changing attitudes to the 24-hour, seven-day-a-week society?
2 What are the likely effects of the 24-hour, seven-day-a-week society on business costs and revenues?

- Changes in social attitudes also encourage a complete rethink of the way in which business is structured. For example, one of the reasons why the Co-operative Bank is so successful in the early twenty-first century is because consumers are happy to put their money in a bank that puts ethics above profits (see Figure 1.44).

Figure 1.44 The Co-operative Bank sells itself to its customers as the ethical bank

The truth is stranger than fiction

One of the most obvious indicators of the 'must have now' society is the astonishing growth in convenience foods. Nearly eight out of ten of us buy convenience foods every week. While meat dishes are the most popular, vegetarian ones are growing in popularity. Now, one in four of us is buying prepared fresh pasta, a food that was almost unknown in the UK a few years ago.

SECTION E *Internal organisation*

<u>**INTRODUCTION**</u>   Sections A–D discussed the external context within which businesses operate. We turn our attention now to focus on the **internal organisation** of business.

No matter how small an organisation is, it still needs to be organised to some degree to ensure that objectives are met. A sole trader with no organised method of sending or receiving invoices would soon find himself or herself in financial trouble which could ultimately threaten the survival of the business. At the other end of the scale, try to imagine the supermarket chain Tesco, which employs thousands of people, operating without any formal system of organising its staff within its stores. Each store would be managed in a different way, which would severely affect the overall profitability of the business.

Critical thinking

The changing shape of organisations

Traditional hierarchies and over-formalised structures are fast becoming an outdated concept. Large organisations are shedding layers of management in a race to become flatter and more responsive to customer needs. Contracting out services and buying in consultancy expertise is also changing the internal function of organisations. Increased competition locally, nationally and internationally means that only the fittest businesses will survive. Some organisations are deciding that to secure a greater share of the market they need to merge with or acquire another company. This is particularly fashionable within the food retailing and financial sectors at the moment.

WHAT DO YOU THINK?

1   To what extent do you think organisations have been affected by the above changes?
2   Are large and small organisations affected to the same degree?
3   How do you think organisations will look in the future?

Chapter 22 *Functional areas of management*

Although organisations may be structured in many different ways and employ different people with different job titles, they will almost certainly all have one thing in common, that is, they all employ **managers**. A manager is very often someone who we aspire to be in business. When we think about managers, we often think of the manager who leads the organisation overall, the managing director, or we think about successful managers who often appear in the media such as Anita Roddick or Richard Branson.

Very often in organisations, there will be more than one manager. This chapter will help you to appreciate what a manager does and how this applies to managers at different levels within an organisation.

What is a manager?

A manager is a leader who ensures that the organisation is achieving or exceeding its objectives in order to satisfy stakeholder interest.

What does it take to be a successful manager?

Figure 1.45 highlights some of the key qualities and skills that a manager might have in today's competitive market place.

What are the functions of management?

Bartol and Martin in their book *Management* (1991) describe the functions of management as planning, organising, controlling and leading:

- **Planning** – setting future goals and objectives and devising a strategy for trying to achieve these aims.
- **Organising** – coordinating the resources of the business, both human and non-human, towards the ultimate achievement of organisational goals.
- **Controlling** – keeping a check on how the organisation is performing by regularly reviewing the progress made towards achieving objectives.
- **Leading** – directing, influencing and supporting employees in the organisation towards the achievement of personal, departmental and organisational goals.

Figure 1.46 explains how objectives are achieved through the functions of management. (It does not consider the impact that external factors may have on the performance of managers.)

Different levels of management within an organisation

As we mentioned earlier, when thinking about managers we often single out the most senior, the managing director.

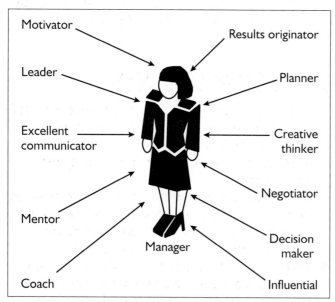

Figure 1.45 *An example of some of the skills and qualities of a manager*

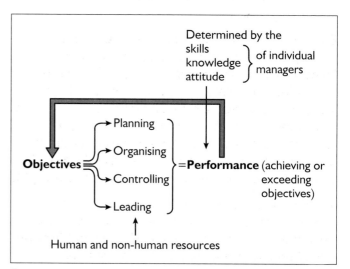

Figure 1.46 *How objectives are achieved through the functions of management*

However, unless an organisation is very small, managers are employed at different levels within the organisation.

The managing director is often the figurehead of the organisation, providing the strategic vision. The decisions that he or she makes will be determining the future of the business, perhaps planning one to five years ahead. This level of management is referred to as **senior/executive** or **strategic** management.

The next level of management may be in charge of a division, function or department within the company. The decisions that these people make will be more tactical in nature and will determine the shape of the business within the next month to a year. This level of management is known as the **tactical/middle** level of management.

The third level refers to the managers who make the decisions on a daily/weekly basis. Including junior managers or supervisors, this is the **operational** level of management.

It is, of course, important to point out that none of the levels of management operates in isolation. Each level would be supporting each other in order to work towards the overall achievement of organisational goals.

Figure 1.47 shows how the different levels of management may be depicted within an organisation.

Table 1.18 illustrates how the different levels of management apply the functions to their roles and gives examples of the types of decision that may be made at each level.

CASE STUDY: SMALL HELPINGS

After having her baby last year, Lucy was disappointed to discover the lack of choice for pre-prepared vegetarian baby food. She therefore opted to make most of the food for her baby herself.

Her business venture really took off by accident. Friends were always interested in what she was making and often used to try her creations. Some busy working mothers asked her to make up some meals for their babies. Everyone told her that she should go into business with such a talent. A trained chef by trade, Lucy felt confident to give it a go. She diligently researched all the regulations for setting up such a venture.

Business blossomed and she was soon too busy to manage from her own kitchen, and decided to invest in a small manufacturing unit. The market for Lucy's frozen vegetarian special baby meals was starting to expand. She persuaded a chain of health food shops to stock it and was also talking to Sainsbury's, Tesco, Asda, Safeway and Boots. She employed more specialist staff to manufacture the products. Business was booming, or so she thought.

With no real business experience, Lucy was convinced that if she continued to develop new recipes and obtain new orders that everything else would be fine. Sure enough, the orders kept flowing.

Lucy now employed 20 people preparing, cooking, packing and delivering the products. She knew that she had some very dedicated people working for her, but how would she retain them if another company sounded more appealing? Lucy was suddenly aware too of the sheer amounts of paperwork that her business was building up. She was so busy chasing new orders that she was unsure exactly what was on her desk or indeed how to actually sort it out. She began to realise that there was more to running a business and being a successful manager than just having a great idea and getting lots of orders. She needed some help.

QUESTIONS FOR DISCUSSION

1 What are the main issues that Lucy must address? Categorise them into strategic, tactical and operational issues.
2 How can Lucy improve her own managerial performance?
3 Do you think that Lucy can manage the business on her own or that she needs some managerial support? If so, how would you organise the management team within the organisation?
4 What future challenges do you think Lucy faces? What advice would you give her to ensure that she is prepared to face these challenges?

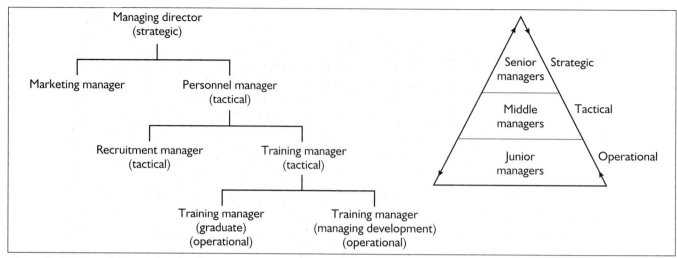

Figure 1.47 How different levels of management within an organisation may be depicted

Table 1.18 How the different levels of management carry out the functions of management

Manager/level	Planning	Organising	Controlling	Leading
Managing director (strategic)	Setting overall future targets and objectives to ensure future survival and development of the organisation	Exploring ways to improve productivity	Reviewing functional budgets against targets set	Supporting and directing tactical level managers as their line manager Role model/source of inspiration for whole organisation
Decision	To expand into Europe within the next five years	To introduce new technology to ensure organisation keeps ahead of competition	To increase or reduce spending in a functional area	To introduce a system of performance appraisal
Personnel manager (tactical)	Compiling and implementing a human resource plan, detailing how many people with what skills, etc. will be needed for the next 12 months plus.	Ensuring that an up-to-date succession plan is in operation	Ensuring that the implementation of the human resource plan keeps within the budget	Motivate, guide and support immediate subordinates Offer advice to internal customers
Decision	To use a recruitment agency to assist with employment decisions	To improve the training and development of supervisors	To seek an increase in the training budget for vulnerable staff liable to be headhunted	To recommend an increase or decrease in staff at a particular level
Training supervisor (operational)	Working out an overall annual training plan for all employees in the organisation	Finding suitable venues for training courses	Implementing the training budget and monitoring spending	Motivating, guiding and supporting immediate subordinates
Decision	To increase or reduce the number and type of a particular course	To change a venue which is not suitable	To purchase some training equipment	To discipline a member of staff

The truth is stranger than fiction

Although more and more women are participating in the workforce, and increasing numbers are entering education in today's world of equal opportunities, we might be led to believe that there are as many top women managers as men. However, a recent report by the International Labour Office does not support this assumption. The report includes statistics from a survey that states that in 1996, out of 300 British companies only 3 per cent of board members were women. In the developing countries the picture was quite different. In Columbia, for example, the percentage of women managers grew from 14 per cent in 1980 to 37 per cent in 1996.

Chapter 23 *The internal structure of organisations*

'Structure is the pattern of relationships among positions in the organisation and among members of the organisation. The purpose of structure is the division of work among members of the organisation, and the coordination of their activities so they are directed towards achieving the goals and objectives of the organisation. The structure defines tasks and responsibilities, work roles and relationships, and channels of communication.' (Mullins, 1993)

This chapter focuses on explaining some of the above concepts in more detail – in particular, how different organisations are structured.

The factors which affect how an organisation may be organised

- **Objectives** – an organisation wanting to expand into Europe would need to be organised in a different way to ensure that customer needs were met, to a business whose market was purely local.
- **The size of the organisation** – an organisation employing three or four people would be organised in a very informal manner. However, when the numbers employed are 3000 to 4000 a more formal system must be in place with clear lines of communication and reporting procedures in order to achieve maximum efficiency and organisational goals.
- **The type of product being produced or the service being provided** – a bespoke jewellery design and production business would have different organisational priorities from a biscuit factory producing thousands of units of output per day. Similarly, a leisure centre providing sports facilities to the local community would be organised in a different way from a call centre providing a national service to customers placing orders for goods purchased through a mail order catalogue.
- **The external economic environment** – managers need to ensure that their organisation is structured in the most efficient way for achieving objectives and keeping up with or ahead of the competition.

This chapter, together with Chapter 24, will explore these factors in more detail and apply them to different organisational settings in order to give you a more thorough understanding of why organisations are structured in different ways.

The organisation chart

The organisation chart illustrates how formal relationships are organised within an organisation and shows the following:

- **Levels of the hierarchy** – the different levels of the organisation representing the degree of authority and responsibility.
- **Chain of command** – the reporting system throughout the organisation, from operators at the lowest level of the hierarchy up to the managing director at the top.
- **Span of control** – this refers to the number of employees who are accountable to each individual manager. There have been many attempts by management theorists to identify what the ideal span of control should be. This very much depends on the type of product or service being produced and the nature of the work involved in producing/delivering the product or service. What is fairly certain is that the span will be narrower towards the top of the organisation than at the lower levels where managers/supervisors may be responsible for several staff.
- **How the work within the organisation is structured** – functionally, or divisionally by product or geography.

The organisation chart does not show the informal relationships that may exist within the company.

The shape of organisations

Tall organisation

The characteristics of a tall organisation are:

- many hierarchical levels
- long chain of command
- small span of control (see Figure 1.48).

Flat organisation

The characteristics of a flat organisation are:

- few hierarchical levels
- short chain of command
- large span of control (see Figure 1.49).

In today's competitive environment, where organisations have to be lean and fit to survive, there has been a greater shift towards flatter organisational structures. Fewer levels

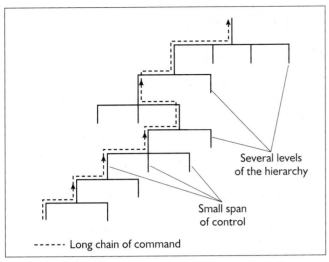

Figure 1.48 A tall organisation

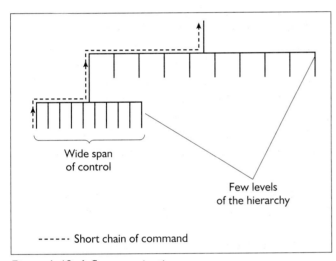

Figure 1.49 A flat organisation

in the hierarchy and a shorter chain of command can enable clearer communications and speedier decisions to be made.

The structure of work within organisations

From entrepreneur to national organisation

An entrepreneur just setting up in business as a chef providing business lunches from home to the workplace, decides that he needs two or three people to help him out. In such a small business, there would be no need for a formal organisational structure. Each person would help out where needed – they would be considered to be **generalists** within the organisation. As the business grows, however, each person may show an interest or a strength in a different part of the operation. It may be necessary at this stage to introduce a more formalised arrangement, for example to put someone in charge of production, marketing and finance. The work would then be organised in a functional way. People's skills now take on a more **specialist** focus. Figure 1.50 shows the transition from an entrepreneurial to a functionally based structure.

As the organisation grows, more functions may be introduced. The levels within the hierarchy may also increase. Figure 1.50 also shows the second stage of the transition. Further expansion may see a change in the customer base from being local to national.

As output increases and more products/services are introduced, the functional structure may become less appropriate. It may be more appropriate to set up **specialist teams** to manage each product area. A textiles company, for example, producing knitwear, hosiery and lingerie may be organised into specialist teams for each product area. Each division would be responsible for marketing, production, finance, etc. within their product area. This type of structure would be called a **product division** structure (see Figure 1.51).

An organisation's customer base may also increase as the business grows. The organisational structure which was appropriate to serve customers locally may not be efficient

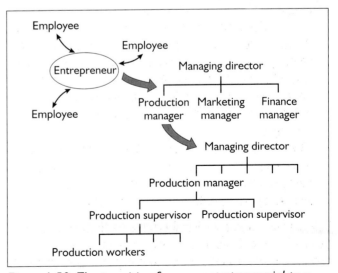

Figure 1.50 The transition from an entrepreneurial to a functional structure

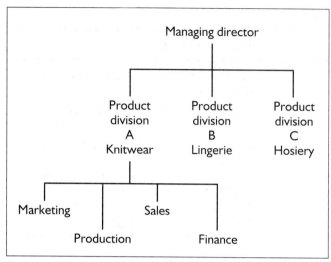

Figure 1.51 A product division structure

for satisfying the needs of national customers. A good example of this type of structure can be found in the retail sector. Very often the company would be split into geographical regions, for example the South West or the Central region. The region would then be split up locally with different stores to respond to the needs of their local customers. This structure would be called a **geographical division** structure (see Figure 1.52).

For both of the structures illustrated in Figures 1.51 and 1.52 to be efficient, decision making has to be **decentralised**. This means that the authority and power for decision making

is delegated from head office to the product division or regional teams. Not all decision making would be decentralised, however – strategic issues would still be a **centralised** function remaining a head office responsibility. The degree to which organisations decentralise their decision making will very much depend on the type of product or service the business offers and the size of the organisation. The success of decision making at this level will be dependent upon the skill and experience of the teams out in the field.

Table 1.19 looks at the advantages and disadvantages of the above organisational structures and Table 1.20 highlights some of the difficulties that arise for managers as a result of inappropriate organisational structures.

There is no secret recipe for ensuring that organisations have the right structure. All of the above factors need to be taken into account. The structure of an organisation may change for essentially two reasons. First, the organisation is evolving and therefore changing as it grows and becomes established. Secondly, an organisation may also be forced to change in reaction to external forces. The crisis could lead to restructuring.

The way that restructuring takes place within organisations is often reported in the business section of quality newspapers. Try visiting *The Sunday Times's* website for some examples – www.sundaytimes.co.uk.

Chapter 24 takes a further look at changing structures and Chapter 25 discusses matrix structures.

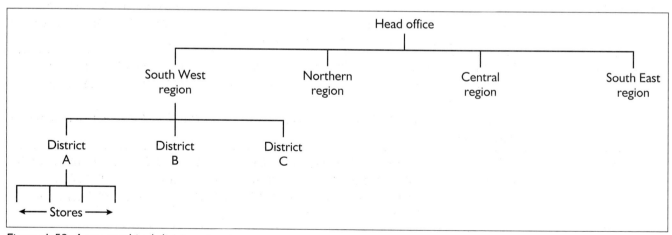

Figure 1.52 A geographical division structure

Table 1.19 Advantages and disadvantages of organisational structures

Type of structure	Advantages	Disadvantages
Functional	Specialisation Efficient use of resources Simple structure	Lack of overall organisational awareness within functions Restricted career opportunities outside function Centralisation of decision making may be slow
Product/geographical division	Closer to the customer Coordination across functions Flexible	Duplication of resources Communications problems across divisions Competition among divisions

Table 1.20 An analysis of inappropriate organisational features

Organisational feature	Potential problems if feature inappropriate
Levels of the hierarchy	Too many – communications difficulties, slow decision making, increase in bureaucracy Too few – span of control too wide (see below), lack of career opportunities, tendency for people in key positions to be overloaded
Chain of command	Too long – problems same as for levels of the hierarchy
Span of control	Too wide – unable to manage individuals effectively, relies on subordinates to be self-motivated, unnecessary stress for manager in charge of subordinates, manager may start to lose control Too narrow – excessive supervision of subordinates, which can lead to subordinates feeling that they have little control over their work
Organisation of work	Work must be organised in the most effective way to ensure that objectives are met. The human element is equally important. If employees are not motivated and well managed and do not have clear career paths, organisational performance will be affected
Centralisation	If decision making is overcentralised the whole process takes a long time. This can lead to organisations finding it difficult to respond to local conditions and potentially loosing their competitive edge Employees may also lack the essential decision making qualities that they need to move up the organisation
Decentralisation	If decision making is decentralised employees must have the skill and experience to cope with this responsibility. Over-decentralisation can lead to lack of control at the centre of the organisation, and local decisions may be inconsistent with strategic objectives. It may also result in increased internal competition

The human resource management (HRM) division had always been located within head office. There were separate departments for recruitment, training, employee relations, remuneration and benefits, and employment legislation.

However, the business was expanding. 'Simple but Stylish' retailing now employed 350 staff and it had just opened its tenth store.

Each store offers consumers a simple but stylish approach to their lifestyle. The three main sections within each store are food, clothing and furniture. Occupying high street locations, each store employs about 35 staff. Initially East Midlands-based, the company is now researching appropriate sites further north and south.

At the moment, whenever an HRM issue arises the store manager has to contact head office. There is very little autonomy at store level for decision making. A recruitment manager will come down from head office to interview, etc. Certain days of the month are set aside for training. Either a training officer visits the store to conduct on-the-job training or employees travel to head office.

As the business expands, this arrangement is clearly becoming impractical. Store managers need to be able to make decisions locally which affect their store. All the store managers have been invited to head office to discuss how they think the HRM division should be structured in order to assist them and the business in moving forward.

QUESTIONS FOR DISCUSSION

1 As a store manager, which areas of the HRM division do you think should be centralised and decentralised? Justify your answer.
2 What would be the costs and benefits of your decision?
3 If a decision is taken to decentralise some of the departments, what are the key issues to consider when implementing such a change?

The truth is stranger than fiction

Manufacturer Proctor & Gamble, well-known for its cleaning products, used to have a very hierarchical functional structure with excessive centralisation of decision making. Within this structure, it usually took about 18 months to introduce a new product. However, by decentralising decision making and introducing cross-functional business teams, the company was able to reduce the time it took to introduce a new product from 18 to four months.

Chapter 24 *Changing structures*

The structure of organisations cannot afford to remain static in today's dynamic customer-focused market place. As Mullins (1993) states: '… Structure should not rest on past achievements but be geared to future demands and growth of the organisation.'

This chapter focuses on the changing structure of organisations. The first part looks at the drivers of change, which have forced organisations to restructure. The second part discusses how organisations have responded to these influences.

Drivers of change

Increased competition

Locally

Over the past three years in the city of Nottingham there has been a variety of café bars opening up – each with their unique image, offering the consumer a relaxing but fun time, but all essentially providing a service to the same market, so that competition is fierce.

Nationally

The competition among the top four food retailers has regularly hit the headlines over the past few years. Sainsbury's, who held the top position for so long and appeared to be virtually untouchable, have taken second place to Tesco for the past four years. At the end of 1998 Tesco, which particularly focuses on price, had a 3.2 per cent greater share of the market than Sainsbury's, which focuses more on choice. A similar battle goes on between Asda and Safeway. Asda increased its market share over Safeway in 1996. At the end of last year, Asda had a 1 per cent lead over Safeway.

Of course, the whole retail sector could be thrown into turmoil following Wal-Mart's recent takeover of Asda.

Internationally – globalisation

A major fact today is that some organisations can no longer survive by serving the local and national market; they need to operate internationally. Increasingly, organisations are operating on a European scale. However, with the relaxation of trade barriers internationally, the **global market place** is becoming much more accessible.

Improved technology

The impact of new technology upon organisations is not a new phenomenon. However, the pace at which technology is changing means that organisations cannot afford to be left behind. The growth of the **Internet** gives both industrial and domestic consumers access to worldwide information at the touch of a button. The government has just unveiled a new **e-commerce** strategy in response to the growing importance of the Internet.

Electronic Data Interchange (**EDI**) has had a huge impact on organisations. EDI allows huge quantities of data to be transmitted via the phone lines from one company to another. This is particularly useful for organisations wishing to place a vast amount of daily orders with their suppliers. EDI has therefore been revolutionary in the retail sector.

Large organisations are increasingly using **Intranet** technology. Similar to the Internet, the Intranet is a way of communicating electronically with customers and colleagues inside the organisation.

Changing consumer lifestyles and tastes

Consumer tastes have changed dramatically over the past decade. With influences from all over the world on our doorstep, consumers are more cosmopolitan. Busy lifestyles have led to a sharp increase in convenience products, from grated cheese in a bag to disposable cameras. Increased awareness of health issues has resulted in an influx of healthy eating products on to the market. This has been complemented by the rapid expansion of luxury health clubs and training gyms.

Home shopping via the Internet and television, together with services such as telephone banking, have eased the burden of fast modern living.

Legislation

Organisations are frequently forced to implement new ways of working as a result of legislation. A debate which is currently going to affect small enterprises quite significantly is the introduction of parental leave. The British Chamber of Commerce has written to the government on behalf of small firms to ask it to revise the proposed 13 weeks. Visit the British Chamber of Commerce's website for more information on how this legislation will affect small companies – www.britishchambers.org.uk.

Management thinking

Contracting out services from within the organisation continues to prove to be a profitable option for employers.

There is also an increased demand for the services of **management consultants**.

As organisations have continued to realise the value of their human resources not only in maintaining but also in improving their competitive edge, increased emphasis has been placed on empowering employees. The value of **teamworking** too has also been recognised as employers strive to ensure they are utilising their human resources most effectively.

The concept of the **learning organisation** has become very popular. This is where the benefits of learning are felt so strongly within an organisation that learning has become part of its culture.

The way that organisations are structured has changed as a result of the above influences. Structures need to be flexible enough to adapt to the constantly changing external environment. Outlined below are some of the strategies that organisations have introduced in response to the changing environment.

The organisational response

Delayering

Bartol and Martin (1991) define **delayering** as: 'The process of significantly reducing the layers of middle management, expanding spans of control, and shrinking the size of the work force.'

Impact on organisational structure
- Flatter structure, shorter chain of command.
- Improved communications.
- Speedier decision making.
- Widens the span of control.
- Increased workload for positions below the layer taken out.

Getting closer to the customer

This may be defined as: introducing strategies that enable the business to find out more about their customer and respond to their needs more effectively.

Impact on organisational structure
- Organisation by location or customer type.
- Decentralisation of decision making.
- Introducing total quality management principles.

Business process re-engineering/re-design

This may be defined as: reorganising the flow of work through an organisation from being functionally organised to structuring the business into teams who manage an entire work process from beginning to end.

Impact on organisational structure
- Changing the hierarchy from specialist functional teams to process-orientated teams.
- The teams work on a whole process from beginning to end. This can lead to improvements in morale because there is a greater sense of ownership.
- Employees are empowered to make decisions. Decision making therefore has to be decentralised.
- Introduction of cellular manufacturing.
- Increased emphasis on becoming closer to the customer and continually improving with this method of organisational design.

If **business process re-engineering** has been implemented successfully, the benefits to the organisation can be significant. In particular, there will be improvements in quality and output.

Figure 1.53 illustrates the difference between a functional structure and the business process teams structure.

Flexible working arrangements

Instead of all employees working similar core hours, the organisation will offer employees the opportunity of working in a more flexible way, for example **part time**, **temporary**, **job sharing**, **homeworking**, **hot desking**, etc. This arrangement offers flexibility for both the organisation and individual employees.

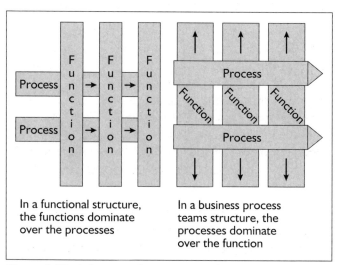

In a functional structure, the functions dominate over the processes

In a business process teams structure, the processes dominate over the function

Figure 1.53 A functional structure and a business process team's structure

CASE STUDY: MARQUEE KNITWEAR

Marquee Knitwear is a family-owned business employing approximately 600 people. The main factory is situated on a small site in the middle of a housing estate. There is no room for development or expansion of the site.

The company manufactures men's jumpers in small, medium, large and extra large sizes. Medium and large are the most popular sizes.

Organised in a functional way, there is a strong sense of pride working within each function. There is a traditional chain of command up through the function to senior management and the chairman. Decision making is highly centralised.

The production process is very traditional. Yarn is machine knitted into shaped panels which are then made up into finished garments. The make-up operation involves two different activities, seaming and linking. The finished garments are inspected and packed before shipping to the customer's warehouse.

Because the knitting machines are so old the mechanics are reluctant to change size unless there is no alternative. This often means that the stock of some sizes builds up while there is little or no stock of other sizes. The collars for the jumpers are knitted separately. There are often problems matching the correct collars to garments. As a result, stock levels have built up to six weeks.

All seaming operators are situated in one building and all linking operators in another. The make-up sequence is as follows: seam shoulders, link arms, seam sides and arms and link collars. There is no way to alter this sequence so garments must travel between buildings in this sequence. There is significant double handling. The average time to unpack and pack a garment is 30 seconds. There is an increased incidence of damage to garments as a result.

The make-up operators are paid individually, based upon the number of garments they process. The method of payment encourages the operators to work as quickly as possible. As operators increase speed there is often a reduction in product quality. Returns and rework often exceeds 10 per cent of the number of garments produced. As a result of inaccurate setting of payment rates by size, the operators can make more money by producing large and extra large sizes. This encourages operators to prioritise large and extra large sizes, with the consequence that at inspection and packing there are often insufficient small and medium sizes to ship complete orders. This causes work in progress to build by a further six weeks.

There is no incentive for teamworking. The operators appear to be motivated mainly by money. The style of management is punitive with supervisors frequently using the disciplinary process to address poor quality or performance.

The company constantly faces increased competition both nationally and internationally. Due to the nature of the company, the strong family involvement and continued success in the past, the company has been relatively untouched by current management thinking initiatives. The chairman is very reluctant to change.

The company cannot afford to continue with current working practices any longer if it is to survive long term.

QUESTIONS FOR DISCUSSION

1 Identify the problems that the company has which are resulting in the build-up of stocks and poor quality output.
2 Do you think that the organisation is structured in the best way? If yes, justify your answer. If no, how would you restructure the organisation? Again you need to justify your answer.
3 What are the drivers of change that have affected Marquee Knitwear?
4 How do you think that the organisation should respond to these changes?

Impact on organisational structure

- Allows the organisation to respond to an increase in demand very quickly due to the flexible nature of employees' contracts.
- The span of control can vary. During busy times, managers and supervisors will see an increase in the number of employees for whom they are responsible.
- Sometimes it is more difficult to build up team loyalty due to the constant changing patterns of employment.
- Consideration must be given to employees who are working away from the original workplace, for example home workers. These employees will not have regular face-to-face contact with office-based employees. Appropriate technology must be in place to ensure that they can communicate and do not become isolated.
- Within this flexible structure there is an emphasis towards empowering employees. This increases the opportunity for decentralising the decision making process.

Mergers and acquisitions

In order to survive in the competitive market place, some organisations are unable to continue trading effectively on their own. They may decide to **merge** with a similar organisation. A recent example would be the merger between the General Accident and the Commercial Union insurance companies. The resulting company is called the Commercial General Union (CGU).

Alternatively, an organisation may decide to strengthen its portfolio by **buying** another business or businesses. For example, the Bradford and Bingley Building Society has recently bought the Black Horse chain of estate agents and Mortgage Express.

In a recent television documentary, the Chairman of Deutsche Bank, talking about how organisations survive today, stated that 'big is not necessarily beautiful, big is essential'.

Impact on organisational structure

- With two organisations effectively joining together, there will inevitably be a duplication of resources. Some positions within the new structure will therefore become redundant.
- The overall structure would need to be revised in order to reflect the changing needs of the new organisation.
- As two or more organisational cultures join together, there will be a significant settling down period while the new culture evolves and employees adapt.

The truth is stranger than fiction

Organisations contract out aspects of their business ranging from cleaning to parts of their production process. As an extreme example, Nike designs and sells sports shoes without stitching a thread itself.

Chapter 25 *The matrix structure*

A **matrix structure** is a combination of the traditional vertical functional structure with horizontal project teams working across the functions (see Figure 1.54).

Characteristics of a matrix organisation

* Two-way flow of information, authority and responsibility.
* Employees have two or more bosses.
* Can be either a temporary or a permanent feature of the organisation's design (see Figures 1.55 and 1.56).

Advantages and disadvantages of the matrix structure

Advantages

* Flexible.
* Decentralisation of decision making and development of managerial skills.
* Effective use of human resources.
* Closer to the customer or product.
* Ideas encouraged.
* Improved opportunities for staff development.

CASE STUDY: ALL CHANGE AT THE BRADFORD AND BINGLEY BUILDING SOCIETY

The Bradford and Bingley has always had a high reputation for its financial advice. However, in order to retain consumer confidence, the company has recently undergone some major changes.

The arrival of a new chief executive in 1996, together with a rapidly changing external market place, led to major changes for both management and staff. Some of these are outlined below:

* Middle and top managers were all enrolled on a management development programme to assist them with the changes they were facing.
* Still recognised by traditional values, the company also realised the significance of becoming more customer focused and flexible.
* Increased competition from the supermarkets and telephone banking sparked a realisation that the consumer wanted not only choice but also speed of response.
* A recent decision to diversify led to the building society buying the Black Horse chain of estate agents from the then Lloyds Bank.
* A matrix-style management, in part replacing the traditional functional structure with staff reporting through their line manager up a traditional chain of command, was introduced. This has been particularly successful in the human resource management and information technology departments.

An example of matrix management in practice was the audit department, which was once viewed as the equivalent of organisational police, swooping in on a department, inspecting the books, and then disappearing until the next year. The department now operates more on a consultancy basis, offering all-year-round help and advice and actually working with departments to improve the service to the customer.

QUESTIONS FOR DISCUSSION

1 Why do you think the Bradford and Bingley thought that it was time to update its image?
2 What were the key changes that were introduced?
3 Why was it important for the Bradford and Bingley to purchase the chain of estate agents?
4 Why do you think that the matrix structure has been successful in the human resource management and information technology departments?

To find out more information about this successful organisation, visit its website at www.bradford-bingley.co.uk.

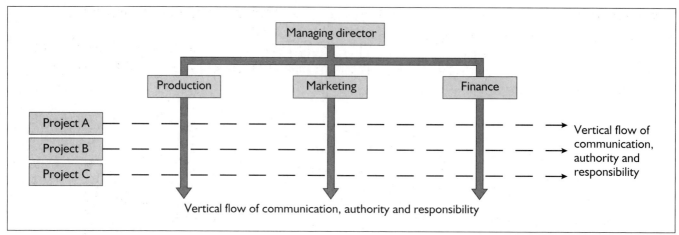

Figure 1.54 A matrix structure

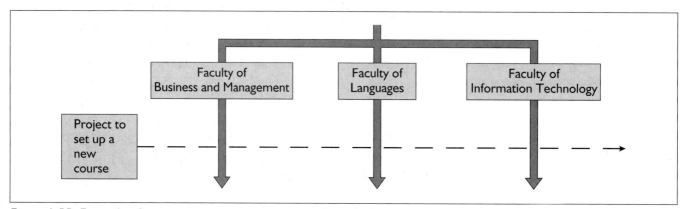

Figure 1.55 Example of a temporary matrix structure within a higher education establishment

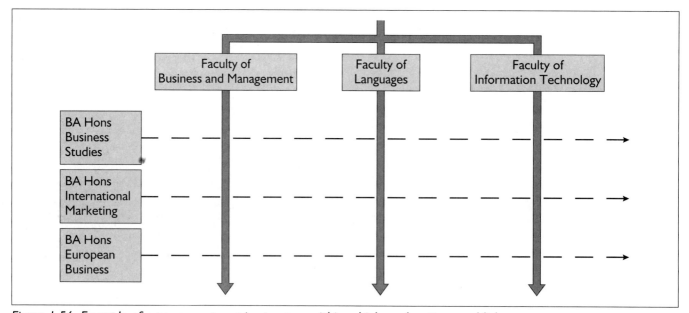

Figure 1.56 Example of a permanent matrix structure within a higher education establishment

Disadvantages

- Potential conflicts of authority and loyalty due to employees having two or more bosses.
- The complexity of having multiple chains of command may cause confusion. It may also lead to difficulty coordinating resources across the functions and the project teams.
- The above issue may result in slow decision making.
- The initial implementation of the structure may be costly.

The truth is stranger than fiction

The success of the matrix structure is dependent upon the effective performance of cross-functional teams.

The concept of teamwork has been around for at least a century. Even in nature, there are parallels. Bluetits and robins used to find the cream on the top of open-topped milk irresistible. With the introduction of aluminium tops, it was the bluetits who quickly learned to peck through the foil. Only a few robins managed to work it out. The bluetits were successful because they flock together in groups. They roam between groups, so when a new skill is learned, it is quickly passed on. Robins, on the other hand, are very territorial and prefer to work alone. If a robin learned the skill this would not be passed on.

Today teamworking is becoming increasingly important in organisations as managers seek to ensure that they are utilising their employee resource to the full.

SECTION F *Communication in business organisations*

INTRODUCTION   It used to be possible to communicate important messages face to face with the whole workforce at once. The nine-to-five working day made this possible. Today, however, with flexible working arrangements, this is no longer an effective method. Employers now have to consider the needs of full-time staff, part-time staff and shift workers, employees working a job-share arrangement, temporary and external staff, and those working from home.

Coupled with an increasingly diverse workforce is the challenge of keeping pace with constant improvements in **communications systems**. This is also vitally important if organisations are going to maintain their competitive edge.

Critical thinking

With the advent of electronic methods of communication, for example personal computers, e-mail, fax machines and mobile phones, organisations have a great deal of choice with regards to which communications system to use. What does not change, however, is the basic model of how communications are sent from the transmitter to the receiver – the essential components of how we communicate remain the same. The challenge within this model for organisations today is ensuring that they choose the most appropriate method and that their communicators have the necessary skills to communicate effectively in a fast global environment.

WHAT DO YOU THINK?

1 To what extent do you think organisations still rely on manual methods of communication?
2 What do you think are the key skills of an effective communicator in today's increasingly electronic environment?
3 Do you think that there will always be a place for manual methods of communication in the workplace, or do you think the future will be completely computerised? Justify your answer.

Chapter 26 *Vertical and horizontal communication*

The way we communicate with each other is very often something that we do not think about. Talking to friends face to face, over the telephone or via the Internet is something that we take for granted. It is, however, frustrating when our message is misunderstood, or ignored.

In organisations, too, the way that employees communicate with each other can lead to distinct competitive advantages or disadvantages depending upon the effectiveness of communication channels.

It is important to consider the process of communication and to appreciate why a message is sometimes misunderstood.

Figure 1.57 outlines the process of communication.

The process of communication essentially involves a **transmitter** or **sender**, sending a message or messages to a **receiver**. The sender must select the most appropriate method of communication: oral, written, electronic, etc. This part of the process is called **encoding**. The sender must then select the most appropriate medium to send the message: fax, e-mail, telephone, etc. The receiver decodes the message through a process of **decoding**. The feedback or confirmation of understanding is then sent from the receiver back to the sender through the same process.

This sounds and appears straightforward and clear. Why then are messages often misunderstood? The communication process can be hampered by the interference of **noise**, which represents a barrier to the effective flow of communication from the sender to the receiver. Some examples of noise include: the choice of an inappropriate method of communication, language difficulties, lack of

interest on the part of the receiver, assuming that the receiver has more knowledge/experience of a particular subject than he or she actually has, actual background noise which interferes with the flow of communication. The causes and consequences of communication failure are discussed in more detail in Chapter 27.

The purpose of communication

The aim of the communication is to convey a message. The purpose of this is to:

- initiate action
- impart or exchange information, ideas, beliefs or feelings
- establish, acknowledge or maintain relationships.

The receiver is more likely to understand and reciprocate the message if it has credibility, and inspires trust and belief, or if it is congenial, appearing pleasant to or compatible with the recipient.

Effective communication

Effective communication depends on:

- clearly defining the objective
- taking account of the needs, attitudes and knowledge of the receiver
- being aware of the potential distractions to distort the message
- selecting the appropriate medium for communication
- checking that the message has been understood through feedback
- listening to feedback and responding.

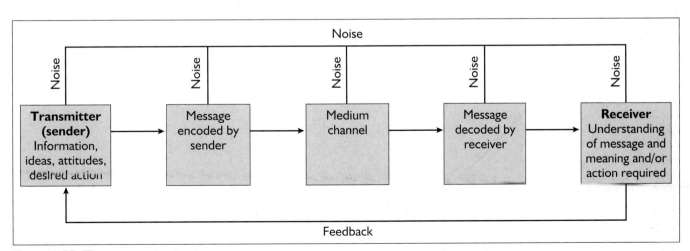

Figure 1.57 The communication process

Communication within an organisation

Vertical communication

Vertical communication is the flow of information up and down an organisation.

Who communicates with whom?
- Manager to subordinate of the same department.
- Subordinate to manager of the same department.

Figure 1.58 illustrates this flow of communication.

Examples of formal communication which might take place between the different parties are:

- from the manager to the subordinate:
  - giving instructions
  - offering advice
  - giving feedback on performance
  - discussing ideas
- from the subordinate to the manager:
  - putting forward ideas
  - reporting on progress with a particular project
  - discussing potential problems which may hinder progress
  - discussing job performance.

Horizontal communication

Horizontal communication is the flow of information across the organisation.

Who communicates with whom?
- Manager to manager across the same and different departments/divisions.
- Subordinate to subordinate across the same and different departments/divisions.
- Manager to subordinate across different departments/divisions.
- Subordinate to manager across different departments/divisions.

Figure 1.59 illustrates this flow of communication.

Examples of formal communication which might take place between the different parties are:

- from manager to manager:
  - discussion of the progress of a particular project
  - sharing ideas regarding the implementation of strategic issues
  - discussion of targets, for example between the sales and production departments
- from subordinate to subordinate:
  - discussion of the progress of a particular project
  - sharing ideas regarding the implementation of tactical/operational issues
  - organising a meeting between departments.

Vertical and horizontal communication

It is, of course, possible to have both vertical and horizontal communication flows within one organisation. A clear illustration of this would be the matrix structure (see Chapter 25).

This chapter has focused on the **formal** channels of communication within the organisation. **Informal** channels

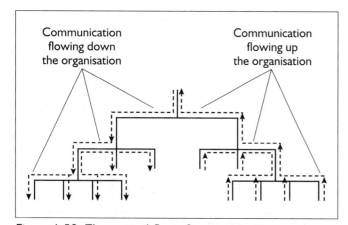

Figure 1.58 The vertical flow of communication

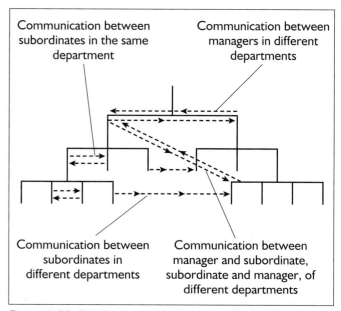

Figure 1.59 The horizontal flow of communication

do not have a set flow up and down or across – communication can take place with anyone within the organisation about anything. Chapter 27 discusses informal communication in more detail.

Group communication networks

When several employees need to work together on a task, it is important that the way that information flows within the group is as effective as possible in order to complete the task efficiently. This pattern of information flow is referred to as the **communication network**. Depending upon the nature of the task to be completed, groups can adopt various communication networks. These may be either centralised or decentralised. The centralised network involves the flow of information through a key person in the group. This type of network is represented as a wheel or a chain (see Figure 1.60). The quality of decision making within this network is dependent upon the skill of the key person.

The circle or completely connected network represents a more decentralised communication network (see Figure 1.61). Here the decision making process is shared; there is no one central figure.

The communication network chosen is dependent upon the task to be completed. Where a quick decision is needed it may be more appropriate to choose a centralised network. However, where the contribution of several people is needed for effective decision making, a decentralised network would be a better choice.

To communicate internally – horizontally, vertically or any other way with employees – organisations are increasingly turning towards developing their own Intranet network. This is a communications system which allows employees to send and receive information via their computer. (For more information about developing an Intranet, visit the website www.intramark.com.)

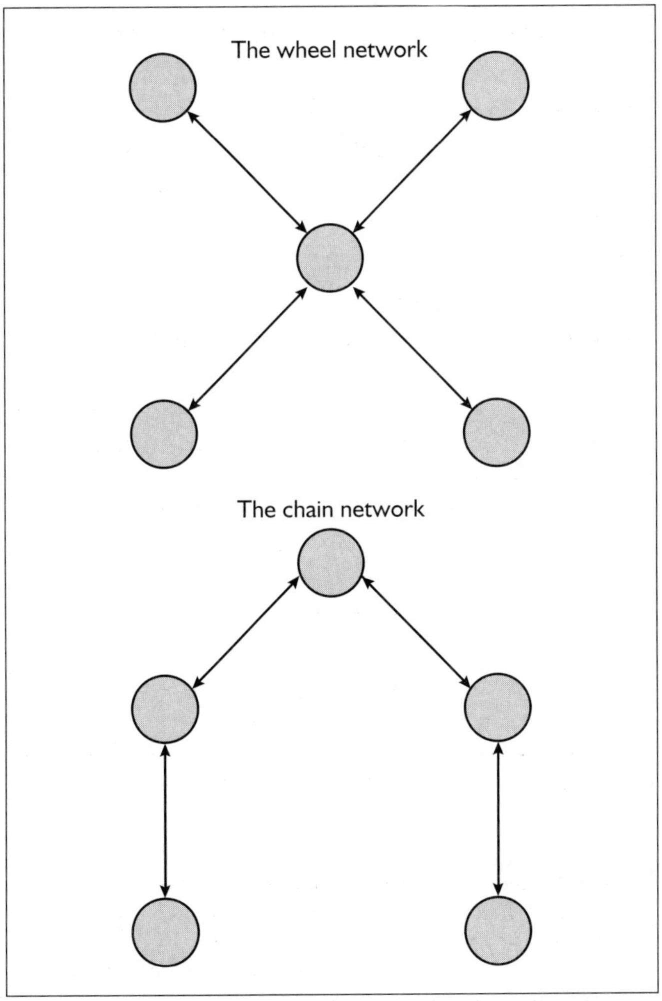

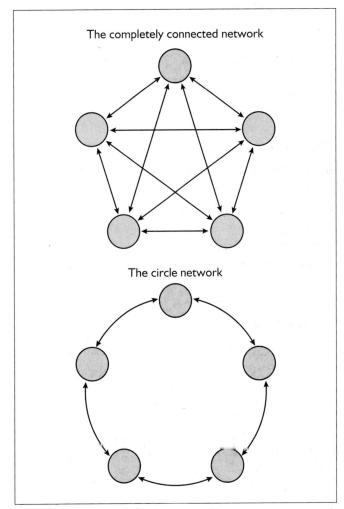

The wheel network

The chain network

Figure 1.60 A centralised network

The completely connected network

The circle network

Figure 1.61 A decentralised network

CASE STUDY: THE COMMUNICATION PROCESS

Imagine that you have been appointed the human resources manager of Marquee Knitwear, a company specialising in the manufacture of men's knitwear supplying several well-known high street stores. There are many tasks requiring your attention and you need to start work quickly. They involve:

- organising training courses for the 300 people who work for Marquee Knitwear
- publicising the Christmas dinner dance
- implementing the company's new appraisal scheme
- setting departmental targets for your own staff
- organising an induction programme for some newly appointed graduate trainees.

QUESTIONS FOR DISCUSSION

1 You need to decide whether the above communication tasks would best be delivered vertically or horizontally throughout the organisation. Justify your answer.
2 What communication channels would you use to successfully organise the induction programme for the new graduates?
3 Choose one of the above tasks and compile a communication process diagram for that task. You need to identify the following:
   - who the transmitter is
   - how the message would be encoded by the transmitter
   - the communication channel to be used
   - how you would ensure that the message had been received and understood by the receiver
   - any 'noise' that may impact on the clarity of the communication.

The truth is stranger than fiction

Although vertical communication is still essential in organisations, effective horizontal communication has taken on a renewed importance as organisations introduce cross-functional teams and reorganise from functionally based to process-dominated structures.

Chapter 27 Methods of communication

The importance of effective communication cannot be understated. A message that is not clearly understood or that fails to reach the receiver is a waste of time, energy and resources. Businesses today, if they are to remain competitive, must ensure that all resources are used effectively. Choosing the most appropriate method of communication is therefore of paramount importance. Herein lies the dilemma, with so many communication channels available to use from.

This chapter discusses the different communication methods and assesses their importance in today's changing workplace.

Formal communication

This is where communication follows company guidelines and respects the structure of the organisation, either verbally or written.

Methods of formal communication

Written
- Memos
- Reports
- Written procedures
- Faxes
- Posters
- Suggestion scheme
- In-house magazine

Verbal
- Company meetings
- Training sessions
- Appraisal interviews
- Team briefings
- Presentations
- Giving instructions
- Giving feedback

Informal communication

Informal communication is often referred to as the **grapevine**. This type of communication does not follow any set structure with relation to the hierarchy. Communication flows through the network of personal relationships that exist within an organisation. This means therefore that communication through the grapevine can flow in all directions.

Grapevine communication can be fast but varies in accuracy. Sometimes it is perceived by employees as a way of spreading rumours or gossip. It is, however, an important part of everyday organisational life. The grapevine can play a useful role in disseminating aspects of the organisation's values and beliefs, which may be central to the cultural understanding of a business. The grapevine can also be used by management to gauge staff's feeling regarding a planned change. By circulating a rumour relating to the change, the management team can test reactions to that change. If there is a positive reaction, management may choose simply to implement the change. If there is a negative reaction, management may choose to modify or withdraw the change.

Electronic communication

The speed with which businesses need to communicate and the distance in terms of operating globally mean that organisations are relying more and more on electronic methods of communication.

Methods of electronic communication

- The Internet
- Electronic mail (e-mail)
- Intranets
- Video conferencing
- Telephones including mobile phones

For an overview of methods of communication on the Internet, visit Freeserve's virtual office website on www.freeserve.net/communication/.

Internal and external communication

The three categories of communication described above contain aspects of internal and external communication. Table 1.21 highlights how each category can be represented in this way.

Choosing the correct method of communication

Clearly, the issue for organisations is not lack of choice when it comes to selecting a method of communication. The issue is choosing the most appropriate medium to ensure that the message is understood and interpreted in the

Table 1.21 Internal and external methods of communication

Communication method	Internal	External
Formal: written		
Memo	✓	
Report	✓	✓
Written procedures	✓	
Faxes	✓	✓
Posters	✓	✓
Suggestion scheme	✓	✓
In-house magazine	✓	
Formal: verbal		
Company meetings	✓	✓
Training sessions	✓	✓
Appraisal interviews	✓	
Team briefings	✓	
Presentations	✓	✓
Giving instructions	✓	✓
Giving feedback	✓	✓
Informal		
Grapevine	✓	
Electronic		
The Internet	✓	✓
E-mail	✓	✓
Intranets	✓	
Video conferencing	✓	✓
Telephones	✓	✓

desired manner (refer back to the process of communication diagram, Figure 1.57 on page 113, for a reminder of how important this stage is).

Chapter 28 highlights the barriers to effective communication and discusses the consequences of choosing an inappropriate channel.

Communication in the flexible firm

Effective communication takes on a renewed importance in today's constantly changing workplace. It is not just the needs of full-time permanent staff that need to be considered. In today's flexible firm there is an increased number of **periphery staff** – part time and temporary – who do not work the traditional core hours and therefore have different communication needs. Teleworkers and people who job share may have less face-to-face contact with their place of work on a daily basis. This does not mean that they are less important. Careful consideration must be given to ensuring that they are kept in touch and up to date. Appropriate methods of communication must be chosen for each category of staff.

Communication for the future

The trends in communication for the future could be summed up as follows:

- **Electronic** – increased use of the Internet, e-mail, laptop computers, mobile phones etc. The paperless office may be a reality in the future.
- **Remote** – this is in terms of employment. More and more employees will be able to work from home, or in other locations apart from their usual place of work. Communication methods must be ready to facilitate this development. The key challenge here will lie in managing such a remote workforce.
- **Interactive** – there will be less and less human contact when we buy goods and services. We already communicate with pre-recorded messages on telephones. Obtaining money from cash machines is also part of our daily routine. With online shopping, banking, etc., this trend is set to continue.

CASE STUDY: THE NEED FOR FLEXIBLE COMMUNICATION

Helen

Helen had just returned to work after having her second baby. She was excited to be back in the cut and thrust again. She worked on Mondays and Tuesdays all day and half a day on Wednesday. She had previously worked full time but this new job share arrangement suited her very well with her change in circumstances. She only saw her job share partner for about half an hour on Wednesday lunchtime to hand over and talk through any issues.

Helen began to have a few concerns about the job. Every Thursday her department had a full meeting to discuss progress made and talk about new ideas for future projects. Although she read the minutes of the meeting each week, she did not feel particularly involved. She also noticed that only her job sharer's name appeared on the circulation list of memos, etc. and although she tried to pass information on to Helen, sometimes important issues were forgotten which made Helen's job very difficult. Helen was beginning to wonder whether this job share arrangement was such a good idea after all.

Chris

Chris had often explained to his boss that he could just as easily do his job from home. It would save nearly two hours a day travelling and he felt he could be much more productive. At last, his boss agreed to give it a trial but was reluctant to spend any money as he felt it would be a waste of resources. Chris had a computer at home which he agreed to use in the short term.

The first couple of weeks were very successful – Chris felt he achieved much more than being in the office with constant interruptions. He had, however, spent most of his time writing reports. He found the arrangement more difficult when he needed to get in touch with people. Not only was he running up a huge phone bill but also he found that people were reluctant to call him back at home.

One night a friend called to find out what Chris thought of the latest staff moves at work and what he thought about the planned merger talks. This was the first that Chris had heard about these issues. He started to feel very out of touch and unimportant. Chris was beginning to wonder whether working from home was such a good idea after all.

QUESTIONS FOR DISCUSSION

1 The case studies represent two flexible ways of working. The arrangements are clearly not working due to communication difficulties. Highlight the communication problems in each case.
2 What methods of communication would you choose for both Helen and Chris to ensure that their flexible ways of working were a success?
3 How would each organisation have to change to accommodate the changing communication needs of both Helen and Chris?

The truth is stranger than fiction

Electronic methods of communication do save us a significant amount of time with our busy lifestyles. We have even found ways to adapt certain methods to meet our needs even further. For example, the answerphone, originally invented to record messages while out of the office or away from home, can also be used to screen calls. If you are too busy to take a message a phone can be left ringing until it connects up to a voice mail system. Calls can then be answered at your convenience. Either way you will never miss an important call again.

Chapter 28 *Communication problems*

People are communicating all over the world 24 hours a day, 365 days of the year. It is inevitable therefore that some of the messages sent will be distorted in some way. The aim of this chapter is to discuss some of the causes and consequences of communication failure and to offer solutions to try to redress the problems. The chapter concludes by looking at the essential skills people need to become effective communicators.

Common communication problems

Language

The sender may use jargon or technical language with which the receiver is not familiar. This often takes the form of abbreviations and shortened versions of words and can be a particular barrier with new employees who are still finding their feet in their new surroundings. Care must also be taken to ensure that the level of complexity reflects the needs of the receivers. This is particularly important in the teaching profession. Another obvious language barrier may be cultural, if the receiver speaks a different language.

Noise

This refers to actual noise which may interfere with the communication process. It also refers to other aspects such as conflicting messages, which the receiver may have to deal with. In this situation the receiver may be unsure how to respond.

Emotional state

This applies to both the sender and receiver. One or both may be upset or angry which may mean that they do not put enough thought into sending the message or indeed listen effectively to the message which has been sent. The receiver may be nervous and this could lead to him or her jumping to conclusions. Instead of interpreting the actual message, the receiver may interpret what he or she thinks the message is saying.

Communication method

If the method chosen is inappropriate for the receiver the message will be distorted. The venue chosen to deliver the message is also of paramount importance. For example, if the sales conference of a multimillion pound company were to take place in the summer in a hotel with few facilities, no air-conditioning and poor food, the level of understanding and participation might be severely reduced. An employee who is reprimanded on the shop floor in front of colleagues may only receive part of the message being conveyed, due to the fact that he or she may be worrying about what his or her colleagues are thinking. A much more appropriate and professional venue would be a quiet office away from the shop floor.

Lack of interest

The message must capture the receiver's interest in order for the communication to be fully understood.

Cultural differences

The receiver's interpretation of the message may be different due to differing cultural experiences and background. Organisations with international outlets have to have an in-depth understanding of the culture of the countries they are trading in. This is to ensure that they do not offend or insult their international business partners or customers, or indeed embarrass themselves by conveying an inappropriate message.

Communication failure could result in any of the scenarios shown in Figure 1.62, the extremes being loss of business and ultimately loss of competitive edge.

Solutions to communication failure

- Ensure all employees understand the importance of effective communication. In order to do this, employees need to appreciate the consequences of poor communication. They also need to be kept up to date with the latest technology and introduced to communication methods which will make their job easier.

Figure 1.62 Consequences of communication failure

- Ensure all employees are effective communicators by conducting the appropriate training. Employees need to be effective listeners. They also need to be able to present information clearly either verbally or in writing or visually. Another important element of effective communication skills is being able to give and receive feedback.
- Ensure that the culture of the organisation is receptive towards encouraging effective communication. If the organisation does not support the above two points then employees may become disinterested. This could then lead to the organisation spiralling down the consequences of communication failure as shown in Figure 1.62.

The ingredients of a successful communicator

- Consider the needs of your audience. Be aware that their needs may vary over time.
- Consider the communication method and venue chosen to distribute the message. Are they the most appropriate?
- Consider your mechanisms for ensuring that your message has been understood.
- Listen carefully to any response to your communication; this is essential to ensure that your message has been understood.

CASE STUDY: ONLY HALF THE PICTURE

It was the start of the new term at Hill Gate College. Staff of the business studies department were hopeful that their head of department, John, would be more organised than last year. However, as the term progressed it was apparent that the same problems still existed.

Every Tuesday morning at 8.45 am there was a departmental meeting. Invariably, John would arrive five to ten minutes late. He always prepared an agenda on the train on his way to work. This gave his staff no time at all to prepare for the meeting. The format of the meetings was always the same: John would talk through the items on the agenda in great detail. This left very little time for his staff to make their contributions which was often done while walking out of the door on their way to the first lesson. Sometimes not all of the agenda items were covered. Instead of being carried forward to the next meeting, they were simply forgotten. This often resulted in staff of the business studies department missing vital information. Students wanting to speak to John in person or on the phone often interrupted the meetings. John would never keep a student waiting, so instead the meeting would be put further behind.

On several occasions important information regarding particular students was not passed on to staff. John would receive a message in the morning and forget to tell the relevant member of staff. The college was so big that staff rarely returned to the business studies departmental room during the day.

John also had another annoying habit. He would keep all of the latest business studies magazines and books to himself. He seemed to have every intention of passing them on to staff but somehow they disappeared into the pile of paper on his desk. How were the staff supposed to write interesting up-to-date lessons without access to this information?

With a college inspection due next term, the staff were determined to sort out the problems within the department. If not, the poor inspection result would reflect upon all of them.

QUESTIONS FOR DISCUSSION

1 Identify the communication problems which exist within the business studies department.
2 What solutions would you recommend to try to improve the communication problems within the department?
3 Do you think that John and his staff would benefit from any communication training? If so, what would you recommend?

Look at BT's website to see how the telecommunications company has solved some of its communication problems while managing an increasingly flexible workforce – www.bt.com/youcan/.

The truth is stranger than fiction

New mobile technologies are freeing people not just from the office, but from the need for any fixed location. It is now possible to dictate e-mails into a mobile phone or connect to an Intranet via a laptop while travelling on a train. Within the office, too, mobile phones are becoming more common. At the BBC where staff change desks regularly and can be hard to track down, employees often end up calling each other's mobiles first. This can be expensive and the corporation has trialled a dual-mode handset, developed by BT and Ericsson, which acts as a digital cordless handset inside the office but switches to a GSM mobile network outside it.

SECTION G *Motivation in business*

INTRODUCTION **Motivation** is defined as the processes or drives that cause people to act in a certain way. In business we need to be able to influence a wide range of people to act in ways which will help us reach our objectives. We need the suppliers of finance to invest in our plans, customers to buy our products, and employees to make our products or supply our services.

In this section we are particularly concerned with motivating employees to maximise their performance, and we will be looking at leading thinkers in this area.

The importance of employee performance to national prosperity has been recognised by government in a number of publications. In 1997 the Department of Trade and Industry jointly with the Department for Education and Employment published a paper *Competitiveness through Partnerships with People* which concluded 'the most powerful resource for change, improved performance and competitive advantage is the people who already work in the organisation'.

Critical thinking

So how do you get the best out of employees? Why do people work, and what can we do to encourage them to become more productive?

Early management techniques assumed that people worked and were motivated solely by money and that providing them the chance to earn more money would motivate them to work harder.

Research has called these assumptions into question. A survey carried out in 1992 asked the hypothetical question that jackpot lottery winners face for real: 'If you had enough money to live comfortably for the rest of your life would you continue to work?' The results are shown in Figure 1.63.

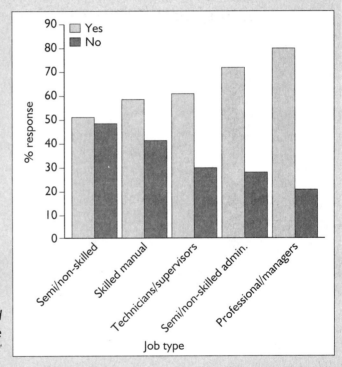

Figure 1.63 Responses to the 1992 survey: 'If you had enough money to live comfortably for the rest of your life would you continue to work?'

WHAT DO YOU THINK?
1 Do people work solely for money? What do you conclude from these results?
2 Why do you think people would continue to work even when they did not need the money?
3 Explain the different responses from each category of job.
4 If you had enough money to live comfortably without working, what would you do?

Chapter 29 Motivational theories

As we have seen above, the people in an organisation are recognised by governments and other leading thinkers as the most powerful resource for improving performance and gaining competitive advantage. In today's free markets all organisations need to compete to survive, so improving the performance of people is vitally important.

Getting maximum performance or productivity from people surprisingly has been a subject that has been studied since the beginning of industrialisation. The Industrial Revolution was brought about by the introduction of machines, which performed repetitive manufacturing tasks much more rapidly, and accurately than people. In recent years a similar revolution has been taking place for clerical tasks where computers have dramatically improved productivity in service industries such as banking.

Providing equipment and machines is one way of improving people productivity. Improving working methods and skills development is another important element.

Frederick Taylor, an American born in 1856, was a pioneer in this area with his **scientific** approach to management. Previously, workers were expected to design their own work methods and to be multiskilled. **Scientific management** involved studying tasks, breaking them down into their component parts, designing the most efficient methods for completing these, and training workers to become experts at one specialised repetitive part of the overall task. Taylor first introduced these ideas in 1911 at the Bethleham Steel Works where he experimented with such tasks as shovelling coke. Taylor designed work methods involving exact shovel sizes and set work breaks. Using such methods output increased by nearly 400 per cent, wages increased by 60 per cent, costs were reduced, and the number of workers fell by over 260.

Henry Ford was another pioneer; he combined mechanisation and scientific management principles to fulfil his dream of producing the first low-cost car, making this new form of transport available to people other than the seriously rich. He is acknowledged as the inventor of the modern-day **production line**, where a product is progressively built as it moves automatically along a line of employees, each of whom fits a specific part. Working in these conditions was not, however, enjoyable – workers became bored and left. This reached such a stage that by 1913 Henry Ford had to double wages to get the best people and keep them.

Experiences such as these led to the realisation that money is not the sole reason for working and to the study of what other factors are important in maximising people productivity.

The dictionary defines **motivation** as 'the mental function or instinct that produces, sustains and regulates behaviour in humans and animals'. **Frederick Herzberg**, a leading thinker, defined motivation as 'the will to work due to the enjoyment of the work itself'.

Leading thinkers – Abraham Maslow

In his article, 'A theory of human motivation' published in the journal *Psychological Review* in 1935, **Abraham Maslow** identified human needs and grouped them into five categories. These categories, he proposed, could be arranged into an order or hierarchy of importance, as shown in Figure 1.64.

Maslow put forward the idea that lower-level needs would require to be satisfied at least in part before progressing to the next level. For example, a starving person would first want to satisfy his or her hunger and thirst before considering the need for a secure home. Similarly, establishing a social life may not be a priority when you have no permanent home or job. Only when you are an established member of a group do you start comparing yourself to others, looking for respect and status. Not until you have grown in confidence and secured your place in society would you start thinking about the achievement of greater things.

Maslow's theory can be used to answer the question why, apart from money, people work. It also gives an insight into why people continue to work when they have enough money to satisfy their needs.

In developed economies most workers earn enough money to satisfy level 1, physiological, and level 2, safety and security, and so the higher levels are important when seeking worker motivation.

Money, however, should not be underestimated as a motivator as it plays a part in meeting each category of need (see Table 1.22).

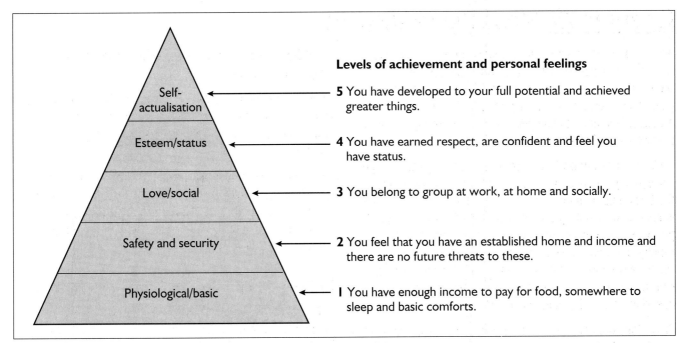

Figure 1.64 Maslow's hierarchy of needs

Table 1.22 How money acts as a motivator

Level	How money helps meet need
1 Physiological	To pay for food and shelter
2 Safety and security	To buy a house, fences, locks and insurance
3 Love	Social activities, pubs, sports and social clubs all cost money
4 Esteem/status	High salaries give people a sense of their value; clothes and cars are symbols of status
5 Self-actualisation	Money can support hobbies, charities and other interests

Living for your work? Or working for a life?

Work, however, should be set in context. Most people achieve their needs through a balance of work, family and social activities, the mix of which will depend on their interests, abilities and the degree to which their work matches their interests and abilities. At the extremes, professional sports people live for their work; and according to a survey of production line workers at a car plant in Luton, other employees work for a life – that is, they are motivated by the needs that high wages provide, for example expensive leisure pursuits, holidays or plans for early retirement.

CASE STUDY: SAINSBURY'S

J Sainsbury plc is one of the world's leading retailers, playing a part in the lives of 15 million customers a week.

Our objectives
To provide shareholders with good financial returns by focusing on customers' needs, adding

value through our expertise and innovation, and investing for future growth.

To provide unrivalled value to our customers in the quality of the goods we sell, in the competitiveness of our prices and in the range of choice we offer.

To achieve efficiency of operation, convenience and customer service in our stores, thereby creating as attractive and friendly a shopping environment as possible.

To provide a working environment where there is a concern for the welfare of each member of staff, where all have opportunities to develop their abilities and where each is well rewarded for their contribution to the success of the business.

To fulfil our responsibilities by acting with integrity, maintaining high environmental standards, and contributing to the quality of life in the community.

Source: www.j-sainsbury.co.uk, June 2000

Sainsbury's annual survey of employee attitudes

Every year Sainsbury's conducts a survey of employee attitudes. The survey is based on a 13-point questionnaire and is sent to all employees. Every store manager is given a 'staff satisfaction measure' based on the results of the questionnaire answered by its own staff.

The latest survey found that the opportunity to grow and develop was the most prized aspect of a good working environment. Second was the desire to work for a well-run company, and third a friendly atmosphere.

The overall measure of staff satisfaction has been found to be closely linked to the level of customer satisfaction.

QUESTIONS FOR DISCUSSION

1. How do the top three aspects of the working environment identified in the staff survey relate to Maslow's hierarchy of needs?
2. How well does the Sainsbury's objective for the working environment match the results of the staff survey, and which aspects of Maslow's hierarchy do they meet?
3. Why do you think that 'satisfied staff' provide satisfied customers?
4. How does staff satisfaction help Sainsbury's provide good financial returns to shareholders?

The truth is stranger than fiction

The Western Electrical Company conducted the Hawthorne studies during the 1920s in Chicago, USA. Two groups of workers were selected to study the effects of workplace lighting. For one group, the light conditions were unchanged. The lighting for the other group was made brighter and dimmer. Levels of output for both groups were measured and no differences were found between the two groups, but observers were surprised to find that in both groups production increased. This effect was called 'the Hawthorne Effect', and was explained by both groups working harder because they were been given special attention.

Chapter 30 *Job design*

In the last chapter we learnt that motivation has an important effect on performance, or productivity, that is, the quantity and quality of work. We also learnt that while money plays an important part in motivating workers, other factors are also important in providing job satisfaction. In this chapter we will look at factors affecting work and how they are used to design jobs that provide satisfaction and result in more motivated and productive workers.

Factors affecting work

Characteristics of the **individual** will affect work performance. We all are different – age, education, experience, intelligence, interests, personality and circumstances vary widely and can affect the way we were are motivated and perform at work.

The **job** itself, the methods and equipment can also have an important effect on performance.

Working conditions – heat, light, comfort and welfare – can also be significant, both in terms of meeting safety and esteem needs. The size of desk, type of chair or style of work clothes have practical working benefits but perhaps an even bigger effect on ego and self-esteem. Social environment, training, supervision and incentives help meet higher level esteem and actualisation needs.

Leading thinkers – Frederick Herzberg

In 1966 **Frederick Herzberg** put forward a new motivational theory. This was based on a series of interviews with a sample of 200 engineers and accountants in Pittsburgh, USA. He asked what actually motivated them at work. He found two types of factors or aspects of work:

- **Hygiene factors** – ones which lead to **dissatisfaction** if not adequate, for example:
  – poor, unsafe working conditions
  – bad, unfair management
  – low pay
  – company policies
  – staff relationships
  – holidays
  – pensions, etc.

These are conditions of work outside or **extrinsic** to the job itself. They correlate to the lower order of Maslow's hierarchy of needs.

- **Motivational factors** – ones which lead to **satisfaction** when present, for example:
  – interesting job
  – recognition of achievement
  – responsibility and decision making
  – the opportunity for achievement
  – promotion prospects
  – personal development and training.

These are dependent on the job content and are **intrinsic** to the job. They correlate to the higher order of Maslow's hierarchy of needs.

Herzberg argued that both sets of factors are important in motivating employees.

In a similar way to Maslow, Herzberg said that the lower-order equivalent hygiene needs had to be met, otherwise these would distract from the higher-order motivating factors.

Providing hygiene factors only, however, will not result in well-motivated staff. For example, a salary increase will remove a sense of injustice, a cause of dissatisfaction, and will give a temporary sense of well-being. It will, however, soon wear off and workers' attention will revert to whether or not they enjoy the job.

So how can managers, having provided appropriate hygiene factors, set about providing the intrinsic job content factors necessary for job satisfaction and employee motivation? Herzberg suggested a number of strategies:

- **Job rotation**, where workers move from one task to another of a similar level on a regular basis. This gives employees a greater variety and interest in their work, providing opportunities for learning new skills and opportunities for achievement. Employees benefit from greater flexibility and the availability of trained cover for holidays and absences.
- **Job enlargement**, where workers are given a wider variety of tasks of a similar level. This can make the job more interesting and lead to a greater sense of achievement as workers are able to see a process through to completion rather than specialising in one aspect of it.
- **Job enrichment**, where employees are given greater depth to their range of tasks rather than simply a wider variety of tasks of a similar level. They take part in decision making and problem solving. They help set

targets and accept responsibility for the organisation and the quality of their own work. Management benefits from having to provide less supervision.

Herzberg used the term **job design** or redesign, which involves looking at the job itself, each of its components and how these can be modified to improve satisfaction.

Job redesign checklist

Can the job be designed to:

- provide a variety of tasks
- produce an identifiable end product or service
- be thought of as worthwhile
- be demanding and provide challenges and targets for achievement

- make good use of the individual's skills
- provide opportunities for further development and training
- allow for contact with other colleagues
- involve working as part of a team
- give opportunities to make suggestions for improvement
- give an area for responsibility and decision making, for example quality?

Benefits of job satisfaction

As we saw from the Sainsbury's staff survey findings, staff satisfaction leads to customer satisfaction.

Well-designed jobs result in benefits both to employees and to employers (see Table 1.23).

Table 1.23 Benefits to employees, employers and organisations resulting from job satisfaction

Employees' benefits	Employers' benefits	Organisational benefits
More interesting work	Better staff motivation	Human resources used to their full potential
Less stress	Fewer staff absences	Higher levels of productivity and quality
Higher self-esteem	Improved productivity, quality and quantity	Improved customer satisfaction
Potential for promotion	More flexible staff	Company growth, profits and prosperity for shareholders, management and staff
Enjoying work		

CASE STUDY: RICHER SOUNDS

Richer Sounds was set up by Julian Richer in 1978 to sell quality hi-fi music systems, and is one of the most successful retailers in the UK (see Figure 1.65). It is featured in *The Guinness Book of Records* for having the highest sales per square foot in the world. What is the secret of its success?

The answer is quite simple: to provide the best quality service for customers from a highly motivated team of employees. Julian Richer's methods have been so successful that he has set up Richer Consulting to help other companies adopt his successful approach. He has also published a book *The Richer Way*.

So how are Richer Sounds staff motivated to provide 'best quality customer service'?

- All staff are called colleagues (definition: fellow worker).

Figure 1.65 Julian Richer outside one of his stores

- All customers are asked to rate the quality of service they have received. Sales people who are rated excellent receive a bonus, while those rated poor are penalised.

- All colleagues are encouraged to submit suggestions to the staff suggestion scheme. All suggestions are acknowledged by Richer and colleagues receive a small reward of between £5 and £25 for each one.
- The basic pay of the sales team is quite low, but high overall rewards can be achieved from customer service and suggestion scheme bonuses and earnings from the company's profit-sharing scheme.
- Each week the company's best performing three stores are given the use of one of the company's luxury cars (two Bentleys and a Jaguar XJS convertible).
- Colleagues can also make use of the company's nine holiday homes.
- There is a well-funded health-care scheme and a hardship fund for staff with financial difficulties.
- Loyalty is rewarded. There is a '5-year club' for staff with five or more years' service. New club members are invited to lunch with Richer at a top-class restaurant such as The Ritz.
- Management recognises staff when they have done well, not just when they have made a mistake.
- Colleagues are encouraged to take on additional responsibilities, for example a member of staff may also be a member of the 'cut the crap' committee. This has the remit to reduce the amount of bureaucracy (unproductive systems and paperwork) in the company.

- One recruitment technique is the 'staff recommend a friend' scheme. A £100 bonus is paid when the new employee completes six-months' service.
- New staff are given comprehensive induction training and all meet Julian Richer.
- Open communication is given a high priority. All staff are issued with Julian Richer's home telephone number.
- Results against target for individual, stores and the company are regularly discussed. Julian Richer produces a monthly video telling staff how they did the month before, details of new developments and giving important personal messages.

Further indicators of Richer Sounds' success include low rates of labour turnover (one to two per cent), absenteeism and theft, plus imitation by other retailers, such as Asda which has adopted many of the Richer policies.

QUESTIONS FOR DISCUSSION

1 What do you think would be the good and bad points of working at Richer Sounds?
2 Consider each of the bullet points above describing 'the Richer Way' and decide which of Maslow's levels of motivation are addressed. Decide also whether they represent Herzberg's hygiene or motivational factors. Justify your answers.

The truth is stranger than fiction

In 1992 the Ford Motor Company acquired Jaguar Cars, the British luxury car manufacturer. Nick Scheele, the new chief executive officer, faced daunting product quality and cost problems plus a serious downturn in orders. In a car manufacturers' comparative customer satisfaction ranking, Jaguar was ranked in a lowly thirty-fifth position, just one place ahead of Lada.

Scheele's reaction was to abolish employee clocking-in procedures and piece work (time-keeping and payment by results) systems. The shop floor workers were given the freedom to move around the factory and responsibility for solving 30 per cent of the identified production problems.

The result was that within a year cost savings of £2,500 per car were made and an improvement in the car manufacturers' comparative customer satisfaction ranking to fifth position.

Since then Jaguar's revival has continued with its new Formula One racing team and the development and introduction of the S range, which has contributed to an 80 per cent growth in sales in the first six months of 2000.

Source: www.jaguarcars.com

Chapter 31 Leadership styles

In Chapter 29 we looked at how motivation can affect employee performance and in Chapter 30 at how jobs can be designed to provide satisfaction and improved motivation. In this chapter we will look at the role of managers and how their leadership style can be developed to get the best out of employees.

Management has been defined as the process of:

- planning
- organising and coordinating
- leading and controlling

an organisation's human and material resources to achieve business objectives.

Another, simpler definition is: getting things done by other people.

An important aspect of effective management is the balance between control and leadership of human resources.

Leading thinkers – Douglas McGregor

In his book *The Human Side of Enterprise* (1960), **Douglas McGregor** describes two extreme views managers can take of staff and how these views can shape leadership style.

McGregor calls these management views **Theory X**, in which the manager assumes the employee to be lazy, and **Theory Y**, in which employees are assumed to want to do a 'good' job. These two extreme assumptions are illustrated in Figure 1.66.

Management styles: autocratic control versus democratic leadership

If a manager believes Theory X, he or she assumes that employees will only work if they are forced to and that threats of punishment are the best way of achieving this. The manager will also believe that employees avoid responsibility, have no ambition, dislike risks, want security and others to take decisions for them.

This belief leads to an autocratic management style, one which involves a high degree of control.

An autocratic manager:

- dominates and controls
- is quick to allocate blame

Theory X managers believe that employees:

- are lazy
- do not want to work
- need control and monitoring.

Theory X managers are autocratic.

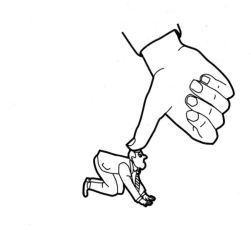

Theory Y managers believe that employees want:

- to work
- to have responsibility
- appropriate rewards.

Theory Y managers are democratic and involve, trust and value employees.

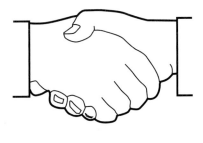

Figure 1.66 McGregor's Theory X and Theory Y

- avoids discussion
- issues instructions without explanation
- does not welcome suggestions from subordinates.

If a manager believes in Theory Y, he or she assumes that employees want to do a good job and need leadership, encouragement and support. The manager will also believe rewards and training are the best way of helping employees achieve their full potential.

This belief leads to a democratic management style, one that involves, trusts and leads employees.

A democratic manager:

- encourages suggestions and discussion of problems
- consults colleagues and subordinates
- involves subordinates in decision making
- recognises achievements of others
- provides training and development.

A continuum of management styles

Tannenbaum and **Schmidt**, two US psychologists, devised their *Continuum of Management Behaviour* in 1958. This set out a framework of management styles, between the extremes of autocratic (control) and democratic (leadership – see Figure 1.67).

As leadership style moves from autocratic to democratic, control decreases and the need for leadership increases. Decision making moves from:

- **tells** – manager makes decisions and tells subordinates what to do
- **sells** – manager makes decisions and explains to subordinates why they should do as he or she says
- **tests** – manager tests subordinates' ability to take decisions for themselves but provides support, or tests his or her own decisions by asking for subordinates' reactions
- **consults** – subordinates take decisions, but consult with manager or vice versa; the manager retains ultimate decision making authority
- **delegates** – decisions are taken by those involved, who have delegated responsibility within defined limits.

Balancing control and leadership

Early management theorists, for example Taylor as we learnt in Chapter 29, concentrated on achieving tasks using the most efficient methods.

Maslow and Herzberg (Chapter 30) considered the needs of employees and showed how meeting these could improve motivation and performance.

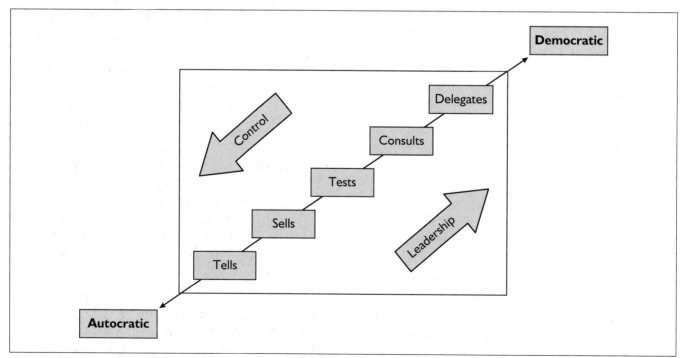

Figure 1.67 Continuum of management styles

McGregor has identified two different and extreme views of employees and the consequent management styles.

Tannenbaum and Schmidt have shown us that between these views there is a wide range of management styles and suggest that the appropriate style will depend on circumstances.

The situational approach to management styles

This pragmatic approach agrees with Tannenbaum and Schmidt that there is no best management style. It depends on the situation (see Figure 1.68).

An **organisation**'s culture or established way of doing things cannot be changed overnight. Systems in particular need time and training to enable change.

A Theory X **leader** will find it difficult or even impossible to transform his or her beliefs and approach. Similarly, a Theory Y leader will feel uncomfortable imposing decisions.

The **subordinates** may not have the necessary skills and attitudes to enable them to respond to the challenges of democratic management. Alternatively, they may not be able to cope with an autocratic manger telling them what to do.

Some **tasks** require urgent action, for example an autocratic decision rather than a democratic debate will be quicker and better when deciding to abandon ship! On the other hand, imposing new hours of work without consultation could lead to unhappy and disruptive employees.

So the best management style will take account of the situation relating to the organisation, the leader, subordinates and the task.

Current trends

In today's environment of

- intense competition
- flexible working
- fewer unskilled jobs (as a result of automation)
- better-educated workers

employees need to be encouraged not ordered about, led and not controlled.

Increasingly, effective managers subscribe to McGregor's Theory Y and adopt a more democratic management style.

Competition has prompted a number of new initiatives. Human resource managers have been actively involved in maximising customer satisfaction through quality assurance programmes. Prompted by the success of Japanese manufacturers, companies in the west have adopted Japanese approaches to quality. A particular feature of these is **quality circles**. These depend upon a very democratic, people-orientated management style and involve employees in helping to identify and resolve quality problems.

Empowerment is a management culture in which all employees are encouraged to participate, make suggestions and take the initiative, thereby reaching their full potential. This is illustrated in the case study on Blue Circle Cement, which also involves **work teams**, where people with complementary skills are given responsibility for tasks and make their own decisions.

There are also a number of other government-sponsored initiatives including **Investors in People** (**IIP**), which focuses on improving organisational performance through identifying and satisfying the training needs of the organisation's people.

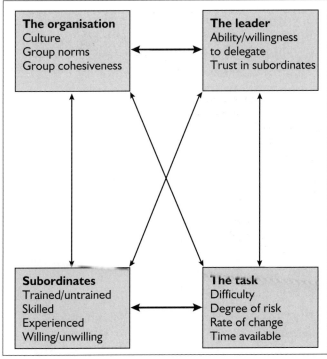

Figure 1.68 The situational influences on management style

Blue Circle Cement is Britain's biggest cement producer and makes about half of the country's needs from eight cement works (see Figure 1.69).

In the early 1980s the UK cement industry was in steep decline and was under threat from low-priced imports due to inefficiency and high production costs.

These high costs were the result of old outdated plant and poor human resource management. There were high manning levels, low wages, long hours (60 hours per week was common) and low morale. Restrictive working practices were the norm, as was strict demarcation between craft and process workers. This meant that workers were not allowed to be multiskilled or flexible. Relations between managers and workers were poor with a 'them and us' culture and little trust. Plant breakdowns were common and resulted in overtime working and as a result higher wages. Not surprisingly, productivity was poor.

The company's Cauldon Cement Works, near Stoke-on-Trent, was founded in 1957 and supplies the West Midlands area. In the early 1980s this plant was chosen for a major £40 million investment to build a highly automated, computer-controlled plant capable of producing 3,000 tonnes of cement a day. The programme for change also involved a radical review of working practices designed, with the new plant, to restore competitiveness.

The management recognised that it would need help with these changes and consulted and gained support from the trade unions. It sought help from the independent Advisory, Conciliation and Arbitration Service (ACAS) which assisted with fact-finding research, analysis and discussion.

A common vision was developed of how the business would run in the future:

> 'To have a highly skilled workforce, working as an integrated team, together with new technology, which would be able to compete with the best in the world.'

Key elements of the new vision were:

- enhanced skills for individuals with fewer job grades (from 14 to 3), leading to greater flexibility
- a new annual hours contract, with a higher rate of basic pay and the elimination of bonus and overtime payments (the annual hours contract involved paying employees a stable wage based on 2,250 hours work per year, made up of 2,028 hours on shift and a further 222 flexi-hours which have to be worked only if there is an operational need)
- a new teamworking approach where everyone works together and has mutual respect
- significant reductions in staffing levels and total labour costs.

Training at all levels, from senior managers down, was a vital part of introducing the new way of working. Both teamworking and skill development was necessary. Every member of staff was required to learn at least four new skills and craft workers at least one new craft. Initial training involved between four and six weeks.

Staff concerns were identified, recognised and addressed at every stage and level of the change process. A common vision was developed, support provided and empowered teams formed.

Figure 1.69 Blue Circle Cement

Table 1.24 Results of Blue circle's change programme

	1985	1990
Cement production	330,000 tonnes	750,000 tonnes
Numbers of employees	548	311
Productivity (tonnes per employee)	622	2,405

Source: *Times 100 Case Study*

Further changes to this agreement were made in 1997 with the introduction of the Way Ahead Agreement. This was designed to harmonise conditions and bring the company, unions and employees together in a business partnership to resolve problems and take the business forward.

Each team was focused on improving customer service and satisfaction, which was summarised in the company's mission statement:

> To be seen clearly as THE LEADER in each of these respects:
>
> * RELIABILITY OF SUPPLY
> * EXCELLENCE OF DISTRIBUTION SERVICE
> * CONSISTENCY OF GOOD PRODUCT QUALITY
> * EXPERTISE OF TECHNICAL SUPPORT
>
> And in these and all other respects
>
> * RESPONSIVENESS TO CUSTOMER NEEDS.

The initial programme took two and a half years to implement and produced dramatic results, as shown in Table 1.24.

When ACAS was independently asked to review attitudes of employees to these changes, there was almost unanimous approval of the changes. Employees found the increased variety and challenges in their jobs stimulating, and the development of team working increased employee involvement and instilled a sense of pride in the job. This led to improvements in commitment and morale.

Continuous improvement since that date has resulted in a further reduction of employees to 223 and a consequent increase in productivity. Similar working practices have also been implemented at other Blue Circle plants.

Blue Circle's success has provided the financial strength to expand overseas in Far Eastern markets and in 2000 to fight off an aggressive takeover bid by LaFarge, a French-based multinational rival.

QUESTIONS FOR DISCUSSION

1. List the major differences between the old style of working at Blue Circle and the new.
2. How would you describe the old and new management styles?
3. Which of McGregor's theories does each style follow?
4. How have the changes in working practices addressed the needs of workers identified by Maslow?
5. What changes have taken place in relation to the factors affecting job dissatisfaction and job satisfaction as considered by Herzberg?
6. What are the benefits to shareholders, managers and workers at Blue Circle of the new way of working?

The truth is stranger than fiction

Newcastle United FC made a poor start to their 1999–2000 season. Ruud Gullit, the manager, dropped star player and England captain Alan Shearer and the team lost to local rivals Sunderland. Gullitt resigned under pressure and Bobby Robson, who was born in the North East and is an ex-England manager, was appointed as his replacement. Shortly afterwards the team won away against CSKA Sophia in Europe and beat Sheffield Wednesday 8–0, with Shearer scoring 5 goals. Shearer finished the season as the club's leading scorer. How did Bobby Robson's appointment so dramatically improve the performance of the team? To what degree do you think management style can affect the performance of sports teams?

End of unit questions

As you have worked through this unit, you will have come across many questions and activities to help you understand the content and internalise your learning. The structure of these does not necessarily reflect the structure of questions you will meet in the exam, however, so the following section provides some exam-type questions by way of example.

Before looking at these questions, you might like to refer back to the 'Examiner Speaks' section (see page vii).

Below is some *general advice*, which refers to ALL the questions in the book, and to any questions you face in your AS-level examination.

- Always look at both the mark allocation and the keyword, which tells you what level of response is required.
- Note that questions usually refer to 'possible' or 'likely' effects and the ways in which the firm 'might' be affected. There is no definitive answer which the examiner is looking for, merely a reasoned discussion of the relevant factors and, where appropriate, a conclusion or, if asked for, a recommendation.
- Always take note of the product involved. What sort of market is likely to exist? What is the production process likely to be?

Note that there is no particular relevance in the total marks allocated to each question, except to illustrate the proportions of the total allocated to each component.

1 Kingsdown Pottery Ltd is a family-run firm, founded in 1948, in which three generations of the Kingsdown family are active. The business has prospered in recent years, particularly since a new design for a medium-priced dinner service was introduced a year ago. This has proved very popular and has increased Kingsdown Pottery Ltd's market share. The market leader, Trent Potteries plc, is rumoured to be about to introduce a rival design. Kingsdown Pottery Ltd is anxious to obtain new investment in order to increase its ability to supply the high demand for its successful product. The board of directors is considering whether to float the company on the stock exchange.

a) i) State any *two* groups of people who are likely to be stakeholders in Kingsdown Pottery Ltd.
(2 marks)

ii) Assess the possible reactions of these two stakeholder groups to a decision by Kingsdown Pottery Ltd to become a plc. **(12 marks)**

b) Analyse the possible effects on Kingsdown Pottery Ltd of the successful introduction of a rival product by Trent Potteries plc. **(9 marks)**

c) Evaluate the ways in which a rise in interest rates might affect Kingsdown Pottery Ltd. **(12 marks)**

Hints for answering

a) This is a Level 1 question, involving knowledge only. You are required to 'state', not 'explain', so a statement naming two groups is adequate.

b) 'Assess' means that Level 4 is required. Think of the possible effects on items like control, dividends, share prices, employment, the future profitability of the firm, the effect on its ordering and distribution policy, depending on which stakeholders you select.

c) This only requires analysis and carries slightly fewer marks than parts (b) and (d). (*Always* look at the mark allocation for each question.) Think of the likely consequences on the market and on demand.

d) This question refers to a macro-economic variable and requires a Level 4 answer. Think about the effect on both sides of the equation, that is, demand (for example consumers' likely spending on pottery) and supply (for example costs, dividends, debts, wage demands).

2 Epsilon plc produces pharmaceutical products on five different sites throughout the UK. It also has a research plant in the north of England. The administrative headquarters are in London. The firm is organised on a traditional basis, with a managing director and directors of production, finance, human resources and marketing, all based in London. Also reporting directly to the managing director are the individual plant managers. There are production and human resource managers in each plant, but finance and marketing are all carried out centrally by department in London. The research plant has a specialist manager who reports directly to the managing director in London.

Recently, the managing director has been made aware of complaints from some of the plant managers that they had not been adequately briefed on recent changes in the strategic objectives of the company; and that financial decisions are taking too long to be made, reducing the ability of the plant managers to formulate tactical objectives and to allocate resources. Also, the board of directors has complained that some plant managers are exceeding their powers and not reporting in sufficient detail to the board. Some plant managers have even been accused of trying to carry out marketing activities.

a) Explain:
   i) a strategic objective
   ii) a tactical objective
   that might exist for Epsilon plc. **(4 marks)**
b) Analyse the possible consequences for Epsilon plc of poor communication. **(10 marks)**
c) Recommend changes which could be made which might improve the management structure of Epsilon plc. **(16 marks)**

Hints for answering

a) This requires that you 'explain' in the context of the business, so a Level 2 response is needed. Think of the context of pharmaceuticals, an industry based on research and development of new products and mass production of long established items.
b) Analysis requires Level 3. Consider the possible effects of inefficient communication for a firm of this structure in this industry. Note that you are *not* required to suggest changes. Indeed, the precise methods of communication that the business uses are not described in the data.
c) This question carries the highest proportion of marks and requires a Level 4 answer. Consider again the context of a headquarters located in London, plants in different areas and a specialist department in the North. Examine the structure in general and within specific plants, remembering the likely aims and objectives of the firm, its product and market. Ideas must be well integrated into the context. It is of little use suggesting, for example, either a matrix or a delayered structure without specific examples to help you justify its application.

And now, here is a question without any hints; you are on your own!

3 Superfood plc owns a large chain of fast-food restaurants and takeaways in the country of Europa, a prosperous democracy in western Europe. Europa has an ageing population. In the next 20 years the proportion of the population under 21 years old may fall by 8 per cent, whereas the proportion of over 60s may rise by 20 per cent.

Recently, there has been a sustained campaign backed by both nutritionists and the medical profession in Europa drawing attention to the dangers of excessive consumption, particularly by the younger generation of fast-food products. The government of Europa has given some support to this campaign. The BSE disease in cattle and its possible spread to humans via the food chain has also been prominently featured in neighbouring countries. There are also rumours, denied by Superfood plc, that it has been using genetically modified ingredients. Superfood plc emphasises that its mission statement is: 'To provide wholesome food at prices that are always unbeatable'.

The Superfood plc chain of outlets relies heavily on the employment of part-time labour, particularly students working at weekends. The majority of the jobs are regarded by the employees as boring and repetitive. Firm control is exerted by local managers, partly on the grounds of health and safety when dealing with food products.

a) Explain what is meant by a mission statement. **(2 marks)**
b) Analyse the possible effects on Superfood plc of the government-backed campaign by nutritionists and medical experts against excessive consumption of fast foods. **(9 marks)**
c) Assess the possible effects on Superfoods plc of the demographic trands referred to in the passage. **(12 marks)**
d) Recommend, with reference to the ideas of *one* theorist, a strategy by which Superfoods plc might ensure that its workforce is well-motivated. **(12 marks)**

UNIT 2 MARKETING AND PRODUCTION

INTRODUCTION Marketing and production are two essential inter-related business functions. Marketing is concerned with finding out what potential customers are looking for and then making sure that their requirements are met – while production is concerned with making products that meet and even exceed customer expectations.

This unit will introduce you to methods of:

1 identifying and satisfying customer demand
2 producing products of appropriate quality as efficiently as possible.

At the end of the unit, you should be able to:
1 use your knowledge in order to evaluate, analyse and apply the most appropriate marketing and production principles to a business depicted in an unseen case study.

SECTION A *Nature and role of marketing*

INTRODUCTION   Marketing is a twentieth-century concept, although markets have existed since the dawn of civilisation.

A traditional market is a place where people meet to exchange goods or services. Originally, markets involved bartering, and some still do, but generally money has become the accepted way of assigning value to goods and facilitating fair exchange. Markets were generally held locally in the centre of towns on a particular day, when farmers would bring food to sell and would use the earnings to buy goods and services from other market traders and craftsmen.

There are still many thriving local markets. A good example is Melton Mowbray, a small Leicestershire town famous for stilton cheese and pork pies, where a large new market has been built for livestock. Every Tuesday the town's streets are filled with market stalls and traders shouting to advertise their wares. The livestock market comes alive with the sounds and smell of cattle, sheep and poultry, the amplified voice of the auctioneer, and crowds of farmers and shoppers.

The value of goods and services exchanged in these traditional ways, however, is a very small proportion of the total market in countries like the UK with developed economic systems. Today, we have shops, supermarkets, catalogues, home deliveries, credit, hire purchase, telemarketing, and the new fast growing e-commerce based on Internet trading and credit cards.

The skill of 'marketing' has also evolved from those simple skills of presenting your wares attractively, shouting out your prices and negotiating the best price. Today, producers are faced with meeting the high-quality standards of demanding supermarket buyers, competition from imports, transporting products around the world, and designing company websites for promotion via the Internet.

Critical thinking: Has the evolution of marketing been good for society?

Marketing may be defined as follows:

> 'Marketing is getting the right goods or services to the right place for the right customers at the right time and at the right price.'

What should marketing be aiming to achieve through this process? Consider the following four alternatives.

1 Maximise consumption

Typically, this is the view of businesses, who see increased consumption of their products or services leading to more sales, more jobs, more profit and greater prosperity. We are bombarded everyday by advertising on TV, radio, posters, newspapers and magazines, through the post and via the telephone. Each advert urges us to buy more food, CDs, cars, clothing, slimming products, holidays, and even items acknowledged to be bad for our health, like cigarettes. Advertising is designed to make us dissatisfied with our current purchasing pattern and to make us want more, different and new things. Fashion spectacles, for example, are designed to stimulate people to buy extra pairs for special occasions, thereby boosting consumption.

The underlying assumption is that the more we consume, the better our quality of life and the happier we become. Our consumption generates jobs and prosperity for others so they also can consume more and enjoy life better.

WHAT DO YOU THINK?

1 Is this a valid assumption? Are we caught up in a rat race to earn more, to buy more such that, as a result, we have insufficient time to enjoy our purchases? Is our increasing rate of consumption depleting the world's resources faster than they can be replaced?

2 Maximise consumer satisfaction

Another view is that the goal should be to maximise consumer satisfaction, not consumption. So, having a second pair of spectacles is fine as long as the result is increased customer satisfaction.

This is difficult to measure, however, and also ignores the environmental impact, depletion of resources and pollution. It also does not take into account the fact that satisfaction of status and ego needs depends on others having *less* or *poorer quality* than we have – that is, there needs to be a degree of exclusivity in ownership. Luxury goods and designer brands meet status and ego needs, for example Porsche cars and Gucci accessories. Neither of these products would satisfy their current customers' needs as well if they were cheap and affordable by everyone!

3 Maximise choice

Some marketers believe that the goal should be to maximise the choice available to consumers. This system enables consumers to choose the products which precisely match their lifestyles and needs. Having a wide range of choice enables a customised lifestyle and more satisfaction.

Maximising choice, however, is costly. Economies of scale in production, storage and distribution are lost as more varieties are held in stock and shorter production runs are necessary. More choice can also result in confusion and wasted time for buyers who find it difficult to choose between very similar products, which offer very few real differences.

Evidence of this is available in any supermarket when choosing a particular brand of beer from metres of shelf space stacked with similar-tasting products.

4 Maximise life quality

Many people believe that quality of life should be the goal that marketers aspire to. This is difficult to pin down and seems to involve a number of considerations:

- the quality, quantity, range and availability of goods
- the effect on the physical environment
- the effect on the cultural well-being of society
- the effect on the equality of all members of society.

The problem with this approach is that if the government, for example, determines what constitutes 'quality of life', then this undermines the operation of a market economy and has political implications.

WHAT DO YOU THINK?

1 Give examples of how the evolution of modern marketing practices has improved the quality of our lives.
2 Consider ways in which conversely marketing has detracted from the quality of our lives.
3 Think of a product or service and consider how you as a marketer would change and develop the way it is marketed.

Chapter 32 *What is marketing?*

Philip Kotler in his book *Marketing Essentials* (1984) defines **marketing** in very broad terms as: 'The human activity directed at satisfying needs and wants through exchange processes'.

Exchange processes involve each side of the exchange giving something of value to the other, thereby satisfying needs. Typically, in modern society money is exchanged for goods (food) or services (car repairs).

Here is a simpler, more focused definition:

'Marketing is getting the right goods or services to the right place for the right customers at the right time and at the right price.'

Probably the most widely accepted definition of marketing is the one developed by the **Chartered Institute of Marketing**:

'The management process responsible for the identifying, anticipating and satisfying of customer requirements profitably.'

We will look at this definition in more detail later, but first we will consider the views of a leading thinker on the evolution of marketing.

Four concepts to guide a company

Philip Kotler, a leading marketer, in his book *Marketing Management: Analysis, Planning and Control* (1984), describes four competing concepts that can be used to guide a company.

The production concept

The production concept holds that consumers will favour those products that are widely available and low in cost. Management in production-orientated organisations concentrates on high-production efficiency and wide distribution coverage.

Perhaps the best example of this approach is Henry Ford, who developed a low-cost production line process for his Model T car which was available only in black! Single-colour production was one factor in reducing cost and improving efficiency. Along with others, it resulted in the production of the first car that could be afforded by people other than the seriously rich.

The product concept

The product concept holds that consumers will favour those products that offer the best quality, performance and features. Management in these product-orientated organisations focuses its energy on making good products and improving them over time.

A good example of this approach is once again the US car industry, which focused on building big, luxurious and powerful cars. It lost sight of the consumers' changing needs for economy and concern for the environment. The result was that Japanese imports of smaller fuel-efficient models won a large share of the US car market.

The selling concept

The selling concept holds that customers, if left alone, will not ordinarily buy enough of the organisation's products. The organisation must therefore make an aggressive selling and promotion effort.

Readers Digest book club offers are good examples: customers are enticed, with direct mail offers featuring prize draws for thousands of pounds, to join a club and regularly purchase books.

The marketing concept

The marketing concept holds that the key to achieving organisational goals lies in determining the needs and wants of target markets and delivering the desired satisfactions more effectively than competitors.

A good example of satisfying the needs of customers is a development announced by EMI, the music group responsible for, among many others, Robbie Williams and The Spice Girls. It plans to develop in partnership with Musicmaker, a US-based Internet company, the facility for customers to make their own CDs, choosing their own favourite songs, artists and playing order, online via the Internet. Initially, Musicmaker will manufacture CDs and post them to customers but eventually customers will be able to download their CDs from the Internet on to their computer at home.

Figure 2.1 shows how Kotler compares the selling and marketing concepts. The selling concept focuses on the company's existing products and applies heavy sales and promotion resources as the means to achieve sales volume as a route to the end profit. The marketing concept focuses on customer needs as the starting point, and uses integrated marketing effort, that is, all of the company's resources working together, to achieve a common goal of customer satisfaction as the means to the end profit.

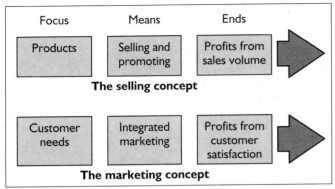

Figure 2.1 The selling and marketing concepts
Source: Kotler 1984

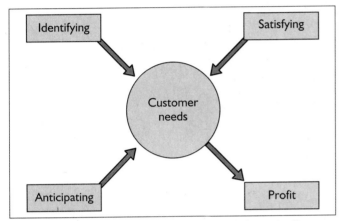

Figure 2.2 The Institute of Marketing's definition of marketing

Customer focus

Looking back at the Institute of Marketing's definition of marketing we can see that it is in accord with Kotler's view that the core of marketing is customer focus. The Institute's definition is illustrated in Figure 2.2.

The scope of marketing practice

The success of manufacturing organisations that have adopted the marketing concept of focusing on customer satisfaction has led to the application of marketing to a wide range of organisational activity:

- **Services sector** – Growth in services, the fastest growing sector of developed economies, has been fuelled by companies providing new and improved ways of satisfying customers, for example ironing services for people with busy lifestyles and luxury hotels which care for pets while their owners are on holiday.
- **Not-for-profit sector** – Charities have needed to compete for funds with the National Lottery and the

proliferation of other good causes. Creative marketing techniques have been used to maintain income. Examples include the following:
- Whiz Kids, which provides wheelchairs for disabled children, has developed adventure holidays, such as trekking in Nepal, which are offered free to people who are able to raise enough sponsorship not only to pay for the adventure but also to make a profit for Whiz Kids.
- Action Aid has introduced schemes to sponsor individual children in countries like Ethiopia. Sponsors receive progress reports on their 'adopted' child, photos and, sometimes, personal letters.
- **Regional development** – Economic regions develop and market support services to potential investors to persuade them to locate their organisations in their region, thereby increasing local employment and prosperity.
- **Special interest groups** – Greenpeace, pro- and anti-fox hunting lobbies and many other organisations are seeking to understand and influence public opinion using marketing principles.
- **Political parties** – Election success depends on understanding the voting public's needs, and developing and communicating policies to satisfy them.

Roles of the marketing function

Marketing has evolved from being a function of sales (responsible for market research, advertising and promotion – see Figure 2.3a), via the situation where it became a department of equal standing with sales (Figure 2.3b), to being the dominant function within an organisation, where sales becomes a function of marketing (Figure 2.3c). It has now reached the point where satisfying customer needs dictates the activity of all company functions (Figure 2.3d), and marketing controls the interaction between the customer and the company, including:

- forecasting sales and cash flows
- prioritising production and delivery schedules
- setting performance standards
- specifying product development requirements.

The development of the marketing function is shown in Figure 2.3.

Competitive marketing

Competition is present and increasing in today's free market economies. Marketing departments therefore have the challenge of providing better customer satisfaction than

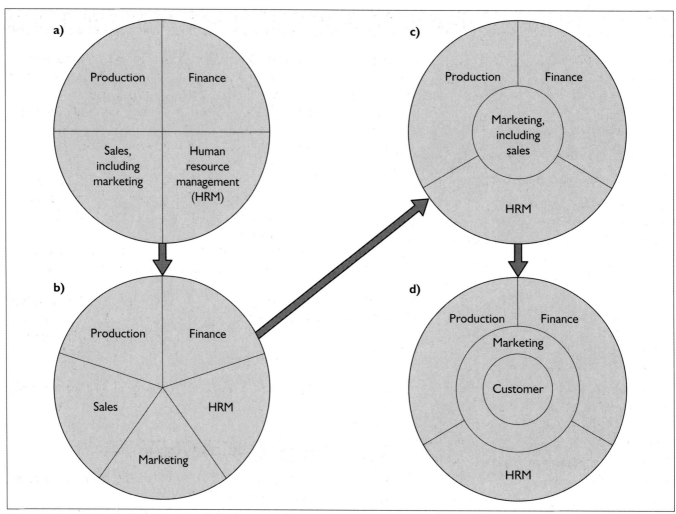

Figure 2.3 Evolution of the marketing function

their competitors. Understanding customers' needs is the key to success. Market research is the activity that seeks to understand and measure customers' needs and levels of satisfaction. Marketing departments, having gathered this information, are tasked with making best use of the organisation's resources to satisfy customers and win new business from the competition.

CASE STUDY: BIRTH OF MCDONALD'S

In a world where there seems to be a McDonald's in every shopping centre, it seems difficult to believe that the first McDonald's fast-food restaurant was opened in the USA just over 40 years ago. In 1996 there were over 21,000 McDonald's restaurants in over 101 countries, generating sales of over US$30 billion, and increasing numbers of similar fast-food burger restaurants such as Burger King following in their footsteps.

The first McDonald's in the UK was opened in Woolwich, south east London, in 1974. The eight hundredth branch was opened in 1997.

What was life like before McDonald's?

Burgers were sold in many restaurants or cafés. Standards of quality varied, but it could be argued that generally service was slow by today's standards, burgers came in different shapes and sizes, and café facilities were often sparse. Staff were often unhelpful, conditions were usually dirty, smoky and noisy, and the toilets were to be avoided! On the other hand, many cafés were, and are, very good, often serving good-value food and being in a well-appointed position.

The dramatic transformation was started by Ray Kroc in 1955 when he recognised that Richard and Maurice McDonald in California, USA, had developed a winning restaurant concept, and bought their chain of seven restaurants for $2.7 million and formed the McDonald's Corporation.

The essence of the McDonald's concept, then as today, is captured in the initials QSC – quality, service and cleanliness. Restaurants are spotlessly clean. Staff are cheerful and friendly. Food is always well-presented, hot and tasty. Customers are served within five minutes. There are no jukeboxes or pool tables. The restaurant is bright and family friendly.

Ray Kroc achieved McDonald's rapid growth by selling franchises, twenty-year licences, enabling people to manage their own McDonald's restaurant. A key element in the success of these franchises has been establishing and continuously developing high-quality standards that are rigorously maintained.

Franchise operators are carefully selected, and given comprehensive training and ongoing support. Franchises benefit from high-quality national advertising, sales promotions, product and service quality monitoring via continuous customer surveys. McDonald's invests heavily in improving the technology of fast-food production and new product development, and works continuously to reduce costs and speed up service.

Key events in the development of McDonald's are:

1963 – Ronald McDonald, the happy clown, made his first TV appearance.
1968 – The Big Mac, two burgers in a three-tier bun, was introduced. It was the 'brainchild' of Jim Delgetti, one of Ray Kroc's earliest franchisees.
1973 – The Egg McMuffin was developed by Herb Preston, another US franchisee.
1979 – The Happy Meal, a meal in a box specially for kids, was introduced.

1984 – McDonald's was the first UK restaurant company to introduce nutrition information on all of its products nationally.
1986 – The first UK Drive-thru restaurants were opened.
1988 – McDonald's sponsored the child achievement awards.
1993 – A Ronald McDonald's house was opened at Alderhay Children's Hospital, a place for parents to stay while visiting their sick children.
1994 – McDonald's was voted the most parent friendly restaurant for the second year running.
1995 – McDonald's sponsored the FA Premiership.
1996 – The McDonald's Vegetable Deluxe veggie burger was introduced. McDonald's gave 1 per cent of all profits to charitable causes.
2000 – McDonald's became global sponsors for the Olympics for the four years 2001–4.

QUESTIONS FOR DISCUSSION

1 What do you think have been the key factors in the growth of McDonald's?
2 Why do you think that the Big Mac and Egg McMuffin product development ideas came from franchisees? Why did McDonald's act on their recommendations?
3 What benefits do you think McDonald's achieves as a result of monitoring product and service quality through continuous customer surveys?
4 Why do you think McDonald's introduced Ronald McDonald, supports children's charities and developed the Happy Meal?
5 To what degree has McDonald's succeeded in implementing the Chartered Institute of Marketing's definition of marketing?
6 McDonalds introduced the McDonald's Vegetable Deluxe veggie burger in 1996, sometime after some of its competitors had introduced veggie burgers. How do you think this could have affected McDonald's sales?

The truth is stranger than fiction

It is interesting to note that car sales staff have achieved a reputation, alongside their double-glazing and time-share colleagues, of using high-pressure sales techniques. Car sales staff are often highly trained, very knowledgeable about their products and skilled at their job. Members of the public, however, have become wary of visiting car showrooms in the fear that they might be approached by pushy staff, interested in earning lucrative commissions, by selling cars that do not ideally match customers' needs and at prices that they cannot afford.

An understanding of this customer fear has been used to advantage by new entrants to the UK car market, Daewoo. It has advertised its policy that a salesperson will not approach a potential customer in its showrooms unless the customer asks for assistance. Daewoo believes that removing the perceived threat of high-pressure sales will encourage customers to visit its showrooms, thereby increasing sales.

Daewoo has achieved success, establishing a significant market share in a competitive market, by instructing sales staff not to approach customers to try to sell cars!

Chapter 33 *Marketing objectives*

Organisational objectives

Different organisations will have different objectives. Commercial organisations seek to maximise profit for their shareholders. Public sector and charitable organisations aim to provide high-quality services at low cost. Political organisations want to win votes, to be elected to office and to satisfy the needs of their voters.

Corporate and strategic planning is the process which:

- defines the organisation's purpose (often referred to as a mission)
- quantifies this in a set of objectives
- considers how best these objectives can be met
- manages and directs the resources of the organisation to meet them.

The process usually involves overall organisational objectives being broken down into functional, departmental and individual objectives, each of which contributes to achieving the organisation's mission and general objectives (see Figure 2.4).

An organisation may, for example, have the objective of increasing profit. One of the functional objectives to achieve this might be for marketing to increase sales of product A. Plans to achieve this could involve setting specific objectives for the advertising and the direct sales departments. Individuals in those departments would then have specific individual objectives for an advertising campaign or additional sales visits to potential customers for product A.

Organisational planning

Planning is the process of establishing an organisation's current position, forecasting future development and determining how it will progress to the point where objectives are met. As mentioned above, it involves deciding how best to meet objectives, and managing and directing resources to meet them.

The broad and general methods of meeting objectives are the organisation's **strategies**. For example, an organisation may have a strategy to increase sales by developing new products.

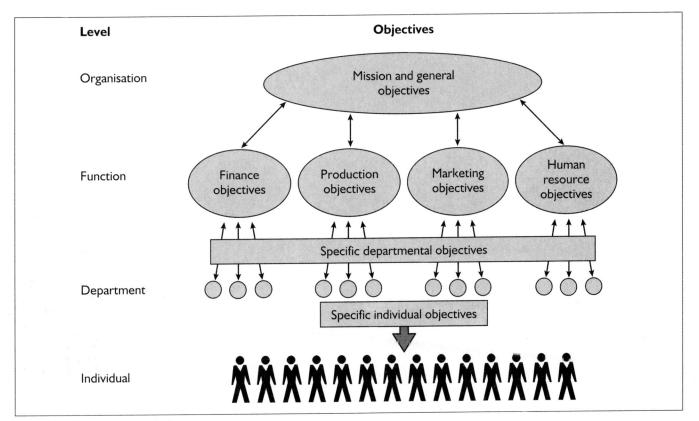

Figure 2.4 Organisational objectives

The more detailed and specific methods of meeting objectives follow the strategic lead and are called **tactics**. For example, an organisation may choose the tactic of developing a low-fat, sugar-free chocolate bar targeted at the health and diet conscious teenage market.

Choice of strategies and tactics will be determined by:

- the organisation's current position, particularly in the eyes of customers in relation to competitors
- the organisation's strengths and weaknesses
- forecasts of how customers' needs (the market) will change in the future
- forecasts of how competition will develop in the future
- new opportunities and threats arising from these changes.

A **SWOT** (**strengths**, **weaknesses**, **opportunities** and **threats**) **analysis** is the term given to this process.

The role of marketing
Planning

We have seen that in marketing-orientated organisations satisfying the customer is the focus of all staff and departments and the marketing department has a key role in this activity acting as the communication interface between the customer and the organisation (see Figure 2.3d).

If we relate this to the planning process, we can see that marketing plays a central role. It is best placed to provide:

- an assessment of the organisation's current position, in the eyes of its customers and in relation to competitors
- forecasts of how customers' needs (the market) will change in the future
- forecasts of how competition will develop in the future.

Market research is the term used to describe this process of gathering information about the market (customers and competitors).

Objectives

Marketing objectives typically will be:

- to increase **sales volume** (number of units) and **value**
- to maintain or increase **market share**, that is, the proportion of the total amount of product or service provided – Tesco, for example, increased its share of the grocery market from 17.8 per cent in 1994 to 24.4 per cent in May 2000
- to improve **customer satisfaction** ratings
- to develop new products or markets.

Choosing a strategy

In the organisational planning section above, we described strategy as the general method by which an objective is achieved. One technique for selecting an appropriate strategy, also mentioned above, is SWOT analysis.

Using information gathered by market research, managers assess the organisation's internal strengths and weaknesses relative to customer perceptions and competitor capability and match these to the opportunities and threats present or developing in the market. A company for example with a top-quality product might use this strength to take the opportunity to increase its selling price and profits. It might also correct a weakness, the lack of export sales, by taking the opportunity to develop export markets. Growth in export sales would help to protect the company against the threat of a recession in its home UK market.

Leading thinkers – Igor Ansoff

Born in 1918, Igor Ansoff published his first book, *Corporate Strategy*, in 1965. Further major books followed, along with more than 90 articles. His ideas relating to the development of strategy have influenced many people in business and business education.

Ansoff is best known for his matrix of strategic options for growth, which compares developing new products and new markets.

In Ansoff's matrix, shown in Figure 2.5, the options are numbered from one to four in order of increasing degree of risk:

1 **Market penetration** – selling more of the same product to the same types of people.

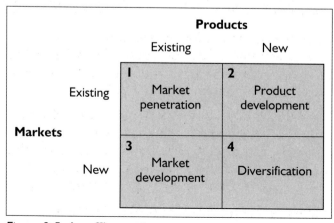

Figure 2.5 Ansoff's matrix

2 **Product development** – selling new products to existing customers.

3 **Market development** – selling existing products to new customers.

4 **Diversification** – selling new products to new customers.

Market penetration – This is possible either by increasing market share at the expense of others, by developing a competitive advantage, or by growing the total market size. Currently, the market for mobile phones is one where companies are achieving growth as result of total market growth.

Product development – This involves a company exploiting the strength of its relationship with customers and using its creative ability to develop new products suited to their needs. Supermarkets are a good example of this. They have gradually moved away from simply selling groceries to a wide range of other products including household goods, clothes, petrol, computers and even cars!

Market development – New customers can be more difficult to develop than products, but where an organisation has significant product strengths this can be a good opportunity for growth. Examples can include selling to export markets, or a different customer type. Lucozade, a high-energy drink, was originally sold to speed recovery from illness, but the company developed a new market among sports people.

Diversification – This involves developing new expertise, both in terms of product and markets and is the highest risk alternative. Often companies, rather than develop their own expertise, will buy another company to achieve their objectives. A recent example is the acquisition by the Ford Motor Company of the Kwik-Fit replacement car tyre and exhaust fitting company. Kwik-Fit was made famous by its 'You can't get quicker than a Kwik-Fit fitter' advertising slogan. Its founder Tom Farmer was paid £1 billion for his company on the understanding that he would continue to manage it, providing the expertise Ford needs to develop an understanding of the new products and markets involved.

Michael Porter in his book *Competitive Strategy* (1980) considered alternative strategies for companies to achieve the objective of growth by market penetration. He suggested that companies needed to develop a competitive advantage by adopting one of three competitive strategies:

- **Cost leadership**, where the company becomes the lowest cost producer and is able to sell at a lower price than its competitors and still make a profit, for example the Freeserve part of Dixons which became Britain's biggest Internet service provider with 1.1 million customers within eight months of the launch of its free service.
- **Differentiation**, where a company makes its products distinctly different from those of its competitors and can charge a premium price. Designer brands are good examples – Nike sportswear baseball caps are often twice the price of unbranded equivalent products.
- **Focus**, where a company targets only one segment or part of the market (see market segmentation, Chapter 40) and decides to pursue either a cost leadership or differentiation strategy as appropriate. Retail examples at either extreme are Poundland (everything costs £1) shops and Harrods, where most products attract a price premium and cost considerably more than £1!

CASE STUDY: TESCO

Tesco is Britain's market leading supermarket retailer employing 200,000 people. Terry Leahy has worked for the company for 20 years, the last two years in the top job of chief executive.

Previously, Leahy was marketing director and in the early 1990s had the task of reviewing the company's marketing strategy. At that time, Sainsbury's was the market leader and much of Tesco's marketing activity was aimed at competing with them.

A massive market research project involving interviewing a quarter of a million people was the starting point of the review. This was aimed at finding out how customers' lives had changed and were changing. It changed Tesco's focus from beating its rivals towards satisfying its customers. The message received from the research was that, more than anything, customers wanted value.

Other findings led to the development of:

- Tesco Clubcard, a customer loyalty (points reward) card
- Metro and Express, high-street convenience stores

- 24-hour shopping
- home shopping, home delivery via the Internet
- retail banking
- a 'computers for schools' promotion.

These initiatives, alongside the focus of cutting costs, reducing prices and thereby providing customers with value, have resulted in Tesco increasing its market share from around 10 per cent to 15.8 per cent by mid-1999. As a result, Tesco is now clear market leader. It came top of the list of Britain's most admired companies in 1998.

Leahy's success as marketing director earned him promotion to the top job two years ago.

What are the secrets of his success? He visits branches on at least one day a week, calling at five or six stores. The purpose of the visits? To listen and to learn.

What are Tesco's objectives for the future? To become a major retailer globally, to rise above its current position of twelfth place in the world.

Leahy's strategies and plans to achieve this objective include:

- export growth in central Europe, Ireland, and South East Asia, involving:

  – six new hypermarkets (stores with over 100,000 sq. ft (about 9300 m^2) of floor space) in Hungary, Czech Republic and Poland
  – the acquisition of Lotus superstores, with thirteen units in Asia
  – a partnership with Samsung superstores, with 25 units in Korea
- opening of new Homeplus hypermarkets in the UK
- developing the traditional UK store format in Ireland
- home shopping delivery service extended from 11 to 100 stores.

QUESTIONS FOR DISCUSSION

1 How did Leahy change the focus of Tesco's marketing when he was marketing director?
2 What was the key message from customers in the survey, and what competitive strategy did Leahy adopt as a result?
3 What is the secret of Leahy's continuing success as chief executive?
4 What is Leahy's objective for the future of Tesco?
5 How could Leahy's strategies be categorised using Ansoff's matrix?

The truth is stranger than fiction

In 1997 BMW, the German luxury car manufacturer, sold record numbers of cars (over 60,000) in the UK but was worried by its success and decided to limit sales the following year to a maximum of 70,000.

Why? BMW's popularity is explained by its exclusivity. It is a premium-priced car that people like to be seen in. BMW is a prestige brand. Drivers of BMWs believe that the car shows the world that they are successful and have made it. BMW's managers believe that too many of their cars on the road will dilute their exclusive, prestige brand and lead to a longer-term decline in sales.

So BMW's strategy, to achieve its longer-term growth objective, is to limit its market share, and protect its prestige brand.

Chapter 34 *The marketing mix*

Having decided on our objectives and selected strategies for achieving them, we need to get down to the detail of marketing our product. True to the marketing concept the first step involves identifying our customers and their needs, and getting to know them well so that we are able to anticipate and satisfy their needs better than our competitors. This will be covered in detail in Chapters 35 to 41. In this chapter we will assume we have done our research on our customers and their needs and will consider how best to meet them.

The **marketing mix** may be defined as follows:

> 'Marketing mix is the mixture of controllable marketing variables that the firm uses to pursue the sought level of sales to target markets.' (Kotler, 1984).

Leading thinkers – E. Jerome McCarthy

There are dozens of marketing mix elements, but in his book *Basic Marketing: A Managerial Approach* (1981) McCarthy popularised **the four Ps approach – product**, **price**, **place** and **promotion**.

The four Ps can be considered to be the four levers the marketing manager can use to control the marketing mix and generate satisfied customers (see Figure 2.6).

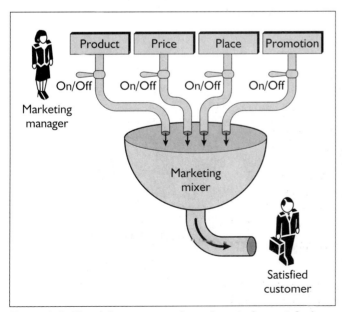

Figure 2.6 The 4 Ps, creating the right mix for satisfied customers

A marketing manager's challenge is to get the right product, at the right price, in the right place (and at the right time) using the right promotion.

The right product

How do you define the right product? Tom Peters (*The Tom Peters Experience*, 1988) says that **perception** is all there is. The perception of a product is a mix of tangible and intangible features. A product can also have a range of indirect rather than direct features. A product consists of a bundle of customer satisfying features, as shown in Table 2.1.

Table 2.1 Product, a bundle of customer satisfying features

Tangible/direct	Intangible	Indirect
Function	Image	Customer service
Colour	Style	Availability of
Size/shape	Reputation	spare parts
Packaging	Quality	Guarantee
Name	Taste	Helpline
Model, luxury	Brand	Training and
or economy		support
Flavour		
Smell		

Customers buy a bundle of satisfaction provided by the product's features that meet their needs and provide benefits. For example:

- a gardener may buy a packet of seeds, but the benefit he or she seeks is a beautiful display of flowers
- when buying clothes the satisfaction bundle the customer is seeking could be a new suit to impress in a job interview or something comfortable and hard wearing for working in a factory, two very contrasting bundles of features.

The marketer's challenge is to understand customers' needs and develop products with a range of features to satisfy them – not a straightforward task, particularly in today's fast-changing world when customers' needs change rapidly and competitors react quickly to follow and overtake their rivals' successes.

To counter these challenges, marketers need to keep their fingers on the pulse of customers' changing tastes and have an awareness of competing products. Prompted by these, new or improved products can be developed to replace today's successes.

The right price

Price is the one element of the marketing mix that generates income – product, place and promotion all cost money. It can be argued that it is the most important element as a result and because it is the factor that consumers find most easy to compare.

Traditionally, companies have set prices by calculating their costs and adding a **margin** – that is, a bit extra – for profit. A marketing-orientated company turns this concept on its head and first decides what price a customer is prepared to pay (the **perceived value**), that is, one that results in a satisfied customer. Having determined this and the acceptable profit level, the company then has to ensure that the product can be manufactured and supplied at or below target cost.

Setting prices

The formula for the traditional approach (cost plus) is:

Costs + Acceptable profit = Selling price.

The formula for the marketing approach is:

Selling price – Acceptable profit = Target cost

How does a customer decide what is good value?

Each of the cost elements has an effect on the perceived value of a product, as will the customer's attitudes and experience. Consider the example of a Rolex watch:

- Promotion – a gold Rolex watch is promoted as the watch of the rich and famous. As a result, students are unlikely to consider this to be a watch for them and would not be prepared, even if they could afford to, to pay a premium price.
- Product – while both will tell the time equally well, most people will pay more for the features of a gold Rolex watch than for a plastic Casio one.
- Place – if tourists were offered gold Rolex watches in a local market, they would expect to pay much less than in a high-class city jewellery shop, even if an authentic guarantee was offered.
- Customers' attitude and experience – a wealthy tourist, who had led a sheltered life, if offered a genuine Rolex

watch in that same market at a bargain price might happily pay $100. A more experienced market trader would more probably haggle and be happy to pay £10 for what he assumes to be a good-quality fake Rolex.

Pricing strategies

Product prices can be set to achieve specific objectives. Strategic pricing falls into three main categories:

- product positioning
- differential pricing
- competitive pricing.

Product positioning

The product price is set at a level which enables the customer to compare a product against competing products on price and quality.

The matrix in Figure 2.7 illustrates this, comparing quality and prices of grocery retailers as an example.

Looking at product quality shows how the premium store Harrods can command high prices by providing high-quality goods in its prestigious food hall in contrast to a motorway services station which may charge high prices for a poor service to hungry motorists who have little choice.

Looking at price, we can see that Aldi, the discount grocer, like the motorway service station, provides lower quality products and services but, in contrast, offers bargain prices.

		Price		
		Higher	**Medium**	**Lower**
Product quality	**Higher**	Premium strategy *Harrods*	Penetration strategy *Marks & Spencer*	Superb value strategy *Tesco*
	Medium	Overcharging strategy *Corner shop*	Average strategy *Sainsbury's*	Good value strategy *Asda*
	Lower	Rip-off strategy *Motorway service station*	Cheap flashy strategy *Kwik-Save*	Bargain price strategy *Aldi*

Figure 2.7 Quality and price comparison

Differential pricing strategies

This is the term given to the situation where a product is priced at different levels in different circumstances. Examples include:

- **volume discounts** – this occurs when customers are given lower prices when they buy larger quantities, that is, more packs, bigger packs
- **trade discounts** – these are given to customers who resell the product, such as a retailer or a builder
- **concessions** – lower prices are often applied to those on low incomes such as pensioners, children or students
- **peak pricing** – many products have times of peak demand when prices are higher such as holidays, telephone calls, electricity; lower, off-peak prices are used to provide an incentive to customers to use these services during less busy times
- **payment terms** – customers may sometimes be offered a discount for prompt or cash payment in situations where 30 days' credit is normal
- **geographic** – prices may be higher in one part of the country than another, which often reflects higher costs (city centres and London in particular) such as restaurants and parking; remote locations such as the Shetland Islands are also charged a premium for products such as petrol
- **promotional** – cheaper prices may be charged as a short-term boost to sales, such as the traditional January retailers' sales.

Competitive pricing strategies

These are strategies that are used to take account of the competitive market situation:

- **Price skimming**. In a situation where a product has no competition, for example a new product or one protected by a patent, then a company can take advantage of this to 'skim off' the cream of the market by charging a high price. Once competition develops the company would then reduce prices to maintain its market share.
- **Expansion pricing**. A company that wants to rapidly expand its market share will set a low price to expand the market size and its share of that market. Generally, this tactic is successful in mass markets, when higher sales volumes result in lower production costs and an increase in profits as a result.
- **Penetration pricing**. When introducing a new product to the market a company may decide to set a low price to win an initial foothold in the market. Low-

cost introductory offers are a good example of this. Dixon's Freeserve Internet service is an extreme example of this: Freeserve became market leader in less than one year.

- **Loss leaders**. This is a form of promotional pricing that is used to attract customers to a retailer. One product such as bread is sold at cost price or lower on the assumption customers will be attracted to the store and will, at the same time, purchase other profit-making items like jam and butter.
- **Price wars**. These occur when a company uses price as an aggressive means of winning business from competitors. This is a successful tactic when a company can see a weakness among its competitors. One example is the supply of petrol, where supermarkets have won business from independent service stations, many of whom have gone out of business because they cannot match the supermarket's low prices and continue to make a profit.

The right place

Having developed the right product at the right price, we now need to make it available to the customer in the right place.

This involves producing products and providing stocks of them in suitable and convenient locations. Too much stock will lead to excess costs, too little to customer frustration and lost sales.

The physical manufacturing of products and distribution of stock will generally be the responsibility of an operations department. It can only provide this service well, however, when the marketing department has provided accurate forecasts of sales demand.

Selecting and developing appropriate channels of distribution is a key area of the marketing mix. The appropriate channels will very much depend on the product and target customer (see Figure 2.8).

Traditionally, consumer goods have gone through the wholesale and retailer channels of distribution to the consumer.

- **Wholesalers** buy and store products in bulk, reducing the need for producers to make small deliveries to retailers and providing a fast supply service to retailers who do not have the facilities to hold large stocks. In recent years the development of logistics (transport and warehousing) companies, able to deliver small quantities

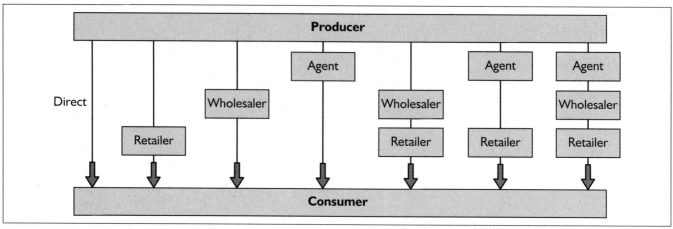

Figure 2.8 Channels of distribution

direct from the manufacturer to the retailer or consumer, and of computerised order processing systems has meant that manufacturers have had less need of wholesalers.

- **Retailers** have also changed and large retailers such as supermarkets have their own regional warehouse systems and the size to buy in bulk direct from producers.
- **Agents** promote a range of producer's products for a commission (percentage of sales) when it is more economic than the producer employing its own sales force, for example export sales.
- **Direct sales** traditionally are via the producer's own sales force who sell to the consumer, for example double glazing. Other fast-growing means of direct sales are mail order (clothing), telephone sales (insurance) and sales via the Internet (books).
- **Marketing managers** need to select channels appropriate to their customers and to develop an appropriate marketing mix of product, price and promotion for each channel and its elements, not an easy task in today's highly competitive environment where consumers expect products and services to be available seven days a week and 24 hours a day.

The right promotion

The right product, at the right price and available in the right places, will not succeed if consumers are not aware of it.

Promotion is the marketing activity that creates a positive image about a product and company. There are four main elements of promotional activity – **advertising**, **sales promotion**, **personal selling** and **publicity**. They all depend on effective communication.

Effective communication depends on:

- sending a clear, persuasive message
- understanding consumer needs, attitudes and knowledge
- winning attention among competing messages
- using a medium that will be seen by the company's target consumers
- consumers receiving and decoding the company's message
- checking understanding through feedback.

The model of effective communication shown in Figure 2.9 has been adapted to the circumstances of promotional activity.

The essence of marketing is understanding **consumers**, the receivers in the communication process, and sending a **message** that will persuade them to buy the product. The message will need to catch their attention, to stand out among the hundreds of **competing advertising**

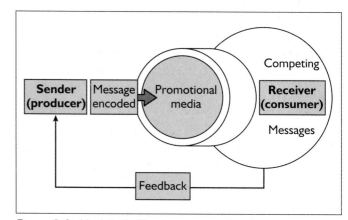

Figure 2.9 Model of effective communication

messages that surround them in their daily lives. It needs to be **encoded** in such a way as to sell subtly but not so subtly that the receiver cannot decode it. The message needs to be sent using **media** that ensure that it will reach the target audience, and there needs to be **feedback** as a means of checking that the message has been received and understood.

Let's look at each of the elements of the model of effective communication in more detail:

- **Consumers**. There will be many and different consumers of products, often with different needs. For a specialist product like a Rolex watch there will be a small elite group of target consumers who will respond to a different message sent through different media than the larger mass market for Casio watches. Similarly, different elements of channels of distribution will need a different approach. A producer of chocolate bars would probably send a personal sales person to call on a wholesaler and use TV advertising to promote to consumers.
- **Message**. Continuing to use the chocolate bar example, the wholesaler's interest would revolve around bulk discounts and payment terms whereas the consumer interest would lie in taste.
- **Competing advertising messages**. We each receive hundreds of promotional messages via various media every day. An effective promotional message needs to stand out from the crowd. The mnemonic AIDA

is used to prompt the stages necessary in an effective promotional message:

- **A** the message should grab the **attention** ensuring product awareness
- **I** attention should be maintained and converted to **interest**
- **D** interest should result in **desire** or **demand** for the product
- **A** desire needs to prompt **action** to buy.

- **Encoding**. In today's sophisticated markets, it is no longer enough to shout 'Best bananas 70p a pound'. The message needs to be subtler. The energy provided by bananas satisfies an important consumer need, and encoding the message using the image of a well-known sportswoman eating one before a game of beach volley ball might be decoded by a consumer as, 'If I eat more bananas I might look better and be fitter!'
- **Media**. There are many different media for transmitting a promotional message, including the following:
  - Advertising, via TV, radio, posters, newspapers, magazines, direct mail, can be classified as mass audience, for example TV (expensive and non-selective), or targeted, such as *Rugby World Magazine* (selective and cheaper).
  - Sales promotion, where the message is often carried on the packaging or on instore leaflets and posters. Generally, these include money-off coupons, special offers, competitions, etc.

CASE STUDY: PETROL STATIONS – THE NEW CORNER SHOPS

Have you noticed how many independent petrol stations and local corner and village grocery shops have closed in recent years – and, as a result, the increasing success of cut-price supermarkets supplying not only the week's groceries but also petrol?

Another recent trend has been the emergence of surviving independent garages as the convenience store for the new millennium, selling not only their traditional snacks and car accessories but also groceries, newspapers, coal, gas, flowers and greetings cards.

QUESTIONS FOR DISCUSSION

1 What elements of the marketing mix are critical to the success of supermarkets?
2 What pricing strategy has resulted in the closure of small grocers' shops and petrol stations?
3 What elements of the marketing mix have been important to the survival of petrol stations whose profits have been squeezed by the availability of cut price petrol?

- Personal selling involves one-to-communication, either face to face or on the telephone. Generally, this takes place in shops, offices and in the home and is usually limited to more expensive and complex products.
- Publicity is usually unpaid for and results from press relations (PR) activity, designed to get a product or company in the news.

- **Feedback**. Promotional activity can be expensive, particularly if it is not working. It is therefore important to test the effectiveness of promotional activity by carrying out research to determine the level of consumer awareness, and then how advertising has affected the consumers' feelings towards the products.

The truth is stranger than fiction

If you take a trip to your local supermarket you will find a vast difference in price between what at first sight seem to be identical products – baked beans.

In May 2000 in a Nottingham supermarket, the supermarket's own brand of economy baked beans was on sale for £0.09. Less than a metre away, a similar-sized can of Heinz baked beans was advertised at the special low price of £0.33, more than 3.6 times more expensive!

Both tins contained the same weight of similarly coloured and tasting beans in a tomato sauce. In supermarkets across Britain there is a similar price difference, but that unique something that the Heinz marketing mix provides ensures that Heinz beans are still the UK's market leader.

SECTION B *Market research*

INTRODUCTION   We learned in the last section that marketing activity should be focused on customers. It is the marketing department's role to understand consumers and to harness company resources to satisfy their needs. Market research is the term given to the activity of gathering the information on markets and consumers necessary to developing this understanding.

Effective market research provides a competitive advantage. If you know and understand markets and consumers better than your competitors you will be better placed to offer products or services that will convert potential consumers into satisfied customers.

In today's rapidly changing and competitive environment, successful organisations establish systems to constantly monitor markets and consumers. The regular supply of information is observed, trends are analysed and the organisation's activities are developed to keep pace with changing consumer expectations and market conditions.

Critical thinking

Our lifestyle and personal data are held on marketing databases. Is this in our interest?

Driven to understand markets and potential consumers better than their competitors, marketing managers are intent on gathering more and more information on each of us.

Store loyalty cards are used to register each time we shop, to record the details of all of the products we have purchased and details of how we have paid, for example by cash or credit/debit card.

Prize draws, guarantee registration cards and customer surveys are used by other companies to gather our personal details, preferences and buying habits.

Specialist companies exist to gather our personal details and to sell this information on to other companies. Years ago databases held little more than our electoral roll details. Today, details of our income, work status and type, credit rating, house type, car ownership, shopping habits, leisure interests, etc. are available for sale to direct marketing companies interested in selling to us via the mail, telephone, fax or Internet.

One of the world's biggest direct marketing service companies is Experian. It is based in Nottingham, has a staff of 11,000 and annual sales of £900 million. Experian is part of Great Universal Stores (GUS) mail order catalogue group. It supplies customer data to hundreds of companies ranging from large multinationals to small specialist local companies. Data held on individuals and households include household composition, ages, gender, length of residency, property type, shareholdings and directorships.

All 44 million UK adults are listed on the Experian database and these can be classified by any of 380 lifestyle profiles, for example 'Mr and Mrs Fit', Mrs Couch Potato', 'Miss Thrifty', etc. The database can also classify households by postal codes (generally groups of 15 houses) into 52 types such as 'chattering classes' or 'clever capitalists'.

Experian claims that the information it provides not only helps marketers to understand and target customers effectively but also improves the lives of consumers who as a result receive product and service offers that match their needs. As more companies use information similar to that provided by Experian we should receive less inappropriate and time-wasting direct mail and phone calls.

Companies that hold personal data on computers are regulated by the Data Protection Act, which gives consumers the right to check their personal details held on computer databases and to have the data corrected if inaccurate.

WHAT DO YOU THINK?

1 How do you feel about the amount of information held on computer relating to you and your family?
2 Is it helpful to receive appropriately targeted product or service offers, for example car renewal insurance offers from competing companies a week or two before your car insurance is due for renewal?
3 How much of a nuisance is it to receive offers that are inappropriate such as car insurance offers when you do not own a car?
4 How do you feel about being stereotyped as belonging to one of 380 lifestyles or one of 52 household types?
5 Do you think it is fair for car insurance rates to vary according to your lifestyle and household category? For example, a teacher in a middle-class neighbourhood will pay less for insurance than a student living in an inner-city area.

Chapter 35 Defining the market

In our introduction to marketing we defined a market as a place where people meet to exchange goods or services. In the past this could have been interpreted literally, but these days in developed economies many more sophisticated methods of exchange exist between suppliers and customers, and this definition needs to be taken metaphorically.

Marketing revolves around the needs of customers, and organisations have to develop an understanding of their target customers. A starting point in this exercise is defining which of the world's six billion citizens are the organisation's target customers.

A product-orientated company is likely to define its target market in relation to potential purchasers of its products. For example, the Lotus Car Company will define its market as potential customers for an upmarket sports car.

A marketing-orientated company will define its target market as those people seeking satisfaction of a particular need, for example a designer clothes company will target those who want to look good and are prepared to pay a premium for products that meet this need.

Companies in each category are likely to limit their market to a particular geographic region as all but a few of the world's big multinational companies have limits to their distribution capability. Many products are also only applicable to certain geographic, economic or cultural regions.

To define its market a company will need to understand the characteristics of people it is targeting, including details of their numbers, location and preferences. Information will also be needed on trends, competitors and other market influences. Market research is a specialist area of marketing that gathers and analyses this information which is used by marketing managers to develop products and services in response to continuously changing customer expectations and market place challenges.

Larger companies will develop a **market research system** as illustrated in Figure 2.10.

The market research system gathers information from the **market environment** and produces reports for **marketing management** who develop and introduce marketing programmes. The effect of these marketing programmes in the **market environment** is evaluated by the **market research system** and fed back to marketing management for monitoring against plans and further development planning.

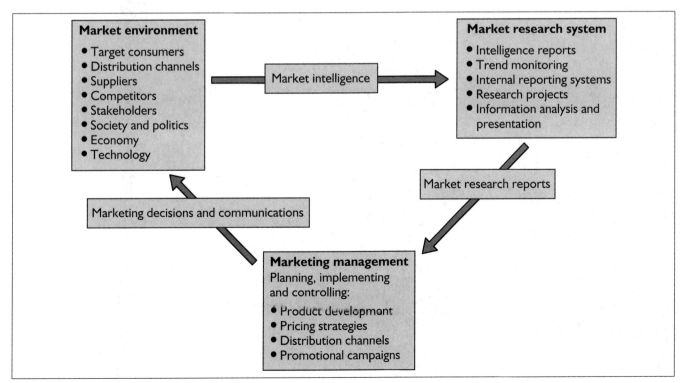

Figure 2.10 A market research system

Market environment

Consideration needs to be given to each of the following:

- **Target consumers**. The location, numbers, preferences, values, demographics, income are some of the factors that can affect behaviour. Current and trend data are of interest.
- **Distribution channels**. How does the target market expect to access the product or service; how might they in the future? How well is your product or service distributed through these channels? What do these channels expect from you?
- **Suppliers**. How reliable are they? Could they help you to improve your product or service? Do they supply your competitors; could they become a competitive threat?
- **Competitors**. How does your competitor's product or service rate against yours on price and quality? How does its market share and customer profile compare with yours?
- **Stakeholders**. Who are your stakeholders? What are their areas of interest? How much influence and power do they have?
- **Society and politics**. How are cultures, tastes and legislation changing and to what degree will these changes affect your markets and consumers?
- **The economy**. What changes are forecast and to what degree will these changes affect your markets, consumers and demand for your products and services?
- **Technology**. How is this changing? What effect could this have on your organisation, products or services and markets? What opportunities or threats might arise for you and your competitors?

CASE STUDY: PRUDENTIAL'S EGG SAVINGS ACCOUNT

Hindsight can provide a very clear picture of how markets develop. Being able to predict how markets will develop makes organisations millions of pounds or in the case of the Prudential's new 'Egg' savings account billions of pounds, as is illustrated by the following summary of press reports in August 1999.

PRUDENTIAL LAYS GOLDEN EGG

Prudential, the financial services, insurance-based organisation, decided to enter the competitive savings account market in the summer of 1998 with their new account called Egg.

Egg was originally launched as a telephone bank with add-on Internet access. Prudential used a market penetration pricing strategy, offering an extremely high interest rate, 0.75 per cent higher than base rate. After a few months, it decided to become the first UK bank only to accept deposits via the Internet.

The new account has been very popular. Savers deposited £6.7 billion in the first ten months. Despite this growth, however, Egg is not making a profit, and does not expect to break even, i.e., start making profits, until 2004.

Despite this Egg is seen as a trailblazer for an entire industry and the new business is estimated to be valued at £3.6 billion. Why?

An online bank has much lower costs than a traditional bank. Transactions are done over the Internet, many fewer staff are required, administration is simpler, there is much less paperwork and no need for networks of thousands of branch offices. As a result, savers can get higher rates of interest on their savings, and loans can also be arranged at lower interest rates. Because of its lower cost base Egg can become profitable on a much lower 'margin', that is, the difference between the interest rate paid to savers and the rate charged to borrowers.

STOP PRESS

Prudential's Egg was floated on the London stock exchange in June 2000 at a share price of £1.70, valuing the company at £1.4 billion.

QUESTIONS FOR DISCUSSION

1. What is the essential requirement for people to open an Egg account?
2. What sorts of people are target consumers for an Egg account?
3. With the benefit of hindsight suggest what consumer, economic and technological trends might have helped forecast the successful launch of Prudential's Egg savings account?
4. What effect will the success of Egg have on traditional banks? How might they react?

The truth is stranger than fiction

To a company like Levi's, the jeans manufacturer, defining the market is very important. First, it must map out the existing groups of jeans buyers, for example the group of trend-setting style leaders, groups of conventional jeans wearers who follow fashion but quite a long time after the trend setters, people looking for jeans to wear at work, etc. Then Levi's need to consider how its various brands such as 501s, Twisted jeans, etc. match each of these segments. Levi's must also consider which retail outlets are used by different groups of customers. The final step is to make sure that the right retailers sell the right Levi's products to the right customers. All this involves a lot of detailed market research and careful planning.

Chapter 36 *Market research*

As we saw in the previous chapter, a market research system gathers information on the marketing environment and prepares reports for marketing management to use when making decisions on the development of marketing strategies.

We listed some of the elements of the market environment as follows:

- target consumers
- distribution channels
- suppliers
- competitors
- stakeholders
- society and politics
- the economy
- technology.

In this chapter we will consider how this information is gathered.

Leading thinkers – Philip Kotler

Philip Kotler, in his book *Marketing Essentials* (1984), outlines the market research process as shown in Figure 2.11.

We will deal with collecting, analysing and presenting the information in following chapters. In this chapter we will cover the first two stages of Kotler's definition of the market research process.

Defining the problem and research objectives

The first step in research is often the most important. The marketing manager and market researcher need to discuss and define the problem and consider and agree the objectives of the research project.

The problems facing marketing managers and researchers can be diverse:

- It may be to identify opportunities for new product development.

- Alternatively, it might be to discover why sales of a well-established product are declining.
- It could be to decide on the most appropriate marketing mix for a new product and to forecast the future sales volumes and values.

If we take the example of the Prudential Egg case study from page 160, the **problem** might have been defined as:

'to identify opportunities for Prudential to develop a new savings account product which is capable of winning new customers from the existing banks and building societies'.

The **objectives** might have been:

- To identify who has savings accounts – how many people, their type and important lifestyle characteristics.
- To identify which savings accounts currently exist, which companies provide them, their characteristics and market shares.
- To identify what customers like and dislike about these accounts and why they chose their current account.
- What suggestions do customers have for improvements to savings accounts?
- What are the trends in the numbers of people saving money?
- What political, social, economic and technological trends may lead to changes in the provision of savings accounts in Britain? Are there any overseas banking practices or trends that may have implications for the UK?

Perhaps a market research brief of the type described above might have prompted the Egg success by identifying that savers wanted better interest rates, and quick and convenient transactions; and that companies in the USA were achieving these goals using online banking.

Developing the information sources

The second stage of research involves determining the specific type of information needed and the best way of gathering it.

Figure 2.11 The market research process

Quantitative and qualitative research

Quantitative research gathers measured numerical data, for example '55 per cent of those sampled preferred the blue metallic colour'. Qualitative data gathers opinions, impressions and motivations, for example 'I like the blue metallic finish because it looks classy and upmarket, and will not show the dirt'. Generally, both types of research are important to marketers. Quantitative data enable the market size and characteristics to be determined. Qualitative data give the insights that enable products and services to be developed to match consumer needs and preferences.

Information sources

A significant amount of information is available to a researcher **internally** within the organisation, for example customer records, product sales data and trends. Researchers can gather primary and secondary data from outside the organisation. **Primary research** consists of collecting information specifically for your project. **Secondary research** uses existing information that has been collected for another purpose. Information sources are shown in Figure 2.12.

Internal information

The widespread use of computers means that companies have large amounts of data which are easy to access and free:

- **Sales figures** – the more detailed these are the better. Sales broken down by geographical area and market segment can be particularly useful.
- **Customer records** – companies often collect a lot of information such as age, sex, size, address, purchase history by product, payment records, etc.

- **Sales reports** – staff who have regular contact with customers can provide a useful source of information on competitor activity, product comparisons, customer trends and opinions. Many companies ask sales representatives to write regular reports providing market research data.
- **Trend data** – information which shows how markets' and customers' behaviour are changing, for example 'more female customers' or 'fewer postal and more telephone orders', can be very useful in developing products and services.

Secondary information (desk research)

Secondary data often provide a broader picture of the whole market. Using reports compiled by others can be much cheaper and quicker than collecting the information yourself. A disadvantage, however, is that you may not be sure of the reliability and the information may not be what you might ideally need. Secondary data include the following:

- **Competitor information**. A wide range of competitor information is generally available such as brochures, catalogues, price lists and other marketing information. Financial information for limited companies is available from the Registrar of Companies. Exhibitions are often good opportunities to gather information, gossip, rumours and customer opinions.
- **Government publications**. The government publishes information on a very wide range of topics. The Office for National Statistics (ONS) coordinates the collection and publication of business and population data. Industrial sectors, for example energy and water

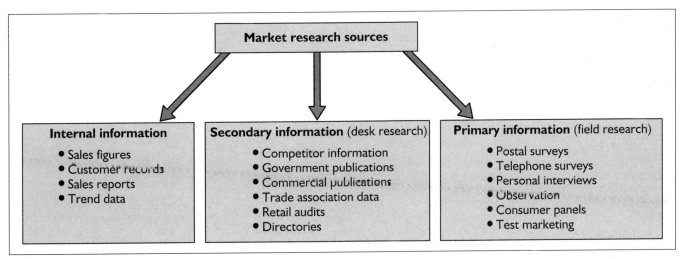

Figure 2.12 Information sources

supply, are classified by Standard Industrial Classification (SIC). Population, household and family expenditure data are collected in national censuses, which take place every ten years. Individual government departments publish a wide variety of other data on, for example:
– education, schools, students, etc.
– health, hospitals, diseases, patients, etc.
– other countries.
The Stationary Office sells copies of these publications.

- **The electoral register**. This details the names and addresses of all those eligible locally to vote in an election.
- **Commercial publications**. Organisations such as Mintel collate and publish reports on different market sectors. Mintel produces a monthly journal containing reports on consumer markets such as alcoholic drinks and toothpaste. These reports are detailed and are up to 20 pages long. Some commercially produced reports can be very expensive. Other organisations such as Dunn & Bradstreet produce reports on individual companies.
- **Trade association data**. Trade associations often publish data and reports specific to their area of interest, for example printing, chemicals, engineering.
- **Retail audits**. The widespread use of EPOS (Electronic Point of Sale) information means that increasingly details of retail sales and trends are available. Best-selling CDs and books lists are good examples. Companies such as A. C. Nielsen collect information on retail sales through supermarkets and large chains and sell these data to manufacturers, which enable them to calculate market share statistics.
- **Directories**. There are numerous directories, usually stocked in libraries, which provide details of companies and product availability. *Kompass* is a buyers' guide that covers the whole of the UK in regions. Other directories relate to specific sectors, for example *The Advertisers Annual* lists all advertising companies.

Primary information (field research)

This is information that does not already exist and needs to be collected by a researcher or a market research agency on the organisation's behalf. One advantage of primary data is that precisely the information that is needed can be collected. Another is that only the organisation commissioning the research has the information – this can give it an advantage over competitors. A disadvantage of primary research is that it can be expensive and very time consuming.

Most primary information is collected either by asking consumers questions or by observing their behaviour. Questionnaires are often used to ask questions (the design of questionnaires is discussed in Chapter 37).

While ideally all consumers would be questioned or observed this is not a practical possibility, so a sample has to be used (see Chapter 38 for information on sampling).

Primary information may be collected in the following ways:

 Postal surveys involve posting a questionnaire to a sample of consumers. This can be done relatively cheaply. However, response rates are often less than 10 per cent and even well-designed questionnaires may be difficult to answer. It is also difficult to get detailed information and opinions.

 **Personal interviews** take place on a one-to-one basis, and enable more complex questions to be asked and explained. This can, however, lead to an element of interviewer bias. Interviews can be time consuming and involve travel. As a result, this is an expensive method of collecting data and the better quality of information can be difficult to justify.

 Telephone surveys are less expensive than personal interviews and are less restricted geographically. They also have the advantage over postal surveys that questions can be explained, but respondents may not be at ease on the telephone for longer than a few minutes.

 **Observation** is a method often used by retailers. Consumers are observed in their stores, to gauge reactions to products and displays. Large numbers of shoppers can be observed at little cost. Observation, however, is limited in that it provides no opportunity to query shoppers' opinions.

 **Consumer panels** involve a group of consumers being consulted over a period of time about a product or products. A typical application might be to review TV programmes. This is a costly method of collecting data but it is effective at building a picture of consumer trends.

Focus groups involve assembling a group of consumers and asking them to discuss in detail their views on a product or service. This is a useful way of developing qualitative opinions on aspects of product design and features.

Field trials are an important part of the development process in which the new product is tested in actual conditions by typical consumers. The objective of field trials is to ensure that performance is as expected and to iron out any potential user problems.

Test marketing takes place after field trials and involves selling the product to a restricted range of customers, generally in a geographic region. This provides an opportunity to test consumer reaction to the 4Ps of Product, Price, Place and Promotion. Results can be used to fine tune the marketing mix and to forecast sales when the product is launched on a wider scale.

Factors influencing market research methods

- **Level of risk**. In some situations the level and potential cost of getting the decision wrong is low and, as a result, there is little justification for time consuming and expensive market research. Trial and error may be a valid alternative.
- **Cost**. Market research can be expensive and so compromises may need to be made in terms of sample size and research method. Research costs need to match not only potential avoidance of risk but also benefits achievable and the available budget.
- **Time**. Some research techniques are quicker than others; agencies can be used to provide additional resources. Markets, however, move increasingly quickly and speed may be needed to gain competitive advantage.
- **Validity, reliability and suitability for purpose**. Given the above restraints, it is important to ensure that the information relates to the problem in hand and that sampling (Chapter 38) and interpretation (Chapter 39) techniques are used to ensure that the information is valid and reliable.

CASE STUDY: HEALTHY ATTITUDE

Reuben Singh, aged 23, is rated as one of Britain's brightest and youngest entrepreneurs. At the age of just 17 he founded his Miss Attitude chain of shops which sell jewellery to teenagers. His business has an estimated value of £45 million (November 1999).

Reuben is currently planning the development of a second major chain, Healthy Attitude, a 24-hour healthy eating fast-food outlet in cities. The first two outlets are due to open before Christmas 1999 and a total of ten sites have been identified. He is confident that he will have a chain of Healthy Attitude stores worth £100 million within five years.

What is the secret of Reuben's success with Miss Attitude and the basis of his confident predictions for Healthy Attitude?

Reuben explains that it all relates to identifying a gap in the market. The Healthy Attitude idea

resulted from months of market research. The gap identified was for the 24-hour availability of healthy and nutritious fast-food in cities. Research identified that while the outlet would appeal to a range of different age groups the restaurants should be staffed by young people and that they should have an emphasis on nutritional education.

QUESTIONS FOR DISCUSSION

1 How might Reuben have set about gathering the information to identify Healthy Attitude's gap in the market?
2 Define the research problem and objectives.
3 To what degree might quantitative and qualitative information be helpful?
4 What information sources might you use and why?

The truth is stranger than fiction

When Renault carried out market research before launching he Renault Twingo, it found out that a large number of people did not like the look of the car. However, it also found that a substantial number of people raved about the car. There were enough enthusiasts to make it worth going ahead with the car – the enthusiasts loved it so much that most were prepared to buy the car. In a similar way, market researchers found that the general public either love or hate the vegetable spread Marmite. Those that like the product are really enthusiastic – leading to the advert 'You either love it or you hate it!'

Chapter 37 Questionnaires

If we recap, by looking back at Kotler's model of the marketing research process (see Figure 2.11 on page 162), we can see that in the previous chapter we have considered the first two stages – defining the problem and research objectives, and developing the information sources. We now move on to the third stage – collecting the information – through the use of questionnaires (this chapter), and sampling techniques (Chapter 38).

Definition, uses and purpose

A **questionnaire** is a list of questions compiled to gather the necessary information required for the project.

Questionnaires are used to prompt questions and record responses. They are commonly used in primary market research and are an essential element of postal or telephone surveys, personal interviews and consumer panels.

A questionnaire is used as a checklist to ensure that all relevant questions are asked. It provides a means of standardising questions so that information gathered by different researchers can be combined and/or compared. A well-designed questionnaire records responses in a manner that is easy to collate and analyse.

Questionnaire design

A good questionnaire starts off by explaining the purpose of the research. This puts the respondent at ease. If only certain classes of respondent, for example home owners, are of interest, then questions designed to eliminate unsuitable respondents should be asked at an early stage to avoid wasted time and effort.

Questions should be sequenced logically, starting with easy-to-answer questions to relax nervous respondents. Difficult, complex or sensitive questions should be left till the end. Do not ask any unnecessary questions. Too many or seemingly irrelevant questions will result in customers failing to respond to postal surveys and cutting short telephone or personal interview surveys.

It is important for questions to be phrased using language appropriate to the target group, and avoiding jargon. Care should be taken to ensure that questions are unambiguous. It is often a good idea to trial a questionnaire with a target group to check that it is easily understood in practice.

Questions need to be posed in such a way as to provide answers that can be collated and interpreted. **Open questions** are ones that encourage the respondent to express opinions and perhaps to talk at length. These are appropriate to obtaining qualitative data from small groups but they are difficult to analyse for larger samples. **Closed questions**, where respondents are asked to choose between options and give specific answers such as yes or no, are generally more appropriate for questionnaires. Care should be taken, however, that questions provide an appropriate range of options and are open enough to avoid bias – that is, that they do not lead respondents to answers that do not accurately reflect their opinions.

Consideration should be given to the collation and analysing of the data gathered on the questionnaire and to how this can be facilitated. Numbering questions and options can often simplify data logging and analysis, particularly if using computers and spreadsheets (see Chapter 39 for analysing results).

Question types
Open questions

These should avoid leading the respondent and bias. For example:

> **How quick and easy was the exercise machine to assemble?** ....

might at first seem a reasonable open question. However, if we look at it more closely:

- it might lead the respondent to comment on the speed and simplicity of the assembly process and this could bias the results, by assuming that speed and simplicity are the prime requirements, which might not necessarily be the case
- the layout of the question does not give the respondent enough space to express an opinion.

The following might be a better approach:

> **Please comment on your experience of assembling the exercise machine.**
>
>
> **If you require more space for comment please continue overleaf.**

Closed questions

These give specific answers such as:

- yes/no
- 17 [age]
- 1.8 metres [height]

Again, at first sight the question

> Was the exercise machine quick and easy to assemble? Yes ☐ No ☐ *Tick appropriate box*

might seem appropriate. This question asks for comment on two aspects of assembly speed and ease, both of which are subjective. One person's expectations of speed and ease will differ from another's. A better approach might be:

> How long did the exercise machine take to assemble? .... minutes

> Did you find the instructions easy to follow? Yes ☐ No ☐ *Tick appropriate box*

Scaled questions

These provide more information and enable a better insight to be gained to respondents' opinions but retain the benefits of ease of analysis afforded by closed questions. They can also be easier to complete. This can be illustrated taking the questions above:

> How long did the exercise machine take to assemble? *Tick appropriate box below.*
> 1 Less than 5 minutes ☐
> 2 5–10 minutes ☐
> 3 10–15 minutes ☐
> 4 Longer than 15 minutes ☐

> How easy did you find the instructions to follow? *Tick appropriate box below.*
> 1 Very easy ☐
> 2 Quite easy ☐
> 3 OK ☐
> 4 Quite difficult ☐
> 5 Very difficult ☐

Prioritising questions

These enable the respondent to state relative importance or preferences. For example:

> When assembling exercise equipment, what matters most to you? *Place the following factors in order of importance by putting a number in each box, where 1 is the most important and 4 the least.*
> Clear written instructions ☐
> Assembly diagrams ☐
> All materials and necessary tools provided ☐
> Speed of assembly ☐

QUESTIONNAIRE

FOOD SURVEY

1 Which of the following is your favourite chocolate bar?

Mars	☐	Toblerone	☐
Bounty	☐	Aero	☐
Galaxy	☐	Other	☐

Please specify: ....

CASE STUDY: DESIGNING A QUESTIONNAIRE

We have learned in this chapter that a questionnaire is a list of questions compiled to gather the necessary information required for a project. We have also learned that questionnaire design and choice of questions are important in terms of getting the right information and being able to analyse it.

Use what you have learned to design a questionnaire to conduct a survey of your fellow students to find out what chocolate bar they prefer and why.

The truth is stranger than fiction

In delivering a questionnaire you can never be absolutely certain whether the respondent is answering the questions seriously. Sometimes therefore constructors of questionnaires put in one or two additional questions which check this. If the respondent answers these questions in a specific way, his or her questionnaire will be eliminated from the survey sample.

Chapter 38 *Sampling*

Having defined our market and objectives, selected our information sources, formulated our questions and compiled our questionnaire, we now turn our attention to deciding whom we will ask. In the ideal world we would ask all of our potential customers. In reality, this would be very time consuming and expensive and we therefore need to select a **sample** to question. The skill of sampling is to select a sample who provide answers which are typical of the whole population.

In selecting a sample two factors need to be decided:

- sampling method (how to choose the right people)
- sample size (how many people).

Sampling methods can be as straightforward as:

- **convenience sampling** – gathering information from the most convenient source irrespective of background
- **judgement sampling** – selecting respondents who, in the judgement of the interviewer, are representative of the population as a whole.

There are advantages to both these methods. However, they are generally outweighed by the disadvantage that interviewer bias is likely to be reflected in the results. The convenience of interviewing passers-by on a street corner, for example, will be offset by the inevitable bias resulting from such a restricted geographic location and time of day.

There are three main 'scientific' sampling methods:

- **Random sampling** – selecting a sample to ensure that every member of the population has an equal chance of inclusion.
- **Quota sampling** – selecting interviewees in proportion to the consumer profile in the market.
- **Stratified sampling** – only interviewing people with the key characteristics required for the sample.

Random sampling

This is not as simple as it sounds. Generally, the starting point is a comprehensive list of the whole population. Where we are dealing with the adult population at large, this is the electoral register. For telephone surveys, then phone books are more useful. Their use can, however, introduce an element of bias, as consumers without telephones and those who are ex-directory are excluded. Other lists might be all car or perhaps dog owners, but lists of these may be more difficult to obtain. Alternatively,

researchers may be interested in the views of businesses, for example newsagents, and these may take some time to collate.

Once you have compiled your population list, then you are faced with the problem of selecting a random sample selection. For this you could use a pin and a blindfold! Alternatively, a computer can be used or a systematic method. A typical system for a sample of 100 from a population of 1,000,000 would be to select every thousandth name (1,000,000 divided by 100 = 1000), having first randomly selected a starting point, for example 396 between 1 and 1000. Sample names would then be number 396, 1,396, 2,396, etc.

Quota sampling

This is generally used when interviewing smaller samples to ensure that a good cross-section of the population is selected. At the simplest level this could involve ensuring that 50 per cent each of men and women are selected. Generally, a wider range of factors is specified and researchers may be given a 'sampling grid' specifying a sample comprising quotas in each category, as shown in Table 2.2.

Table 2.2 Quota sample grid for adult lager beer drinkers

	%	Quota
Men	75	300
Women	25	100
Ages		
18–24	38	152
25–34	21	84
35–44	16	64
45+	25	100

Stratified sampling

This involves selecting a sample of only those with the key characteristics of those relevant to the study. For example, if developing a new lager beer for young men, then the sample would be restricted to the sample stratum of men between ages 18–24. Within this stratum, a sample could be interviewed on a completely random basis or on a quota sample grid, related to weekly earnings for example.

Another basis of stratified sampling involves taking into account that some customers are more important than others. Consider, for example, a greengrocer with 500 regular customers, 50 of whom are restaurants who buy in bulk and account for 30 per cent of sales. A 10 per cent random sample of 50 customers including five restaurants would not take into account the relative importance of the restaurant customers. A stratified sample of 50 customers would take this into account by **weighting** the sample to include 30 per cent of restaurants:

$$50 \times 30\% = 15 \text{ restaurants}$$

This would reflect their importance relative to the value of their purchases.

Sample size

The larger the sample, the more likely it is that it will be typical of the whole population. Questioning your sample, whether by post (the cheapest), by phone or personally (the most expensive) costs money. How should a marketing manager decide on the right sample size?

The first consideration should be: how **valuable** is the information? The information gathered will be used in decision making. What are the benefits (costs) of getting the right information? What are the risks (costs) of getting the wrong information? The second consideration is: how **accurate** does the information need to be? A smaller sample will be less accurate, but if this level of accuracy is acceptable, then costs can be reduced.

When consumers show a clear preference for one option, for example the red packaging (65 per cent) over the blue packaging (35 per cent), then a small sample will be sufficient to be sure the results are **representative**. When responses are more finely balanced, for example 52 per cent versus 48 per cent, then a larger sample will be needed to provide a high level of confidence in the accuracy of the results.

So what size of samples are used in practice? Perhaps the best-known surveys are political opinion polls, which are used to predict the voting intentions of Britain's 44 million voters. These use quota samples of between 1,000 and 1,500 respondents and generally are good predictors of election results. Smaller samples may be used for smaller populations and where the results are less finely balanced. Frequently, samples of 100 respondents will be used to determine the opinions of retail consumers.

CASE STUDY: RESEARCHING THE MARKET

Imagine you are the marketing manger of a soft drinks company and want to research the market for a new 'healthy' and 'environmentally friendly' soft drink.

Define your market (Chapter 35) and decide on some objectives for your research (Chapter 36). List these according to whether you feel qualitative or quantitative information is required.

For each objective note a suitable market research source and suggest a research method and sample size for those objectives for which you decide require primary research. Briefly explain the basis on which you selected the research source, method and sample size.

The truth is stranger than fiction

Checking on international swimmers' and athletes' use of controlled substances involves international testers using random, quota, and stratified sampling techniques to try to cut out substance abuse. During the late 1990s one Irish swimmer, who was surprised to be asked to give a sample, added whisky to her urine sample. She was banned from the sport – for doctoring the sample.

Chapter 39 *Interpreting results*

Having gathered a mass of market research information, it can be a daunting task to make sense of it. Information will need to be summarised, classified and presented in a format that aids understanding, interpretation and presentation of results.

Data logging sheets

A **data logging sheet** is a useful way of summarising primary research results. It generally takes the form of a spreadsheet or grid matrix (table), which can be generated either manually or more quickly by a computer using spreadsheet software.

Responses to questions are 'tallied' in each category, totals counted and percentages calculated.

This can be illustrated using the example of the exercise machine assembly questions from Chapter 37 (see Figure 2.13).

Data logging sheet: exercise machine assembly questionnaire

Question

Response	Tally of responses e.g. ＨＨＨ ＨＨＨ ＩＩ = 12	No. of responses	% of total respondents
How long did the exercise machine take to assemble?			
Less than 5 minutes		15	15
5–10 minutes		36	36
10–15 minutes		40	40
Longer than 15 minutes		9	9
Total respondents		100	100
How easy did you find the instructions to follow?			
Very easy		5	5
Quite easy		27	27
OK		32	32
Quite difficult		34	34
Very difficult		2	2
Total respondents		100	100
When assembling exercise equipment, what matters most to you?			
Clear written instructions		9	9
Assembly diagrams		47	47
All materials and necessary tools provided		29	29
Speed of assembly		15	15
Total respondents		100	100

Figure 2.13

Presenting results

Many people find statistics difficult to understand and interpret. It is often helpful to present results in a summarised format, in tables or graphically. As with data logging sheets, these techniques can be applied manually. Computers and spreadsheet software, however, such as Microsoft Excel, can save a lot of time and effort.

Averages

One way of summarising information is to calculate the **average**. An average is a measure of central tendency. It is used to find the number which is representative of a group of numbers, that is, the middle value.

The arithmetic mean is the most frequently used measure and is commonly referred to as the average. Other measures are the median and the mode.

We will use the following example to illustrate how the different types of averages are calculated:

> 15 people were timed assembling an exercise machine and they took 7, 8, 9, 9, 10, 10, 11, 11, 11, 12, 13, 13, 14, 15 and 16 minutes.

The **arithmetic mean** is calculated by totalling the sum of all the numbers in the group and dividing them by the number in the group:

$$\text{Arithmetic mean} = \frac{\text{Sum of all the values}}{\text{Total number of values}}$$

$$= \frac{7 + 8 + 9 + 9 + 10 + 10 + 11 + 11 + 11 + 12 + 13 + 13 + 14 + 15 + 16}{15}$$

$$= \frac{169}{15}$$

$$= 11.3$$

The **median** is the value of the middle number and is found by arranging the numbers in order and selecting the middle number in the list. It is particularly useful when there are extreme values in a series of numbers that would otherwise distort the arithmetic mean:

$$\text{The position of the median} = \frac{n + 1}{2}$$

where *n* is the number of values.

In our example:

$$\text{Median} = \frac{15 + 1}{2} = 8 \quad \text{(that is, the eighth number in the list, which is 11).}$$

The **mode** is the most frequently occurring item in a list of numbers. In our example 11 occurs three times and is the mode.

Tables

Tables are often referred to as spreadsheets, especially when produced on a computer. A table is a matrix structure where data are placed in titled rows and columns.

Tables are particularly useful for presenting detailed and specific data where there are two variables. For example:

Consumer product preferences by age range

Consumer age ranges	Product			
	a	**b**	**c**	**d**
0–19	13	15	8	12
20–29	16	19	12	15
30–39	33	41	27	21
40+	12	14	19	9
Total	74	84	66	57

Graphical presentations

Pie charts

Pie charts are used to show how proportions of the whole sample have responded. Figure 2.14 shows a pie chart which has been constructed using the data from the logging sheet (Figure 2.13) relating to the time taken to assemble an exercise machine. For many people a pie chart is much easier to interpret than a series of figures or a table.

Bar charts

Similarly, **bar charts** can be effective in comparing results or responses. Figure 2.15 shows a bar chart that has been constructed using the data from the logging sheet example relating to the easiness or otherwise of the assembly instructions. A bar chart can provide an instant picture of results which is much quicker to interpret than a series of figures or a table.

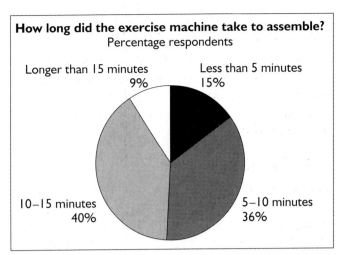

Figure 2.14 A pie chart

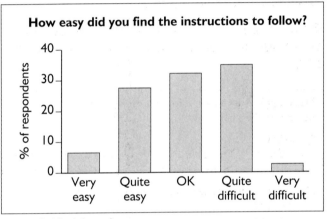

Figure 2.15 A bar chart

Graphs

Graphs are another way of displaying data. They show the relationship between two variables in either the form of a straight line or a curve, for example, advertising expenditure and the sales of cans of cola (see the following table and Figure 2.16).

Sales of 'Fizzy' cola versus advertising expenditure

Month	Sales value (£000s)	Advertising expenditure (£000s)
April	160	15
May	260	20
June	350	25
July	490	28
August	570	29

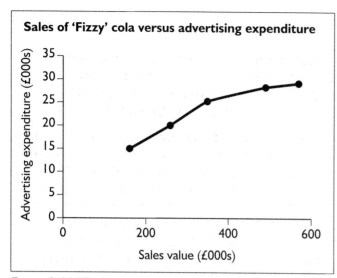

Figure 2.16 *The relationship between two variables presented as a graph*

Graphs are also useful for displaying trends such as monthly sales (see Figure 2.17).

Charts and graphs such as those shown in Figures 2.16 and 2.17 can be generated quickly and easily on computers using standard spreadsheet software.

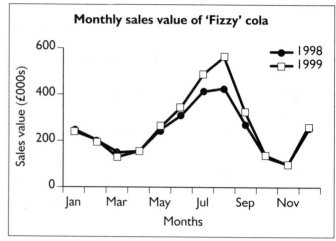

Figure 2.17 *Using a graph to display trends*

Monthly sales of 'Fizzy' cola (£000s)

Year	Jan	Feb	Mar	Apr	May	Jun	Jul	Aug	Sep	Oct	Nov	Dec
1998	250	200	160	150	240	310	420	430	280	130	100	260
1999	240	210	140	160	260	350	490	570	320	140	100	270

The truth is stranger than fiction

A survey carried out by the publishers EMAP in the late 1990s revealed a new group of consumers whom they labelled 'Tweenies'. Tweenies are 10-to-12-year-olds. The research showed that for this group wearing the right sports brands such as Adidas and Nike is a must. This group is not interested in their elder siblings' aspirations but is determined to create its own group identity. As Tweenies grow older they develop individual tastes, but at this age being part of a group is most important.

Chapter 40 *Probability*

If we remind ourselves of the purpose of market research, to collect information that enables us to identify and anticipate customer requirements, we are able to see that the outcome of market research is a prediction of consumer behaviour. Often, significant expenditure is risked on the basis of these predictions. It is reported, for example, that the confectionery manufacturer Cadbury's invested £14 million on the launch of its new Fuse chocolate bar in 1996. If market research had been wrong and the product had flopped, then Cadbury's would have wasted £14 million. Other projects, such as the Channel Tunnel, involve investments of hundreds and even thousands of millions of pounds.

When risks of this size are involved managers are obviously interested in the degree of accuracy of predictions of customer behaviour. The likelihood that predictions will be accurate is termed **probability**. Complex statistical techniques can be applied to calculating probabilities. In this chapter, however, we will limit ourselves to a few basic considerations.

Sampling and **bias** are important influences on the accuracy of predictions. As we discussed in Chapter 38, larger samples increase the probability that the sample will be representative of consumers. This needs to be offset against higher costs. It is also important to select a sample that has been chosen carefully to reflect the target consumer, otherwise the results may be affected by bias. Another potential source of bias is the questions asked and the way in which they are asked (see Chapters 36 and 37).

When looking at statistical data it is important to look behind the raw numbers. **Averages** can be misleading. Making predictions based on the arithmetic mean of a very close range of values is likely to have a high probability of being accurate. A prediction on an average based on a very wide range of values has a much higher probability of being misleading. The use of other measures – the median and the mode – can give a better insight in these cases. An advanced statistical technique called **standard deviation** can be used to give a better insight into predictive probability of averages.

Correlation, that is, whether one factor causes another, can be another important consideration. For example, if sales increase at a time of increasing advertising expenditure this could be seen as being the result of the advertising. Before deciding to maintain or increase advertising expenditure, however, it is important to look behind this first assumption to check that the sales increases have not been caused by some other factor.

In the example of 'Fizzy' cola sales on page 174, looking at Figure 2.16 you could assume the sales are increasing as a result of advertising. If you look at Figure 2.17, however, you should spot that sales increase during the period April to August each year. This is described as a seasonal factor – hot weather increases the demand for soft drinks. This seasonal effect it appears is having more impact on sales than advertising. In this example, as in real life, looking at other potential causes for the effect (sales increase) could save thousands of pounds in wasted advertising.

There are various advanced statistical techniques, **regression** for example, that can be used to give a better insight into the correlation between one factor and another.

Sales forecasting

Sales forecasts are usually based on previous sales results. As mentioned above, however, these can only provide a guide. Many factors can affect sales, for example competition and consumer trends, and these and their likely effects need to be identified and taken into account in our forecasts.

Graphs, as we have seen in Chapter 39, can be useful in interpreting results. They enable seasonal trends to be spotted as in the 'Fizzy' cola example. Sometimes, however, seasonal variations can hide the underlying trend. One technique that can be used to smooth out peaks and troughs and see the longer-term trends more clearly is the use of **moving annual totals** (**MATs**).

This technique involves adding up the sales for the previous twelve months each month and plotting the result (see Figure 2.18).

From the graph in Figure 2.18 it can be seen clearly that sales grew during July, August, September and October, but levelled off towards the end of the year reverting to the static sales pattern at the beginning of the year. On this basis, all things being equal, a marketing manager might conclude that the increased advertising during June to August resulted in increased sales growth during the

Monthly sales of 'Fizzy' cola (£000s)

Year	Jan	Feb	Mar	Apr	May	Jun	Jul	Aug	Sep	Oct	Nov	Dec
1998	250	200	160	150	240	310	420	430	280	130	100	260
MAT*												2930
1999	240	210	140	160	260	350	490	570	320	140	100	270
MAT*	2920	2930	2910	2920	2940	2980	3050	3190	3230	3240	3240	3250

* MAT = moving annual total

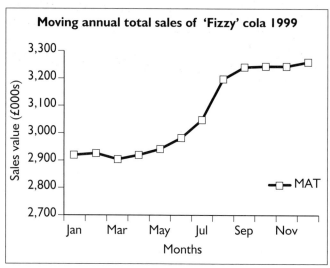

Figure 2.18 Moving annual totals

following months which fell back when advertising was reduced to previous levels.

Based on the above, the marketing manager might forecast that in 2000 sales will show little growth and will follow the seasonal pattern of 1999 unless further advertising expenditure is used to stimulate sales growth.

In summary

Understanding the needs of customers and anticipating their future needs is vital to success in today's dynamic markets. Increasingly, sophisticated market research systems provide more and more detailed consumer information on which to base forecasts. When assessing that information and making decisions to use expensive resources, marketing managers need to question the validity of the data presented. How reliable are the data? Are they based on a representative sample size? Is there an element of bias in the results? How strong are the correlations between factors? All these play a part in gauging the probability, the likely accuracy, of forecasts, which can make or lose companies millions of pounds and must be taken into account as part of the decision making process.

The truth is stranger than fiction

Marketers need to be able to quantify wherever possible the impact of marketing activities. For example, a marketing plan should show estimates of the likely impact of marketing activities based on probabilities. Marketers will then track the impact of their marketing activity, comparing projected results with actual results.

Of course, it is often difficult to make accurate estimates of the likely success of new products. For example, in 1998 Internet shoppers spent an estimated £406 million. It was then estimated that this figure would rise to £1 billion in 1999. The reality was that Internet sales were double this figure!

Chapter 41 *Market segmentation*

As a marketing-orientated organisation gathers more information and begins to understand its customers better it recognises that their needs vary and different types of customer have different opinions, preferences, tastes and purchasing characteristics. Customer types with similar purchasing characteristics are called **market segments**. Marketing managers may choose to:

- market one product to all market segments, for example Heinz baked beans (see Figure 2.19)
- market different products to different market sectors, for example Cadbury's chocolate – Dairy Milk, Bourneville, Wispa, Fuse, Milk Tray, etc. (see Figure 2.20)
- market one product to one segment, for example a Rolls Royce motor car (see Figure 2.21).

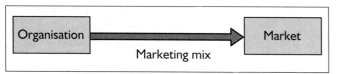

Figure 2.19 Mass marketing

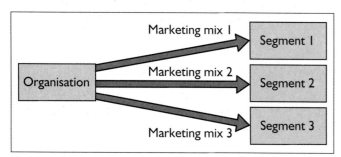

Figure 2.20 Differentiated marketing

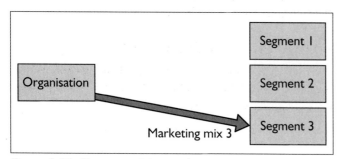

Figure 2.21 Target or niche marketing

Current trends – micro marketing

Recent advances in information and communications technology have resulted in much better customer data and the ability to define market segments more accurately. An example is the case of Experian, one of the world's biggest direct marketing service companies, which was described on page 157.

Customer services and delivery systems have also improved and this has led to more direct-to-the-consumer sales (see 'The right place', Chapter 34, page 153).

The development of e-commence making use of the Internet for targeting, promotion and order processing will add further impetus to precisely targeted direct-to-the-customer marketing.

The marketing evolution is set to continue:

Mass marketing

↓

Differentiated marketing

↓

Target marketing

↓

Micro marketing.

Leading thinkers – Michael Porter

Michael Porter in his book *Competitive Strategy* (1980) considered alternative strategies for companies to achieve the objective of growth by market penetration.

He suggested that companies needed to develop a competitive advantage by adopting one of three competitive strategies:

- **cost leadership**, where the company becomes the lowest cost producer and is able to sell at a lower price than its competitors and still make a profit
- **differentiation**, where a company makes its products distinctly different from those of its competitors and can charge a premium price

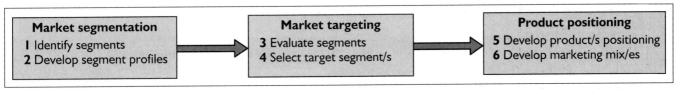

Figure 2.22 *The market segmentation process*

• **focus**, where a company targets only one segment or part of the market and decides to pursue either a cost leadership or differentiation strategy as appropriate – for example Gucci, the designer fashion accessories company, supplies highly differentiated products to an exclusive target market.

The market segmentation process

Philip Kotler in his book *Marketing Management: Analysis Planning and Control* (1984) depicts this as a three-stage process (see Figure 2.22):

1 market segmentation
2 market targeting
3 product positioning.

As shown in Figure 2.22, the process may be broken down into six steps.

1 Identify segments

Review the market and identify clusters of consumers – segments – with similar purchasing characteristics.

2 Develop segment profiles

Study the segment clusters and identify common characteristics that can be used to profile the segment.

These characteristics may be based on the following:

• **Age**. For example, elderly people are increasingly seen as an important affluent market segment.
• **Sex**. For example, adverts for a number of small hatchback cars are targeted at women drivers.
• **Social class**, which may be further categorised into six socio-economic classes:
  A – higher managerial, administrative or professional
  B – middle managerial, administrative or professional
  C1 – supervisory or clerical or junior management
  C2 – skilled manual workers

D – semi- and unskilled manual workers.
E – casual or lowest paid workers and the unemployed.
Expensive luxury goods are generally targeted at socio-economic classes A and B.

• **Religion**. For example, an Internet website, Jewishnet.co.uk, the equivalent of the *Yellow Pages* for the Jewish market segment, was set up in 1999 by a 17-year-old schoolboy and has been so successful that it has been valued at £5 million.
• **Geographical**. For example, outdoor/country clothes targeted at consumers in rural areas; home security products targeted at consumers in inner-city areas.
• **Lifestyles**. For example, young affluent professionals are targets for Next's ranges of clothing.
• **Ethnic groups**. For example, make-up for different skin colours.

3 Evaluate segments

Having profiled the segments, the next stage is to determine their size and purchasing power. The level of interest in a product is another key consideration in evaluating its potential.

4 Select target segment/s

Matching objectives and capabilities against the evaluation in 3 enables the segments with the best potential for profit to be selected.

5 Develop product/s positioning

This involves evaluating the product/s against competing products and presenting them advantageously in the eyes of the consumers in the market segment/s.

6 Develop marketing mix/es

The final stage involves developing a mix of product, price, place and promotion suited to the market segment and the positioning you want to achieve within it.

VW, the German multinational car maker, acquired Rolls Royce Motors in 1998. This followed the acquisition of Skoda in 1991. With its long-standing Audi and Seat brands, VW has a wide range of car models, which it markets globally. This is an excellent example of differentiated products developed for different market segments.

QUESTIONS FOR DISCUSSION

1 Carry out your own market research with the object of gathering information on the range of models available under these four brands.
2 Use your market research findings to describe the various brands and models and the market segments at which they are targeted.
3 Describe for each model how the marketing mix has been developed to match its market segment.

The truth is stranger than fiction

VW has evolved from the original Volkswagen car, which was developed over 60 years ago when Hitler was the German Chancellor. The name 'Volkswagen', literally translated from German as 'people's wagon', described the car which was designed as a utilitarian, low-cost car for the mass market. The car's rugged reliability and unique shape earned it the 'Beetle' nickname and a cult following among the young. Old Beetles are collectors' items and can be sold for more than their original new cost. Around the country, most cities and many towns have Vee Dub Clubs of enthusiastic owners.

The original car is no longer made in Germany; some are still made in Brazil and are exported to Europe. Meanwhile, VW has developed a replacement for the Beetle. It has a body style reminiscent of the old Beetle but its target market segment is very different from the original people's car for working-class families. The new Beetle is sporty and stylish and has a premium price to match. Its target market segment is the young, image conscious and affluent (see Figure 2.23).

Figure 2.23 The recently discontinued VW Beetle and the new-style upmarket Beetle

SECTION C *Product*

<u>INTRODUCTION</u> A **product** is something that is offered to the market which can be:

- a good such as a computer or a bread roll
- a service such as insurance or a personal manicure
- a place such as a holiday resort
- a person such as a film or pop star (see Figure 2.24).

The marketing strategy that is designed for an organisation will depend on the type of product on offer. For example, you would use a different marketing mix to promote a can of beans than you would to promote a chart-topping band!

A product offers the purchaser a range of **benefits**. It will be composed of several elements. On the surface, there are often clear tangible benefits – things you can touch and see. Tangible features of a product include:

Figure 2.24 Today, 'stars' like Robbie Williams are one of the most sought-after products

- shape
- design
- colour
- size
- packaging.

The intangible features are not so obvious. These include the **reputation** of a firm ('You can be sure of Shell') or the corporate **brand image** (like the Shell logo).

There are extra features to be considered such as:

- after-sales service
- availability of spare parts
- guarantees
- customer-care policy, etc.

A product is made up of a range of features which serve to meet customer requirements. A customer buying a new car may not simply want a family saloon. Additional requirements may be things like:

- a blue car
- four doors
- low petrol consumption
- a well-known name
- a long guarantee
- credit facilities
- after-sales servicing
- a proven safety record.

The more benefits a company can provide for customers, the more likely it is to be able to sell its product and get a 'good price' for it. Competition is all about creating more benefits than the rival product.

Most organisations produce more than one product. The **product mix** is the complete range of items made by the organisation.

Critical thinking: KitKat

No matter how effective the promotion and packaging, a firm will find it very difficult to market a product which fails to satisfy a consumer need. KitKat owes much of its success to a unique dual appeal – as a four-finger chocolate bar (known in the confectionery trade as a countline), sold at corner shops and newsagents, but also as a two-finger biscuit sold in supermarkets. It is a product that has endured because of its wide appeal across the age ranges and to both sexes.

Altering the actual product is potentially a very hazardous act for an established brand name as it risks altering the consumer perceptions of quality built up over decades. Tampering with the recognised core qualities could well damage the integrity of the brand. For KitKat, these intrinsic elements of the brand, or unique selling points, include the:

- chocolate fingers
- foil and band wrapping – unique in the countlines market and seen as an important feature which encourages involvement and sharing by consumers
- well known strapline – 'Have a Break, Have a KitKat'.

In spite of the risks of altering the product, the two-finger bar and multipacks were introduced in the 1960s to meet the increased needs of supermarket shopping and, more recently, Orange, Mint and Dark Chocolate KitKats have been available for limited periods. In the third week that KitKat Mint was available, it more than doubled total KitKat sales.

WHAT DO YOU THINK?

1 How do you think a particular brand like KitKat is able to capture the public imagination over a long period of time?
2 Is a KitKat just a chocolate biscuit/bar, or is there something more to justify its lasting appeal?
3 Why is packaging important to a successful product?
4 Why might it be a mistake to tamper with an existing established brand?
5 Can you think of examples where existing brands have been altered successfully?

Chapter 42 *Branding and packaging*

Each product requires a different, appropriate and cost-effective combination of branding and packaging.

Branding

A **brand** consists of a range of features which help to identify the products of a particular organisation. These may include its name, a symbol, term or other creative element. For example, consider the Coca-Cola brand. It consists of a number of distinctive features (see Figure 2.25).

It is not surprising that Coca-Cola is the best-known brand name in the world. It was The Coca-Cola Company that created the distinctive red and white robes of Santa Claus as part of a Christmas advertising campaign.

A product like Coca-Cola has a distinct advantage over rivals in that its brand name has come to be associated with the product. Other examples of this are:

- Hoover for vacuum cleaner
- Sellotape for sticky tape
- Pritt Stick for paper glue
- Durex for contraceptive sheaths.

What has happened is that in the course of time marketing of these products has been so successful that the public has come to associate the brand with the product. Of course, it helps to be the first in the market, for example the Sony Walkman or the Dyson Cyclone, but having established a new product it is essential to secure its presence by ongoing advertising and promotion.

Branding is important for consumers because it is a form of product differentiation which communicates quickly and effectively a lot of information about a product range – it helps consumers to make key decisions in the market place.

The uniqueness of a brand comes from its physical characteristics (for example the taste and unique ingredients of Coca-Cola) plus its image (that is, its logo, advertising, etc.) which are usually created by the manufacturer through advertising and packaging.

When we talk of a product's **consistency**, we mean not only the consistency of its quality and performance, but also of its design, advertising and packaging.

Image is also important. Our image is the way that others see us. Whether we like it or not, it is our public face. People quickly form opinions about us from the way we dress, walk and talk, from where we live and work, and our interests.

In the same way, every product conveys an image to the consumer. This can be a positive or a negative image, depending largely on how the product is designed and presented.

Packaging

Packaging is the way that goods and services are presented to the customer. It can give added benefits to a product, such as an attractive design, protection during transport, ease of access and so on.

However, packaging can also add considerably to the cost of production. The heavier and bulkier the packaging, the higher the cost of moving the goods around. The more packaging used, the more material that needs to go into the packets, etc., and, of course, the more packaging created, the greater the environmental cost of disposing of it. Firms therefore need to think very carefully about the advantages and disadvantages of packaging.

The following checklist would help a company to evaluate the effectiveness of its packaging:

- **Weight of packaging**. To what extent does the weight of the packaging add to the costs?
- **Shape of packaging**. To what extent does the shape of the packaging add to costs, and potential damage to the product?
- **Protection**. Does the packaging protect the product in the desired way?

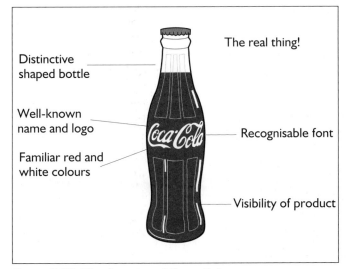

Distinctive shaped bottle

The real thing!

Well-known name and logo

Recognisable font

Familiar red and white colours

Visibility of product

Figure 2.25 The features of Coca-Cola

By the late 1990s the Boots 17 cosmetic range was a mature brand which had been around for 30 years. Its target market was 15- to 19-year-olds. Boots decided that it was time to change the image of the brand from a relatively low-cost one to one which is 'with it' and for 'girls with attitude'.

In order to get the new brand message across a number of objectives were established:

- To develop 17 as the teenage make-up brand.
- To evaluate its logo styles and packaging features to ensure an appropriate fit with the 17 personality portrayed through the advertising.
- To match the consumer understanding of 17 with its new brand personality.
- To deliver the positioning in-store with new merchandising units.

The message to be delivered in advertising was that the 17 range would make girls feel great and in control (see Figure 2.26).

Research indicated that 17 had a strong appeal to its target market. The street-cred of 17 was good and there was a good fit with the perception of 17 with a fun, confident and daring lifestyle. The advertising strapline 'It's not make-up, it's ammunition' was the major contributor to the brand's image.

The packaging, however, was not well received and was not recognised as delivering the promise of the advertising campaign. The old packaging was felt to:

- undervalue the brand
- cheapen the range of products
- suggest a basic product portfolio
- lack desirability.

It was important to raise the status of the brand so that it would reflect the personality and lifestyle of its users – becoming a brand in its own right.

In 1998 therefore a new range of packaging was designed for 17, based on extensive market research carried out with the target audience. The research showed that the favourite packaging for 15- to 19-year-olds had:

Figure 2.26 The Boots 17 range is targeted at 15- to 19-year-olds

- unusual materials (such as matt finish)
- dark colours (which were not plastic-looking)
- recognisable markings (such as logos and designs)
- chunky, rounded shapes
- consistency across a range of products
- a touch of silver or gold
- practicality (pocketable, easy to use, with mirrors or applicators)
- conformist shapes.

QUESTIONS FOR DISCUSSION

1 Why is brand image so important in marketing?
2 How did Boots manage to revive its brand image for 17 after 30 years?
3 Why is packaging such an important part of the product? Use the 17 case study to explain why.

- **Convenience**. Is the packaging easy to handle by the consumer and distributors?
- **Design**. Is the packaging eye-catching? Does it help the consumer easily to distinguish the product from rivals? Does the packaging match the overall emphasis of the firm's marketing? For example, if the organisation claims to be environmentally friendly, does the packaging support this?
- **Information**. Does the packaging display the required information about the product in an appropriate way? For example, are the cooking instructions on ready-prepared meals easy to find and large enough to read?
- **Environmental considerations**. To what extent is the packaging wasteful of materials? How easy is it to recycle the packaging?

The truth is stranger than fiction

In 1999 Heinz spent £32 million on relaunching its Heinz Tomato Ketchup. This involved creating a standardised bottle around the globe which would have:

- a new '57 varieties' label on the neck
- the same distinctive shape bottle and label everywhere
- 'established 1869' on every bottle.

Chapter 43 *Product analysis techniques*

There are a number of marketing tools related to the product and product development including the product life cycle, product portfolio analysis and the Boston Matrix.

The product life cycle

Markets are in a constant state of change. Over a period of time tastes and fashions alter and the technology used to produce goods and services will move on. As a result, there will always be demand for new products and old products will become redundant.

Which of the following (if any) have you seen recently:

- a black and white television
- an instamatic camera
- a Ford Anglia motor car
- a radiogram
- a reel-to-reel tape-recorder
- a vinyl record?

The **product life cycle** is a useful mechanism for planning changes in marketing activities. It recognises that products have a finite market life and charts this through various phases. The sales performance of any product introduced to a market will rise from nothing, reach a peak and then, at some stage, start to decline. The life cycle can be further broken down into distinct phases:

- **The introductory phase**. During this period it is necessary to create demand. Growth is slow and volume is low because of limited awareness of the product's existence.

- **The growth phase**. Sales then rise more quickly. It is during this phase that the profit per unit sold usually reaches a maximum. Towards the end of this phase, competitors enter the market which reduces the rate of growth.
- **Maturity**. In this period most of the potential customers have been reached. However, there will still be plenty of scope for repeat purchases. Competition from sellers in the market becomes stronger and new firms enter the market.
- **Decline**. The product becomes 'old' and sales start to fall. Perhaps a new or improved product will have entered the market (see Figure 2.27).

Injecting life into the product life cycle

In the previous chapter we saw how Boots injected new life into its 17 range of cosmetics. The life cycle of a product may last for a few months or for hundreds of years. To prolong the life cycle of a brand or a product, an organisation may inject new life into the growth period by readjusting the ingredients of its marketing mix (see Figure 2.28).

The readjustment of the marketing mix might involve one or several of the following activities:

- **Change or modify the product** – to keep up with or ahead of the competition. For example, in 1990 Nestlé introduced the blue Smartie to improve its competitiveness against M&M's. Since then, the company has introduced a range of novelty Smarties including the Cola Smartie in 2000.

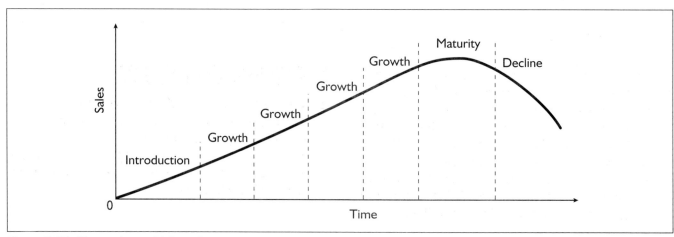

Figure 2.27 The traditional life cycle

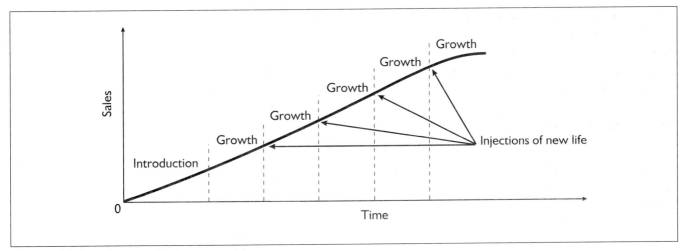

Figure 2.28 *Injecting new life into a product*

CASE STUDY: PRODUCT LIFE CYCLES

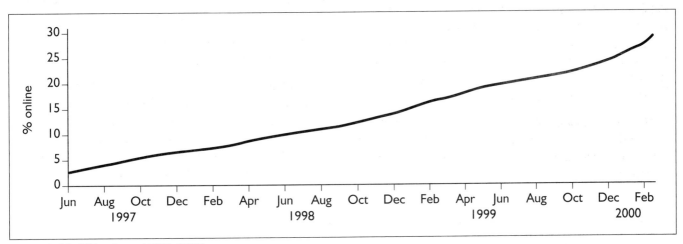

Figure 2.29 *UK online, 1997–2000*

The concept of the product life cycle is perhaps best understood when related to real products and current developments. For example, it is possible to argue that while the Mars bar is still in a state of maturity, other products are in decline. In 1999 Heinz nearly withdrew its Salad Cream from production because the market was disappearing. In contrast, Internet use in the UK is in a period of strong growth as illustrated by Figure 2.29.

QUESTIONS FOR DISCUSSION

1 Identify products which are currently (a) in decline, (b) at the maturity stage, and (c) experiencing rapid growth.
2 What strategies have the companies responsible for these products adopted in order to respond to the life cycle stage?

- **Alter distribution patterns** – to provide a more suitable place for consumers to make a purchase. This is very common today with many firms changing their distribution patterns to sell through the Internet. For example, the frozen food retailer Iceland has changed its name to Iceland.com to emphasise its new pattern of distribution using the Internet.
- **Change prices** – to reflect competitive activities. For example, in 2000 a number of educational book publishers offered free copies of some texts to teachers in order to develop an interest in the texts.
- **Run a promotional campaign**. The Guinness campaigns have helped to extend the life of a well-established product.

Consumers and the life cycle

Looking at the life cycle from the angle of consumers provides important insights into changes in a market and their influence upon strategies. For example, in the introductory phase of the life cycle 'early adopters' try products. As the product moves into growth, more consumers become adopters. As the life cycle of the product moves on, competition will intensify. The number of competitors operating in the market will increase as it nears maturity. Organisations will fight to retain their market share and this might lead to product diversification and price cutting. Consumers will become more selective about their purchases. During maturity suppliers will depend on repeat purchases. Usage will fall during decline. This life cycle is shown in Table 2.3.

Product portfolios

Businesses with a single product are always likely to be vulnerable to variations in the market place. By spreading investment across a range of products, an organisation reduces its risks.

Most companies produce a range of products, each of which has its own life cycle. By using life cycles, companies can plan when to introduce new lines as old products go into decline. The collection of products that a company produces is known as a **portfolio**.

In Figure 2.30 t_1 represents a point in time. At that point product 1 is in decline, product 2 is in maturity, product 3 is in growth and product 4 has recently been introduced. This helps to avoid serious fluctuations in overall profit level and ensures that the most profitable products provide support for those which have not yet become quite so profitable.

Table 2.3 The consumer and the life cycle

Stage	Users/buyers
Development	Few trial or early adopters
Growth	Growing number of adopters
Shakeout	Growing selectivity of purchase
Maturity	Saturation of users
	Repeat purchase reliance
Decline	Drop off in usage

WHAT DO YOU THINK?
Can you identify four products in the portfolio of a well-known confectionery manufacturer like Cadbury-Schweppes, Mars or Nestlé which are at different stages of the product life cycle?

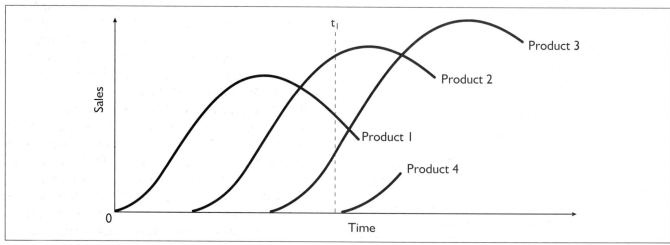

Figure 2.30 A product portfolio

Portfolio analysis

Perhaps the best-known method of analysing a product portfolio to see its balance was devised by the **Boston Consultancy Group**. The technique is based on the 'experience curve' which shows that the unit costs of adding value fall as cumulative production increases (see Figure 2.31).

Gains in efficiency stem from greater **experience**. The Boston Consultancy Group argued that as a rough rule, average cost per unit fell by 20–30 per cent with each doubling of experience. Greater experience stems from:

- reductions in cost from large-scale production
- the elimination of less-efficient factors of production
- increased productivity stemming from using better techniques and learning effects
- improvements in product design.

Companies which have a high market share should be able to accumulate more experience. Therefore companies should strive for a high market share. Market share is measured in comparison to the market share of the nearest rival:

$$\text{Relative market share of Coca-Cola} = \frac{\text{Market share of Coca-Cola}}{\text{Market share of Pepsi-Cola}}.$$

The Boston Consultancy Group believes that a ratio of 2:1 would give a 20 per cent cost advantage.

WHAT DO YOU THINK?

Can you think of companies which have at least a 2:1 advantage over their nearest rivals in particular markets?

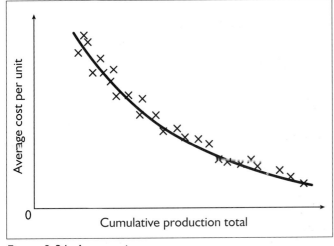

Figure 2.31 An experience curve

Product portfolio and market growth

The Boston Consultancy Group argued that the faster the growth of a particular market, the greater the costs necessary to maintain market position. In a rapidly growing market, considerable expenditure will be required on investment in product lines, and to combat the threat posed by new firms and brands. This is one of the reasons firms are investing so much in websites today.

To summarise, the Boston Consultancy Group identified two key elements in the analysis of a product portfolio:

- The greater the cumulative experience, the greater the cost advantage.
- The faster the growth of a market, the greater the cost of maintaining market position.

On the basis of these two general rules, the Group devised a **portfolio matrix** which is illustrated in Figure 2.32.

The matrix identifies four main types of products:

- **Stars** are those classes of products which compete in rapidly expanding markets. They take up large sums of cash for investment purposes. However, they also yield high cash returns. On balance, they provide a neutral cash flow, but generally, they will go on to be the cash cows of the future. For example, the Internet bookseller Amazon.com has found its core product – book delivery – largely to fit this criterion. It has a very high turnover of books but as yet (2000) is not making any profits from the operation.
- **Cash cows** have a high market share in markets which are no longer rapidly expanding. Because the market is relatively static they require few fresh injections of capital. Advertising and promotion will be required to inject fresh life from time to time. However, the net effect is of a positive cash flow. Cash cows provide the bread and butter of a company in the form of profits. The food manufacturer Heinz has a number of power brands which are cash cows such as Heinz Tomato Ketchup and its popular baby foods.
- **Question marks** have won a relatively low market share in fast-growing markets. Can these be turned into market leaders? What needs to be done to improve their performance? These are just some of the key questions which help to determine the viability of such products. The company knows that such products may go on to be powerful earners, but at the same time they may prove to be a drain on resources. What should be done with question marks? For example, this book will initially be a

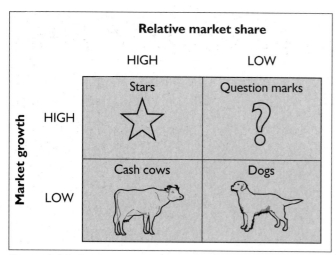

Figure 2.32 Product portfolio matrix

category, with the expectation that eventually they will become cash cows.

In order to manage the development of product success effectively, it is important to have a balanced portfolio of products at any moment in time. A company will require a number of cash cows to provide the bread and butter of the organisation. At the same time it is important to develop the cash cows of the future by investing in the stars. Fortunately, the stars will pay their own way. A company will therefore need to prop up its question marks and cut out its dogs.

question mark as it enters the rapidly growing market for AS Level – hopefully, it will rapidly become a cash cow!

• **Dogs** are products with a low market share in a low-growth market. Research indicates that these are products which are relatively poor competitors. As such they will generate a negative cash flow. For example, a producer of jam which has failed to capture the public imagination would be in this position.

In terms of cash flow, the product portfolio matrix can be redrawn as in Figure 2.33. Cash generated by the cash cows is used to help in the development of the question marks. The purpose of this is to increase the market share of the question marks in order to move them into the star

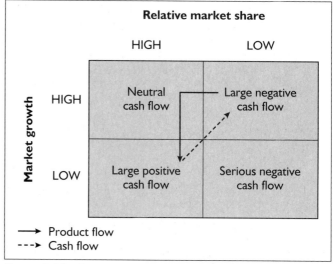

Figure 2.33 Cash flow and product flow

The truth is stranger than fiction

An organisation does well to bear in mind the simple principle known as Pareto's rule. This suggests that 20 per cent of time and effort put in tends to produce 80 per cent of the results. An extension of this idea is that 20 per cent of the product portfolio will account for 80 per cent of sales and profits. For example, a large percentage of Coca-Cola's sales and profits comes from one drink, Coca-Cola; the ice-cream manufacturer Wall's depends heavily on the sales of Magnum, etc.

SECTION D *Pricing, promotion and place*

INTRODUCTION   In addition to providing the product that consumers want successful marketing also involves choosing the right price, creating an attractive promotional mix and providing the most appropriate place for customers to come into contact with the product (involving selecting the most suitable channels of distribution).

Critical thinking: wine websites are next to crash

In 1999 there was a rush to set up websites for many types of e-commerce. Unfortunately, in 2000 many of the firms moving into Internet trading crashed in the first half of the year, as people realised that these companies would not yield the expected returns.

A popular new form of e-commerce was wine trading. A substantial number of Internet sites were set up to sell wine, cutting out the costs of having a High Street presence, and other forms of advertising. Internet wine traders were able to purchase supplies of wine in response to consumer demand, shipping in wine from France, Germany, etc.

Having a website can be a useful promotional tool for wine because many wine consumers have access to the Internet. Also, selling through the Internet enables the seller to offer discounts on a range of popular and other difficult-to-obtain wines.

By the mid-2000 the web directory Yahoo! listed 24 online wine-sellers for the UK – but that did not include newer sites, including itswine.com, chaired by the former managing director of the Majestic Wines warehouse chain, winetoday.com, which is owned by the giant New York Times company, or Virgin Wines.

However, it is widely felt by experts that many of these new dotcom wine sellers will go out of business. It is likely that only a small number of sites will prosper, and they will be the ones with good brand names among wine users or which have a well-known name they can use, such as Virgin. The rest are doomed to niche business which might keep a family business going, but they are never going to be significant dotcoms.

The trouble with selling wine over the Internet is that there is very little value added by being online. There isn't much different there that you can't get from a mail order catalogue or just walking into a store.

The competing wine sites are now all locked in a desperate struggle to win market share, through offering cheaper prices or quicker delivery and by running a series of promotional activities such as discounts for first time buyers.

WHAT DO YOU THINK?
1   Why is the Internet a good medium for selling wine to people?
2   What are the drawbacks of selling wine using the Internet rather than more traditional methods of distribution?
3   How could an Internet wine-seller capture the attention of the public more effectively than rivals?
4   How important is pricing in determining the success of Internet wine-sellers?
5   Access one of the websites mentioned in the case study. How effective a marketing tool is the website?

Chapter 44 *Pricing methods*

Choosing an appropriate method of pricing a product is a difficult decision. For example, recently I started a General Studies magazine aimed at sixth formers (see Figure 2.34).

Pricing is important to the business, as we have seen in the case study above, because it will help to determine the level of sales revenue made.

Sales revenue = Price per unit × Number sold.

If the price is set too low you will not be able to cover your costs; set a price too high and you may not get enough demand for your product (see Figure 2.35).

Figure 2.34 Front cover of General Studies Review aimed at sixth formers

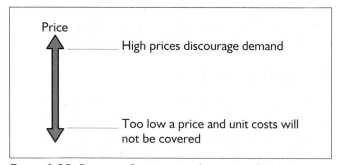

Figure 2.35 Danger of setting too low or too high a price

The secret is getting the price just right. Market research will help an organisation to assess the right price at a particular moment in time.

The elasticity of demand for a product is an important determinant of price. Price elasticity of demand is a measure of how much consumer demand will respond to rises or falls in price of a product.

$$\text{Elasticity of demand} = \frac{\text{Percentage change in quantity demanded}}{\text{Percentage change in price}}.$$

Consider the example of a magazine which is priced at £5 per copy and which sells 1,000 a month. The publisher is considering altering the price in order to increase revenue. Table 2.4 shows what will happen to the total revenue should the publisher decide to increase the price.

Table 2.4 Effect of increasing the magazine's price

Price (£)	Quantity demanded (copies)	Total revenue (£)
6	500	3,000
5 (current)	1,000	5,000
4	1,100	4,400

An increase in price of 20 per cent (from £5 to £6) would lead to a 50 per cent fall in demand (from 1,000 copies to 500 copies). Total revenue would fall from £5,000 to £3,000. In this case demand is said to be elastic because the proportionate change in quantity demanded (50 per cent) is higher than the proportionate change in price (20 per cent).

$$\text{Price elasticity of demand} = \frac{50\%}{20\%} = 2\tfrac{1}{2}.$$

Demand is elastic for values of greater than 1. In this case the measure of elasticity is $2\tfrac{1}{2}$ (or more accurately $-2\tfrac{1}{2}$ because price and quantity demanded are moving in opposite directions).

If we now examine the reduction in price from £5 to £4 we see the following results. The price reduction is 20 per cent. The increase in demand is 10 per cent (1,000 to 1,100). Revenue falls from £5,000 to £4,400. This is because demand is inelastic for the price fall – the proportionate change in price (20 per cent) is greater than the proportionate change in demand (10 per cent).

CASE STUDY: *GENERAL STUDIES REVIEW*

The difficulty is in knowing what is too high a price, and what is too low a price. In either case, it is essential to cover your costs. The danger of charging too high a price is that you may not generate enough revenue to cover your costs.

General Studies Review is published three times a year, is 44 pages long and includes a range of articles designed to interest and broaden the knowledge of intelligent sixth formers. The magazine has a colour cover, and a two-colour layout including photographs and drawings. The magazine is accompanied by a website.

After carrying out some preliminary market research it was decided to price the magazine at £25. This would enable a school or college to buy a single copy of the magazine for the library. However, it was hoped that schools would subscribe to multiple copies on behalf of interested sixth formers. Therefore a differential price list was constructed offering different price charges depending on the numbers of magazines ordered. In the event, a variety of subscriptions were taken out – some subscribers took one copy, others two, some five, etc. (see Figure 2.36).

SUBSCRIPTION APPLICATION

Description	Quantity	Price
General Studies Review £25 per year – published termly – reduction for quantity		

Please return this form to: Peacock Press, FREEPOST HX 2488, Hebden Bridge, West Yorkshire, HX7 5BR. Tel: 01422 886157 e-mail: jeremy@recordermail.demon.co.uk.

2 subscriptions	£20.00	each subscription
5 subscriptions	£17.50	each subscription
10 subscriptions	£15.00	each subscription
20 subscriptions	£13.75	each subscription

Special rates for 30+ subscriptions

Figure 2.36 Subscription application form showing differential price list

QUESTIONS FOR DISCUSSION

1 Why was the price set at £25 for a single subscription? What might have been the danger of setting the price at this level?
2 Why are much lower prices set for bulk subscriptions? What is the danger of offering bulk discounts?

$$\text{Price elasticity of demand} = \frac{10\%}{20\%} = \frac{1}{2}.$$

Again, the figure is $-\frac{1}{2}$ because price and quantity are moving in opposite directions.

The simple lesson for pricing is that:

- you can raise the price and increase your revenue if demand is inelastic
- you can lower the price and increase your revenue if demand is elastic
- if you raise the price, your revenue will fall if demand is elastic

- if you lower the price, your revenue will fall if demand is inelastic

There are a number of pricing strategies that businesses can use including skimming, penetration, competitive, psychological, cost-based and market-based pricing.

Skimming pricing

At the launch of a new product, there will frequently be little competition in the market, so the demand for the product may be somewhat inelastic. Consumers will have little knowledge of the product. **Skimming** involves setting a reasonably high initial price in order to yield high

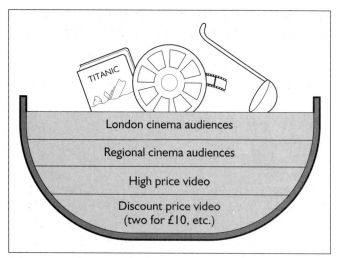

Figure 2.37 Skimming Titanic

initial returns from those consumers willing to buy the new product. Once the first group of customers has been satisfied, the seller can then lower prices in order to make sales to new groups of customers. This process can be continued until a larger section of the total market has been catered for. By operating in this way the business removes the risk of underpricing the product.

The term skimming comes from the process of skimming the cream from the top of a milk product. An example of this type of policy is seen with blockbuster films like *Titanic* (see Figure 2.37). Initially, the film will be shown at a high price in London cinemas, then at a slightly lower price in the regions. A video is then released of the film at a high price. Eventually, the video may be sold at a low-price discount.

Penetration pricing

While skimming may be an appropriate policy when a seller is not sure of the elasticity of demand for the product, **penetration pricing** is appropriate when the seller knows that demand is likely to be elastic. A low price is therefore required to attract consumers to the product. Penetration pricing is normally associated with the launch of a new product for which the market needs to be penetrated (see Figure 2.38). Because the price starts low, the product

may initially make a loss until consumer awareness is increased.

A typical example of penetration pricing is that of the men's magazine *Loaded*. When it was first introduced it was a new concept – the idea of having a 'laddish men's magazine'. Initially, it was launched with a relatively low price, coupled with discounts and special offers. As the magazine rapidly penetrated the market, sales and profitability rose. Prices were then pushed upwards.

Penetration pricing is particularly appropriate for products where economies of scale can be employed to produce large volumes at low unit costs. Products which are produced on a large scale are initially burdened by high fixed costs for research, development and purchases of plant and equipment. It is important to spread these fixed costs quickly over a large volume of output. Penetration pricing is also common when there is a strong possibility of competition from rival products.

Competitive pricing

Competitive pricing simply involves selecting prices with the competition in mind. Firms which have little power to determine prices in the market will have to refer to the market in selecting price.

The major variants of competitive pricing are as follows:

- **Setting a price at the current market price**. This is typically the case for petrol retailers in towns and cities were customers have plenty of choice and have a good knowledge of prices charged by different sellers. Another example is that of fruit and flower sellers in a local market – if they fail to sell their produce, then the product will spoil. Their pricing decision is thus heavily dependent on the market.
- **Discount pricing**. This involves selling goods at a price which is less than the market leader. A number of businesses know that if they charge the same price as the market leader, then people will choose to buy from the market leader – they are thus forced to discount. For example, supermarkets like Morrisons sell at

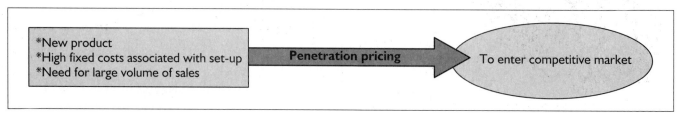

Figure 2.38 Environment appropriate for penetration pricing

discount prices relative to Tesco and Sainsbury's, Superdrug sells at discount prices relative to Boots, Wranglers sells its jeans at a discount relative to Levis, and so on. Supermarket own-brand goods are another example of discounted pricing.

> **WHAT DO YOU THINK?**
> Why are supermarket own-brand beans always sold at a discount to Heinz beans?

Psychological pricing

Consumers have a feel for what is the 'right price' for a product. It is therefore important for the producer or seller to understand the psychology of the consumer, that is, why consumers buy products, what makes them feel that a price is appropriate. The danger of charging too high a price is that consumers may instinctively feel that they are not getting value for money, that they are being 'ripped off'. However, if the price is too low, then consumers may feel that there is something wrong with the product or service that they are being offered. Figure 2.39 shows the **psychological 'right price'** for a pair of trainers.

Cost-based and market-based pricing

In choosing a pricing method the price setter will tend to lean towards pricing according to **costs** or according to market-based considerations such as **demand** and the level of **competition**.

Any study of how firms price products in the real world inevitably reveals a very high proportion of businesses using no other basis than a **mark-up** on the cost of providing the product or service concerned. Information about costs is usually easier to piece together than information about other variables such as likely revenue. Firms will often therefore simply add a margin to the unit cost.

The **unit cost** is the average cost of each item produced. If a firm produces 800 units at a total cost of £24,000, the unit cost will be £30.

Talk to many owners of small businesses and they will tell you that they 'cost out' each hour worked and then add a margin for profits; or they will simply mark up each item sold by a certain percentage. For example, fashion clothes are frequently marked up by between 100 and 200 per cent. The process of cost-plus pricing can best be illustrated in relation to large firms where economies of scale can be spread over a considerable range of output.

For a large firm, unit costs will fall rapidly at first as the overheads are spread over a larger output. Unit cost then becomes relatively stable over a considerable quantity of output. It is therefore a relatively simple calculation to add a fixed margin (for example 20 per cent) to the unit cost. In Figure 2.40 the firm is able to select a target output to produce (Q) and to set a price that will be 20 per cent higher than the unit cost of production.

While cost-plus pricing is very popular, there are many dangers associated with it. If the price is set too high, sales may fall short of expectations; and if the price is set too low, then potential revenue is sacrificed. However, the greatest danger of cost-based pricing is that it indicates a

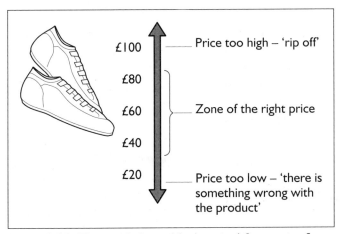

Figure 2.39 The psychological 'right price' for a pair of trainers

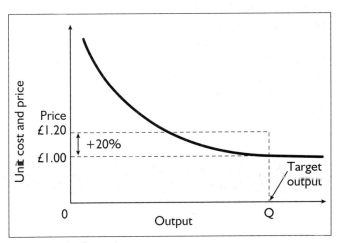

Figure 2.40 Cost-plus pricing

production-orientated approach to the market. Emphasis on costs leads to tunnel vision that looks inwards at the company's product rather than outwards to the customers' perception of the product.

In contrast, market-based pricing has far more of a marketing orientation based on an understanding of customer perceptions (for example psychological pricing, penetration pricing and skimming) and of rivals (competition-based pricing).

The truth is stranger than fiction

When Michael Marks first started trading in the UK as a travelling hawker (door-to-door seller) he carried a tray round his neck with the slogan 'Don't ask the price, it's a penny'. Marks & Spencer have certainly moved up market since then. In a similar way, when Jack Cohen, the founder of Tesco, started trading his motto was 'Pile them high and sell them cheap' – he was a discount pricer. Today, Tesco is in a position as market leader to charge higher prices than its rivals (although most of its prices are very competitive) with smaller market shares.

Chapter 45 _Techniques of promotion_

Promotion is all about communicating – telling existing customers and potential new customers about a product. The aim is to persuade customers to buy the product.

The **promotional mix** comprises all the marketing and promotional activities of the marketing mix and includes personal selling, advertising, sales promotion, public relations, sponsorship and advertising media. In designing an effective promotional mix a strong emphasis should be placed on cost-effectiveness – getting value for money from promotion for the organisation.

Promotional methods can be divided into two types:

- **Non-controllable methods** are marketing messages which take place on the basis of word of mouth, personal recommendations and a consumer's overall perception of a particular product or service. For example, consumers' opinions are influenced by factors such as whether their family has regularly used the product. A brand heritage, character, colour and image will also have helped to create brand loyalty and influenced regular purchasing patterns. On the other hand, public displeasure with a particular organisation, country or range of products might discourage purchase. For example, in recent years buyers have been hostile to purchasing tuna that is caught by methods that may maim or kill dolphins.
- **Controllable methods** are marketing messages which are carefully directed to achieve the objectives of an organisation's promotional campaign such as advertising and sales promotions.

Personal selling

Personal selling is when a company's sales team promotes a product through personal contact. This can be carried out over the telephone, setting up a meeting, in retail outlets or in old-fashioned 'door-to-door' selling.

As a general rule, the more highly priced, individual or technically complex a product is, the greater will be the need for personal selling, in order to best communicate the features and benefits of the product. For example, the selling of machinery to industrial users will largely be done by personal selling through sales representatives.

The key benefit of personal selling is that it offers the potential customer individual attention.

Personal selling is useful in order to:

- introduce a new product to an appropriate audience
- develop an awareness and interest in the product
- explain how a product or service works, and to demonstrate technical details
- obtain orders for the product, and even to deliver it
- encourage the trialling of products and test marketing
- gain rapid feedback about customer perceptions of the product and suggestions for ongoing improvements.

Disadvantages of personal selling are that it is costly and labour intensive, and that some potential buyers are not happy about being visited by a sales representative.

Advertising and advertising media

Advertising is a method of communicating with groups in the market place in order to achieve certain objectives. Advertisements are messages sent through the media which are intended to inform or influence the people who receive them (see Figure 2.41).

Advertising is any paid form of non-personal presentation and promotion of ideas, goods or services by an identifiable sponsor.

Advertisements may be used:

- to promote goods or services
- to develop the image of the organisation.

The starting point for an advertising campaign is to produce an advertising plan. This will involve allocating a budget to a range of activities designed to meet advertising objectives. There are seven steps in an advertising campaign:

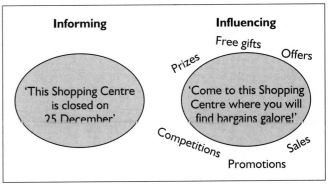

Figure 2.41 The difference between informative and persuasive advertising

1 Identify the target market.
2 Define advertising objectives.
3 Decide on and create the advertising message.
4 Allocate the budget.
5 Develop the media plan.
6 Execute the campaign.
7 Evaluate the effectiveness of the campaign.

Types of advertising media

Advertising messages may be sent through a variety of media forms, such as TV, radio, the press and on Internet websites (see Figure 2.42).

Promotional materials supplied with a product, promotional events or company brochures are known as **publicity** and although they are not regarded as advertising, they do support the advertising process.

At all stages in the advertising process it is important to assess how effectively advertisements have contributed to the communications process. In order to measure objectives, **DAGMAR – Defining Advertising Goals for Measured Advertising Results** – has become a fundamental part of good advertising practice.

In other words, before any advertising campaign is started, an organisation must define its communications objectives so that achievements can be measured both during and after the campaign.

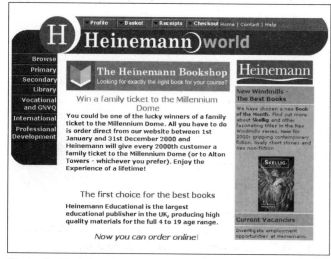

Figure 2.42 Advertisement on a website

Broadcast media

Broadcast media include commercial **television** and commercial **radio**. TV is the most powerful medium – it reaches 98 per cent of households, and viewing figures for some programmes can exceed 20 million. TV advertisements are usually of a highly creative quality, helped by both sound and colour. Messages are dynamic as they have voice, images, movement and colour, and can be repeated over and over again. The main disadvantage of such an expensive medium is that it is sometimes difficult to target a broadcast to a particular group of consumers.

The development of digital television has meant that viewers have far greater choice of television. It has also led to a fragmentation of television audiences – no longer are they tied to the staple channels. From the advertisers' point of view, however, this means that they are able to target specific audiences, for example those that watch a nature channel, a sports channel, etc.

Today, there are more independent local radio stations (ILRs) than ever before and a number of independent national radio stations (INRs) including Classic FM and Virgin. Radio is a good way of communicating a sense of urgency and action. Advertisements are low-cost in comparison with those of TV. One problem with radio, however, is that many regard it only as a background medium.

Posters

Posters include **hoardings** and **screens**, and are particularly useful for providing frequency and supporting the images created through the broadcast media. If an outdoor medium is well sited, its impact may be considerable. Posters can be in colour and there is a wide choice of locations and sites with little competition from other advertising matter. In fact, many posters become a sole attraction in places such as railway platforms, where people have little to do except look at an advert.

Posters do, however, suffer from the intrusions of noise and clutter from the immediate environment. Some may even go unnoticed. They may also be subject to vandalism such as graffiti, and many people feel today that hoardings intrude on the environment.

In the late 1990s media companies in London used the medium of projecting images on to public buildings such as the Houses of Parliament in order to capture public attention and press coverage. Today, the authorities are fighting back, and the standard fine levied by Westminster council in 2000 for a projective on a public structure such as a building or a bridge was £2,000.

CASE STUDY: CLEAN & CLEAR

Clean & Clear is a medicated skincare range targeted at female teenagers. The range consists of treatment products that help to get rid of existing acne as well as preventative products. The range was launched by Johnson & Johnson in the UK in 1992.

Between 1993 and 1996, Johnson & Johnson adopted advertising that had been developed in the USA, 'Girls Talking', which featured confident girls talking about how they didn't worry about spots because they used Clean & Clear. The product made significant gains, and by 1996 had 14 per cent of the market. However, Johnson & Johnson was keen to make Clean & Clear the number one product in the market.

Research by the company into customer perceptions showed that some of the responsibility for the failure to dominate the market lay in the advertising. Advertising awareness is the extent to which potential customers are able to identify the messages given out in advertisements and to identify the characteristics of a brand as they are put across in the advertisements. It was felt that the US advertising was not having enough impact on British teenagers.

The advertising agency responsible for developing new advertising therefore carried out some research among UK teenagers to find out what 'real' teenagers talk about. With the help of video diaries, the result of giving video cameras to teenage girls over the Christmas period, the advertising agency was able to develop new scripts that incorporated shrewd insights from real conversations between UK teenage girls.

Two scripts were chosen which worked very well in trials. One that was chosen was called 'Big Bum', and had the following script. One girl is trying on a pair of jeans.

Girl 1:   How do they look? They make my bum look big, don't they?
Girl 2:   What bum?
Girl 1:   Come on. It sticks out a mile!
Girl 2:   It's a good job you don't have spots to worry about as well – we'd be here all night!
Voiceover: Clean & Clear's lotion is clinically tested to effectively remove dirt and grease. So no matter what, you'll feel confident your skin is beautifully clean and clear!
Girl 1:   So how does this look?
Girl 2:   Great!
Girl 1:   Are you sure?
Voiceover: Clean and clear and under control.

Source: Johnson & Johnson

By the middle of 1998 Clean & Clear had won a position as the preferred choice among teenage girls.

QUESTIONS FOR DISCUSSION

1 Why is television advertising particularly appropriate for a product like Clean & Clear?
2 Why do you think that the 'Big Bum' advertising campaign was so successful?
3 What other means of advertising would be appropriate for a product like Clean & Clear?

Cinema

Though **cinema** has declined in relative importance as an advertising medium, it tends to be popular with the young and is a good way of targeting a specific type of audience. A cinema has a captive audience, and the physical size and loud volume of advertisements makes them impossible to ignore. The quality of sound and vision helps the audience to recall cinema commercials better than those on television. The size of cinema audiences fluctuates widely and is dependent on the popularity of the film being shown. Commercials tend to be shown once during a programme and are not reinforced unless the recipient is a regular cinema attender.

Website advertising

Because of the large numbers of consumers with access to the Internet, and because it attracts an international audience, web-based advertising has become very popular.

One advantage of a website is that it is relatively easy to monitor the number of hits to that site. Many sites are also of a specialist nature. It is therefore possible to use a website for targeted advertising, for example sports goods on a sports site, gardening equipment and materials on a gardening site, etc. In addition, there are sites dedicated to advertising purposes such as advertising job vacancies.

In deciding on the cost-effectiveness of using the Internet as an advertising medium, firms need to consider whether their adverts will be viewed by the user who may just browse through the contents of a web page without paying any attention to the adverts.

WHAT DO YOU THINK?

1 Which websites are you familiar with which would be particularly suitable for advertising specialist products? How could adverts be made to stand out on these sites?

2 How could the advertiser monitor the effectiveness of advertising on a website?

Publicity

The term **publicity** refers to non-personal communications about an organisation and its products. In many cases, where publicity is provided free of charge by the press, publicity will not be paid for. However, this is not always true, as many organisations provide materials themselves as part of their own approach to developing publicity (advertorials in magazines for example). As we will also see, there is a fine dividing line between publicity and public relations and sales promotional activities. Whatever the case, it is very important that publicity is compatible with other areas of the promotional mix.

Activities involving publicity may include the following:

- **Sales literature**. Organisations may produce a lot of literature which accompanies their products and activities, for example leaflets, brochures, magazines, calendars, etc.
- **Signage**. The names of some organisations may appear in a variety of places which are noticed by consumers, for example on football hoardings.
- **Vehicle livery**. This may help to provide a form of publicity, particularly if an organisation has a large fleet and the livery is distinctive, for example Harrods delivery vans.
- **Stationery.** Distinctive headed paper, invoices, pencils, pens, etc. provide a reminder of an organisation or product.
- **Point-of-sale materials**. These are designed to help consumers with product choices at the point of sale. They may include racks, displays, videos and interactive materials. An effective point-of-sale display attracts customers' attention and encourages them to approach and inspect the product before making the decision to buy.

Public relations activities

Public relations (**PR**) is the planned and sustained effort an organisation makes to establish, develop and build

---

CASE STUDY: 'ONLY THE BALLS SHOULD BOUNCE'

At the Lawn Tennis Championships at Wimbledon in the summer of 2000 the tennis star Anna Kournikova was involved in an advertising campaign for a new sporting bra with the strapline 'Only the balls should bounce'. The campaign received extra exposure when a streaker with the slogan 'Only the balls should bounce' scrawled across his midriff danced on to the Wimbledon court where Anna Kournikova was playing.

As the umpire shouted, 'New balls please!', the streaker dived over the net and did a forward roll on the court. He danced around the court for around 90 seconds before two policemen caught him and covered him with a towel.

QUESTIONS FOR DISCUSSION

1 How might the streaker have provided extra publicity for the initial advertising campaign?

2 Do you think that it is possible to engineer campaigns to have this sort of ongoing publicity effect?

relationships with its many publics, for example shareholders, customers, employees, the community at large, etc.

The purpose of public relations is therefore to provide an external environment for the organisation in which it is popular and can prosper. Building goodwill in such a way requires behaviour by the organisation which takes into account the attitudes of the many people who may come across it and its product.

Whereas many of the other promotional methods are short term, public relations is long term, as it may take a long time for an organisation to improve the way people think about its products and activities. For example, just think about the sort of public relations problems that chemical and oil companies have in a world where consumers have become increasingly environmentally conscious.

WHAT DO YOU THINK?
What sorts of PR activities do you think an oil company should engage in?

According to Frank Jefkins, PR involves a transfer process which helps to convert the negative feelings of an organisation's many public faces into positive ones (see Figure 2.43).

There are many different types of public relations activities:

- **Charitable donations** and **community relations** are good for an organisation's image, and often provide lots of good publicity as well as helping to promote and provide for a good cause.
- **Corporate hospitality** at major sporting events such as the FA Cup Final and the Grand National provides organisations with an opportunity to develop customer relations.

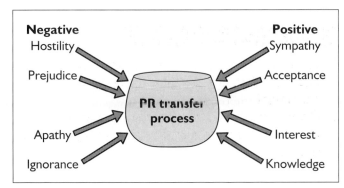

Figure 2.43 The PR transfer process

- **Press releases** covering events affecting the organisation, such as news stories, export achievements, policy changes, technical developments and anything which enhances the organisation's image, are a useful form of PR. **Press conferences** are used to cover newsworthy events which are of interest to a variety of media.
- **Visits** and **open days** are used to improve the invited guests' understanding of what the organisation stands for.
- **Sponsorship** of sporting and cultural events provides the opportunity to link an image, usually a major organisation, with a particular type of function. An example is the NatWest Trophy in cricket. The sponsoring organisation is thus perceived to be more than just a profit making business – it is seen to have a stake in the community at large.
- **Corporate videotapes** have become increasingly popular as a method of providing a variety of interested parties with information about a company's activities.
- **Corporate websites** have become a very popular way of presenting the public face of an organisation. This is particularly true in the case of the provision of educational materials for schools. The site can be designed to deal with the most common queries from members of the public and to provide information in a way that best projects the company's image.
- **Product changes**, such as no testing on animals or environmentally friendly products, can provide considerable PR benefits.

Sales promotion methods

Sales promotion is a group of techniques used to encourage customers to make a purchase. These activities are short term and may be used:

- to increase sales
- to help with personal selling
- to respond to the actions of competitors
- as an alternative to advertising.

Sales promotion is the function of marketing which seeks to achieve given objectives by the adding of value to a product or service. The essential feature of sales promotion is that it is a short term inducement to encourage customers to react quickly, whereas advertising is usually a process that develops the whole product or brand.

As you walk down your local high street or shopping mall, you will see many different examples of sales promotions. Such promotions may serve many different purposes. For example, **competitions**, **vouchers** or **coupons** and **trading stamps** may be designed to build customer loyalty and perhaps increase the volume purchased by existing customers. **Product sampling** is a strategy that is often used to introduce new products into the market place. **Clearance sales** of overstocked goods will increase turnover during part of the year in which business might otherwise be slack. Many sales promotions are carried out in response to the activities of competitors to make sure that the organisation keeps its competitive edge.

There are two main types of sales promotion:

- Promotions assisting with the sale of products to the trade.
- Promotions assisting the trade in selling products to the final consumer.

Selling into the pipeline describes promotions which move products from the manufacturer into the distribution system. **Selling out of the pipeline** describes promotions which trigger the end-user to make a purchase (see Figure 2.44).

There are many different types of sales promotion:

- **Dealer loaders** are among the inducements to attract orders from retailers and wholesalers. They may include a 'free case' with so many cases bought such as buy six, get two free, etc.
- **Competitions** may interest dealers and consumers. For dealers they may be linked to sales with attractive prizes for the most successful dealer. **Scratch cards**, **free draw** and **bingo cards** are popular promotional methods for consumers.

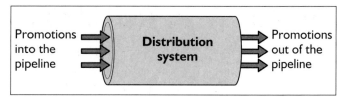

Figure 2.44 *Promotions into and out of the pipeline*

- **Promotional gifts** such as bottles of spirits, clocks, watches or diaries are also used to induce dealers to purchase.
- **Price reductions** and **special offers** are usually popular with consumers. They can, however, prove expensive as many consumers would otherwise have been prepared to pay the full price.
- **Premium offers** may offer extra product for the same price. **Coupons** which offer money off or money back may also be attractive incentives for consumers. These may appear in magazines, be distributed door to door or appear on packaging.
- **Charity promotions** can be popular with younger consumers, who collect box tops or coupons and send them to a manufacturer, which then makes a donation to charity.
- **Loyalty incentives** may be an important element in sales promotions. Dealers' loyalty might be rewarded with bigger discounts, competitions and prizes or even having their names published as stockists in advertisements. For consumers, loyalty incentives may be in the form of 'cash back', free gifts or a variety of other tangible benefits.

The truth is stranger than fiction

Advertising people are constantly seeking opportunities to promote a product or brand. One such opportunity arose in the Women's Football World Cup. When the US captain scored the winning goal in the final she raised her shirt above her head in the way that footballers typically do to celebrate. Immediately, the image was snapped up by the makers of the sporting bra that she was wearing – to head an expensive advertising campaign for a range of sportswear.

Chapter 46 *Channels of distribution*

There are a number of major channels of distribution including direct sale, wholesalers, retailers, mail order and the Internet. In choosing an appropriate channel of distribution it is important to examine the cost-effectiveness of the method chosen.

Direct selling

Direct selling involves contacting customers without the use of an intermediary (see Figure 2.45).

While direct selling has been a prominent part of selling in **business-to-business** (**b2b**) markets (for example for machinery and equipment), today it is becoming an increasingly prominent part of **business-to-consumer** (**b2c**) markets.

E-commerce is paving the way for a worldwide electronic market place. Twenty per cent of Internet users are European, with the majority in the UK and Scandinavia, 67 per cent are North American. In 1998, 16 million Europeans made purchases over the Internet generating 165 million euros in revenue. This will rise to 3 billion euros in 2002, representing a growth of approximately 2000 per cent. The euro is increasing the use of e-commerce in the European Union (EU), allowing consumers and businesses easily to compare prices and buy products across the European market.

An e-commerce survey carried out by CommercNet in September 1999 showed that 27 per cent of British adults now use the Internet regularly. Of this 27 per cent, 44 per cent log on every day and about a third have purchased goods online and about a half use the Internet for comparing prices. The survey showed that the UK Internet users demographic profile is very similar to that of North America in the mid-1990s. UK Internet users, however, are embracing e-commerce much more rapidly than their North American counterparts.

Figure 2.46 shows that a large percentage of online buyers have children. This may be due to these people having less time to get out than people without children. The Internet offers a much wider selection of the items illustrated; for this reason these markets are growing faster than others.

There are a number of other methods of direct selling:

- **Television selling** is increasing in importance, particularly through digital TV and the development of specialist shopping channels. One of the biggest hurdles to TV and Internet selling has been difficulties associated with credit card fraud. Credit card companies are developing new forms of credit card where it is much harder to engage in fraudulent activity.
- **Radio selling**. Businesses such as car showrooms, kitchen unit manufacturers and even colleges advertise on radio and provide follow-up details of their location or telephone numbers. Many radio stations also have programmes where listeners can ring up and either swap or sell goods.
- **Factory shops**. Many producers sell direct from their premises.
- **Telesales**. This originated in the USA as a fast-action sales tool. When first developed in the UK it was regarded as intrusive and established a poor reputation.

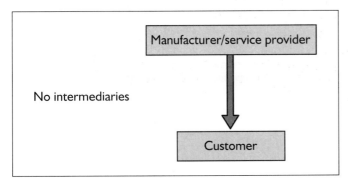

Figure 2.45 Direct selling

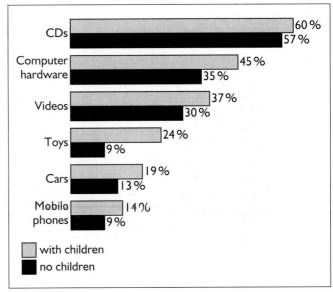

Figure 2.46 *Percentage of online shoppers who intend to buy (1999)*

Since then telesales have become far more focused, with organisations carefully targeting customers and providing a number of supporting services to develop and maintain the telesales relationships. For example, many companies use 'carelines' to monitor the reactions of customers to new telesales promotions. The great advantage is a massive reduction in sales expenses and more time which can be spent on selling.

- **Door to door**. Many organisations try to sell their goods directly into local communities either through door-to-door catalogue sales or by arranging other activities, parties and promotions. For example, Betterware, Tupperware and Anne Summers are widely known for their different techniques for reaching customers. Parties and other events may be of help for a number of products such as clothing and jewellery. Agents sell on behalf of the host organisation and usually receive a commission on their sales.
- **Pyramid selling**. This involves setting up a network of salespeople to sell on your behalf. Each salesperson takes a commission from their sales and then also takes a commission from the sales of anybody they manage to get to join in the selling process. The more people they encourage to join, the larger the commission as they stand at the top of the pyramid they have established. Some consumer goods, restaurants and many other areas rely on this form of selling.
- **Mail order catalogues**. Mail order firms either sell goods through agents or by members of the public ordering a free catalogue. Some firms have their own delivery service while others use the Royal Mail or other carriers. As mail order firms cut out the 'middlemen', they have the opportunity to sell goods at competitive prices. They are also able to use computerised methods for handling orders and stocks and sell from large warehouses situated in locations where rates are cheap and communications links are efficient.

Indirect selling

Whereas direct selling methods are zero-level channels which do not use an intermediary, indirect selling methods use one or more channels of distribution through which goods are transferred from the producer to the end-user. These channels consist of one or more individuals or organisations who help to make the products available for the end-user (see Figure 2.47).

Wholesalers

These stock a range of goods from competing manufacturers to sell on to other organisations such as retailers. Most

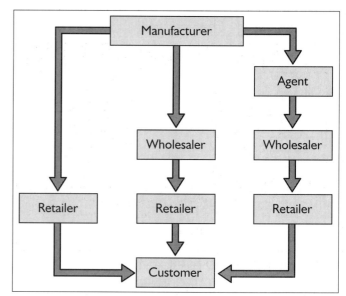

Figure 2.47 Indirect sales channels

wholesalers take on the title to the goods and so assume many of the risks associated with ownership. They may provide a range of services which include the following:

- **Breaking bulk**. Manufacturers produce goods in bulk for sale but they might not want to store the goods themselves. They want to be paid as quickly as possible. A number of wholesalers buy the stock from them and generally payment is prompt. The wholesaler then stocks these goods, along with others bought from other manufacturers, on the premises, ready for purchase by retailers.
- **Simplifying the distribution process**. The chain of distribution without the wholesaler would look something like Figure 2.48. Manufacturer 1 has to carry out four journeys to supply retailers 1, 2, 3 and 4, and has to send out four sets of business documents and handle four sets of accounts. The same situation applies to each of the manufacturers, so that in total 16 journeys are made and 16 sets of paperwork are required. (This is a simplification because in the real world thousands of different transactions might be involved.)

The wholesaler can simplify the costs and processes of distribution:

- by cutting down on journeys, fuel and other costs
- by reducing the amount of paperwork – invoicing, administration, etc.

With a wholesaler the distribution process is simplified, as follows:

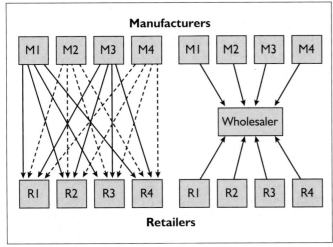

Figure 2.48 *The chain of distribution*

- **Storage**. Most retailers have only a limited amount of storage space. The wholesaler can be looked upon as a huge cupboard for the retailer. Provided the retailer agrees to take supplies at regular intervals, the wholesaler will perform this important storage function. With the growth of cash-and-carry facilities, it has become easier for the retailer to stock up on supplies that are running down.
- **Packaging and labelling**. The wholesaler will sometimes finish off the packaging and labelling of goods, perhaps putting on branded labels for supermarkets.
- **Offering advice**. Being in the middle of the process of distribution, wholesalers have a lot of market information at their fingertips. In particular, wholesalers know what goods are selling well. They can advise retailers on what to buy and producers on what to make.

Retailers

The French word *retailler* means 'to cut again' – and the retailer breaks bulk in dealing with the final consumer. There are many different types of retail outlets including the following:

- **Independent traders**. According to the Census of Distribution, an independent trader is an organisation with fewer than ten branches. A typical number is one or two branches. The market share of these has been declining, particularly in food. The best opportunities today for independent traders often rest with finding a niche in the market, for example speciality foods and clothing.

- **Multiple chains**. These are usually owned by companies and run by professional managers. The Census of Distribution defines a multiple as having more than ten branches. Some are specialist stores such as The Body Shop dealing in cosmetics, others are variety chains like Marks & Spencer with food, clothing and other items. Some key features of multiples are:
  - centralised buying
  - concentration on fast moving lines
  - merchandise is well known
  - they are located in busy shopping areas
  - high volume of sales enables low prices
  - shops project a strong corporate image.
- **Supermarkets**. A supermarket is defined as a store with at least 200 square metres of selling area, using mainly self-service methods and having at least three check-out points. The layout of a store is designed to speed customer flow and reduce time spent shopping. Today, there is intense competition between the supermarkets. Tesco is the market leader, followed by Sainsbury's and then Asda which is owned by the US giant Wal-Mart. Supermarkets have thrived with the development of brand names, the increasing number of working women with less time for shopping, and consumer preferences for easy shopping at low prices. They have high turnovers at a low mark-up – by maximising sales they are able to spread their operating costs over a large output in order to minimise unit costs.
- **Hypermarkets**. These are very large supermarkets. They have a massive selling area and offer a wide range of household goods at discount prices. As well as food and clothing, they stock lines as diverse as DIY equipment, motoring accessories, cosmetics, children's toys and hardware. Their aim is to provide cheaply for all the basic shopping needs of an average household. By buying and selling in huge quantities they are able to operate at very low costs per unit sold. They will focus on lines which sell well and will regularly monitor sales for each square metre of selling space.
- **Department stores**. The Census of Distribution defines a department store as one with a large number of departments and employing more than 25 people. They are to be found on 'prime sites' in the centre of many towns and cities. A department store is divided into separate departments, each with a departmental manager and staff. It provides a very wide range of services and goods so that customers can do all their shopping under one roof. The store generally provides a high standard of service and comfort with carpeted floors, a café, exhibitions and displays (see Figure 2.49).

Figure 2.49 The modern department store offers a wide range of goods

Department stores continue to be a force in the market place with their reputation for quality goods. However, while it is true that department stores have an up-market image, they can also offer discounts on many items. Department stores include many famous names such as Harrods and the John Lewis Partnership. Over the past decade they have moved towards customer self-selection. They have also operated with a policy of 'leasing' shopping space to other retail names with a compatible image – this makes for better use of space and is an added attraction for many customers.

- **Co-operative retail societies**. The co-ops have a proud history of seeking to help shoppers in poorer communities. However, they have struggled to win the continued loyalty of shoppers in the face of competition from larger supermarkets. For many years the co-ops focused on sharing profits with their shoppers. Today, their main point of difference from other stores is a heavy focus on ethical trading – dealing fairly with suppliers and avoiding all forms of exploitation.

- **Discount stores**. Specialist companies like Argos, Dixons and Comet concentrate on selling large quantities of consumer durables at discount prices. The aim of these stores is to produce a high level of profit by means of a very high turnover of stock. As the name implies, they attract custom by the discounts they offer. In recent years, these stores have moved away from the original warehouse-like service, and have increasingly begun to offer credit and other facilities. Discount stores tend to be located at edge-of-town positions. They are well-stocked with a wide range of brands. Recent examples are discount toy sellers and discount pet-food sellers. They are located near to high densities of population.

Mail order

Mail order was discussed under the section on direct selling at the beginning of this chapter (see page 203). Many goods sold by this method are paid for on credit terms.

Distribution through the Internet

Online shopping is a rapidly growing trend and many companies have moved into this new area, particularly electrical retailers, sellers of music and video, computer software, and major grocers.

Table 2.5 shows online shopping forecast sales by product categories.

Table 2.5 Online shopping: forecasts by product categories, 1999–2005

	1999		2005	
	Online/TV shopping (£m)	Online as percentage of retail sales	Online/TV shopping (£m)	Online as percentage of retail sales
Grocery	165	0.2	4,960	4.9
Clothing and footwear	5	0.01	1,843	4.0
Computer software	122	9.97	1,502	51.9
Electricals	18	0.17	993	7.6
Music and video	85	2.87	782	20.4
Books	106	5.15	473	18.3
Health and beauty	1	0.01	355	2.5
Other	79	0.17	1,625	2.4
Total:	581	0.29	12,533	5.0

Dixons Group specialises in the sale of high-tech consumer electronics such as domestic appliances, personal computers (PCs), photographic equipment, communications products and related financial and after-sales service. Included in the Dixons Group are:

- Dixons, the leading retailer of consumer electronics with the latest range of TV, video, PCs, photographic and communications technology
- The Link, a nationwide specialist in mobile phones
- @Jakarta, the games console and PC software specialist
- Currys, the UK's largest chain of electrical stores
- PCWorld, the UK's largest chain of computer superstores.

Changing technologies offer opportunities for moving into new fields of business. Dixons has been instrumental in bringing PCs, software and the Internet into the home. The Dixons Group is now dealing with its customers on the high street, in its out-of-town locations and now directly in the home over the Internet (see Figure 2.50).

Shopping habits are changing rapidly and late-night and Sunday shopping are now an accepted part of our modern lifestyle. The current trend in Internet shopping may well be the key to the future of retailing and open doors to an entirely new retail proposition.

One application of e-commerce is the use of the Internet for business. It is revolutionising businesses because of its speed, reliability and accessibility. Building on the expertise of the Dixons Group in electronic and electrical retailing the advantages of e-commerce provide an obvious way for the Group to add value to its current proposition and meet changing customer needs. In 1997 Dixons established both its corporate

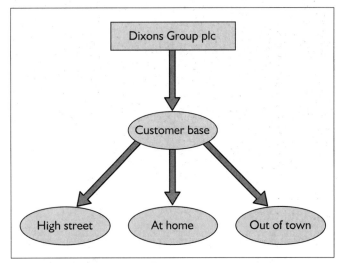

Figure 2.50 The Dixons Group

website and one of the first customer fulfilment websites in the UK through which customers could purchase over 1,500 lines online. In 1999 Dixons launched PC World and @jakarta sites.

Electronic retailing:

- allows customers to browse through a store's products to obtain information, before they go to the retail outlet to make the purchase
- allows customers to buy direct from the Internet in the comfort of their own home
- adds value to the Group's existing products and services
- allows the Group to communicate with its customers before its competitors.

QUESTIONS FOR DISCUSSION

1 How is the Dixon's Group able to gain a competitive advantage over rivals?
2 What distribution advantages does the Dixon's Group gain from having a range of inter-related businesses?
3 Why is the Dixon's Group embracing e-commerce in such a big way?

By 2010 online sales are estimated to rise to 15 per cent of all sales.

Online distribution enables producers and sellers to slash costs, because they are able to dispense with expensive retail premises. Shoppers are able to view goods from the comfort of their own homes. The cost of setting up an online store is also a lot less than using traditional methods. Large-scale online retailers still need to set up warehousing facilities and the logistics of getting goods from manufacturers to the final consumers.

Online trading has tremendous potential and it is not surprising that many entrepreneurs are rushing to get into this field. However, there are considerable difficulties associated with this approach. Even Internet companies like the bookseller Amazon, which has a very high turnover, are not yet in a profitable position. Online sellers also need to develop highly sophisticated websites if they are to be able to build up the sorts of customer relationships enjoyed by traditional sellers who are better placed to build up face-to-face links. Online retailers need to sort out problems associated with delays in orders arriving, and mistakes in the make-up of orders. While, initially, it appeared that the Internet would provide opportunities for many new traders to enter markets, it now seems that established firms are best placed (on account of their huge resources) to adapt the Internet to their own ends.

The truth is stranger than fiction

Egg, the online bank, is launching an electronic wallet for its customers. An electronic wallet is a way of storing customer details centrally so that, instead of keying in information each time, they can be transmitted directly by clicking on a secure symbol. The need to key in the same details repeatedly is a major deterrent to shopping on the Internet. Experts say 70 per cent of customers give up at this stage.

SECTION E *Operational efficiency*

INTRODUCTION It is through its operations that an organisation is able to satisfy the needs and wants of consumers.

Operations are the processes and acts which an organisation performs (often of a practical nature) to satisfy customers. For example, your hairdresser may wash, colour, cut and dry your hair, while holding an entertaining conversation with you – all of these are operations (see Figure 2.51). They will take place in a particular physical location, for example in a hairdressing salon (or at your house in the case of a mobile hairdresser).

In order to meet customer requirements an organisation must organise its methods of production so as to meet these needs efficiently.

Figure 2.51 *Cutting hair is just one of several operations performed by a hairdresser*

Operations need to be designed to use available resources in the best possible way. Operations management is therefore crucial to the success of an organisation.

The nature of the operations depend on the good or service being produced. Operations in schools and colleges, for example, take place in classrooms, assembly halls, on the playing fields, in the college office, etc. and include teaching and learning, the organisation and running of sports fixtures, and so on.

Operations in restaurants take place in the kitchens and in service at the tables, and include the preparation and construction of menus, the preparation and cooking of food dishes, etc.

The production function

Production is the process of using resources to add **value** to a product or a service and so meet the customers' needs. In a manufacturing company, this will involve buying in raw materials and then transforming them into finished products which can be distributed to the market (see Figure 2.52).

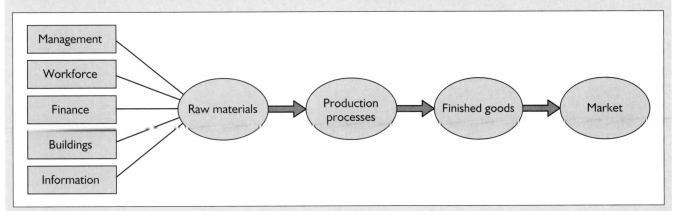

Figure 2.52 *The production process of a manufacturing organisation*

In service industries, the production function involves organising resources efficiently to offer the final consumer the best value and quality. The finished good may be a Premiership football match, a visit to the manicurist, having your funds looked after securely in a bank and so on.

Transforming your resources

Operations involve converting inputs into finished outputs. Figure 2.53 shows how operations management facilitates this process by successfully transforming inputs into desired goods and services. (Note that there needs to be a feedback loop to ensure that if outputs do not conform with the required standards, changes can to be made to inputs and/or operations.)

A useful distinction can be made between **transforming resources** and **transformed resources**:

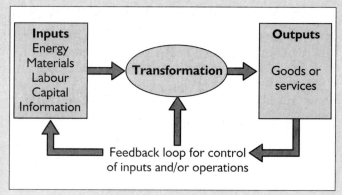

Figure 2.53 The transformation process

- managers, employees, machinery and equipment are transforming resources
- the resources that they transform are the materials and information which they process.

Operations management

Organisations depend upon the management skills of their operations (production) managers. They need to be able to organise operations to produce products that satisfy consumers.

You may hear the expression that production is at the 'sharp end' of business activity. In other words, if production does not produce the right goods, then the organisation will fail. Targets have to be met and standards kept up. Failure to meet targets and standards can be disastrous.

Production management involves controlling and coordinating the organisation's resources such as finance, capital equipment, labour and other factors. Timetables and schedules will need to be set out to show how these resources will be used in production.

Efficient production sets out to:

- keep costs to a minimum
- keep quality standards as high as possible
- meet the needs of customers
- maximise the use of plant and equipment
- keep down the level of stocks to the minimum requirement.

Critical thinking: Shojinka

Since the 1980s UK industry has adopted many Japanese business practices. Of these, 'flexible working' is one of the most commonly used. *Shojinka* means 'flexibility in the number of workers at a workshop to adapt to demand changes'. Shojinka is most significant when demand is decreased. For example, let us assume that on a production line five workers perform a job which produces 1,000 units. If the production quantity of this line was reduced to 800 units (80 per cent of the original total), the number of workers can or should be reduced to four (= 5×0.80); if the demand fell to 200 units (20 per cent of the original total), the number of workers can or should be reduced to one (= 5×0.20).

There are three important factors that help organisations to achieve the Shojinka concept:

- Proper design of **machinery layout**. For example, Toyota car factories have U-shaped production lines. These make it possible to widen or narrow a worker's responsibility in response to demand changes.

- Versatile and well-trained workers, that is, **multifunction workers**. Toyota, achieves this through **job rotation**, whereby workers will regularly try out new jobs and develop new skills.

- **Continuous evaluation** and periodic revision of the standard operations routine. This makes it possible (through increased efficiency) to reduce the number of workers required to produce given levels of output (even in periods of increased demand).

WHAT DO YOU THINK?

1 How does the concept of Shojinka enable an organisation to become more efficient?
2 What are the advantages of increased efficiency through Shojinka?
3 What criticisms could be levelled at Shojinka?

Chapter 47 Methods of organising production

There are four main ways of organising production:

- **Job production**. One job is completed at a time before moving on to the next. An example might be the completion of a designer wedding dress.
- **Batch production**. This involves dividing the work into a number of different operations. Each operation is completed on the whole batch before moving on to the next. An example would be a batch of iced buns where each batch goes through several different baking stages.
- **Line and continuous flow production**. This involves mass production. Once work has been completed on one operation, the job moves on to the next without stopping. The production of bottled beer on a production line might be one example. Continuous flow will involve running the production line for 24 hours a day, perhaps every day of the week.
- **Just-in-time production**. Just-in-time approaches involve producing and delivering goods just in time to be sold, partly finished goods just in time to be assembled into finished goods, parts just in time to go into partly finished goods, and materials just in time to be made into parts ('just in time' is examined in Chapter 50).

Job production

Job, or 'make complete', production is the manufacture of single individual items by either one operative or a team of operatives. Ships and bridges are built in this way. It is possible for a number of identical units to be produced in parallel under job production, for example several ships of the same type. Smaller jobs can also be seen as a form of job production, for example writing this book, hand-knitting a sweater, rewiring a house. Job production is unique in that the project is considered to be a single operation which requires the complete attention of the operative before he or she passes on to the next job (see Figure 2.54).

Benefits of job production

- The job is a unique product which exactly matches the requirements of the customer, often from as early as the design stage. It will therefore tend to be specific to a customer's order and not in anticipation of a sale. For example, someone doing a customised spray job on a motorcycle will first discuss with a customer the sort of design he or she would like. A detailed sketch will then be produced on a piece of paper. Once the sketch has

Figure 2.54 Job production – the construction of Twickenham rugby sports stadium

been approved, the back of the sketch will be traced on to the relevant piece of the motorbike. The background work will then be sprayed on with an airbrush before the fine detail is painted on. Finally, the finished work is handed over to the customer, who will pay for a unique product.

- As the work is concentrated on a specific unit, supervision and inspection of work are relatively simple.
- Specifications for the job can change during the course of production, depending on the customer's inspection, to meet his or her changing needs. For example, when a printing firm is asked to produce a catalogue for a grocery chain, it is relatively simple to change the prices of some of the goods described in the catalogue.
- Working on a single-unit job, coping with a variety of tasks and being part of a small team working towards the same aim provides employees with a greater sense of purpose.

Disadvantages of job production

- Labour, plant and machinery need to be versatile in order to adjust to a range of relatively specialised tasks associated with the same job. Trying to provide the right type of tools, equipment and labour to cope with such a range of specialised operations may be expensive.

- Because job production is unique, costing is based on uncertain predictions of future costs and not on the experience of past events. For example, the Channel Tunnel project cost twice as much as originally forecast.
- Unit costs tend to be high. For example, there will be fewer economies such as bulk purchasing and the division of labour.

Batch production

The term **batch** refers to a specific group of components which go through a production process together. As one batch finishes, the next one starts.

For example, on Monday machine A produces a type 1 engine part (for an aircraft engine), on Tuesday it produces a type 2 engine part, on Wednesday a type 3 engine part and so on. All engine parts will then go forward to the final assembly of different categories of engine parts.

Batches are continually processed through each machine before moving on to the next operation. This method is sometimes referred to as **'intermittent' production**, as different types of job are held as work in progress between the various stages of production.

Benefits of batch production

- It is particularly suitable for a wide range of nearly similar goods which can use the same machinery on different settings.
- It economises on the range of machinery needed and reduces the need for a flexible workforce.
- Units can respond quickly to customer orders by moving buffer stocks or work in progress or partly completed goods through the final production stages.
- It allows economies of scale in techniques of production, bulk purchasing and areas of organisation.
- It makes costing easy and provides a better information service for management.

Disadvantages of batch production

- There are considerable organisational difficulties associated with batch production. For example, sequencing batches from one job to another to avoid building up excessive or idle stocks of work in progress is difficult in terms of routing and scheduling.
- There is a time lag between an initial investment in material and its eventual transfer into cash upon the sale of a product.

- The time spent by staff on problems of paperwork, stock control and effective plant utilisation can be lengthy.
- Part of a batch has to be held waiting until the rest is completed before moving on to the next stage.

Flow production

Batch production is characterised by irregularity. If the rest period in batch production disappeared, it would then become flow production. **Flow production** is a continuous process of parts passing on from one stage to another until completion. Units are worked on in each operation and then passed straight on to the next work stage without waiting for the batch to be completed. To make sure that the production line can work smoothly, each operation must be of equal length and there should be no movements or leakages from the line, for example hold-ups to work in progress.

For flow production to be successful, there needs to be a continuity of demand. If demand is varied this will lead to a constant overstocking of finished goods (or periodic shortages, if the flow is kept at a low level). Apart from minor differences, all flow products need to be standardised as flow lines cannot deal with variations in the product.

Achieving a smooth flow of production requires considerable pre-production planning to ensure that raw materials are purchased and delivered on time, that sufficient labour is employed, that inspection procedures fit in with the process and that all operations take the required time.

Continuous flow production is an extension of line production. Today, in many organisations the production line works 24 hours a day for six or more days a week, perhaps with one day being allocated to maintenance. Examples are food processing, and oil refineries. Maximum use is made of plant and operatives' work shifts to ensure the continuous flow of products.

Benefits of flow production

- Labour costs will tend to be reduced as comprehensive planning and often investment will generate economies in both the type and numbers of those employed.
- Deviations in the line can be quickly identified.
- As there is no rest between operations, work-in-progress levels can be kept low.
- The need for storage space is minimal as there is no waiting period between processes.
- The physical handling of items is reduced.

In the UK today, the beer and lager market is dominated by a few large breweries. These firms are able to produce high outputs at a low average cost per unit. The brewing process is controlled by a central computer which checks that the mixing of ingredients has taken place correctly and takes regular readings of temperature and fermentation.

Used bottles from pubs and other outlets are returned on pallets containing several crates at a time. The crates are lifted off the pallet automatically and a machine picks up the bottles before passing them down a line into a washer. The bottles are then checked for faults by an electronic device. The bottles are automatically filled and an electronic eye checks that the contents reach a certain level in the bottle (see Figure 2.55).

The machine line then automatically labels and caps the bottles. The bottles are automatically placed on crates which are passed on to a pallet which is automatically stacked on an out-going lorry.

The production line works using a continuous flow of production. The same type of bottled or canned beer can be produced around the clock, every day of the week. The whole process has been designed to eliminate the need for labour. Labour is only required to manage the computer, maintain machinery and keep an eye on it in case it breaks down.

Figure 2.55 Continuous flow production in a brewery

QUESTIONS FOR DISCUSSION

1 Why does lager and beer production lend itself to continuous flow production techniques?
2 How does the continuous flow production method for beer and lager benefit the manufacturer?
3 Can you see any potential problems with using the continuous flow method for producing lager and beer?

- Investments in raw materials are more quickly converted into sales.
- As material and line requirements are easy to assess, weaknesses are highlighted and control is more effective.

Disadvantages of flow production

- It is sometimes difficult to balance the output of one stage with the input of another, and operations may function at different speeds.
- Flow production requires constant work-study.
- Providing a workforce with diverse skills to cater for circumstances such as cover for absence may be

difficult and expensive, and regular absences can have far-reaching effects.
- Parts and raw materials need to arrive on time.
- Maintenance must be preventative to ensure that machinery breakdown does not cause the flow to stop.
- If demand falters, overstocking may occur.

Just-in-time manufacture

It is possible to argue that **just-in-time manufacturing (JIT)** should be regarded as a method of production in its own right. The authors of this book certainly feel that it should be given this importance and JIT is the subject of Chapter 50.

Capacity utilisation

A key aspect of successful operations management is to be able to utilise existing capacity in the most efficient way. **Capacity utilisation** is measured by actual output as a proportion of maximum capacity. For example, if a firm is capable of producing 10,000 units but only produces 5,000, then it is only producing at half of its capacity. This is wasteful because it will continue to incur costs on its unused capacity – rent and rates, for example, will still be paid on a factory building that has shut down.

The formula for capacity utilisation is:

$$\text{Capacity utilisation} = \frac{\text{Current output}}{\text{Maximum possible output}} \times 100.$$

A major problem for the firm operating with spare (unused) capacity is that it still has to incur the fixed costs associated with that unused capacity. For example, if a school has capacity to take 1,000 pupils and it only operates with 500, then it is operating at half of its capacity. Examining one of the fixed costs – the caretaker's salary of £20,000 per annum – we can see that:

- when the school is operating at full capacity, the caretaker's salary is spread over 1,000 students, that is:

$$\frac{£20,000}{1,000} = £20 \text{ per student}$$

- when the school is operating at half capacity, the caretaker's salary is spread over 500 students, that is:

$$\frac{£20,000}{500} = £40 \text{ per student.}$$

The same applies to all of the school's other fixed costs. In situations where fixed costs per unit are too high, then economies have to be made. In education, in recent years we have seen the merging of schools with some school premises being closed and jobs being cut. The process of reducing spare capacity is known as **rationalisation**.

At any one time an organisation has so much plant, equipment and labour available to carry out its operations. Efficient operations management involves making sure that this capacity is used in the best possible way. The most efficient method will be the one which yields the maximum return relative to the quantity of factors of production employed.

By measuring productive efficiency a firm is able to:

- identify inefficiencies and eradicate them
- identify areas for improvement
- analyse how effectively it is using resources
- make comparisons of productivity within the organisation
- make comparisons between organisations
- establish clear plans and targets for improving efficiency.

Outputs are produced by a range of factors of production, so we can measure productivity in the following way:

$$\text{Productivity} = \frac{\text{Output}}{\text{Labour} + \text{Materials} + \text{Fixed Assets}}.$$

In practice, productivity is usually measured by dividing output by the number of hours of labour employed.

Another way of measuring efficiency is:

$$\text{Productive efficiency} = \frac{\text{Sales revenue}}{\text{Factors of production employed}}.$$

In industries where capital is a significant factor of production this can be calculated by:

$$\text{Productivity of capital} = \frac{\text{Sales revenue}}{\text{Value of capital items}}.$$

The truth is stranger than fiction

Because of the high demand for seaside rock, and because of modern production techniques, rock with standard messages can be produced using a continuous flow approach. However, there are potential pitfalls, for example associated with the misspelling of a message. One year several tons of Blackpool rock had to be recycled because a disenchanted employee had changed the message inside the rock to 'F... off'.

Chapter 48 *Economies/diseconomies of scale*

It is often the case that a business will benefit from producing on a larger rather than a smaller scale. However, to produce on a large scale it is necessary to have a large enough market for the product.

We use the term **economies of scale** to describe the advantages that a firm gains from being able to produce larger outputs at lower unit costs (than by producing smaller levels of output).

Of course, today, many modern consumer goods are produced to sell to millions of consumers every day. The production line in a Coca-Cola canning or bottling plant runs for 24 hours a day, and the production of Mars bars will take place around the clock for almost 365 days a year. Producers of mass-market goods are confident that it is worthwhile to produce on a large scale because they know (as a result of market research evidence) that they will be able to sell large quantities.

Mass producers are able to spread their overheads over large production quantities. For example, Coca-Cola may invest heavily in a very expensive television advertising campaign. The campaign may be able to be used globally – in Mauritius, and Madagascar as well as in Mexico, the USA and France. The advertising will help to promote each and every can or bottle of Coca-Cola sold throughout the globe. Spread the cost of the campaign over each can or bottle and it is obvious that the advertising cost per can is practically zero. Compare that with a much smaller producer of soft drinks and it is clear why Coca-Cola is at such an advantage. Indeed, in recent years some other soft drinks manufacturers have left the market because they realise that they simply cannot compete against large-scale producers like Coca-Cola and PepsiCo.

Types of economy of scale

In business there are two main types of economy of scale:

- **Internal economies** are the advantages to an individual firm stemming from the growth of that firm to a large scale. For example, a supermarket chain expands from having one or two small shops in a particular region of the country, to opening larger supermarkets, and then hypermarkets in its home region. It then becomes a national chain of hypermarkets and supermarkets.
- **External economies** are the advantages accruing to firms in an industry resulting from the general growth and development of that industry. For example, a

number of firms producing similar products set up in an area, to be followed by firms supplying components to the industry and firms providing ancillary services to the industry, followed by the improvement of transport links to that region.

Internal economies of scale

Internal economies of scale can be illustrated. The scale or size of production is usually measured by the number of units produced over a period of time. If the scale of production increases, average unit costs over most production ranges are likely to fall because the firm will benefit from economies of scale. All businesses will aim for the scale of production which best suits their line of work and this will be achieved when unit costs are at their lowest for the output produced. Beyond this point a firm will start to find that inefficiencies push average costs up and diseconomies of scale account for this (that is, the disadvantages of growing too large).

If output increases faster than the rate of inputs, average unit costs will be falling and a firm is said to be benefiting from increasing returns to scale. Beyond the point at which average unit costs are at their lowest the increase in output will be less than the increase in input, so that average unit costs are pushed up and the firm is suffering from decreasing returns to scale (see Figure 2.56).

There are five main types of internal economy of scale.

1 Technical economies
Large-scale producers use techniques and equipment which cannot be adopted by small-scale producers. For example,

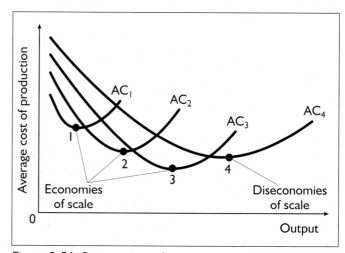

Figure 2.56 Returns to scale

a firm might have four machines each producing 1,000 units per week at a unit cost of £2; as the firm becomes larger these could be replaced by one machine which produces 5,000 units per week at the lower unit cost of £1.75. If small firms tried to use such specialised machinery, costs would be excessive and the machines might become obsolete before the end of their physical life. (Economic lifespan of machines may be shorter than their physical life because demand for the goods produced by the machines will diminish before the machine wears out.) An essential by-product of higher-tech operations is that processes are simplified and standardised so that cost reductions can be made in other areas such as labour.

Many economies of scale fit into the category of technical economies. An important technical economy relates to 'increased dimensions'. For example, a double-decker bus will be able to take at least twice as many passengers as a single-decker coach but each will require one driver. A larger hotel will probably be able to get by with a single reception desk (the same as for a small hotel). Increase the dimensions of a cylindrical storage tank in a factory and its capacity to hold liquids will increase at a faster rate than the quantity of materials required to construct the tank, etc. Technical economies thus relate to a wide number of ways in which it becomes possible to better organise production by expanding the scale of operations.

2 Labour and managerial economies

In larger organisations highly skilled workers can be employed in jobs which make full use of their specialised skills whereas in a small business unit they might have to be a generalist ('jack of all trades'). This element of division of labour therefore avoids the time-wasting element caused by the constant need to switch from one type of job to another. In the same way, a larger firm can also employ a number of highly specialised members of its management team such as accountants, marketing managers, human resource managers, etc., in the hope that the improved quality of work and decisions made by this more qualified workforce will reduce overall unit costs.

3 Commercial economies

Commercial or trading economies are concerned with the benefits that large firms gain in terms of buying and selling when compared with smaller firms. The large firm is generally able to win considerable discounts in purchasing raw materials and supply because of the value of a large order when compared with a smaller one. The reputation of the large firm may also lead to it being viewed as a safer

business risk than a smaller firm. The costs of transport per unit will be much lower with larger loads. Larger firms are also able to organise the selling of their products more effectively. For example, if you can sell all your output to one or a few buyers, the cost of making the sale will be a lot lower than if you are dealing with thousands of separate customers.

4 Financial economies

As larger companies tend to present a more secure investment they find it easier to raise finance. For example, during periods of recession when businesses require periods of extended credit, many large companies are kept afloat by securing bank loans whereas smaller organisation with similar problems are often treated less favourably. Larger firms are in a better position to negotiate loans at preferential interest rates. A further financial advantage to large firms is their ability to raise capital by issuing new shares on the stock exchange. The larger the share issue, the lower the cost per pound raised from the share issue, because the costs of the share issue such as payments to specialist firms involved in helping with the share issue are spread.

5 Risk-bearing economies

Large firms have the possibility of carrying out a range of activities, rather than 'putting all their eggs in one basket'. This is called **diversification**. They may decide to produce several products rather than one; or they may sell goods in different markets, for example in France, Spain, Greece and India as well as the UK; or instead of just selling goods to one age range, they may produce products which appeal to different age ranges such as one breakfast cereal for young children, another aimed at teenagers, a third aimed at the weight-conscious middle-aged. A clear advantage of diversifying is that the firm is able to cater for a range of markets and tastes rather than having a narrow customer focus. For example, supermarkets that are able to provide a range of products to meet a customer's 'total food and drink needs' will win business across the full range of food and drink categories.

External economies of scale

External economies of scale are ones that all firms in an industry or region can benefit from as a result of general developments external to a specific organisation. There are three main types of external economy.

1 Economies of concentration

If firms operating in a particular sector concentrate in a particular locality, then benefits will occur. For example,

CASE STUDY: ARE SMALL SIXTH FORMS ON THE WAY OUT?

Small sixth forms are under pressure (see Figure 2.57). The government published a White Paper on the future of education in mid-1999 requiring Ofsted, the Office for Standards in Education, to examine the effectiveness of school and college sixth forms. Those which are too small will have to collaborate, those that fail to improve will have to close or merge. Increasingly, schools are having to account for the costs of running a sixth form and for the quality of sixth forms. Some of the paperwork associated with the White Paper suggested that small sixth forms offer 'poor value for money'.

There are 1,800 schools in England with their own sixth forms. Only a third have more than 200 students; 25 per cent have 100 or fewer, and 6 per cent have 50 or fewer. The figures indicate that size does matter. Colleges are 20 per cent cheaper than schools, yet get roughly the same exam results. Sixth forms with 200 or more get results nearly twice as good on average as those with 50 or fewer. Value-added measures, which purport to measure teaching performance, suggest similar students do just as well wherever they go (see Table 2.6).

Table 2.6 Comparisons by cost and results

	Annual cost per student	Results: A level point scores*
Schools	£7,380	
Further education colleges	£5,910	
Sixth form colleges	£6,250	
School sixth forms (200+ students)		18.6
Sixth form colleges		17.2
Tertiary colleges		14.2
Schools (50 or fewer students)		10.8
General further education colleges		9.0

* where 10 = A and 2 = E

Heads of small sixth forms complain that the bald statistics say nothing about the intake of students. You can hardly condemn a tiny sixth form in an area with a poor academic record for achieving low average results if it is offering opportunities its students would otherwise miss.

However, at the heart of the Education Minister's plans is the ability of sixth forms to offer a much broader range of subjects than at present.

The government has introduced a tough new course for academic sixth formers – up to five subjects in the new half-an-A-Level AS exam and three subjects topped up to the full A level. It is a regime much easier to introduce in a large institution offering 35 or so A levels than a small one offering a dozen.

Figure 2.57 A small sixth form class

QUESTIONS FOR DISCUSSION

1 Why do you think that sixth form colleges have lower costs per student than school sixth forms?
2 Why do you think that school sixth forms with more than 200 students appear to get the best A level results?
3 Explain how a large school sixth form might benefit from each of the following economies of scale:
   • technical economies
   • labour and managerial economies
   • commercial economies
   • financial economies
   • risk-spreading economies.
4 How might a large sixth form suffer from diseconomies of scale?
5 What might be the advantages of studying in a school with a small sixth form?
6 From your own experience of A level study, how could the efficiency of the organisation of your studies be improved by a change in the scale of the operations?

---

many advertising agencies are concentrated in the Soho area of London. As a result, many other firms providing services to the industry such as specialist editing facilities are located in this area, benefiting all of the advertising agencies in Soho – and leading to reductions in unit costs of production. Often, when industry concentrates in a particular region, then transport and communications links will be developed creating benefits to all firms in a region or locality.

2 Economies of information

Industries will often create information services designed to benefit all participants in the industry. Today, this is particularly true in the field of the provision of Internet information services.

3 Disintegration

Firms producing components or supplying specialist machinery might well be attracted to areas of specialised industries as well as where there are firms to help with maintenance and processes. The term **disintegration** is used because individual organisations do not have to do everything themselves in an integrated way – they can farm out non-core activities.

Integration

Organisations can take advantage of economies of scale by ploughing back profits and gradually expanding their operations. **Organic growth** of this kind is, however, often a slow process.

A quicker and more dynamic process is through **mergers** or **takeovers.** These involve combining a number of businesses under a single organisation. Merging increases size and enables companies to benefit from economies of large-scale production. Some firms merge in order to increase the benefits of specialisation. Others do so in order to diversify and so cut down risk.

Horizontal integration

A company may take over another which produces similar goods and which is involved at the same stage of production, for example the merger of two ice-cream manufacturers (see Figure 2.58).

Vertical integration

Some products are made in stages which may be carried out by several firms. Vertical integration therefore involves the joining together of firms at different stages of production.

Backward vertical integration would be the takeover of a supplier (for example the ice-cream firm taking over a dairy farm), and forward vertical integration would be the takeover of a firm at a later stage of production (for example taking over a chain of ice-cream vans). These are shown in Figure 2.58.

Lateral integration

This is integration between two business which produce similar products. For example, a bleach and cleaning fluids

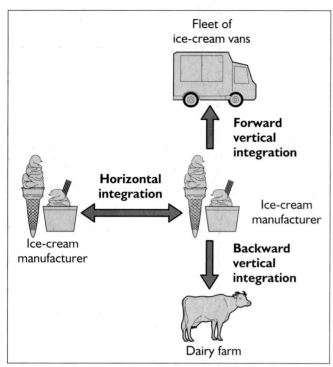

Figure 2.58 *Types of integration*

company might take over one that produces toilet rolls. The products fit into the general category 'cleaning' and will be able to be distributed through similar channels enabling the reduction in unit costs.

Conglomerate integration

Another way of maximising risk-bearing economies is for a firm to acquire businesses which are not connected in any way with its present activities. A **conglomerate integration** can provide wide diversification.

The problems of operating on a large scale

Having outlined the benefits of operating on a large scale one might expect all firms to be large. However, this is not the case. Indeed, 95 per cent of all firms in the UK have a turnover of under £1 million. This is either because they are in the early stages of growth or because there are considerable advantages to being small in the markets that they operate in. The ability that a firm has to specialise and to enjoy economies of scale depends on the scale of the market. Today, there are many niche markets which are suitable for small business such as those selling specialist CDs over the Internet, antique shops focusing on particular types of antiques, specialist pet shops and many more. In such markets there would be little scope to operate on a large scale. The large-scale producer would find itself with spare capacity which would drive up unit costs.

In many markets economies of scale can only be obtained up to a given level of production. Beyond that diseconomies of scale set in – often associated with the difficulty of managing too large a business. A good example of this would be a secondary school. As the school gets larger it is possible to employ a greater variety of specialist teachers and specialist managers. However, if the school grew too large, then relationships between people would become more impersonal, management difficulties would arise, and discipline might be more difficult to maintain.

The truth is stranger than fiction

Today, competition in the international car market is so intense that firms must use economies of scale to their full potential. The secret is to produce high-quality car components to the best-quality standards and in very large quantities to drive down unit costs. In the car industry this has meant that the French manufacturers Peugeot, Citroen and Renault all put exactly the same engines into their vehicles, enabling the greatest possible mass production advantages.

Chapter 49 Stock control

In an ideal world, where businesses know demand well in advance and where suppliers always meet delivery dates, there would be little need for stocks. In practice, demands vary and suppliers are often late and so stocks act as a protection against unpredictable events.

Businesses hold stocks in a variety of forms:

- **Raw materials** and **components** are stocks that the business has purchased from outside suppliers, and are awaiting processing.
- **Work in progress** is work that is being processed as part of the organisation's operations.
- **Finished goods** are ones that are waiting to be sold. The firm may hold on to them to await demand to pick up or because it delivers the goods in batches.
- **Consumable goods** (for example stationery).
- **Plant** and **machinery spares**.

The aim of any **stock control system** is to provide stocks which cater for uncertainties but which are at minimum levels and so ensure that costs are kept low while, at the same time, not affecting the service to customers.

Balancing stocks at the right levels is of fundamental importance to the business. The keeping of low stocks or excessively high stocks can have harmful effects. High stocks will represent money lying idle when it could be put to better use, whereas low stocks could result in not being able to take on and meet orders. Table 2.7 illustrates the disadvantages of having the incorrect stock levels.

Table 2.7 *The problems of incorrect stock levels*

Low stocks	High stocks
Difficult to satisfy consumer demands	Increased risk of a stock item becoming obsolete
Leads to a loss of business	Risk of stock losses increased
Leads to a loss of goodwill	Costs of storage high
Frequent ordering required and handling costs higher	Can tie up a company's working capital

Buffer stocks can be built up as a preventative measure against running out of stocks due to unexpected variations in demand. A minimum level will be set, below which it will be hoped that stocks will not fall, though this may depend upon the lead time between placing an order and its receipt.

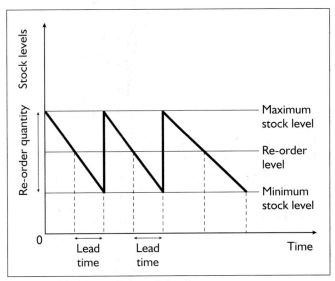
Figure 2.59 *Managing stock levels*

Figure 2.59 illustrates an ideal situation in which stock never falls below the set minimum stock level or goes above the set maximum stock level. Stocks will be replenished just at the point at which the minimum stock level is about to be breached. (In this example should the replacement stock not arrive on time the firm will at least be tided over by the buffer stock.) In reality, delivery times, reorder quantities and rates of usage will vary and either a continuous or periodic review system will monitor and control the levels.

At regular intervals stock is counted and accurately recorded so that trading results can be calculated. The physical counting of stock can be time consuming and it is inevitable that inaccuracies creep in. After stock is counted it is checked against records so that discrepancies can be investigated.

Managing stock

Managing stock involves making sure that a business does not have too much stock or too little stock at any moment in time. There are a number of approaches to this:

- **Economic order quantity (EOQ)** – this is the level of stocks which minimises costs. Getting the EOQ right involves taking into account the costs of holding stock. Costs will rise with the amount of stock held, and the average costs of ordering stock will fall as the size of the order is increased.

- **Fixed re-order interval** – this involves re-ordering stock at set time intervals. For example, each week the firm may re-order stocks, quantities depending on shortfalls.
- **Fixed re-order levels** – this involves ordering set quantities of stocks at variable intervals.
- **Kanban system** – this approach was developed in Japan and is looked at in more detail in the next chapter. A *Kanban* is simply a signal that more stocks, parts, etc. are required in a manufacturing operation. In some production environments a container is used as the Kanban. When an empty container is returned to the supplying operation this is a signal that more needs to be produced.

You should be able to illustrate a stock control chart by means of a graph. An example is shown in Figure 2.60, where:

- 20,000 units are used every month
- the **maximum stock level**, above which stocks should not rise, is 50,000
- the **opening stock** is 50,000
- the **minimum stock level**, below which stocks should never fall, is 30,000 (this provides a buffer stock against delays in delivery)
- the **re-order quantity** is 20,000 units (the same quantity as is used up every month)
- the **lead time** is half a month (about two and a half weeks). This is the time between the order being placed and the date it is lodged in stock.

Buffer stocks are always important because of the danger of late delivery of stock.

The importance of stock rotation

It makes sense to use old stock first in order to ensure that stocks do not deteriorate, go out of fashion or pass their sell-by date. A system of **stock rotation** will help to make sure that stock does not go out of date. For example, supermarkets will put new stock at the back of shelves so that customers use the old stock first. A simple rule of effective stock rotation is **First In First Out** (**FIFO**).

Computerised stock control

Nowadays, stock control in most organisations is carried out using computers. Bar coding has made this a simple operation. Scanning stock items means that a centralised stock controlling computer has an accurate account of the precise number of items in stock at a particular moment in time. For example, when you visit an Argos store you can check whether the item that you want is in stock. In the same way, your local Argos store has an up-to-the-minute record of what is or is not in store. Where stocks have fallen below a given level an automatic re-order code is fed into Argos's distribution system, so that it will be very unlikely to have items out of stock.

Most systems are programmed to order stock automatically when the re-order level is reached. Today, therefore stock

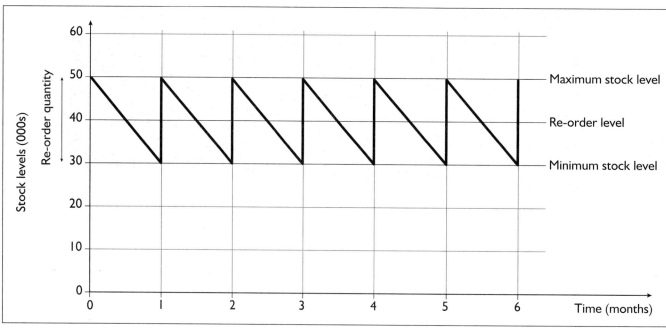

Figure 2.60 Using a graph to illustrate a stock control chart

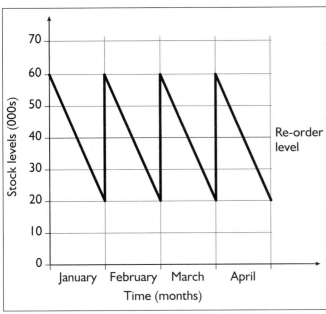

Figure 2.61 Stock control at Quality Sweets

Figure 2.61 shows a stock control chart for Quality Sweets for its stocks of tin boxes, which are needed for an exclusive range of sweets that it produces for the UK market.

QUESTIONS FOR DISCUSSION

1 What are (a) the lead time, (b) the minimum stock level, (c) the re-order level, and (d) the re-order quantity for tin boxes?
2 Why in the real world might the company need to alter lead times, minimum stock levels, re-order levels and re-order quantities at various times in the year?

control systems have become an essential feature of effective operations management – they are programmed on the basis of statistical patterns built up over a period of time. An effective automated stock control system can save an organisation millions of pounds simply by making sure that the organisation never has too many or too few items in stock.

The truth is stranger than fiction

Today, supermarkets use intelligent stock control systems to give them a competitive edge over rivals. Supermarkets generally buy stocks on credit, perhaps paying for them a month or even longer after receiving delivery. Using automatic stock control systems they can get the stock on the shelves and into the customer's trolley almost immediately. What this means is that the supermarket effectively receives cash for items it has not paid for – and is earning interest or profit on the transaction. Suppliers could thus be seen as lending the supermarkets money.

Chapter 50 Just-in-time (JIT) and just in case

Just-in-time (**JIT**) manufacturing is one of the strengths of the Japanese production system and is one which has enabled Japan to have a highly productive economy.

Just-in-time production is a very simple idea:

- Finished goods are produced just in time for them to be sold, rather than weeks or months ahead.
- The parts that go into a finished product arrive just in time to be put together to make the final product, rather than being stored (at some cost) in a warehouse.

The idea is to run a company with the smallest possible levels of stock and work in progress. Clearly, this needs careful planning:

- All sources of uncertainty must be removed from the manufacturing process. There must be absolute reliability of production targets, supplies and levels of output achieved.
- The time to set up machines must be reduced to a minimum so that components and finished products can be produced in small batches as and when required.
- Bottlenecks must be eliminated.

Using a JIT system requires a complete reorganisation of the traditional factory. Traditionally, factories have been organised into 'shops', each working at a particular stage in producing a final product. With a JIT system the factory is reorganised so that people are grouped together around the products they produce. They may need to have access to a family of machines (such as a lathe, a milling machine, a drill and a grinder), as shown in Figure 2.62.

Kanban systems

Just-in-time manufacturing involves producing the required items, to the required quality and in the right quantities at the precise time they are required. It can be seen as a waste elimination process.

The use of Kanban systems is one way to achieve the goals of JIT. *Kanban* is Japanese for 'card' or 'signal' and it is the method used by a customer to instruct a supplier that it needs more parts. The customer might be a factory operative requesting supplies within the factory. The customer could also be a machine or a procedure that requires the parts, stocks or supplies (see Figure 2.63).

The notion of the Kanban reverses traditional thinking about operations. Traditionally, operations start with step 1 in the chain of production and work through step 2 to step 3, etc. Kanban works from the other end. The end-customer drives the process, creating a demand at the final stage of production, driving demand all the way back down the line. In this way there should be no overproduction or

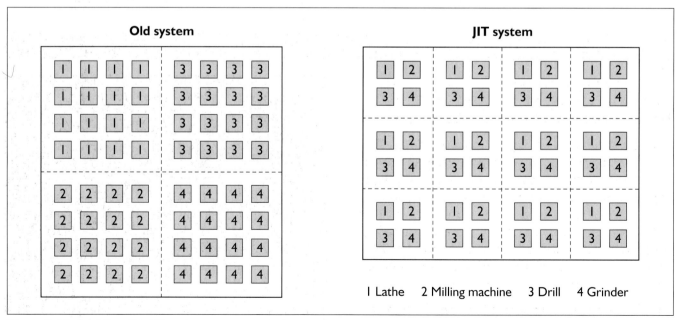

1 Lathe   2 Milling machine   3 Drill   4 Grinder

Figure 2.62 Adopting the JIT system

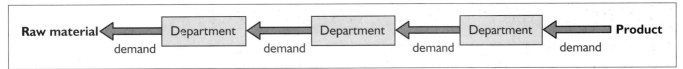

Figure 2.63 The Kanban pull system

underproduction, because production is determined by demand.

A Kanban does not have to be a card – it could be an empty container that needs filling, or a space on the floor or shelf.

There are three main types of Kanban:

- conveyance Kanban – used as a signal that material should be withdrawn from a store and sent to a particular place
- production Kanban – used as a signal for a production process to start
- vendor Kanban – used to signal to a supplier to send parts of materials (the supplier is usually external to the company).

In some production environments a container is used as the Kanban. When an empty container is returned to the supplying operation this is a signal that more needs to be produced. The container must be labelled and coded so that the correct products are produced within the necessary time scale. No parts are produced without a Kanban card, and each full container will only contain its stated number of parts. The aim of the Kanban system is gradually to reduce the number of Kanbans and the time period should be made shorter, that is, months, weeks, days, hours. The shorter the period, the more efficiently the system is running.

In a manufacturing environment like a car assembly plant, a conveyance Kanban would be used to advise the warehouse that an operative requires a part. For example, an operative is fitting a gearbox to a car. The operative takes possession of the new gearbox to fit and takes a Kanban card, which has the relevant stock numbers, descriptions, etc. and may even be colour coded for priority level. This card is sent, taken or passed back to the warehouse. The operative then fits the new gearbox. By the time he has done this his next gearbox is just arriving for the next car. If it takes two hours to fit a gearbox the Kanban card may be colour coded accordingly so that the warehouse knows it has two hours in which to deliver the next gearbox.

A just-in-case approach

The Japanese just-in-time approach is usually compared with the **just-in-case** approach which involves holding extra stocks just in case they are needed. Many

CASE STUDY: LEAN WORKING AT JAGUAR

The Jaguar S-Type car production line at Castle Bromwich, Birmingham, uses a range of modern Japanese methods of production (see Figure 2.64).

Lean production is an approach to operations management which involves minimising the use of the major business resources of materials, people, capital, floor space and time. Lean production involves the standardisation of work processes to cut out waste. The standard is the best identified method of operation at a particular moment in time and one that will be continuously monitored and improved by the individual operator.

The first stage in introducing lean production at Jaguar was to ask workers to operate in small

Figure 2.64 A Jaguar S-Type on the production line

teams with a group leader – known as cellular work. The teams (cells) were introduced to a series of new approaches designed to enable them to work more effectively.

One of the most significant changes has been creating continuous flow systems of production based on a just-in-time approach. Previously, groups of employees had focused on set processes in the production of Jaguar cars using batches of components. The work area for a particular process would be cluttered with components which resulted in a cramped working environment and less floor space.

The new approach is to cut down stocks of components in the work space to the numbers required to keep production flowing smoothly. Teams press a signal button to call for fresh stocks when they are required. A quick response from a central store enables new parts to arrive at work stations just in time for them to be used. This cuts out waste in a number of ways. For example:

- less floor space is required
- cells are able to work in an uncluttered work area
- walking (physically moving about between operations) is minimised
- fewer components are damaged from standing around in batches on the work space floor.

One of the greatest measures of improved working systems at Jaguar has been to match the supply of new cars coming off the line at Castle Bromwich to the demand from Jaguar customers. Given the demand for Jaguar cars, production managers are able to calculate the volume of cars that need to come off the production line in any one week. Produce too few and the company will not be able to meet demand; produce too many and it will have waste or rising inventory (a build-up of stock). The solution is to run the production line at the speed necessary to match demand patterns while retaining quality.

Lean manufacturing requires 'thinking' at all levels within the organisation. The key opportunities for reducing waste are as follows:

- Remove over-production. Producing too much too soon takes up storage space and involves extra handling. Parts and products which have to wait to be used can be damaged, or become obsolete, leading to wasteful scrap.
- Eliminate time spent waiting for parts to arrive.
- Reduce conveyance (that is, moving things around the factory). Some conveyance is necessary, but it does not add value to the product.
- Eliminate over-processing, that is, processing which goes beyond what the customer requires or processes which don't add value to the product.
- Reduce inventory, that is, the build-up of stock. Only the minimum amount is required to get the job done. Having too large inventories causes interest charges and storage costs, uses up space and creates extra handling.
- Decrease wasteful movement by improving work plans and the management of parts and production facilities.
- Eliminate the need for repair. Not getting it right first time is wasteful.

QUESTIONS FOR DISCUSSION

1 How does Jaguar's just-in-time approach enable the company to match supply to demand for the product?
2 How does this enable the company to reduce costs and maximise profitability?
3 How does a just-in-time approach enable the elimination of waste?
4 What is lean production? How does this help to improve operations management?

commentators feel that the just-in-case approach is outmoded in a world in which it is important to be competitive and flexible, and to cut out costs.

Under the traditional just-in-case approach a business will hold stocks of raw materials, components, work in progress and finished items. The manufacturer will seek wherever possible to produce large quantities of products in order to benefit from economies of scale, even when sales are falling. A standard joke about Rover in the late 1990s was that there were only two things that you could see from Space – the Great Wall of China and stockpiles of unsold Rover cars!

With a just-in-case approach stocks will be ordered less frequently but in greater bulk, enabling large-scale purchasing economies and reduced distribution costs in getting those stocks to the plant.

Under just-in-case there is less need to create zero-defects because there are always extra supplies to deal with errors.

WHAT DO YOU THINK?

What do you see as being the main advantages of just-in-case and just-in-time?

The truth is stranger than fiction

In the late 1990s an earthquake which rocked the Japanese city of Kyoto made many manufacturers think twice about just-in-time approaches. Their just-in-time philosophy had meant that they had no stockpiles of goods. When the earthquake struck, a number of small suppliers were affected. The loss of just one or two components brought the whole production line of many producers to a standstill for quite a long while.

SECTION F *Quality*

INTRODUCTION   In the early part of the 21st century there is a greater emphasis in UK business on quality than ever before. Quality means more than simply providing what the business considers to be a 'good product'. Rather it means providing an excellent product, which is fit for the purpose that the customer wants the product for. The emphasis in quality is on meeting and exceeding customer expectations and requirements.

In the second half of the twentieth century the impetus towards improving quality came from Japan. The Japanese realised that producers could not simply assume that they knew their market, and that because they produced high-standard products these were the right products for the market. The Japanese set out to find out what customers wanted, and then at every stage in the production of goods there was an emphasis on quality. The Japanese concept of 'kaizen' involves continual improvement of products and processes. Today most British and American companies have learnt from the Japanese.

Critical thinking

In late September 2000 Lord Puttnam, the Oscar-winning film maker and chairman of the new General Teaching Council (GTC) set up, in effect, to police teaching, said he wanted to stop a tiny minority of staff damaging the morale and image of Britain's 400,000 schoolteachers. He stated that up to 10,000 weak or incompetent teachers should be taken out of classrooms to relieve the burden on skilled and conscientious colleagues. The GTC will regulate the teaching profession in the same way that the General Medical Council regulates doctors. Lord Puttnam stated that 'Teachers who are not pulling their weight in schools have an effect on their colleagues who are doing an excellent job . . . every teacher in Britain knows which of his or her colleagues are pulling their weight. Slowly, through the competency procedures, we are hoping to help the 97.6 per cent of teachers who are doing an excellent job and possibly deal with the 2.4 per cent who are not. In this way we can ensure quality.'

WHAT DO YOU THINK?
1 What do you think Lord Puttnam meant by 'ensuring quality'?
2 How could the GTC help to make sure that quality is improved in the education process?

Chapter 51 _Quality control, quality assurance and Total Quality Management_

For much of the twentieth century manufacturing techniques used in the UK were borrowed from the USA. In the early days of the century the emphasis in the USA had been on scientific management and the creation of the efficient factory system.

The efficient factory system was based on a division of labour into specialist tasks, the creation of single-purpose machines and machine tools, and mass production to benefit from economies of scale. Employees were trained to do a limited range of tasks, and they worked with specialist machinery. The classic example of this was the car industry. So-called scientific managers used **work-study**. In work-study, first the work method is improved by making it simpler to do as well as more efficient; next the improved method is timed, which provides a time standard; then workers are trained in the standard method. Finally, jobs are scheduled, supervised and controlled with reference to the standard method and time.

This approach removed ground-level employees from the decision making process. They were simply there to carry out the orders of the quality engineers, work-study engineers, production engineers and inspectors. US and UK industry came to be dominated by this top-down approach, which was the dominant form of managing industry up until the 1980s. Large-scale, mass-production industries were able to continue in this way for many years, because of lack of competition in the national market. However, all of this was to change from the 1970s and 1980s as Japanese industry became a considerable force in world markets.

Leading thinkers – W. Edwards Deming

After World War II, Japan set out to rebuild its industry, large swathes of which had been destroyed. It was fortunate to have the help and support of W. Edwards Deming. Deming's key idea was that quality control involved defect prevention rather than defect detection.

This was just what the Japanese needed as a way of stopping problems occurring in production, rather than in successfully finding them at final inspection. Dr Deming was invited to Japan in 1950 to lecture on quality to Japanese companies. Today, many of these companies publicly acknowledge their debt to his lectures. The main lobby in car manufacturer Toyota's Tokyo headquarters, for

example, has three photographs in it – of Toyota's founder, of the current chairman and of Dr Deming.

The basic message that Deming took to Japan is quite simple and is set out in Table 2.8.

Table 2.8 The traditional approach versus the Deming approach

Traditional approach	**Deming approach**
Inspection is the key to quality	Produce defect-free goods – eliminate inspection
Quality control is a cost	Good quality increases profits
Buy from the lowest cost suppliers	Buy from suppliers who are committed to quality
Play suppliers off against each other	Work with suppliers
Quality comes from quality control	Quality comes from top management commitment

Leading thinkers – Taiichi Ohno

In parallel with what it was learning from Dr Deming about productivity, Toyota was developing an approach to production under the guidance of Taiichi Ohno, a production engineer working for the company.

Recognising that Dr Deming was advocating low levels of inventory as an aid to quality control, Toyota removed assembly-line buffer stocks completely, allowing workers to stop the line (also known as Poka-Yoka – see below) if there was a problem. Ohno also developed other techniques such as just-in-time and the Kanban system.

From quality control ...

It is possible to identify three stages in the development of quality:

1 Quality control.
2 Quality assurance.
3 Total Quality Management (TQM) (see Figure 2.65).

Quality control is an old idea. It is concerned with detecting and cutting out components or products which fall below set standards. This process takes place after these products have been produced. It may involve considerable

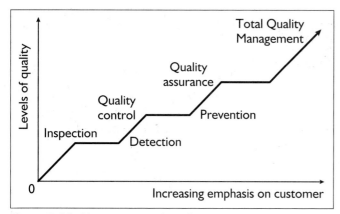

Figure 2.65 Moving to total quality management

waste as defective products are scrapped. Quality control is carried out by quality control inspectors. Inspection and testing are the most common methods of carrying out quality control.

Quality assurance occurs both during and after the event, and is concerned with trying to stop faults from happening in the first place. Quality assurance is concerned to make sure that products are produced to predetermined standards. The aim is to produce with 'zero defects'.

Quality assurance is the responsibility of the workforce, working in cells or teams, rather than an inspector (although inspection will take place). Quality standards should be maintained by following steps set out in a quality assurance system.

Total Quality Management goes beyond quality assurance. It is the most complete form of operations management. It is concerned with creating a quality culture, encouraging everyone in the workplace to think about quality in everything they do. Every employee sets out to satisfy customers, placing them at the centre of the production process.

Companies like Tesco and Cadbury-Schweppes have been following this policy for a long time. It involves providing customers with what they want, when they want it and how they want it. It involves moving with changing customer requirements and fashions to design products and services which meet and exceed their requirements. Delighted customers will pass the message on to their friends.

Customer preferences will constantly change – the organisation therefore has to provide new ways of responding to changing tastes, needs and wants. For example, leading hotels like the Savoy in London are continually improving their service even though guests are already delighted with the service they receive.

Quality Circles

Quality Circles are an important part of the TQM process and are an important way of increasing participation in organisational activities. The **Quality Control Circle** (**QCC**) is made up of volunteers (five to ten in number) who work together on quality-related issues. The circle can be divided up into subcircles of five members.

The Quality Circle has an overall leader who is capable of training the leaders of the subgroup. This person coordinates the groups and helps in inter-Circle investigations. All the members of the group are involved in continuous self and mutual development, control and improvement.

The basic purposes of a Quality Control Circle are:

- to contribute to the improvement and development of projects
- to respect human relations and establish a happy workshop that offers job satisfaction
- to deploy human capabilities fully and to draw out potential.

QCCs have been employed widely in the car industry in the UK and also in service industries such as banking and finance.

The way in which Quality Circles can contribute to solving problems in an organisation is shown in Figure 2.66.

Organisations can measure the effectiveness of their QCC programmes in terms of improvements in quality, reductions in cost, and improvements in attitude (see Table 2.9).

Table 2.9 Measurement of effectiveness of QCC programmes

Improvements in quality measured by:	• defects per worker hour • scrap/unit of manufacture • customer return data, etc.
Reductions in costs measured by:	• total cost of manufacture • failure costs • cost of sales, etc.
Improvements in attitudes measured by:	• turnover of labour • absenteeism levels • reductions in accidents • quality of production, etc.

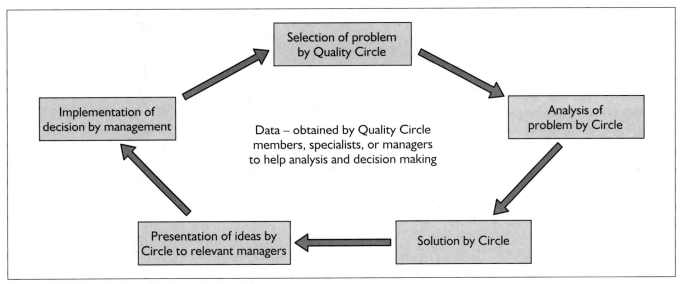

Figure 2.66 The Quality Circle problem-solving process

The Jaguar plant at Castle Bromwich, Birmingham, has taken to heart Japanese ideas about Total Quality Management. On the production line, employees are organised into cells. Each cell has a meeting area alongside the production line where cell members are able to discuss quality-related issues. Each cell has a team leader. At the heart of the meeting area is an Information Centre which is based on a 'three-minute management approach' of communicating work problems in simple visual diagrams that anyone can understand in three minutes. The charts highlight issues, events and progress.

Under the new working arrangements at Jaguar, work teams have been encouraged to take responsibility for their own work. Work must be standardised so that everyone knows what they are accountable for and they can ensure quality standards. However, within each cell, team members will be responsible for writing their own work element sheets. In this way the team takes ownership for the processes and the amount of time involved in carrying out work.

Borrowing another idea from Japan – the Yamazumi board – the responsibility of each worker is outlined in a series of work elements. These work elements are shown in a vertical column on a flat white screen, the Yamazumi board. The value added activities of each employee are shown in green and non-value added activities in red. The height of each vertical element represents the time needed to carry out the element, for example nine seconds. By examining the Yamazumi board it is possible to reallocate some work elements from some production workers to others in order to create greater fairness of work distribution.

Another purpose of work teams is to discuss their work in order to identify ways of reducing the time spent on non-value added activities, that is, to eliminate waste – the purpose of lean production.

Through working together to identify solutions to common work problems a cell of workers can develop a sense of group identity and a shared sense of responsibility for improving their work. Cell members feel that they are making a genuine contribution, and that their ideas are part of the decision making process.

QUESTIONS FOR DISCUSSION

1 Why might the approach outlined in the case study lead to improvements in quality and to higher work motivation?

2 Do you think that it is possible continually to improve quality in this way?

3 How does the approach outlined differ from the old-fashioned quality inspection approach?

The truth is stranger than fiction

Japanese managers believe that it is important to avoid muri, muda and mura to ensure effective JIT and Total Quality Management methods.

Muri – meaning excess – is about avoiding the previous western approach to stocks of Economic Order Quantities (EOQs). JIT systems require the ordering of lots of smaller sets of new stocks.

Muda – meaning waste – involves getting rid of the influence of the old end of production inspectors who actually often increased waste. It involves defining the production line cells of workers as having the responsibility for problem solving and decision making. Errors can therefore be detected before they happen, rather than after they have happened.

Mura – meaning unevenness – involves avoiding the western buffer stock principle. Buffer stocks are based on the assumption that someone at an earlier stage of production will make a mistake. If you can eliminate mistakes (unevenness of production), then there is no need for a buffer stock.

Chapter 52 *The training gap*

An organisation will struggle to produce quality goods and services if it does not employ quality people. It can seek to recruit people with the right skills and qualities, or it can create the right skills and qualities within the organisation through an effective training and development programme, or it can do both.

There are a range of approaches to training and development which are investigated in this chapter including induction, on-the-job and off-the-job training, multiskilling and retraining.

Training

Training includes all forms of planned learning experiences and activities which are designed to make positive changes to performance and other behaviour involving the acquisition of new knowledge, skills, beliefs, values and attitudes. Learning is generally defined as 'a relatively permanent change in behaviour that occurs as a result of practice and experience'.

At any one time an organisation needs to be aware of the training needs of its employees. The training need of an organisation is the gap between the future level of skills and other capabilities that the organisation identifies as being needed to meet its objectives, and the level of skills and capabilities that its workforce will have without training (see Figure 2.67). Training involves closing that gap.

In recent years we have seen an emphasis in business organisations on a principle of Japanese management known as **kaizen** which translates as continuous improvement. Continuous improvement takes place by continually identifying small steps which will improve quality.

As a result, many organisations have developed training programmes which are concerned with helping employees to develop kaizen. Kaizen is most likely to occur when employees are empowered to make decisions for themselves. Training employees to become empowered decision makers often involves quite a radical change in attitudes. People who have previously been told what to do are now being asked to become decision makers. At the same time supervisors and managers are being asked to take on a team leader role. Many organisations which have adopted this new approach to quality start off by training team leaders to work in new teamwork situations. They then work to build their teams, often by carrying out simulation activities in which members of a team are encouraged to start working together as a team. These problem solving activities do not have to be work related.

It may take a considerable time before employees have been trained to accept new work roles.

Examples of new approaches to quality

British employees are being trained in a number of new approaches to quality including the 5 S's and Poka-yoka.

The 5 S's

In Japan the 5 S's are seen as being fundamental to quality and productivity. The purpose of the 5 S's is to communicate targets, measurements, analysis and achievements to employees. Visible management is the concept of displaying data in a very visible manner in the workplace – often by means of **Andon** (easy-to-see display boards). Self-discipline (or 'housekeeping') is another key ingredient.

The 5 S's are designed to enable individual employees to develop a world-class working environment:

1 **Seiri** (proper arrangement of work) – sort through what you have, identify what you need and discard what is unnecessary.

2 **Seiton** (orderliness) – set things in order, establish a location for all essential items, make this space self-explanatory so everyone knows what is going on.

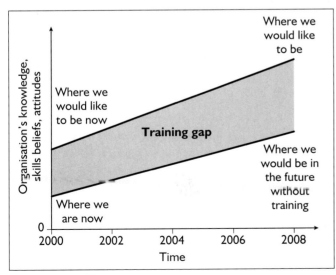

Figure 2.67 The training gap

3 Seiso (cleanliness) – clean equipment, tools and workplace; keep the workplace spotless at all times.

4 Seiketsu (clean up) – maintain equipment and tools, keep the workplace clean.

5 Shitsuke (discipline) – stick to the rules scrupulously and make them a habit.

UK companies like Rolls Royce and Jaguar have trained their employees in the principles of the 5 S's.

Poka-yoka

Poka-yoka was first introduced at the car manufacturer Toyota and the term means 'mistake proofing'. In 1961 Shigeo Shingo, an industrial designer at Toyota, visited an electric company in Nagoya. The plant manager explained a recurring problem that was costing money and time: the operatives were assembling simple on and off switches, but they often forgot to put both springs in the switch.

Shingo observed the operation and suggested it should involve a checklist of some kind. Rather than assuming that workers should assemble perfectly every time he recognised that mistakes would be made and they should guard against this. He suggested a new approach:

- At the beginning of every operation two springs should be taken out of the box containing hundreds of springs and placed into a small dish.
- The springs were then enclosed into the switches.
- If any of the springs were remaining in the dish, the worker would hopefully realise that he or she had left a spring out and switch could be re-assembled.

The Poka-yoka system minimises defects by carrying out feedback and action immediately.

Poka-yoka is a set of rules and techniques designed to 'mistake proof' a process or product. It is based on two primary principles:

- Designing a product or process so that a defect cannot be made.
- Designing a product or process so that if a defect *is* made it is immediately obvious and can be corrected.

WHAT DO YOU THINK?
How would you go about training workers who were not familiar with kaizen, Poka-yoka and the 5 S's to change their existing work practices to adopt the new approaches?

Development

Development approaches individuals and their motivation from a different angle from that of training. While training is typically concerned with enabling individuals to contribute better to meeting the objectives of the organisation, personal development is more concerned with enabling individuals to develop themselves in the way that best meets their own individual needs. Hopefully, training and development will come together. By helping individuals to develop themselves they will be more inclined and better able to contribute to helping the organisation to meet its objectives.

Identifying development needs go well beyond training requirements. For example, an individual may need development for life after work (retirement), or may want development for career opportunities which lie outside the organisation, or the individual may seek personal development through education which is not strictly job related. However, by looking after individual development needs an organisation is best placed to create a committed workforce.

Induction

Induction is concerned with helping a new employee settle into a job and often into a new organisation. Employees are far more likely to resign during their first few months than at any subsequent time, particularly during times of high employment. Troubles in 'fitting in' can be tackled through a good induction programme.

Induction marks the start of the relationship between employer and employee and is of fundamental importance in setting standards and patterns of behaviour. Good induction procedures have three main objectives:

- To help employees settle into their new environment.
- To help employees understand their responsibilities.
- To ensure that the organisation receives the benefit of a well-trained and motivated employee as quickly as possible.

Employees will best be able to contribute to the quality objectives of the organisation if they are quickly introduced to empowered ways of working, to understanding clearly organisational objectives, and to understanding how they and their job fit into the organisation.

There are major advantages in providing induction material in advance of the joining day. It calms nerves, smoothes the transition into the new workplace and can speed the induction process by helping the new employee to prepare.

CASE STUDY: RETRAINING WORKERS AT MARCONI

At the end of the 1990s, Marconi Electronic Systems decided to reorganise its workforce into production cells, that is, work teams which have complete responsibility for the completion of manufacturing jobs.

Initially, it was decided to try out the new approach to cellular production in a pilot cell. The company sent a letter to all employees, asking for volunteers to work in the pilot cell. This gave management the opportunity to do three key things:

- To start to communicate plans to all employees.
- To make it clear that a change in operating practice would be required.
- To give all personnel the opportunity to be involved.

To begin with, employees were cynical about the initiative, although eventually there were more than sufficient volunteers from each of the key areas required. A random selection process was then employed which ensured that there were enough people with the right skills to staff the pilot cell which initially consisted of five people.

It was decided to develop a training programme specifically aimed at teamwork and tailored to the specific needs of the cell. The training programme was carried out by the company training department together with external consultants. The five-day training programme consisted of the following elements:

Phase 1. Manufacturing simulation – a one-day activity designed to help cell members understand the disadvantage of having work in progress and to help them identify ways of reducing lead times.

Phase 2. Setting the team structure – a one-day activity designed to provide team members with the knowledge, understanding and skills of how to build and develop team spirit.

Phase 3. Teamwork activities – a one-day team-building activity designed to help team members understand how they could contribute to meeting individual and team objectives, and to broadening their teamworking capabilities.

Phase 4. Team challenge – a one-day outdoor team challenge designed to weld the team together and to give members the opportunity to practise their team skills.

Phase 5. Review – a review day to examine ways of building on and improving the team-building programme.

A major change that was introduced early on was to overhaul the housekeeping arrangements completely in the area that the cell would be working. An external contractor was employed to paint, clean and tidy the whole cell in time for the hand over. The Japanese 5 S's housekeeping programme was chosen as a model for the cell.

Unfortunately, on the first day that the cell took over its new area it was subject to mischief making which put the change process under pressure. When the team left for the lunch break, a coolant tank in the cell work area was tampered with, causing coolant to leak out over the floor. Although a potential disaster, the cell team heard of the problem while queuing for lunch and immediately returned to clean up the area. This event helped create a real team feeling and demonstrated to the whole workforce that the team itself wanted the project to be successful.

QUESTIONS FOR DISCUSSION

1 How do you think that the training programme outlined above would have helped to create a teamwork approach?
2 What do you see as being the key changes that needed to take place in order to introduce the new way of working?
3 Why is training important in managing change in the workplace?

As well as the basics like conditions of employment, job descriptions and instructions about the first day at work, the pre-employment pack can contain staff handbooks, house journals and press cuttings.

On-the-job training and off-the-job training

On-the-job training involves training people in their place of work. This could be done by an experienced worker demonstrating the correct way of performing a task or by a supervisor coaching an employee by talking him or her through the job stage by stage. Job rotation involves switching employees between a range of tasks in order to develop their skills in a number of areas and to give them a general feel for the key operations of the organisation.

Off-the-job training is any form of training which takes place away from the immediate workplace. The firm itself may organise an internal programme based within its on-site facilities or pay for employees to attend a local college or university for an external development scheme. This approach to training will include more general skills and knowledge useful at work, as well as job-specific training.

For example, in the area of quality management it is very important for employees to have a good understanding of statistics analysis. Employees therefore may be trained externally to the organisation in areas such as working out the mean, variances, process distributions, random sampling and measurement errors. They will learn to read and to construct charts such as Gantt charts. This will enable employees to work better in teams and to contribute to decision making. Control charts enable employees to identify any abnormalities within production, so that they are better able to contribute to Total Quality Management.

Multiskilling

Multiskilling is a key feature of modern business life. Prior to the 1980s employees tended to concentrate on a narrow range of skills enabling them to be productive in large-scale organisations which focused on producing in bulk. However, the Japanisation of industrial management communicated the important lesson that organisations needed to be flexible. Employees need to be able to solve work-based problems themselves rather than waiting for another expert to come to their aid. Wherever possible therefore flexibility means training employees so that they have the full range of skills required in their work area. At a simple level, if a light bulb needs changing they should be able to change it without waiting for a qualified electrician.

Increasingly, therefore, employees have been trained to be multiskilled. In a supermarket, if the queues are getting too long it should be possible to call for queue busters to come and solve the problem. Rather than people saying 'That is not my job', they need to be trained to take responsibility for a variety of work. The implication is that the multiskilled worker will receive better rewards but their extra productivity will justify this. The multiskilled worker is also more likely to enjoy and be motivated in their work.

Retraining

A feature of the modern business world is that while new jobs are being constantly invented, old jobs are becoming redundant. The flexible worker needs to recognise that job security is a thing of the past, and that he or she needs constantly to update skills and abilities if he or she is going to be employable.

Most people will need to be **retrained** throughout their lives. The modern concept is of lifetime learning and training. It is not enough just to be trained once – you need to be constantly retraining and upskilling in order to be able to gain employment in a flexible labour market. Organisations need constantly to retrain their employees in order to upgrade the quality standards of the products and services they produce. Today, it is the intelligence of people and their ability to interface with a range of customers which quality organisations value – these organisations therefore need to invest heavily in training and development.

The truth is stranger than fiction

In 2000 the Xerox organisation spent £2,000 on training for every single one of its employees.

End of unit questions

As you have worked through this unit, you will have come across many questions and activities to help you understand the content and internalise your learning. The structure of these does not necessarily reflect the structure of questions you will meet in the exam, however, so the following section provides some exam-type questions by way of example.

Before looking at these questions, you might like to refer back to the 'Examiner Speaks' section in the Introduction (see page viii) and to the general advice at the start of the Unit 1 questions.

Note that there is no particular relevance to the total marks allocated to each question, except to illustrate the proportions of the total allocated to each component.

The first question is in the form of a case study. This is similar to a data question, except that all the questions asked are related to one piece of data, which needs to be studied at the start of the examination. (It is assumed that this data is not pre-issued before the day of the examination.)

1   Jewels of London Ltd is a package-holiday company which promotes itself in New York, Washington DC, Boston, Los Angeles, Chicago and Philadelphia. The company arranges luxury two-week holidays to London for US tourists. The holiday price includes air fare, hotel accommodation, guided tours to the sights of London and escorted excursions to places of historic interest within easy reach of London, such as Windsor, Stratford-upon-Avon and Stonehenge. Tickets to concerts, shows and plays in London are also arranged for the clients on request. Top-class hotels are used. The first-time traveller to London has particularly been targeted. Many of the clients are retired people and are, of course, relatively wealthy.

The tourist business is very competitive, especially in London, but Jewels of London Ltd aims at the top segment of the market, namely socio-economic groups A and B. The business has obtained a significant market share of this exclusive segment in the five years of its existence and its brand name is becoming increasingly well known in the cities of the USA in which it promotes itself. Clients have been very complimentary about the holidays and many have indicated that they would use Jewels of London Ltd again, if new holiday packages were introduced. Promotion is done through brochures issued to travel agents in the six US cities and by advertisements in glossy travel magazines. Word-of-mouth promotion by satisfied clients has led to bookings from other USA cities by friends and relatives of clients who have enjoyed Jewels of London Ltd's holidays. Indeed, some prospective clients have approached the firm directly instead of going through travel agents in the USA and some have requested quotation of a price excluding air travel, wishing to incorporate the holiday as part of a longer tour of Europe that they intend to make.

The directors of Jewels of London Ltd are anxious to take advantage of the firm's success by expanding into new markets. There are three plans on the agenda for the next board meeting, but the firm will only have the resources to select one in the first instance.

The ideas are:

A To promote the firm more widely across USA and in Canada.

B To seek new customers, by promotions in Australia and New Zealand.

C To extend the itineraries of clients' holidays, by including visits to and stays in other historic cities, such as York, Chester and Edinburgh.

a) Explain the importance to Jewels of London Ltd of having established a good brand name.   **(5 marks)**

b) Analyse the reasons why Jewels of London Ltd may have decided to segment its market, targeting socio-economic groups A and B in the US market.   **(15 marks)**

c) Consider the methods of market research which Jewels of London Ltd might employ in order to estimate demand for each of the three plans under review and recommend the most suitable method for them to use.   **(20 marks)**

d) Assume that Jewels of London Ltd decides to extend its holidays to include other areas of Great Britain. Assess the ways in which the firm could ensure that high quality is maintained in this venture and discuss the consequences for the firm if this is not achieved.   **(20 marks)**

e) Evaluate the promotional methods used by Jewels of London Ltd and suggest any improvements that could be made, assuming that its target market remains in the USA.   **(20 marks)**

Hints for answering

General points

Read the extract carefully before looking at the questions. There are no figures or appendices, so you only have to read the passage. Try to get a picture of the firm, its product and its market, both in terms of likely customers and competitors.

Specific questions

a) This asks for explanation in context, so there would probably be two marks for a Level 1 description or demonstrating of knowledge of branding and three marks for an explanation of its importance to this firm in this market.

b) Level 3 is required. Why would a firm target a rich, US market? Think about profit margins, competition and branding, for example.

c) Level 4 is required. The question does *not* require details of questions to be asked in questionnaires, or how to evaluate and present findings, though sampling *is* relevant. In other words, the theoretical base is the only starting point. Consider the *aim* of the research and the *cost-effectiveness* of the methods used to satisfy this aim. Consider the target markets. Would they change (for example the first-time traveller to Britain might not be targeted for trips to other cities)? Would different methods be used for the three different plans?

d) The assumption stated in the question does *not* mean that this is the best plan or the one that should be recommended. It has merely been selected so that the examiner has a peg to hang a particular question on! Think about the clients – elderly and rich. The comfort of travel and accommodation, good guides and interesting visits are important. How could this be guaranteed? Are ideas like TQM and benchmarking relevant? What are the consequences for their main product if quality is not up to standard on the new one?

e) Are there any new ideas which might work in the US market? Would direct selling be a good idea? Could videos be used? Could individual packages and flexibility be promoted? Always bear in mind the target market and the need for cost-effectiveness.

Now, here is an ordinary data response question.

2 Warren and Matthews is a long-established partnership, trading as builders' merchants. It supplies materials to firms in the building trade, having a regular clientele of about 20 small building firms in the area. Both Warren and Matthews are in their late 50s and wish to reduce their commitment in preparation for selling the business and retiring, but at the moment they consider themselves overworked. This is partly because of their inability to find a new stores manager to replace Ted Bates, who recently retired after many years' valuable service, and partly because of the high turnover of labour in the firm and the need to employ several part-time workers.

In recent years both the turnover and the profits of Warren and Matthews have declined as larger firms with the advantages of economies of scale have come to dominate the market. In addition, there has been a rising number of complaints from customers concerning the quality of some of the materials and about some items not being in stock, causing delays in delivery. Warren and Matthews has always tried to hold sufficient items of the basic items of stock, relying on long-established good relations with its suppliers, both for quick delivery of the less usual items and also for replenishment of its more popular materials. Recently, however, the suppliers have appeared to make mistakes (which they have vehemently denied), sending incorrect items to Warren and Matthews, and causing shortages and stock outs to occur. These problems had never seemed to happen when Ted Bates was in charge or ordering.

a) Explain, with examples, how lack of economies of scale may handicap Warren and Matthews.(**8 marks**)

b) Analyse the possible causes of Warren and Matthews's recent problems concerned with the quality and quantity of their stocks. (**12 marks**)

c) Recommend measures which Warren and Matthews could take which might help them to overcome the firm's problems. (**20 marks**)

Hints for answering

a) This is a Level 2 question, where marks will be awarded for explaining and illustrating economies of scale and for applying them to the context (for example bulk buying, larger and well-trained workforce, wider range of stocks, financial economies).

b) There are several reasons which might apply, such as the workload of the partners, the lack of forecasting and planning, or problems at the suppliers' end. How predictable would the demands of Warren and Matthews' customers?

c) This carries half the marks for the whole question and therefore needs a thorough Level 4 approach, so ideas must be realistic and cost-effective. There are several problems to consider. Areas to examine include training for quality (note the profile of the workforce given in the data), stock control theory (usage, buffers, lead times, relations with suppliers [are *they* having staff problems?], JIT and JIC), and methods of competing with larger firms through the marketing mix.

And now, here is another short case study for you to try (no hints this time!).

3 Barlow's Biscuits Ltd produces a range of biscuits. There are four main varieties in its portfolio. The nutty slice is the firm's oldest product, but its popularity has decreased and it is now bringing in little profit. The chocolate delight is the major money-spinner, having been popular for many years. Sales of the jam whirl are growing rapidly, with increasing orders being received monthly. The cream crunchie is the newest product, introduced six months ago after a great deal of research of both product and market. Barlow's Biscuits Ltd has high hopes for this product, despite the fact that there have been a few minor problems in its initial production. The biscuits are sold in packets of four, six and ten, and assortments are also made up into tins, incorporating six other products in the firm's portfolio, these being manufactured solely for the purpose of adding variety to the tins of assorted biscuits.

The products are made on a batch production basis. The firm tries to allocate a certain day for the production of a specific variety, but this is not always possible. Sales of the nutty slice no longer require such regular production, whereas the jam whirl has had to have extra production runs devoted to it recently. Batches are arranged so that cleaning time can be allocated for some of the machinery while other processes are going on, but this coordination does not always occur and there can be both bottlenecks in production and periods when resources are not fully or efficiently utilised. This occurs especially when extra production runs of unscheduled varieties have to be made because of large or unexpected orders.

Stock control is also difficult. Because of the inability to forecast and plan production with complete accuracy, an experiment with JIT stock ordering had to be abandoned. In any case, the firm has several different suppliers for the different ingredients used, some of which have a comparatively short shelf life.

Quality is controlled by an end-of-line inspection process, which visually checks the product and samples 0.5 per cent. Recently, the number of rejects found has risen from an average of 1 per cent to 1.5 per cent, with as much as 3 per cent of the cream crunchies found to be faulty. Some of the experienced employees, who have worked for the company for many years and show a definite pride in their work, have complained that there is a flaw in the recipe for this product, causing the ingredients to become overheated if the process is not tightly controlled. They claim that some of the newer operators do not take sufficient care. Some of the ingredients also seemed not to be of the required quality, or had not been stored in the appropriate conditions.

The products are distributed to wholesalers. Most of the feedback which the company receives about the market comes from these wholesalers. However, Barlow's Biscuits Ltd has been approached by a supermarket chain, enquiring whether it would be interested in negotiating a contract for one year to produce an 'own label' biscuit assortment. The company would deal directly with the supermarket for this contract, but there is some concern about whether it could cope with this new demand, which could be quite large, without putting at risk the business's core activities, or changing its production methods at some cost.

a) i) Draw a product life cycle diagram and insert in the appropriate places the firm's main four products. **(8 marks)**

ii) Recommend a suitable pricing policy for each of the four products mentioned. **(12 marks)**

b) Suggest changes which could be made to improve the quality problems of Barlow's Biscuits Ltd. **(20 marks)**

c) Evaluate the distribution policy of Barlow's Biscuits Ltd, justifying any alternatives you may suggest. **(16 marks)**

d) Assess, with reference both to the information given in the passage and anything else you would wish to know, whether Barlow's Biscuits Ltd should negotiate a contract with the supermarket for the manufacture of 'own label' biscuits. **(24 marks)**

UNIT 3 FINANCIAL MANAGEMENT

INTRODUCTION   We only have to look in the financial pages of any newspaper to see the extent to which external confidence in the management of any large business organisation is determined by its financial performance. Shareholders and other external stakeholders keenly await information about the financial performance of a business.

This unit will introduce you to:

1   the structure and use of accounting and financial information as an aid to financial management and decision-making.

By the end of the unit, you should be able to:

1   analyse the profitability and liquidity of a business by interpretation and analysis of financial and accounting data
2   assess how this position may have arisen
3   understand budgeting and break-even analysis.

SECTION A *Financial accounts*

INTRODUCTION   Every business has to meet internal and external reporting requirements, to show its financial health and to meet legal and other requirements. This section looks at the various needs of users of accounts, focusing on the information they require about the financial performance of a business organisation. These users include internal users of information such as managers and other employees, as well as external users such as shareholders and creditors. Financial information will serve a variety of different purposes for each of these users, depending upon their different needs.

Critical thinking

At one stage or other all businesses started on a very small scale. When Richard Branson started Virgin or Anita Roddick started The Body Shop, each had to think carefully about the financial needs of the organisation, as well as about how to use various snippets of information from their finances as and when those became available. Running a business is more than just recording what comes in and then paying for goods and services from this pot of money. For example, with so much of the information coming from documentary records such as invoices, cheques, paying-in slips and credit notes, business people have to think carefully about what all the information generated by such paperwork means for their businesses.

WHAT DO YOU THINK?
1 If you were in a position of starting your own business, what financial information would you consider to be:
  a) the *most* important?
  b) the *least* important?
2 Explain how you would deal with much of the financial information you would be generating.
3 Assuming that the business would be likely to remain small in the near future, how would you organise your paperwork and finances?
4 What help might you look for?
5 As the business began to grow, how would you further develop the methods you use for looking after your finances?

Chapter 53 Use of accounts

Where businesses do well, there are many rewards and benefits for the individuals and organisations affected by their actions. On the other hand, if businesses perform poorly, there is a similar knock-on effect, with a range of consequences for both individuals and organisations.

For example, the downturn in the fortunes of high street retailer Marks & Spencer saw an increase in the amount of stock it bought from overseas suppliers. This had a dramatic effect upon many businesses within the UK who had developed 'under the wing' of the company and had come to depend upon its business over many years.

Accounting and financial records for users of financial information

In order to make judgements about business activities, individuals require accounting information from an accounting system. **Accounting** acts as an information system by processing business data so that those parties either interested in or affected by the business can be provided with the means to find out how well or badly the organisation is performing (see Figure 3.1).

Business data are the inputs for the accounting system. The output is financial information. Financial information can then be fed to those who require such information.

Accounting information

Accounting information may be used both within and outside an organisation. It involves providing important data which may form the basis for decisions to be made. In order to clarify what we mean by accounting information, it is perhaps best to explain what we mean by accounting.

Accounting is concerned with identifying, measuring, recording and reporting information relating to the activities of an organisation:

- **Identifying information** – this involves capturing all of the financial data within a business related to how it is performing. For example, this would include all information about the sales of goods to customers, data about the payment of expenses such as wages and rent and also information about the purchase of any stock, as well as data concerning the purchase of new vehicles and machinery.
- **Measuring information** – money, in the form of pounds and pence, is used as the form of measurement of economic transactions. In the future, the form of measurement might change to become euros, the European Union single currency. For accounting purposes, instead of saying that a business had sold ten cars in a week, which would be meaningless unless you knew the value of the cars, it would be more useful to specify the value of the cars. For example, ten cars valued at £15,000 per car would mean a turnover during the week of £150,000.
- **Recording information** – accounting data and information must be recorded either into hand-written accounting books or upon a suitable computer package such as a specialised accounting package or a spreadsheet.
- **Communicating information** – the reporting of financial information may take a variety of different forms. For example, although some financial information may be required and extracted from the accounts weekly, such as sales totals, there are standard financial statements such as profit and loss accounts and balance sheets which have a set format for reporting the activities of organisations.

It is important that throughout the accounting process accounting information is:

- **reliable** – free from errors and bias
- **comparable** – accounting information should be comparable with information from other organisations
- **relevant** – accounting information should relate to many of the decisions which have to be made about the business

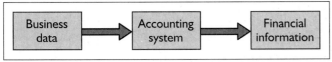

Figure 3.1 The transformation of business data into financial information

Table 3.1 The differences between financial and management accounting

Financial accounting	Management accounting
Subject to accounting regulations to ensure that reports/statements follow a standard approach	Reports are only for internal use so no restrictions are necessary
Provide a broad overview of the whole business using totals	Information extracted relates to parts of the organisation where it is used to help with a particular decision
Provides information up to a particular date	Will look at future performance as well as at past performance
Produces general statements and reports	Produces reports with a specific decision in mind
Quantifies information in monetary terms and values	May have non-financial information such as stocks

- **understandable** – information should be capable of being understood by those at whom it is targeted.

Financial and management accounting

The process of accounting can be divided into two broad areas:

- **Financial accounting** is concerned with the recording of financial transactions and the preparation of financial reports to communicate past financial performance.
- **Management accounting** involves looking to the future, using a knowledge of past performance where relevant to aid the management of the business.

A number of distinctions can be drawn between these two areas (see Table 3.1).

WHAT DO YOU THINK?
Which of the following would fall into the realms of financial accounting, and which would be management accounting?

a) Recording transactions from source documentation.
b) Calculating what the profit is likely to be over a range of outputs for the launch of a new product.
c) Producing financial statements to show what has happened to the business during the past year.
d) Advising a business upon its tax liability.
e) Creating a budgetary system to improve control over the costs within a business.
f) Setting the prices of products or services.

Critical thinking

It has been said that the number of accountants is increasing so rapidly that by the end of the twenty-first century the entire nation will be accountants! Have we become an accountancy-obsessed country? In order to become a qualified accountant, a person must have passed rigorous examinations to become a full member of one of the following accounting bodies:

- the Institute of Chartered Accountants in England and Wales (ICAEW)
- the Institute of Chartered Accountants in Ireland (ICAI)
- the Institute of Chartered Accountants in Scotland (ICAS)
- the Association of Chartered Certified Accountants (ACCA)
- the Chartered Institute of Management Accountants (CIMA)
- the Chartered Institute of Public Finance and Accountancy (CIPFA).

Users of financial information

All businesses differ in one way or another. Some may be very small, such as the 'corner shop' serving a local community as a newsagent, sub-post office and a place to purchase essential groceries. Others may be multinationals which include famous brand names and operate all over the world. As a result, many of these types of business will have different legal structures, with different types of people interested in the sorts of financial information that they generate.

What is **financial information**? For you, it might be your income from a Saturday job, the cost of your bus fares

The ICAEW is the largest professional accountancy body in Europe, and its qualification allows members to call themselves chartered accountants and use the designatory letters ACA or FCA. It is recognised all over the world as a prestigious qualification.

Established by Royal Charter in 1880, the ICAEW today has a membership of over 115,000 worldwide. Around half of its members are employed in industry, finance and commerce, with the other half employed in the 'profession' in firms of auditors such as Deloitte & Touche and PriceWaterhouse Coopers.

Over recent decades the range of professional activities carried out by chartered accountants has expanded to include financial reporting, taxation, personal finance, corporate finance, financial management and information technology.

Accountants undergo lengthy and rigorous training and must pass examinations to qualify for membership of the ICAEW. They are also required to maintain high standards of professional conduct and competence.

The Research Board of the ICAEW is the largest private sector sponsor of accountancy research in the UK. As part of its role it commissions papers for publication and supports conferences on a wide range of accountancy issues.

One of the key areas of the ICAEW is practice regulation. Although it has always given guidance to members on ethical matters and dealt with complaints about members through its professional conduct system, since the mid-1980s the ICAEW has regulated and monitored its members' activities in the areas of investment advice and insolvency licensing.

Twenty-two district society offices provide member support, and the ICAEW's technical enquiry line receives 20,000 individual requests for advice each year. Newsletters and a range of activities are also tailored to the interests of members.

QUESTIONS FOR DISCUSSION

1 Why do 'accountants' need to be members of a professional body?
2 Describe the main purpose of the Institute of Chartered Accountants.
3 How does the ICAEW support its members?

For more information on the ICAEW, visit its web site: www.icaew.co.uk/

---

and telephone calls and the purchase price of a car you may wish to buy. If you were then asked to describe financial information from a business, it is not vastly different. You might talk about **profits**, **sales**, **costs**, accounting statements such as **balance sheets** and **profit and loss accounts** or simply the **cash** within a business. These different examples of financial information help to show that financial information includes *any information on activities within a business that are expressed in some form of monetary term.*

There are many different stakeholders both within and outside a business organisation who will have their own needs and requirements as users of accounting information (see Figure 3.2). It is easy to understand that within a business financial information is required for record-keeping and decision making purposes. This is important as accounting information is useful for those who need to make decisions within a business. It is also easy to understand that owners of a business, particularly if they take little active part in running it, are going to want information about how the organisation is performing so that they can monitor their investment.

However, there are other less obvious parties who are interested in financial information. For example, in the town of Barnard Castle in County Durham, there is a large Glaxo Wellcome factory. The pharmaceuticals company employs many people from the local community and is the largest employer not just in that town, but also in that part of

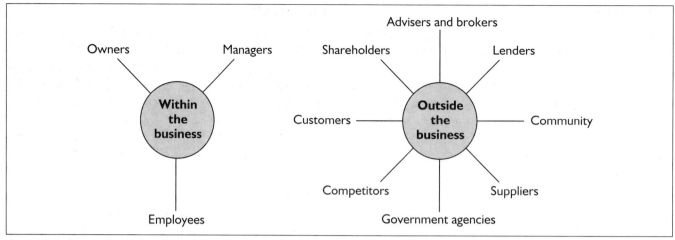

Figure 3.2 *Internal and external stakeholders to a business*

County Durham. There are many associated businesses locally that rely on this factory, and, if it ever closed, it would be a huge loss to residents in the town. Local residents and the community therefore rely upon the success of this factory and the improving position of Glaxo Wellcome in the world pharmaceuticals market. There are therefore many individuals and businesses in County Durham who are interested in the financial information made public by this organisation.

Owners/shareholders

The interests and priorities of business owners are varied. Sole traders and partners are more likely to be involved in the daily management of the business and act as internal stakeholders. In many ways, their interests may be more akin to those of an employee. As these people know the business intimately, they will probably rely less on a formal reporting system to know how well the business is doing.

Though the concerns of shareholders who take little or no active part in a business are less 'hands-on' than those of more traditional owners, there are concerns which are universal to all business owners, even if they do not possess informal information channels. For example, they will require information concerning:

- **profitability** – whether the business makes efficient use of resources to provide the desired financial return
- **liquidity** – whether the business has the ability to generate cash to ensure continued trading and to make dividend payments
- **state of financial affairs** – the nature of the business's assets and liabilities

- **financial structure** – the nature and value of the business's loans in relation to the amount invested by the owners
- **future prospects** – an evaluation of the business's future prospects, having regard to the firm's external environment and its adaptability to change.

Managers

Every level of management, from junior managers to directors, will be concerned about the performance of the organisation, and will have a particular interest in information relating to their own responsibility, such as management accounting information, which will help them to improve their decision making capabilities and run their part of the business more efficiently. Financial information is important for the effective management of a business. Information concerning the recent past can be used to monitor and control operations, and financial projections are a vital component of decision making.

WHAT DO YOU THINK?
Choose one of the following roles:

- chief executive
- marketing director
- personnel manager
- purchasing manager
- production director.

Make a list of ten types of financial information that the person in your chosen role might require. Briefly explain in each instance how they might use that information.

Employees

Employees will be concerned with job security as well as how the business is going to develop, so that they can ascertain whether there are opportunities for promotion. Important sources of information for individual employees, as well as employee groups such as trade unions, will be financial reports that may have been published for public consumption or be part of employee packs or information. Employees will also want to know about the business's financial solvency so that they can support their wage claims.

Advisers and brokers

Advisers and brokers may require the same sort of information as owners, particularly if they are stockbrokers advising their clients about the nature of their investments. Business analysts may require further information about company performance, so that they can advise their clients accurately.

Lenders

The primary concern of lenders such as the financial institutions is the ability of the organisation to pay interest and make repayments on the loans advanced. Although the information needs of lenders will be similar to those of owners, they will be particularly interested in cash flow, the assets the business owns and its ability to pay its debts.

Customers

Customers want to know that their supplies are secure, not just in the short term but also in the future. This is particularly important when customers want to develop long-term trading relationships with their suppliers. They may also be interested in the size of the profits their suppliers are making. Large profits would be an example of market exploitation. Consumer groups and industry watchdogs may analyse financial information on behalf of customers.

Community

Areas depend upon the success of local businesses. If a business is doing well, it is helping the local community to prosper not simply by providing employment but also by paying wages to people who then spend money in the community which, in turn, provides employment for others. Many organisations also become involved in a wide range of community projects. Individuals living close to a business may also be interested in the impact of an organisation's activities upon the environment.

Competitors

Competitors will be interested in the activities of other organisations within their industry. Financial information from companies may be freely available. Other information may be published in the press or be available from data research agencies. Looking at the activities of competitors may help organisations to think ahead and fine-tune their own strategies.

The truth is stranger than fiction

The good news is that accounting firms within the UK are growing. The bad news is that the rate of growth has slowed down from an average of 14 per cent during 1999, to 11 per cent during 2000. The top five accounting firms in terms of size are PriceWaterhouse Coopers (PWC), KPMG, Ernst & Young, Deloitte & Touche and Arthur Andersen.

Chapter 54 *Capital and revenue expenditure*

When making purchases it is important for a business to distinguish between the sorts of spending. For accounting purposes there are two forms of expenditure:

- **capital expenditure**
- **revenue expenditure**.

Capital expenditure is incurred to purchase fairly permanent resources that are required to carry on a business. Examples include property, machinery, motor vehicles, furniture and computer equipment. These items are also called **fixed assets** and would normally last for more than one year.

Revenue expenditure includes all amounts paid in the day-to-day operation of a business. This includes wages, purchases of stock and payment of expenses such as electricity, advertising and repairs. Table 3.2 shows how capital and revenue expenditure differ.

> **WHAT DO YOU THINK?**
> Classify the following items of expenditure into capital and revenue expenditure:
>
> **a)** a computer purchased for use in the business
> **b)** a computer purchased by a computer retailer for resale
> **c)** a garage purchasing a car for resale
> **d** an office extension
> **e)** office redecoration
> **f)** insurance for a motor vehicle
> **g)** carpet for an office.

Table 3.2 *The differences between capital and revenue expenditure*

Item	Capital expenditure	Revenue expenditure
Property	To buy land and buildings	To pay rent and rates
Building work	To improve the building, for example alterations and extensions	To maintain the building in good order, for example redecoration
Goods bought for resale to customers	No	Yes
Equipment, motor vehicles, furniture, fixtures and fittings used in the business	Purchase price, delivery and installation	Running costs – power and maintenance
Marketing and selling costs	Only for fixed assets used, for example delivery vehicles and office equipment	All other expenditure
Management and administration	Only for fixed assets used, for example office equipment	All other expenditure

CASE STUDY: ARK GEOPHYSICS

When Ark Geophysics, a software company in the geophysics industry, was first established, its founders Richard Gleave, Kitty Hall and Andy McGrandle had to ask themselves a lot of questions:

- What equipment would they need?
- Would there be enough work to generate the income they required?
- Could they meet a repayment schedule?
- How would they be affected by their competitors?
- What were their financial needs?

They began by carefully researching their revenue expenditure, that is, the day-to-day running expenses of their business, such as rent, office expenses, electricity, telephone, etc. They also looked at their capital expenditure on large or fixed items such as computers and office equipment. They tried to work out what they would have to pay out and when their income would next come in. Then they drew up projections of cash flow in a business plan. This outlined how their proposals would work. It was shown to several banks. Soon they were being offered finance from a variety of sources. This process of planning had helped the business to 'start up'. Today, Ark Geophysics is a successful company.

Financial planning

Every business requires some form of **financial plan**. In the short term, it may simply want to pay its suppliers or decorate the office, but in the long term financial planning should:

- provide an opportunity to examine the objectives of an organisation

- provide long-term direction which enables managers to focus beyond current issues
- provide a framework upon which budgeting decisions can be made
- enable long-term decisions to be made about investments and borrowing
- establish a benchmark of success against which performance can be monitored and controlled.

The financial planning process is shown in Figure 3.3.

The problem with planning, however, is that the process can be time consuming and there may be a failure to respond to unforeseen circumstances which have not been included in the plan.

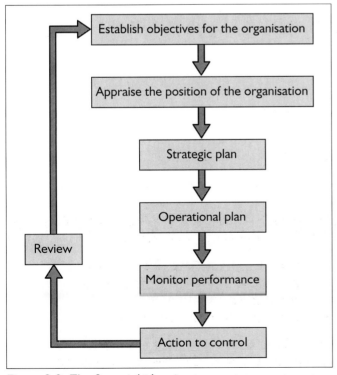

Figure 3.3 The financial planning process

CASE STUDY: A CHANGING INDUSTRY

In the new millennium, public houses are having to change or gradually die. This is happening at a time when regulators are dismantling old brewery empires to allow greater competition. But while many large operators are sprucing up The George & Dragon or The Red Lion, new operators have become increasingly popular with different groups of customers.

Surrey Free Inns has created a chain of concept superpubs called the Litton Tree. These use town-centre sites vacated by retailers who have headed for the out-of-town retail parks. The Litton Tree pubs are large and appeal to a wide range of clientele depending on the time of day. During the day the pubs offer food and drink to town-centre workers and shoppers, while at night the young flock there because of the entertainment and music.

A slightly better established newcomer is J D Wetherspoon, which converts well-positioned properties such as old banks into pubs. Another operator, Regent Inns, has gone public and quickly spread its format from its London base into the Midlands and the north of England. Its formula is for large outlets where young singles like to meet and drink. Irish pubs have also developed, with successful brands such as O'Neills, and town and city centres have seen the birth and development of wine and café bars. With the spit and sawdust image rapidly disappearing, the industry is having to respond to higher customer expectations.

QUESTIONS FOR DISCUSSION

1 What are the main external influences that have caused the changes to the pubs sector?
2 Describe the pubs that are flourishing within your area.
3 What strategic initiatives are likely to be required by pub operators over the next few years?
4 What are the variables that might influence any forecasting for pubs?
5 How difficult is it to develop a financial plan as a pub operator?
6 What should a financial plan include?

The truth is stranger than fiction

Goodbye Humber Bridge ... welcome the debt-free Millennium Bridge. For the 'Golden Gate of Europe' is set to be renamed to coincide with an ambitious project to light it at night as part of a national initiative to push and promote Great Britain.

The Prime Minister Tony Blair is anxious that all ports and points of entry into this country 'make a statement for Britain' and be 'a positive experience' for foreign visitors. As a result, the dawn of the new century is set to start with good tidings for the city and the whole of East Yorkshire.

The new Millennium Bridge will be lit at night thanks to a unique partnership between business leaders and local government. The old Humber Bridge's massive debt will be wiped away and a new package to relaunch the finances will be announced. Talks will be held shortly with a self-made city millionaire who wishes to contribute a six-figure sum to the project.

The City, East Riding and neighbouring authorities on the South Bank aim to use the Millennium Bridge as a high profile brand to identify and market the region. A Bridge Board source said: 'For years the Humber Bridge has suffered from a negative image – a white elephant tag. The new name, high profile and cathedral-style lighting will take us into the new Millennium with style. The Humber Bridge's enormous debt is more than £400 million and there had been genuine concern the huge costs may fall on local council tax payers.'

Chapter 55 *Depreciation*

Fixed assets or the long-term assets owned by a business such as machinery and office equipment are acquired in order to earn profits. But although their use is not limited to a single accounting period, they do not last forever. Most businesses have expectations about the future lifetime of their assets. They will wish to show a true asset value in the balance sheet and to charge the cost of its depreciation to the profit and loss account.

Depreciation may be defined as:

'the measure of the wearing out, consumption or other reduction in the useful life of a fixed asset, whether arising from use, time or obsolescence through technological or market changes'.

There are a number of different methods of allowing for depreciation. The most common are:

- the **straight-line** method
- the **reducing balance** method
- the **machine hour** method
- the **sum-of-the-digits** method.

Straight-line method

The most frequently used method is the straight-line or equal-instalment method of depreciation. This charges an equal amount of depreciation to each accounting period for the life of an asset. The instalment is calculated by the following formula:

$$\text{Depreciation} = \frac{\text{Cost of asset} - \text{Residual value}}{\text{Expected useful life of asset}} .$$

For example, a machine which is expected to last five years costs £20,000; at the end of that time its **residual value** will be £5,000.

$$\text{Depreciation charge} = \frac{£20,000 - £5,000}{5 \text{ years}}$$

$$= £3,000.$$

	Year 1 £	Year 2 £	Year 3 £	Year 4 £	Year 5 £
Cost	20,000	20,000	20,000	20,000	20,000
Accumulated depreciation	3,000	6,000	9,000	12,000	15,000
Net book value	17,000	14,000	11,000	8,000	5,000

Reducing balance method

The reducing balance method calculates the depreciation charge as a fixed percentage of **net book value** from the previous period. This method allocates higher depreciation costs to the earlier years of an asset. It can be argued that this system is more realistic, as it caters for the increased expense of repairs and running costs as machinery becomes older.

For example, a machine is purchased by a business for £20,000 and its expected useful life is three years. The business anticipates a residual value of £4,320 and thus wishes to depreciate it at 40 per cent.

	£	Accumulated depreciation £
Machine at cost	20,000	
Depreciation Year 1	8,000	8,000
Net book value	12,000	
Depreciation Year 2	4,800	12,800
Net book value	7,200	
Depreciation Year 3	2,880	15,680
Residual value	4,320	

Machine hour method

The machine hour method relates depreciation to use rather than time; therefore depreciation is calculated on the basis of the number of hours a machine has been worked. The depreciation charge per hour is calculated as follows:

$$\text{Depreciation charge per hour} = \frac{\text{Cost of asset} - \text{Residual value}}{\text{Expected lifetime of asset in machine hours}} .$$

For example, a machine is purchased for £34,000 with an estimated life of 10,000 machine hours and a residual value of £4,000. The depreciation rate would be:

$$\frac{34,000 - 4,000}{10,000} = £3 \text{ per machine hour.}$$

Therefore, if the machine was used for 2,000 hours in Year 1, 3,000 hours in Year 2 and 1,000 hours in Year 3, depreciation would be charged as follows:

	Depreciation charge £	Accumulated depreciation £	Cost of asset £	Net book value £
Year 1: 2000 × £3	6,000	6,000	34,000	28,000
Year 2: 3,000 × £3	9,000	15,000	34,000	19,000
Year 3: 1,000 × £3	3,000	18,000	34,000	16,000

Sum-of-the-digits method

The sum-of-the-digits method is similar to the reducing balance method in that higher levels of depreciation are charged in earlier years. However, it uses digits rather than percentages as a simplified way of working out the depreciation charge. Digits are allocated in a descending order to each year of the life of an asset and a charge is worked out for each digit used.

For example, a machine is purchased for £15,000 and is expected to last for three years, after which it will be sold for £3,000:

Year	Digits
1	3
2	2
3	1

Sum-of-the-digits = 6.

A weighted charge is then calculated as follows:

$$\frac{\text{Cost of asset} - \text{Residual value}}{\text{Sum-of-the-digits}} = \frac{15,000 - 3,000}{6}$$

$$= £2,000 \text{ per digit.}$$

	Digits	Depreciation charge £	Accumulated depreciation £
Year 1	3 × 2,000	6,000	6,000
Year 2	2 × 2,000	4,000	10,000
Year 3	1 × 2,000	2,000	12,000

CASE STUDY: DEPRECIATION SOLUTION

Depreciation Solution is software designed for businesses to provide them with fixed asset management. Depreciation Solution provides the users with unprecedented flexibility in managing assets with extensive calculation capabilities.

Whether it is being used by a practising accountant with many clients or a corporate accountant managing assets for a business, Depreciation Solution turns the tedious and time-consuming task of fixed asset management into an efficient and organised process.

Powerful asset sorting capabilities allow the way asset data is presented to be customised specifically to meet asset management needs – in an instant. Virtually every component of depreciation information is available for use as sorting criteria, and columns can be arranged in the order required.

Depreciation Solution's versatile report writing capabilities mean that the user can meet any depreciation reporting need.

QUESTIONS FOR DISCUSSION

1 What are the benefits of using software to calculate and manage an organisation's fixed assets?
2 How might Depreciation Solution be used?

WHAT DO YOU THINK?

Bognor Regis, a car hire business, purchases new cars which they keep for four years before selling. Second-hand vehicles fetch around a quarter of their new price. In 1999, 2000 and 2001, the company buys six vehicles at £18,000 each. Choose a method of depreciation and show how these cars will depreciate during their life span.

The truth is stranger than fiction

It is now possible to get your vehicle depreciation calculated online. If you visit www.insidecentralflorida.com/shared/autos/calculators/depreciation.html, the site will automatically work out, on the basis of the cost of the vehicle and the expected period that you will own it for, how much depreciation you will lose each year.

Chapter 56 *Profit and loss account*

Final accounts

A business's **final accounts** are usually produced once a year by a firm of outside auditors or accountants. As well as helping the owners of a business to revise and fine tune their business strategies, final accounts provide a broad picture of how an organisation is performing and may be presented to the Inland Revenue and lenders of money such as banks. Final accounts comprise the financial documents shown in Figure 3.4.

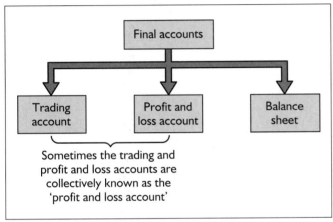

Figure 3.4 Constructing final accounts

Critical thinking

In complete contrast to the term 'knowledge-based' economy, it is sometimes said that we generate far too much information to be able to use it. For example, if the decision makers in a business have an excessive quantity of data to consider, this might delay the decision making process and also hinder them in making critical choices between alternatives. What sort of information generated by an accountant might (a) help and (b) hinder decision making processes?

The trading account

As the **trading account** is usually linked together with the **profit and loss account**, with the trading account appearing above, they are sometimes collectively called the profit and loss account.

The trading account can be likened to a video giving ongoing pictures of an organisation's trading activities. For many business organisations, trading involves buying and selling stock. The difference between the value of the stock sold (sales) and the cost of producing those sales – which may be the production costs of manufactured goods for a manufacturing company, or the cost of purchasing the supplies for a trading company – is known as the **gross profit**.

The trading account simply shows how gross profit is arrived at, that is:

Net sales – Cost of sales = Gross profit.

The trading account includes only the items in which an organisation *trades*. For example, if a small supermarket buys tins of baked beans and sells them to its customers, then the cost of purchasing these and the amounts received from selling them will appear in the trading account. However, if the supermarket's owner decided to sell the business's van, this would not be included in the trading account as he or she is not in the second-hand vehicle business.

1 **Sales** are often described as **turnover**. Sometimes goods which have been sold are returned inwards as **sales returns**. Obviously, these should not be included in the sales figures because they have come back to the business. Net sales, which are the final sales figure, are therefore:

Sales – Returns inwards (Sales returns) = Net sales.

2 As with sales, some **purchases** may have been returned, but in this instance the returns will have been outwards (as **purchases returns**). Purchases may also include the cost of transporting the goods to the organisation, which must be added to the cost of buying goods and is known as **carriage inwards**. Net purchases, where there is carriage inwards and purchases returns, could therefore be:

Purchases + Carriage inwards – Returns outwards (Purchases returns) = Net Purchases.

3 The final 'cost of sales' figure must take into account the value of **stocks**. **Opening stock** is effectively a purchase as this will be sold in the current trading period. On the other hand, **closing stock** must be deducted from the purchases as this will be sold next year.

4 The calculation for **cost of sales**, including a full set of adjustments to purchases and stocks, would therefore be:

The Trading Account of D Cork for the year ended 31 December 2000

	£	£	£
Sales			21,000
less Returns inwards			1,000
Net sales			20,000
Opening stock (1 January 2000)		4,500	
Purchases	12,100		
Carriage inwards	300		
	12,400		
less Returns outwards	500		
Net purchases		11,900	
		16,400	
less Closing stock (31 December 2000)		3,700	
Cost of sales			12,700
Gross profit			£7,300

Figure 3.5

Opening stock + Purchases + Carriage inwards – Returns outwards (Purchases returns) – Closing stock = Cost of sales.

All of the above are shown in the trading account illustrated in Figure 3.5.

WHAT DO YOU THINK?

Prepare accounts for each of the following sets of figures:

1 M. Atherton on 31 December 2000. His figures are as follows: closing stock £4,100; returns outwards £700; carriage inwards £400; purchases £15,300; returns inwards £500; opening stock £3,900; sales £34,800.

2 J. Gallian on 31 December 2000. Her figures are as follows: closing stock £3,200; returns outwards £550; carriage inwards £324; purchases £10,125; returns inwards £650; opening stock £4,789; sales £15,000.

Critical thinking

So far all of the organisations we have looked at have assumed that a gross profit is made. What would happen if the cost of sales was greater than the net sales figure?

The profit and loss account

The profit and loss account may be drawn up beneath the trading account, and covers the same period of trading. The gross profit (or gross loss) figure becomes the starting point for the profit and loss account.

Some organisations receive income from sources other than sales. These may be **rents** received, **commission** received or profits on the sales of **assets**. As these are extra income, they are added to the gross profit.

In addition, every organisation incurs **expenses** and a range of **overheads**, and these are deducted to show the true **net profit** (or **loss**) of the business. These expenses might, for example, include:

- rent of premises
- carriage outwards
- discount allowed
- gas
- electricity
- stationery
- cleaning costs
- insurances
- business rates
- depreciation
- bad debts
- interest on loans
- sundry expenses
- motor expenses
- accountancy and legal fees.

Net profit = Gross profit + income from other sources – expenses.

Net profit is the final profit in the business and will belong to the owner (see Figure 3.6).

It is important to note that trading accounts will only apply to organisations that *trade* in goods or that are involved in the process of manufacturing. Service sector businesses such as a dentist, an estate agent or a solicitor will not require a trading account because they are not

The Trading and Profit and Loss Account of D Cork for the year ended 31 December 2000

	£	£	£
Sales			21,000
less Returns inwards			1,000
Net sales			20,000
Opening stock (1 January 2000)		4,500	
Purchases	12,100		
Carriage inwards	300		
	12,400		
less Returns outwards	500		
Net purchases		11,900	
		16,400	
less Closing stock (31 December 2000)		3,700	
Cost of sales			12,700
Gross profit			7,300
add other income:			
Discount received			2,000
			9,300
less expenses:			
Electricity		510	
Stationery		125	
Business rate		756	
Interest on loans		159	
Advertising		745	
Depreciation – motor vehicles		1,000	
Insurances		545	
Sundry expenses		124	
Total expenses			3,964
Net profit			**£5,336**

Figure 3.6

The Profit and Loss Account of U Afzaal for the year ended 31 December 2000

	£	£
Income from clients		4,100
add other income:		
Rent received		1,400
		5,500
less expenses:		
Electricity	412	
Insurances	124	
Sundry expenses	415	
Travel expenses	147	1,098
Net profit		**£4,402**

Figure 3.7

buying and selling goods. Instead, their final accounts will consist simply of a profit and loss account and a balance sheet. Instead of starting with gross profit, their profit and loss account will start by listing the various forms of income such as fees received (see Figure 3.7).

The truth is stranger than fiction

The Ohio State University has an Accounting Hall of Fame. Established in 1950, its purpose is to honour accountants who have made significant contributions to the advancement of accounting since the beginning of the twentieth century. The names of the elected persons are inscribed on a scroll, and a photographic portrait of each person elected, together with the citation, are permanently displayed in the corridors of the Fisher College of Business.

Chapter 57 *Balance sheets*

Whereas the trading account provides an ongoing picture, a **balance sheet** is a snapshot of what an organisation owns and owes on a particular date. A balance sheet is a clear statement of the **assets**, **liabilities** and **capital** of a business at a particular moment in time (normally at the end of an **accounting period**, for example a quarter, a year, etc.).

Looking at the balance sheet can thus provide valuable information because it summarises a business's financial position at that instant in time.

Critical thinking

Surely people in business would know what they own and what they owe? So, why would they need a balance sheet? To whom might they show the balance sheet, and how might they use it as part of running the business?

The balance sheet 'balances' because the accounts record every transaction twice. For example, if you lend me £100

we can say that:

- I owe you £100 (a liability or debt)
- I now have £100 (an asset, something I own).

There is thus a dual nature to every transaction, which in its simplest terms shows what is added and what is subtracted as a result of every business transaction.

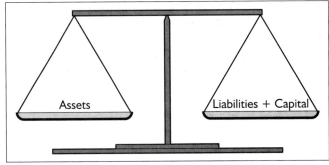

Figure 3.8 Calculating the balance sheet

Beavis Walker is a large firm of chartered accountants. Its expertise has become increasingly global as it takes on clients working in an international market place. The client profile of the firm includes listed companies, professional and other partnerships and small private companies, as well as sole traders and expanding businesses. The services provided by Beavis Walker include:

- accounting
- audit
- company secretarial
- tax advisory and consultancy
- tax compliance
- litigation support
- corporate finance
- corporate recovery
- special purpose
- other services.

For example, its accountancy services involve:

- advice on complex as well as simple accounting issues
- preparation of accounts in compliance with relevant requirements
- preparation of periodic management accounts
- preparation of trust accounts and pension scheme accounts
- advice and assistance on management information systems
- profit and loss, cash flow and balance sheet projections.

QUESTIONS FOR DISCUSSION

1 What problems might an accountant face when working with companies that are becoming increasingly global?
2 Why will the accounts for small businesses like sole traders, illustrated by the accounts within this chapter, differ from those for large businesses such as fully listed public companies?

Look at Figure 3.8. As you can see, a balance sheet is represented by a simple formula, which underlies all accounting activity.

At the end of a trading period a business will have a number of assets and liabilities. Some of these will be for short periods of time, while others will be for longer periods. Whatever the nature of the individual assets and liabilities, the balance sheet will balance.

WHAT DO YOU THINK?
Make a list of six probable assets and six probable liabilities of a corner shop. Do the same for a public house.

As you work through this section, look at the balance sheet illustrated in Figure 3.9.

Every balance sheet will have a heading, containing the name of the organisation as well as the date upon which the snapshot is taken.

The asset side of a balance sheet is normally set out in an **inverse order of liquidity**. This means that items that may be difficult to convert into cash quickly and are therefore the least liquid appear at the top of the list of assets. By looking down the order it is possible to gauge the ease with which successive assets can be converted to cash, until we come to the most liquid asset of all, cash itself.

The Balance Sheet of D Bicknell as at 31 December 2000

	£	£	£
Fixed assets			
Land and buildings			80,000
Machinery			13,200
Motor vehicles			8,700
			101,900
Current assets			
Stocks		9,700	
Debtors		3,750	
Bank		2,100	
Cash		970	
		16,520	
less **Current liabilities**			
Creditors	8,000		
Value added tax owing	1,000	9,000	
Working capital			7,520
			109,420
less **Long-term liabilities**			
Bank loan		9,000	
Mortgage		30,000	
			39,000
NET ASSETS			£70,420
Financed by:			
Capital			70,000
add Net profit			5,286
			75,286
less Drawings			4,866
			£70,420

Figure 3.9

Fixed and current assets

Assets can be divided into fixed assets and current assets.

Fixed assets tend to have a life-span of more than one year. They comprise items that are purchased and generally kept for a long period of time. Examples of fixed assets would be premises, machinery and motor vehicles. When a business buys fixed assets it does so by incurring capital expenditure.

Current assets are sometimes called 'circulating assets' because the form they take is constantly changing. Examples of current assets are stocks, debtors, money in the bank and cash in hand. For example, a business holds stocks of finished goods in readiness to satisfy the demands of the market. When a credit transaction takes place, stocks are reduced and the business gains debtors. These debtors have bought goods on credit and therefore owe the business money; after a reasonable credit period payment will be expected. Payments will have to be made on further stocks, so that the business has a cash cycle: 'cash' or 'bank' changes to 'stock', then to 'debtors', back to 'cash' or 'bank', and then to 'stock' again (see Figure 3.10).

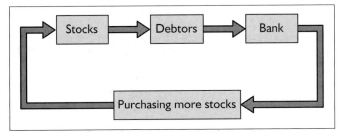

Figure 3.10 Current (circulating) assets

Current liabilities

Current liabilities are debts which a business needs to repay within a short period of time (normally a year). These liabilities include **creditors**, who are suppliers of goods on credit for which the business has been invoiced but not yet paid. They may also include a bank **overdraft** which is arranged up to a limit over a time period and is, technically, repayable on demand. Other current liabilities may include any short-term **loans** and any **taxes** owed (see Figure 3.9).

Working capital

The balance sheet is set out so as to show **working capital** because this is always an important calculation for an organisation, as it indicates how easily the business can pay its short-term debts. Working capital is the ratio of current assets to current liabilities and is shown as the formula:

Working capital ratio = Current assets : Current liabilities.

It is important for an organisation to maintain a sensible ratio. The level of ratio depends on the type of business, and the likelihood that funds will be required quickly to meet liabilities (for example creditors demanding repayment quickly). For most businesses a ratio of 2:1 is regarded as a sign of careful management, but some businesses have lower ratios.

Working capital is important because it provides a buffer to 'keep the wolf from the door'. Many businesses have suffered the consequences of having too many of their assets tied up in liquid assets.

Long-term liabilities

A long-term liability is sometimes called a **deferred liability** as it is not due for payment until some time in the future. By convention, in a set of accounts this means longer than one year. Examples for a sole trader could include a **bank loan** or a **mortgage**.

Capital

As we saw earlier, **capital** is provided by the owner of the business and is therefore deemed to be owed to the owner by the business. The balance sheet keeps an updated record of the amount owed by the business to the owner.

During a year's trading the owner's capital may be increased by the inflows of **profits** (profits for the period) and decreased by outflows of **drawings** (money or other assets taken out of the business for personal use). Having taken these into consideration, a new capital figure is calculated at the end of the year. So the balance sheet shows how the capital has increased (or decreased!) since the last balance sheet was prepared.

Most sole traders employ an accountant to draw up their accounts. Nevertheless, whoever prepares the accounts, it is the sole trader who remains responsible for their

accuracy and for correctly declaring the amount of the profits. The tax authorities will need to be satisfied that the accounts supplied to them represent the true results of the business.

It is essential to keep full and accurate records from the day the business starts trading. Well-kept books make the preparation of the annual accounts easier, and save the accountant's time (so keeping down the fee charged).

In this chapter we only consider the accounts of a sole trader. In the next chapter, when we look at how to interpret financial information, we also look at the final accounts of limited companies.

WHAT DO YOU THINK?
From the trial balance of G. Archer shown in Figure 3.11, draw up the trading and profit and loss account for the year ended 31 December 2000, together with her balance sheet at that date. The closing stocks were valued at £10,300.

Trial balance of G. Archer as at 31 December 2000		
	£	£
Stock at Jan. 2000	12,700	
Sales		81,250
Purchases	18,325	
Electricity	1,451	
Stationery	1,526	
Business rate	1,845	
Loan interest	3,955	
Advertising	2,150	
Sundry expenses	1,205	
Land and buildings	161,000	
Machinery	4,900	
Motor vehicles	18,300	
Debtors	12,100	
Bank	4,250	
Cash	325	
Bank loan		10,000
Mortgage		20,000
Creditors		4,300
Drawings	9,350	
Capital at Jan. 2000		137,832
	253,382	253,382

Figure 3.11

The truth is stranger than fiction

There has always been pressure for accountants to engage in irregular accounting practices. According to an article by Lawrence Cunningham, a US professor of law, pressure upon accountants to use these is more critical in companies facing tougher competitive conditions.

Chapter 58 *Working capital management*

In the last chapter we saw that **working capital** is the difference between current assets and current liabilities. Current assets are either in the form of cash or in a form that can soon lead to cash, and current liabilities will soon have to be paid for with cash. A prudent ratio of current assets to current liabilities is considered to be 2:1, although most businesses operate with a slightly lower ratio than this. The working capital ratio will usually depend to some extent upon the type of business and the nature of its operations.

Working capital is often considered to be the portion of the capital that 'oils the wheels' of business. It provides the stocks from which the fixed assets help to produce the finished goods. It allows the salesforce to offer attractive credit and terms to customers, which creates debtors.

Organisations that do not have sufficient working capital lack the funds to buy stocks and to produce and create debtors.

The **operating cycle** expresses this connection between working capital and the movements of cash. It can measure the period of time between:

- the purchase of raw materials and the receipt of cash from debtors
- the time when cash is paid out for raw materials and the time when cash is received from sales (see Figure 3.12).

Example

A business buys raw materials on two months' credit and holds them in stock for two weeks before issuing them to the production department from which they emerge as finished goods. These are held on average for six weeks before sale. Debtors take three months to pay. The cash cycle would be:

	Months
Raw materials credit from suppliers	(2)
Turnover of stock of raw materials	0.5
Turnover of stock of finished goods	1.5
Debtors' payment period	3.0
Cash cycle	5.0

Not only does this cycle show the time ingredients; it also shows that income from debtors should be more than enough to cover any manufacturing costs and overheads encountered.

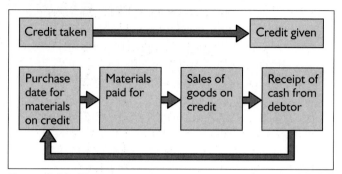

Figure 3.12 *The operating cycle*

> ### WHAT DO YOU THINK?
> 'Industry and commerce would rapidly come to a halt if goods could only be sold to buyers able to pay cash on delivery.' Discuss your thoughts about the degree of truth within this statement.

The dangers of insufficient working capital are therefore clear to see:

- A business with limited working capital will not be able to buy in bulk and could miss out on any opportunities to obtain trade discounts.
- Cash discounts will be lost as the business will avoid paying creditors until the last possible opportunity.
- It will become more difficult to offer extensive credit facilities for customers. By shortening the credit period, customers may well go to alternative suppliers.
- The business will be unable to innovate. Limited finances will hinder its ability to develop new products or improve production techniques.
- The business's financial reputation as a good payer may be lost.
- Creditors may well take action. As capital becomes squeezed, a business will be forced to finance its activities by overdrafts and trade credit. A point could well be reached where its future is dependent upon the actions of creditors.
- **Overtrading** could take place. This is where a larger volume or production of orders takes place, without sufficient working capital to support it. This then leads to a complete imbalance in the working capital ratio.

As a result of problems with working capital, there are a number of options. These may include the following:

- Reducing the period between the time cash is paid out for raw materials and the time cash is received from sales. This helps to provide funds for regeneration. However, although the improved efficiency of the cash cycle may improve working capital, actions taken may be unpopular with creditors.
- Fixed assets such as land and buildings may not be fully utilised, or space may be used for unprofitable purposes. Space could be rented, sold or allowed to house a more profitable operation so that cash flow could be improved. A business's cash flow might be improved by selling assets and leasing them back, although this may commit an organisation to heavy leasing fees.
- A company could review its stock levels to see if these could be the subject of economy measures. If the stock of raw materials is divided by the average weekly issue, the number of weeks' raw materials held in stock can be calculated. The problem with this is that the business might then lose out on trade discounts or have problems obtaining supplies.
- Many businesses employ a **credit controller** to help manage cash flow and control the debtors. A credit controller will vet new customers and set them a credit limit, ensure that credit limits are not exceeded and encourage debtors to pay on time. Credit controllers are often caught in a conflict with sales staff who wish to offer attractive credit terms and the accounts department which wants debtors to pay quickly and so increase the business's working capital.
- As we will see, the use of **cash budgets** can be an important control mechanism which can be used to predict the effects of future transactions on the cash balance of a company. Cash flow forecasting or cash budgeting can help an organisation to take actions to ensure that cash is available when required.
- A number of short-term solutions are available to increase working capital. Companies might extend their overdraft or bring in a **factoring company** to buy some of their debtors and provide them with instant finance. It might be possible to delay the payment of bills, although this obviously displeases creditors.

When a business can no longer pay its debts it may go into **liquidation.** This may be ordered by a court, usually on behalf of a creditor. This may then be followed by

CASE STUDY: DEVELOPING PROBLEMS

A petition for bankruptcy may be presented by:

- a creditor, either on his or her own or with other creditors, where £750 or more is owed
- the debtor
- the Official Petitioner, where a criminal bankruptcy has been made
- the supervisor of a debtor's Individual Voluntary Arrangement.

There are a number of grounds for the process to start, the main ones being that the debt is above the level of £750 and is unsecured and to be paid at some certain time. An Official Receiver is appointed to act as a trustee from the date of the bankruptcy order until a trustee takes control. The Receiver will then decide whether to call a creditors' meeting or appoint a licensed insolvency practitioner to act as trustee of the bankrupt estate. There are a number of offences associated with bankruptcy including:

- concealment of property
- concealment of papers
- false statements
- fraudulent disposal of property
- absconding
- fraudulent dealing with property on credit
- failure to keep proper accounts
- gambling.

QUESTIONS FOR DISCUSSION

1 Describe a situation in which a creditor might present a bankruptcy petition.
2 What is an Official Receiver, and what would he or she try to do?
3 Use an example to discuss why one of the restrictions listed above is placed upon bankrupt individuals.

receivership, where independent accountants supervise the sale of the different parts of the business. But sometimes, while the business is struggling to survive and meet the demands of creditors, a **white knight** appears on the scene to launch a rescue bid and save the business.

The truth is stranger than fiction

'He stood calmly at the entrance while the packed room fell silent. Over one hundred people had spotted the man who desired immortality but would compromise glorification. Tall, bronzed and immaculately dressed (bright blue suit, white shirt and dazzling red bow tie), Robert Maxwell, alias "the publisher", glanced at his watch to judge whether the precise moment had struck for his next public appearance.

'... Eight floors above hums the nucleus of a growing empire. Even higher, on an adjoining building, is a heliport for the publisher's favoured mode of transport to and from the capital. In the garage below is an immaculate Rolls-Royce. Sixty-four years earlier, the dollar billionaire was born into a community whose poverty and hardship would be unimaginable for those who were now witness to his ease amid wealth and power.' (Tom Bower, Maxwell: The Outsider, Viking, 1992)

Chapter 59 _Company accounts_

So far, our analysis of accounts has centred upon those of a sole trader. Before looking further at how to interpret and analyse financial information, we are going to look at another type of business organisation, that of a company. Accounts of a company are prepared on a similar basis as those for a sole trader, but there are some important differences in the appropriation of profit and in the organisation's capital structure.

As we have seen in earlier chapters, a limited company has:

- a legal identity separate from that of its owners
- owners who are known as shareholders, who have limited liability
- a management which is delegated to a board of directors, who may or may not be shareholders
- a commitment to pay Corporation tax on any profits made.

WHAT DO YOU THINK?

Why do these differences mean that company accounts have to be presented in a different way from those of a sole trader?

Companies must comply with the **Companies Acts**, and the **Companies Registration Office** controls their formation. There are two types of limited companies:

- **public**, which have their shares traded on the stock exchange
- **private**, for which there are restrictions on the trading in their shares.

To set up a limited company, it is necessary to go through a number of legal procedures. This mainly involves the presentation of various documents to the Registrar of Companies. All limited companies must produce a Memorandum of Association (see page 21) and Articles of Association (see page 22) to receive a Certificate of Incorporation.

Shares

There are a number of types of **securities**. These may include:

- **ordinary shares** – dividends/profits for these are normally expressed as a percentage of the nominal value of the shares or as a monetary value per share

- **preference shares** – these carry a preferential right to receive a dividend
- **debentures** – these are split into units in the same way as shares, but are in effect loans to the company which may be secured on specific assets.

The capital of a company is split into shares that are recorded at a **nominal value**. Nominal values might be at 5p, 10p, 25p, 50p or £1. For example, a company with 10,000 shares issued at a nominal value of £0.50 has a share capital of £5,000, and this would be disclosed in the capital section of the balance sheet. The difference between the **issue price** paid by the shareholder and the nominal value is the **share premium**.

Reserves

Limited companies rarely distribute all of their profits, a proportion of which are usually retained in the form of reserves. There are two forms of reserves:

- **Revenue reserves**. Sometimes known as **distributable reserves**, these are left as the balance of the 'profit and loss account' or 'retained profits'. To give shareholders confidence in the funding of the business, directors may decide to transfer some of the profit and loss account balance into a **general reserve**. In doing this, directors are communicating their intention not to use those funds for dividends. As this reserve is created out of distributable profits and can be used for dividends, it is still a revenue reserve.
- **Capital reserves**. These cannot be used to fund dividend payments. They may include **revaluation reserves** which occur when property is revalued and also share premium, the value of the higher amount than the nominal value.

The trading/profit and loss accounts

The trading account of a limited company is similar to the trading account of any other type of organisation. However, in the profit and loss account:

- directors' fees or salaries may be included, because these people are employed by the company and their fees and salaries are an expense
- debenture payments, being the same as loan interest, may also appear as an expense.

	£	£
Net profit		250,000
less Corporation tax		100,000
Profit after taxation		150,000
less Proposed dividends:		
Ordinary shares	70,000	
Preference shares	20,000	90,000
		60,000
less Transfer to General Reserve		40,000
		20,000
add Retained profit from previous year		30,000
Balance of retained profit carried forward		50,000

Figure 3.13 An appropriation account for a company with a net profit of £250,000

The appropriation account

Beneath the profit and loss account of a company will appear the **appropriation account**. This is designed to show what happens to any profit and how it is divided (see Figure 3.13).

Corporation tax

Corporation tax is the first charge on profits and has to be paid to the Inland Revenue. **Proposed dividends** are the portion of the profits paid to the shareholders. After dividends have been paid, it is possible to allocate profits to reserves. Any profit left over at the end of the year, after taxes and shareholders of all kinds have been paid, is added to the balance of profit from the previous year to give the new retained profit:

Balance of profit at end of year = Net profit from current year + Retained profits from previous years – Corporation tax – Dividends – Transfers to reserves.

WHAT DO YOU THINK?

Hussain Ltd has just announced a net profit of £300,000. Prepare the appropriation account for the end of December 2000 from the following details:

- The taxation rate is 25 per cent.
- There are 500,000 ordinary shares of £1 each.
- A dividend of 10 per cent is proposed.
- There are 300,000 10 per cent preference shares of £1 each, fully paid. The 10 per cent dividend is to be paid.
- £50,000 is to be transferred to general reserve.
- Retained profit from the previous year was £125,000.

The balance sheet

In the balance sheet of a company, the fixed and current assets are presented in the same way as in any other balance sheet.

The current liabilities are the liabilities due to be paid within twelve months of the date of the balance sheet. In addition to those which normally appear in this section, limited companies also have to show Corporation tax which is due to be paid during the next twelve months, as well as ordinary and preference share dividends to be paid. Long-term liabilities may include debentures.

At the beginning of the 'Financed by:' section of the balance sheet, details will appear of the authorised capital, specifying the type, value and number of shares that the company is authorised to issue. These are in the balance sheet for interest only, and their value is excluded from the totals. Issued capital contains details of the classes and numbers of shares that have been issued (obviously the issued share capital cannot exceed the authorised).

Reserves are shown beneath the capital. Reserves and retained profits are the amounts the directors and shareholders decide to keep within the company. Shareholders' funds comprise the total of share capital plus reserves.

Example

From the trial balance of Happy Ltd shown in Figure 3.14 and the notes below, we can prepare the trading, profit and loss and appropriation account and the balance sheet for the year ended 31 December 2000 (see Figures 3.15 and 3.16). The following notes are attached:

- The closing stock is £12,250.
- Corporation tax is charged at 25 per cent of profits.
- There is a 6 per cent dividend on ordinary shares.
- The 10 per cent preference dividend is to be paid.
- £2,000 is to be allocated to the general reserve.
- Authorised share capital is 400,000 ordinary shares of £1 each and 100,000 10 per cent preference shares of £1 each.

Trial Balance of Happy Ltd as at 31 December 2000	Dr £	Cr £
Stock at 1 Jan. 2000	21,300	
Sales		118,100
Purchases	35,000	
Electricity	8,000	
Stationery	5,000	
Business rate	1,300	
Loan interest paid	1,000	
Debenture interest paid	800	
Advertising	3,200	
Sundry expenses	1,350	
Directors' salaries	12,000	
Land and buildings	320,000	
Machinery	24,000	
Motor vehicles	12,000	
Debtors	7,100	
Bank	23,200	
Cash	500	
Bank loan		10,000
10% debentures		8,000
Creditors		500
General reserve		4,000
Retained profit at 31 Dec.		35,150
Issued share capital:		
200,000 ordinary £1 shares		200,000
100,000 10% £1 preference shares		100,000
	475,750	475,750

Figure 3.14

The Trading, Profit and Loss and Appropriation Account of Happy Ltd for the year ended 31 December 2000

	£	£
Sales		118,100
Opening stock	21,300	
Purchases	35,000	
	56,300	
less Closing stock	12,250	
Cost of sales		44,050
Gross profit		74,050
less Expenses:		
Electricity	8,000	
Stationery	5,000	
Business rate	1,300	
Loan interest paid	1,000	
Debenture interest paid	800	
Advertising	3,200	
Sundry expenses	1,350	
Directors' salaries	12,000	
		32,650
Net profit		41,400
less Corporation tax		10,350
Profit after taxation		31,050
less Proposed dividends:		
Ordinary shares	12,000	
Preference shares	10,000	22,000
		9,050
less Transfer to general reserve		2,000
		7,050
add Retained profit from previous year		35,150
Balance of retained profit carried forward		42,200

Figure 3.15

The Balance Sheet of Happy Ltd as at 31 December 2001

	£	£	£
Fixed assets			
Land and buildings			320,000
Machinery			24,000
Motor vehicles			12,000
			356,000
Current assets			
Stocks		12,250	
Debtors		7,100	
Bank		23,200	
Cash		500	
		43,050	
less **Current liabilities**			
Creditors	500		
Proposed dividends:			
Ordinary shares	12,000		
Preference shares	10,000		
Corporation tax	10,350	32,850	
Working capital			10,200
			366,200
less **Long-term liabilities**			
Bank loan		10,000	
10% debentures		8,000	
			18,000
NET ASSETS			348,200
Financed by:			
Authorised share capital:			
400,000 ordinary shares of £1			400,000
100,000 10% preference shares of £1			100,000
			500,000
Issued share capital:			
200,000 ordinary shares of £1 fully paid		200,000	
100,000 10% preference shares of £1 fully paid		100,000	
			300,000
Reserves			
General reserve		6,000	
Balance of retained profit		42,200	
			48,200
SHAREHOLDERS' FUNDS			348,200

Figure 3.16

From the trial balance of Sad Ltd shown in Figure 3.17 and the attached notes, prepare the trading, profit and loss and appropriation account and balance sheet for the year ended 31 December 2000.

You have been informed that:

- the closing stock has been valued at £3,400

- Corporation tax will be charged at 25 per cent of profits
- the 10 per cent share dividends are to be paid
- £3,000 is to be allocated to the general reserve
- authorised share capital is the same as issued share capital.

Trial Balance of Sad Ltd as at 31 December 2000

	£	£
Stock at 1 Jan. 2000	7,300	
Sales		123,400
Purchases	12,500	
Electricity	4,100	
Advertising	3,200	
Business rate	800	
Salaries	16,000	
Directors' salaries	18,000	
Loan interest paid	4,400	
Debenture interest paid	1,000	
Land and buildings	124,000	
Motor vehicles	16,000	
Debtors	7,000	
Bank	15,000	
Cash	1,000	
Bank loan		25,000
10% debentures		10,000
Creditors		4,000
General reserve		3,000
Retained profit at 31 Dec. 2000		4,900
Issued share capital:		
50,000 ordinary shares (£)		50,000
10,000 10% preference shares (£)		10,000
	230,300	230,300

Figure 3.17

The truth is stranger than fiction

In 1967 AEI was taken over by GEC. AEI had forecast a profit for that year of £10 million, but when the figures were published they showed a loss of £10 million. The result showed that accountants at the time were using completely different methods to prepare and forecast financial statements.

Chapter 60 _Analysis of final accounts_

Accounting ratios are not simply the domain of the accountant. There are many users of accounts who will require a range of accounting ratios to make judgements and influence decisions related to the business. These include the following:

- Lenders of money will want to use the ratios to find out how well the business can meet its repayments.
- Managers within the business will want to use the ratios to improve the way in which they manage the business and make decisions that affect the future.
- Customers will want to be sure that supplies will be sustained in the future, and that their suppliers can meet their commitments.
- Creditors will want to know that the business they supply can meet their payments. They might also want to know more about how long they will expect to wait for payment.
- Employees and their representatives have a key vested interest within the business. They want to know about the financial strength of the organisation, whether there is a likelihood of redundancies and what the long-term future is for the business.
- Government departments will wish to find out about the tax liabilities of the business.
- Shareholders will want to know not only that their investment is secure but also what the returns are likely to be on that investment for the near and distant future.

Performance ratios

Performance ratios help to measure how successfully an organisation is being run and/or how well management is handling different aspects of the business. As with all accounting ratios, these ratios need to be compared with previous periods or with similar types of organisations. There are a number of different ratios including:

1 stock turnover
2 debtors' collection period
3 creditors' payment period
4 asset utilisation
5 asset turnover performance
6 proprietary ratio.

Stock turnover

Stock turnover is a very important measure of the number of days' stock that is held on average. The value of

the stock is related to sales revenues to find the number of times that it has been 'turned over' during the period. It can be measured in two ways:

1 $$\text{Stock turnover (times per year)} = \frac{\text{Cost of sales}}{\text{Average stock}}$$

where:

$$\text{Average stock} = \frac{\text{Opening stock} + \text{Closing stock}}{2}$$

For example, a stock turnover of 26 times per year would mean that two weeks' stock is held. Stock turnover refers therefore to the average time an item of stock is held in stores before it is used or sold. The adequacy of this ratio depends heavily upon the type of business sector within which an organisation is operating. For example, a greengrocer would expect a much higher stock turnover than a furniture business. In order to improve their efficiency and performance many organisations today hold smaller stock levels than in the past. Remember that high stock levels soak up investment with assets that are not performing for the business. Some organisations operate a just-in-time policy by having just enough stock to meet current demand. As a consequence they have a higher stock turnover.

2 $$\text{Number of days' stock held on average} = \frac{\text{Average stock}}{\text{Cost of sales}} \times 365 \text{ days.}$$

WHAT DO YOU THINK?

1 Work out the stock turnover figures for a business from the following figures:

(£000)	2000	2001	2002
Average stock	260	380	500
Cost of sales	1,200	1,600	1,900

2 Explain the implications of the changes in stock turnover during this period.

Debtors' collection period

The **debtors' collection period** is calculated using the formula:

$$\text{Debtors' collection period} = \frac{\text{Debtors}}{\text{Average daily sales}}$$

Average daily sales are calculated by dividing sales over the year by 365. This ratio shows the average number of days it takes for debtors to pay for the goods sold to them by the organisation. Although there is considerable variation and this is often dependent upon the industry, the normal accepted debt-collection period is between 30 and 60 days. It may be possible to improve the efficiency and performance of the business by reducing this period. Customers who are late in paying their debts are receiving free finance for their business. This ratio indicates the average number of days of credit received by customers before they provide a payment. Comparisons are usually made from one year to another.

WHAT DO YOU THINK?

In the group profit and loss account for The Boots Company for the 12 months up to 31 March 1999 turnover was £5,044.6 million. At that time the group balance sheet showed debtors of £402.2 million. Net assets at that time were £1,780.6 million, ordinary shareholders' funds were £1,780.2 million and tangible assets were £1,788.6 million. Calculate:

1 the average number of days it takes for the debtors of The Boots Company to make their payments
2 the asset turnover performance for The Boots Company over this period
3 the proprietary ratio.

Comment upon how these ratios might help managers to make decisions about how to improve the financial performance of the company.

Of course, it is helpful to remember the basics of good debtor control, namely:

- **Invoice quickly**. As soon as the goods have been delivered and accepted, invoice!
- **Invoice correctly**. If your customers want you to attach a copy of the purchase order, or quote the order number, make sure that you do. Ensure that your invoice is clear and well laid out.
- **Check creditworthiness**. Find out whether your customers are able to pay and their reliability. If you agree to a level of credit, keep to it.

WHAT DO YOU THINK?

Interview a business manager with some responsibility for accounts to find out the debt-collection period in his or her organisation, and ask how the company seeks to reduce it.

Creditors' payment period

The **creditors' payment period** measures the speed that the organisation takes to pay its creditors. It is calculated using the formula:

$$\text{Creditors' payment period} = \frac{\text{Creditors}}{\text{Average daily purchases}}$$

Average daily purchases are calculated by dividing purchases for the year by 365. This ratio is particularly useful for businesses that constantly buy and sell goods. These types of business organisations would prefer a longer creditors' payment period than debtors' collection period, as this provides the organisation with leeway to collect money before it pays its creditors.

Asset utilisation

Asset utilisation indicates how efficiently fixed assets are being used to generate sales. It is measured by:

$$\text{Asset utilisation} = \frac{\text{Sales}}{\text{Fixed assets}}$$

Asset turnover performance

A more appropriate ratio than asset utilisation is considered to be that of **asset turnover**. This ratio measures the efficiency of net assets in generating sales. It is calculated by:

$$\text{Asset turnover performance} = \frac{\text{Sales}}{\text{Net assets}}$$

Net assets for the purpose of ratio analysis are:

Fixed assets + Current assets – Current liabilities.

The ratio examines the efficiency of the organisation and helps managers to understand how well they are using net assets for running the business. The ratio will depend upon the type of business concerned and the sector within which it operates. For example, a fast-food retailer with high turnover and few assets will have a higher figure than a heavy engineering business which has large capital assets.

Proprietary ratio

The **proprietary ratio** shows the proportion of owners' funds to the tangible assets of an organisation. The tangible assets of an organisation are the tangible fixed assets plus the current assets. The formula is calculated by:

$$\text{Proprietary ratio} = \frac{\text{Ordinary shareholders' funds}}{\text{Tangible assets}}$$

Tangible assets are those assets with material substance and would not include patents and goodwill, as these would have less value if the business was sold. It would be usual to have a minimum ratio of around 0.5:1.

Solvency ratios

Solvency ratios are sometimes known as **liquidity ratios**. They refer to: (a) the ability of an organisation to convert short-term or current assets into cash to cover payments as and when they arise, and (b) the liquidity of long-term areas within the balance such as the ease with which interest can be paid or the relationship of long-term loans to capital. In the short term, stocks are the least liquid of the current assets because they must first be sold (usually on credit) and the customer is then provided with a payment period before payment is made. As a result, there is a time lag before stocks can be converted to cash. There are a number of different ratios including the following:

1 working capital
2 working capital ratio or current ratio
3 acid test ratio
4 gearing ratio
5 interest cover.

Working capital

Working capital is required to finance an organisation's everyday activities. It is calculated by:

Working capital = Current assets − Current liabilities.

Managing working capital involves making sure that a business has sufficient stocks to meet the needs of customers, enables such customers to become debtors, and has liquid funds which give it the ability to pay creditors.

Working capital ratio or current ratio

The **current ratio** is an important way of measuring an organisation's ability to settle current liabilities (short-term debts). It is measured using the formula:

CASE STUDY: CALCULATING THE CURRENT RATIO

The following figures reflect the current assets and current liabilities of a small business:

	£	£	£
Current assets			
Stocks:			
Raw materials	500		
Work in progress	300		
Finished goods	800	1,600	
Debtors		1,000	
Cash/bank		400	
		3,000	
less **Current liabilities**			
Trade creditors	500		
Tax due	300		
Loan interest due	200	1,000	
Working capital			2,000

QUESTIONS FOR DISCUSSION

1 What is the working capital ratio of this business?

2 If trade creditors increased by £1,500, what action should the business take?

$$\text{Current ratio} = \frac{\text{Current assets}}{\text{Current liabilities}}$$

Clearly, some current assets are more liquid than others, and the time factor involved in transferring them to cash is something an experienced manager should be able to estimate. A prudent ratio is sometimes 2:1. This may not be the case if stocks form the bulk of the value of current assets. Companies have to be aware that bank overdrafts are repayable on demand and that figures extracted from a balance sheet, while reflecting the position of current assets and liabilities at a particular moment, do not reflect the current assets/current liabilities ratio at other times. In practice, most businesses operate with a ratio slightly lower than 2:1.

Acid test ratio

The **acid test ratio** is sometimes known as the **quick ratio** or **liquidity ratio**. One major problem for some businesses is that they are not able to convert stocks rapidly into cash. Organisations therefore often use a more severe ratio to test whether they have the ability to meet current liabilities. This is called the 'acid test ratio' and does not include stock in the liquid assets of the business. The acid test ratio is measured by:

$$\text{Acid test ratio} = \frac{\text{Current assets} - \text{Stocks}}{\text{Current liabilities}}$$

The acid test ratio is sometimes referred to as the **Plimsoll line** of a business. The Plimsoll line is a line drawn on a ship's hull. If the ship sinks below this line in the water, then it is in danger of sinking.

WHAT DO YOU THINK?
Look at the final accounts of any business by extracting this information from a balance sheet. Find out the current ratio and acid test ratio of the organisation. Comment upon the figures you extract. Discuss the positioning of the Plimsoll line of this business.

Gearing ratio

Working capital and gearing ratios help us to understand how well an organisation can meet its short-term liabilities. The **gearing ratio** is a good indicator of the longer-term financial stability of an organisation. It is calculated as follows:

$$\text{Gearing ratio} = \frac{\text{Long-term loans (including debentures and preference capital)}}{\text{Ordinary shares and reserves}}$$

Gearing makes a direct comparison between the long-term capital in a business provided by ordinary shareholders and that provided through long-term loans and preference shares. Using the above formula, we can say that a company is:

- **low-geared** if the gearing is less than 100 per cent
- **high-geared** if the gearing is more than 100 per cent.

The higher the gearing, the less secure is the investment of ordinary shareholders. For example, it is said that gearing of more than 100 per cent is not good for a business organisation. This is because debt adds to the expenses of the business and its ability to meet all of its commitments.

Interest cover

The **interest cover** is clearly closely linked to the gearing of a business. Managers within an organisation that is highly geared must think carefully about how easily they can make interest payments and what margins of safety they have built into the business, particularly if interest rates change. Interest cover is calculated as follows:

$$\text{Interest cover} = \frac{\text{Profit before interest and tax}}{\text{Interest paid in the year}}$$

If the ratio is 1 or 2, then the business is only earning enough to cover interest charges. For example, if the business made profit before interest and tax of £50,000 and interest paid was £25,000, the ratio would be 2, which is low. The higher the interest cover, the easier an organisation will find it is able to meet its commitments to its debts. A ratio of 3 would provide the minimum level of safety required.

Profitability ratios

Although business organisations have a range of business objectives, for most the main objective is to make a profit. The profitability of an organisation should be looked at by looking at the general profitability of an investment made or at the profits that the business makes on its sales, based upon information supplied through the profit and loss account.

Gross profit percentage

Sometimes known as the **gross profit ratio** or **profit percentage**, this ratio is extracted from information within the trading account. It simply relates gross profit to sales revenue. For example, if the ratio is 35 per cent, it means that for every £1,000 of sales, 35 per cent of these sales will be gross profit. It is calculated by:

$$\text{Gross profit percentage} = \frac{\text{Gross profit}}{\text{Sales}} \times \frac{100}{1}$$

The gross profit percentage should be relatively consistent and should be calculated at regular intervals. If it suddenly rises or falls, the reason should be investigated. For example, if the percentage falls it could mean that stock is being stolen or damaged. Alternatively, it could mean that the cost of stock is rising and that the increase has not been passed on to the consumer through rising prices.

Net profit percentage

The **net profit percentage** indicates the net profit as a percentage of sales. As with the gross profit percentage, the net profit percentage should remain consistent from year to year. It should also be possible to compare the net profit percentage of organisations within the same type of industry. It is calculated by:

$$\text{Net profit percentage} = \frac{\text{Net profit}}{\text{Sales}} \times \frac{100}{1}$$

If the gross profit percentage is consistent, then any changes in the net profit percentage could indicate an increase in overheads as a proportion of sales, and a need to make economies or cut costs.

Operating profit percentage

The net profit percentage is charged after interest has been paid on loans. It can be argued therefore that when making comparisons between businesses, it is difficult to do so, because one might be highly geared and financed with a considerable amount of loans, while another might be financed with capital from the owner. The **operating profit percentage** is calculated by:

$$\text{Operating profit percentage} = \frac{\text{Profit before interest and tax}}{\text{Sales}}$$

Return on equity

When investing in a business, it is important that the investor thinks about alternative investments and other uses for the money. For example, what would be the point of investing in a business that provides a 2 per cent return, when a building society would provide less risk and a higher return? **Return on equity** (**ROE**) is calculated by:

$$\text{Return on equity} = \frac{\text{Net profit (after tax and preference dividend)}}{\text{Ordinary share capital and reserves}} \times \frac{100}{1}$$

Return on equity indicates how well a business has used its financial resources in the interests of ordinary shareholders.

Return on capital employed

Whereas ROE only takes into account ordinary shareholders' investments, the **return on capital employed** (**ROCE**) adopts a wider measure of the methods for financing a business, by taking into consideration preference shares and debentures.

Capital employed is calculated as follows:

Ordinary share capital + Reserves = Equity
Equity + Preference shares + Debentures
= Capital employed

Return on capital employed is calculated by the following formula:

$$\text{Return on capital employed} = \frac{\text{Net profit} + \text{Interest on debentures}}{\text{Ordinary shares} + \text{Reserves} + \text{Preference shares} + \text{Debentures}} \times \frac{100}{1}$$

There are many reasons for adopting this wider definition. In particular, a business has use of these resources and so it is therefore a better measure to take these into account when working out profitability.

Dividend yield

A number of ratios are much more specially aligned to the needs of larger companies, particularly those quoted on the London stock exchange, as public limited companies. The **dividend yield** relates the shareholders' dividend to the market price of the share. It is calculated by:

$$\text{Dividend yield} = \frac{\text{Ordinary share dividend}}{\text{Market price per share}} \times \frac{100}{1}$$

Dividend yield can be obtained by looking at the information about shares in the financial press. It provides an investor or a potential investor with a good guide to the annual percentage return paid on a share. Dividend yield as a raw measure, however, ignores wider profits or earnings such as retained profits that give investors more capital growth than increased income.

Earnings per share

Earnings per share (**EPS**) measures the amount of profit made by each share, after tax and preference dividends have been paid. This is an important determinant of the value of each share. It is calculated by:

$$\frac{\text{Earnings}}{\text{per share}} = \frac{\text{Net profit after tax and preference dividends}}{\text{Number of ordinary shares}}$$

This provides the ordinary shareholder with key information about the earning capacity of each share and enables comparisons to be made with previous years in order to develop a good understanding of performance.

Earnings/dividend yield

The **earnings/dividend yield** relates the shareholders' dividend to the market price of the shares. It is calculated by:

$$\text{Earnings/dividend yield} = \frac{\text{Earnings per ordinary share}}{\text{Market price per share}} \times \frac{100}{1}.$$

This shows the return earned by the company on each share and includes not just the part paid to investors but also the amount kept within the company to increase the value of the capital owned by ordinary shareholders.

Price/earnings ratio

The **price/earnings ratio** is sometimes called the **P/E ratio**. The P/E ratio compares the current market value of a share with the earnings per share. It shows the amount that each share is earning and provides the ordinary shareholder with key information about the earning capacity of each share. It is calculated by:

$$\text{Price/earnings ratio} = \frac{\text{Market price per share}}{\text{Earnings per share}}$$

If a share has a market price of £8.00 and the earnings per share in one year are £1.60, the P/E ratio would be 5. The person owning the share would have a share value five times that of its earnings. A low P/E ratio would indicate to investors that the share price would not be experiencing much growth in the near future.

Dividend cover

The **dividend cover** illustrates the difference between an organisation's margin of safety and the amount it has to pay out in dividends. It is calculated by:

$$\text{Dividend cover} = \frac{\text{Net profit after tax and dividends}}{\text{Ordinary dividends}}$$

This is a useful ratio to work out how easily a company can pay dividends to its ordinary shareholders. A ratio of between 5 and 10 would provide a secure margin of safety, with profit exceeding dividends by more than five times.

The truth is stranger than fiction

Accounting ratios are not infallible. Sometimes a decision that results in the worsening of a ratio can produce a better result for the business. For example, an expanding business would require more capital. This might cause the return on capital to fall, even though the business would be earning more profits. It is important to be aware that absolute values are sometimes more important than relative ones shown by ratios.

Chapter 61 *Profit versus cash/accounting information*

Profit versus cash

Whereas cash is a liquid asset owned by the business which enables it to buy goods and services, profit is a surplus arising from trading. It is therefore possible for a business to be selling goods at a higher price than they cost and to be making a profit but, if creditors have not been paid, for it to be having cash flow problems.

A business must look carefully at its cash flow to ensure that use of its most liquid asset resource is economically utilised. For example, if a business holds too much cash it could be sacrificing profits, and if it holds too little it could run out! The solution to the problem involves getting the balance just about right.

The opportunity cost of holding too much cash would be the interest that could otherwise be earned. If interest rates are high, businesses will be sacrificing income by holding cash: they would prefer to hold the lowest possible cash balances so that they can earn interest from the rest. In times of inflation, businesses will wish to hold higher levels of cash in order to finance the increasing price of transactions.

> **WHAT DO YOU THINK?**
> In what circumstances do you usually hold cash, rather than save it or spend it?

According to economic theory, there are three motives for holding cash:

1 The **transactionary motive**. In order to meet commitments such as wages, materials and other payments, a business requires cash. Cash is the 'life-blood' of the organisation which circulates and enables it to meet obligations as and when they arise.
2 The **precautionary motive**. If cash flows are uncertain in the future it would be sensible to hold a sufficiently large balance of cash to deal with any problems that may arise.
3 The **speculative motive**. Sometimes it might be worth holding cash just in case any profitable opportunities arise.

Management information systems (MIS)

A small business may be run by one person. That person may know the business inside out and may have no need for a formal accounting system. But as soon as a business grows, the management function is performed by people who are more specialised and may be removed from day-to-day activities. In this case some form of **management information system** (**MIS**) is required.

CASE STUDY: FALLING PROFITS FORCE COMPANIES TO BORROW MONEY

There is a close connection between profits and liquidity, as shown during 1999 and 2000 when borrowing by companies on the financial markets reached record levels. A study in *Economic Trends* (Office for National Statistics, 2000) argued that part of the reason for this surge in borrowing was that companies had been maintaining dividend payments to shareholders, despite the fact that for many their profits had been falling. This meant that although profits were falling, companies were still paying strong dividends and many needed to develop the cash flow to be able to do so. In fact, dividend payments remained steady during both 1999 and 2000. UK companies faced a squeeze on profits, but maintaining payments to shareholders was providing businesses with a tighter liquidity position.

QUESTIONS FOR DISCUSSION

1 What does the case study say about the connection between profits and liquidity?
2 Is it possible for a company making small profits to be liquid?

A management information system uses data to provide meaningful information to enable its users to make appropriate decisions in pursuit of business objectives.

T. Lucey, in *Management Information Systems* (1998), defines a management information system as:

'a system using formalised procedures to provide management at all levels in all functions with appropriate information, based upon data from both internal and external sources, to enable them to make timely and effective decisions for planning, directing and controlling the activities for which they are responsible'.

The nature and type of business has a bearing upon the sort of information generated by its MIS. Information may be internal information generated within the business, or external information generated outside the business but relevant to the business (see Table 3.3).

WHAT DO YOU THINK?
What sort of information, both accounting and otherwise, is of value to the managers of a school or college? You may wish to ask your school bursar or college administrator/accountant questions to find out more about the sort of information held within management information systems. Having found out the nature and type of information, find out how it is used.

Management information may be used for the following:

- **Strategic planning**. The strategic planning process uses both internal and external sources of information. In a dynamic and changing business environment information is geared towards helping an organisation use strategic planning in order to adapt.
- **Management control**. This is the 'process by which managers ensure that resources are obtained and used effectively and efficiently in the accomplishment of the organisation's objectives'.
- **Operational control**. This ensures that tasks are carried out efficiently. At the operational level, tasks have been specified and methods determined. Information for operations is geared to the needs of those who have the responsibility of executing tasks with the minimum of expenditure on resources.

Limitations of accounting information

An essential function of management is to make decisions, and decisions have to be made whenever there are alternative courses of action. The main problem of any accounting system is that information reflects data from the past and present and enables predictions only to be made about the future. Time pressures can be imposed on managers which constrain their ability to collate sufficient information. Also, the information extracted from the accounting system may prove to be unmanageably detailed. The problems may be numerous. Many decisions will require information not only from accounting systems, but also about external factors such as:

- current tax rates
- the current state of the economy
- the market value of shares, if listed
- the state of the market
- goodwill and corporate reputation
- industrial relations.

Table 3.3 Types of information generated by management information systems

Type of business	External information	Internal information
Car manufacturer	Industry-wide innovations Economic information Trade regulations Market share Political changes	Production figures Quality tests Waste figures Output per worker Lead times
Supermarket chain	Market shares Competitors' prices Demographic changes Competitors' innovations	Sales per employee Stock levels Production lines Number of stock-outs

Clearly, nothing can be forecast with absolute certainty. No matter what research takes place and however competent the accounting team, business involves taking risks.

Although accounting information has reduced the unpredictability, it will never eliminate it, and there will always be a need for human judgement.

The truth is stranger than fiction

We always think of computers as our reliable friends, helping us to be more efficient and enabling us to compete more effectively. However, a recent survey showed that computer downtime costs British industry more than £1 billion per year.

Chapter 62 Sources of business finance

Every modern organisation needs to draw upon sources of finance. It needs to have funds to carry out its activities. The financial problem for an organisation is similar to that of an individual. If I want to visit the cinema, then I will need to have cash in my pocket. If I want to buy a relatively expensive item such as a DVD player, then I will probably need to be able to draw on my bank account using a cheque book or cash machine. At other times, I may buy goods on credit, such as borrowing money to purchase a car.

Sources of finance are the people and organisations that provide finance for an individual or an organisation. **Methods of finance** are the form in which the funds are provided.

> ### WHAT DO YOU THINK?
> Think about the methods of finance that your household draws upon. Rank these in order of the length of time that these funds are required for. Why is it that some methods of finance are required for longer periods than others? What are the sources of finance used within your household?

Organisations have available to them a number of sources of finance. These include:

- individuals
- organisations providing venture capital
- banks and other financial institutions
- suppliers
- government
- profits retained by the business.

By drawing on these sources of finance, organisations have available to them a number of methods of finance. In choosing what type of finance to draw upon, they may consider:

- the length of time for which they need the finance
- the cost of raising the finance in one way rather than another
- the flexibility of the finance, that is, how easy it is to change from one form of finance to another, for example by transferring a long-term loan into a short-term one.

Table 3.4 Methods of finance used by different types of organisations

	Sole traders	Partnerships	Private limited companies	Public limited companies	Non-profit organisations
Personal funds	*	*	*	*	*
Shares			*	*	
Mortgage	*	*	*	*	
Grants	*	*	*	*	*
Gifts					*
Loans	*	*	*	*	*
Profit retention	*	*	*	*	*
Trade credit	*	*	*	*	*
Overdraft	*	*	*	*	*
Leasing and hire purchase	*	*	*	*	*
Trade credit	*	*	*	*	*
Factoring	*	*	*	*	

Methods of finance can be ranked in order of the length of the term which they are typically used for. Going from the shortest term to the longest term we have: trade creditors, overdraft, leasing and hiring, borrowing (loans), profit retention and capital.

Table 3.4 shows the methods of finance used by different types of organisations.

Owner's capital

The business owners are the ultimate risk takers, as they provide the business with capital and only expect a return if the business proves to be profitable. Providers of owners' capital benefit most when the firm is successful, but stand to lose the most if it fails. The form these funds take depends on the legal form of the business.

Unincorporated businesses are made of individuals acting as sole traders and groups of individuals who set up in partnership. Their businesses are simple to set up but are not recognised by the law as being separate from the owners. The assets (what the business owns or is owed) and liabilities (what the business owes) of the business belong directly to the owners or partners. This means, therefore, that when a partner leaves or joins the business, the inconvenient situation arises of one partnership ceasing and another commencing. In addition, the owner may be forced to transfer more personal wealth into the firm if the business cannot generate enough funds to pay its debts. Generally speaking, unincorporated businesses are relatively small and are only able to raise limited amounts of capital. However, there are some very big partnerships which have access to vast sums of capital such as accountancy partnerships and major City law firms.

Share capital

Unlike sole traders and partnerships, companies are legal identities quite separate from those of their owners. This enables easier exit for investors who wish only to tie up their money for a limited period of time, as the company's ability to trade is unaffected by changes in its ownership. The capital contributed by the owners of the business is divided into **shares**. Hence an owner is called a **shareholder**.

Shareholders enjoy limited liability as the maximum amount they can lose in the business venture is the amount they paid for the shares they hold. Shareholders receive benefits from profits earned in the form of cash **dividends** and an increase in the **value** of their shares.

A **private limited company** is one that restricts the rights of members to transfer their shares and limits the ability of the public to subscribe for its shares. Membership of the **Alternative Investment Market** (**AIM**) is often seen as a halfway stage between a small company and a fully listed company on the London stock exchange.

A fully **listed company** on the London stock exchange has almost limitless opportunities to raise fresh capital from the market as long as it abides by its rules. For example, a public company has a number of methods open to it for the **issue** of shares:

- It can create a public issue by **prospectus**. An issuing house will organise the issue by compiling a prospectus, accompanied by an advertisement and an invitation to buy shares. This can be an expensive method, and up to 7 per cent of the money raised by the issue can go to meet the costs.
- An **offer for sale** exists where a public company issues shares directly to an issuing house which then offers them for sale at a fixed price. This is also an expensive method and is best used when the size of the issue is too small to need a public issue by prospectus.
- A **rights issue** is a cheaper method, whereby existing shareholders are offered further shares at an advantageous price.
- A **placing** avoids the expense of going to the market by placing shares with a number of investors through an intermediary. Since this method avoids the market, the stock exchange keeps an eye on these transactions.
- With an **offer by tender**, an offer is made to the public but the company states a minimum price below which shares will not be offered. Buyers then have to indicate the price they are willing to offer for the shares.

Most capital is normally raised through the issue of **ordinary shares**, which are commonly called **equities**. An ordinary share is a fixed unit of ownership giving the holder the opportunity to share in the profits or losses. Ordinary shares carry voting rights at shareholders' meetings. Shareholders elect the board of a company and can sanction the level of dividends proposed. **Authorised capital** is the amount of share capital a company is empowered by its shareholders to issue. **Issued capital** is the actual amount of share capital that has been issued. In other words, a company may hold back part of its authorised capital to issue at a later date.

Deferred shares are sometimes called **founders' shares**. These are issued to the people who originally set up the business. Sometimes these shares have superior voting rights relative to other shares to ensure that the founders keep a substantial part of the power and influence within a company.

Preference shares are a less flexible class of share. Owners of these shares are not, strictly speaking, owners of the company. Their exact rights are set out in the company Articles of Association. Holders of these shares have preferential rights to receive dividends if profits exist and, in the event of a company going into liquidation, will receive the face value of their shares before the ordinary shareholders are paid. However, dividends on preference shares are limited to a fixed percentage of **par value** (the face value of the share).

Some companies issue **cumulative preference shares** and this avoids the difficulty of having to pay preference shareholders if profits are too small. The holder of a cumulative preference share will receive arrears of dividends accumulated from the past in later years. With **redeemable preference shares** the company can buy back the shares from the shareholders; redemption can be made from profits or reserves, or it may be financed by a fresh issue of shares. **Participating preference shares** receive dividends above the fixed rate when ordinary shareholders have been paid if the company has done well in a particular year.

There are many advantages of using risk capital instead of alternative sources of finance, including the following:

*   If the business has had a bad year, the company is under no legal obligation to pay shareholders.
*   Unlike loans, whereby the principal has to be returned at the end of a period on a contracted date, the company does not have to pay back the share capital.
*   Interest on loan capital is an overhead which reduces profits, whereas share capital does not create overheads.

However, there are several disadvantages of issuing risk capital. For example:

*   it can be expensive to issue shares
*   companies have to undergo the rigorous financial requirements of the London stock exchange to be listed, and then demands for shares are subject to the uncertainties of the marketplace
*   the creation of more shareholders may dilute the influence of the founders of the company and affect their ability to make decisions.

WHAT DO YOU THINK?

In a world where it is easier for large firms rather than small businesses to raise finance, why do small businesses continue to exist?

CASE STUDY: THE BIRTH OF THE BODY SHOP

The presentation of a business plan can be just as important as the facts and figures contained within it. This was a lesson learned by Anita Roddick when she approached her bank manager for the start-up capital to open her first Body Shop.

She came up with the name after finding her first premises between two funeral parlours in Brighton. She had a good idea and a well-developed business plan, so in 1976 she went to see her bank manager in her Bob Dylan T-shirt, with her two small children in tow. She thought that her enthusiasm and energy would convince the bank manager to believe in her. Sadly, she was turned down. So, next time she went she decided

to 'dress up like a bloke' in pinstripes and leave the kids behind. After walking into the bank, she came out with a £4,000 loan.

Today, the company has a market value of more than £200 million, operates in 47 countries around the world and makes 400 products.

QUESTIONS FOR DISCUSSION

1   What lesson did Anita Roddick learn about approaching her suppliers of finance?
2   Describe the sort of information she would have included in her business plan.

Venture capital

Another form of capital for a business is **venture capital**. Venture capital companies provide finance in return for an equity (ordinary) shareholding in the company and an element of control. 3i is the largest venture capital company of this type. In recent years, the law has changed to allow companies to buy back their capital if certain safeguards have been met.

Profit retention

One of the most important sources of finance for business is profits that have been ploughed back. Initially, profits are subject to Corporation tax, payable to the Inland Revenue. Then a proportion of what is left over is allocated to shareholders as dividends. The directors will recommend how much profit should be distributed in this way. The board needs to satisfy shareholders while at the same time ensuring that sufficient funds are available for **reinvestment**.

Borrowing

Borrowing is an important part of business activity. The charge for borrowing is **interest**, and a crucial element in calculating the interest charge is the amount of risk involved with the loan. For example, longer-term loans tend to carry higher rates, as will loans made to small businesses with an unproven track record.

Bank loan

Bank loans are taken out for a fixed period, repayment either being in instalments or in full at the end of the term. Banks generally provide funds on a short- to medium-term basis, with relatively few loans over more than ten years' duration. Details of bank loans are as follows:

- Source – main clearing banks and merchant banks.
- Cost – in addition to interest charges levied at so many percentage points over base rate (for example 3 per cent over base), there may be arrangement fees and a security fee.
- Limit – banks are unlikely to lend more than the owners are putting into the business. In particular, the banks need to be convinced of the owner's commitment to the enterprise before they will pledge their own funds.

Debentures

Large, publicly quoted organisations may borrow money by issuing **debentures**. A debenture is a certificate issued by a company acknowledging a debt. The debt is paid at a fixed rate of interest and the certificate states the terms of repayment at the end of the period of debt. It is thus a long-term loan which can be traded on the stock exchange, that is, the holder of a debenture can sell it on to someone else. A debenture holder is not a shareholder but a creditor. This means that interest payments are an expense to the company and are allowable against profits.

Although holding debentures is much less risky than holding shares, their value in the market place will vary according to interest rates. For example, a debenture that pays a 10 per cent rate of interest will be worth 10/8 or 1.25 per cent of its face value when interest rates are 8 per cent; if interest rates rise to 15 per cent it would only be worth 10/15 or 0.66 of its face value. Thus, if interest rates rise, the value of the loan falls and vice versa.

Bank overdraft

An **overdraft** is the most frequently used form of short-term bank finance and is used to ease cash flow problems. Arrangements are made between the customer and the bank to include an agreed limit on an account beyond which the customer will not draw. Interest is calculated on the level of the overdraft on a daily basis. Often a bank will make a special charge for arranging an overdraft and committing the bank's money, whether the withdrawal facilities are used or not. After an agreed period, the bank will examine the account and make a decision about whether to revise or reinstate the limit.

Whereas the accounts of personal customers will usually show a regular input of income per month and a regular pattern of expenditure, this is not the case with business customers who are dependent upon debtors paying their bills. As a result, it is easy to understand why business customers often slip into an overdraft situation and need this flexible form of short-term finance.

Hire purchase

Hire purchase (HP) allows the business to use an asset without having to find the money immediately. A finance house buys the asset from the supplier and retains ownership of it during the period of the hire-purchase agreement. The business pays a deposit and then further payments to the finance house, as stipulated in the agreement. At the end of the agreement, ownership of the asset is passed to the business. Details are as follows:

- Source – finance houses, often subsidiaries of the clearing banks and equipment suppliers.
- Cost – the payments made by the business under the HP agreement are in excess of the cash price of the asset. The difference is the finance charge required by the finance house.
- Limit – the finance house will want to be sure that the company's profits will be well in excess of the planned repayments and that it has a good payment record on existing HP agreements and other debt arrangements.

Leasing

Leasing an asset provides similar benefits to hire purchase in that a leasing agreement with a finance house (**lessor**) allows the business (**lessee**) to use an asset without having to buy it outright. The real distinction between the two forms of finance is that leasing does not confer an automatic right to eventual ownership of the asset. It is a very popular form of finance for company vehicles, office equipment and factory machinery.

The benefits of leasing are that:

- it enables a business to have complete use of an asset without having to use risk or loan capital to finance it
- leasing payments are an expense and are charged to the profit and loss account before tax is assessed
- leasing enables businesses to change their equipment more often and thereby keep up to date with technology
- tax allowances can be claimed by the lessor and be filtered through to the lessee in lower lease payments.

Although leasing enables the lessee to manage expenditure more easily, the lessee does not own the equipment. If income falters, lease payments may impose a considerable burden on a business; furthermore, loans cannot be secured on assets that are leased.

Factoring

Trade debts mean that money can often be tied up for as long as six months. For a business requiring cash quickly this can be a real problem. A **factoring company** may offer immediate payment of part of the amount owed to a business – normally around 80 per cent – with the balance being paid when the debt is settled. This provides an immediate way for a business to improve its cash flow. In return the factoring company will charge a fee which includes interest and administration charges.

Commercial mortgages

A **mortgage** is a loan secured on land and buildings and can either be used to finance the purchase of the property, or to provide security for a loan applied to some other purpose. It is a long-term financing arrangement of typically 10–30 years. Details are as follows:

- Source – financial institutions, such as insurance companies and pension funds as well as the banks.
- Cost – interest on amount outstanding.
- Limit – values of the property and income are the basis for determining the maximum mortgage permissible.

Sale and lease-back

This involves a business selling its freehold property to an investment company and then leasing it back over a long period of time. This releases funds for other purposes in the business.

Loan Guarantee Scheme

The government guarantees the repayment of 70–85 per cent of a medium-term bank loan (2–7 years) in return for a 2.5 per cent annual premium. The scheme enables banks to lend money to businesses of less than 200 employees for projects that would otherwise be thought too risky.

Suppliers

Suppliers are a valuable source of finance for many businesses. Just as the business may give credit to its own customers, the firm may be able to negotiate **credit terms** with its suppliers. Credit terms are typically 30 days from date of supply or the end of the month following the month of delivery, that is, 30 to 60 days.

Public–Private Partnerships (PPP)

Over recent years the government has forced its departments and local authorities to look for finance for capital projects. By doing this it has created a new industry – **Public–Private Partnerships**, which used to be known as **Private Finance Initiatives** (**PFIs**). The aim of public–private initiatives is to use the private sector to manage and run projects or institutions which have been traditionally associated with the public sector.

Some commentators have criticised the initiative because they feel it is a smoke screen behind which the government reduces the amount it makes available for a capital project by encouraging the private sector to take on more responsibility. For example, a public–private initiative might be to run and build a new school. Instead of the local authority paying for the building, under the Public–Private Partnership, it would be built by the private sector and then leased back. One issue would be how much influence the private investor would have over the running and maintenance of the school.

The Channel Tunnel rail link is a Public–Private Partnership and is set for completion in 2003. It is claimed that Public–Private Partnerships provide an alternative way of looking at investments in the public sector, with opportunities existing for new prisons, hospitals, colleges and public buildings as well as for roads, light-rail systems and bridges.

The European Union

The European Union provides a range of finance for businesses, such as loans or loan guarantees for investment projects.

WHAT DO YOU THINK?

Identify the most relevant sources of finance for each of the following organisations:

1 A school wishes to replace its existing photocopier with a more elaborate version which it wants to pay for over a period of time.
2 The Queens' Medical Centre wishes to build a new hospital wing on vacant land close to its existing site.
3 Prakesh Patel needs a new computer system costing £5,000 for his business.
4 A medium-sized company wants to expand its factory building. The cost will be £500,000.
5 A small firm is having temporary problems with its cash flow.

The truth is stranger than fiction

Some companies qualify for government grants and other concessions such as 'tax holidays'.

SECTION B *Budgeting*

INTRODUCTION   As well as recording financial information and making judgements about the effectiveness of the information, businesses need to manage their finances. **Budgets** help people within businesses to plan, to set targets and to control their expenditure. To understand how budgets are used you need to know what they are, how they work, and their particular purposes. You also need to be able to understand what **variances** are and describe how they are used.

Remember that financial planning involves defining objectives and then developing ways to achieve them. To be able to do this a financial manager must have a realistic understanding not just of what is happening at any one time, but also of what is likely to happen within the business in the future.

Critical thinking

Budgeting is something that helps not just businesses but also individuals. Make a list of your income sources over the next three months. For example, your income may come from working, pocket money, birthday presents, repayment of loans, etc. Identify when you expect each of these sources to yield income, and then make a list of your expenditure over the same period. Again, think of all of your expenditures and be realistic. For example, there may be a concert you wish to go to; you may need money for socialising, clothes or special events, as well as for playing sport, bus fares, and regular expenditures. Find out *either* how much you will have left at the end of the three months *or* how much you need in order to finance all of the things you wish to do.

WHAT DO YOU THINK?
1 How difficult was it to engage in the financial planning process above?
2 Given this process of planning, how will you deal with any unexpected expenditures as and when they arise?
3 Why might it be necessary to constantly readjust your budget during this process?

Chapter 63 *The role of budgeting*

Looking into their future helps all organisations to plan their activities so that what they anticipate and want to happen can actually happen. This process of financial planning is known as **budgeting**. It is considered to be a system of **responsibility accounting** because it puts an onus on budgeted areas to perform in a way that has been outlined for them and its success will depend upon the quality of information provided. Businesses that do not budget may not be pleased when they view their final accounts. Budgeting helps the financial manager to develop an understanding of how the business is likely to perform in the future.

Budgeting and people

We all budget to a greater or lesser extent. Our short-term budget may relate to how we are going to get through the coming week and do all the things we want to do. Our slightly longer-term budget may involve being able to afford Christmas presents in two months' time. Our longest-term budget could involve the planning necessary to afford the car tax, MOT and motor insurance which all fall due in ten months from now. Also, when can we afford in the longer term to replace the car?

WHAT DO YOU THINK?
Identify a range of activities in which you participate that you think could be helped by some form of budgeting. For example, these may include your personal finances, or some club responsibility. Explain how, in each instance.

Budgeting and business

In exactly the same way, businesses try to see far into the future. The problem is that, the further one looks into the future, the more difficult it is to see accurately.

A budget is a financial plan which is developed for the future. Many businesses appoint a budget controller whose sole task is to coordinate budgetary activities. A short-term budget would be for up to one year, a medium-term budget would be for anything from one year to five years, and a budget for a longer period than this would be a long-term budget.

Wherever budgeting takes place it is important to draw upon the collective experience of people throughout the business. A budgeting team might consist of representatives from various areas of activity. The team will consider the objectives of the budgeting process, obtain and provide relevant information, make decisions, prepare budgets and then use these budgets to help to control the business.

Benefits of budgeting

Budgeting provides a valuable benchmark against which to measure and judge the actual performance of key areas of business activity. There are therefore many benefits of budgeting including the following:

- It helps to **predict** what the organisation thinks will happen. Given the experience within the organisation, it helps to show what is likely to take place in the future.
- It creates opportunities to **appraise alternative courses of action**. Information created for budgeting purposes forms the basis of decisions that have to be taken. The research necessary for budgeting will look at alternative ways of achieving the organisation's objectives.
- Budgets set **targets**. If communicated to people throughout the organisation, the budgets will help them to work towards the targets which have been set.
- Budgeting helps to **monitor and control performance**. This can be done by studying actual results, comparing these to budgeted results and then finding out why differences known as **variances** may have taken place. This is a useful starting point for some kind of action designed to deal with a particular problem in the business. Sometimes variances are bad, while at other times they may be good. Whatever the causes of the variances, they are a useful starting point to deal with issues within the business.
- Budgets are fundamental to the process of **business planning**. They provide a series of quantitative guidelines which can be used for coordination and then followed in order to achieve the organisation's business objectives.
- Budgeting can be used as a source of **motivation**. As part of the consultation process, budgets help to keep people involved. They also help to create **goal**

congruence, so that the aims and objectives of the individual are the same as that of the organisation.

- Budgets are a form of **communication**. They enable employees from across the organisation to be aware of performance expectations with regard to their individual work area.

Budgeting may also have some useful spin-offs. Every year the business is reviewed and this gives members of the various departments a better understanding of the working of the organisation as a whole. In fact, by participating in the budgetary process they feel that their experience is contributing to policy decisions.

It also increases cooperation between departments and lowers departmental barriers. In this way members of one department can become aware of the difficulties facing another department. By being involved in the budgetary process, non-accountants also appreciate the importance of costs.

In reality, budgeting may take place in almost all parts of an organisation. Budgeting should also be viewed as something that is ongoing and as a source of useful information and guidance for managers.

The process of budget setting

The process of setting budgets has to be set within the context of the longer-term objectives and strategies at the highest level of management of any organisation. The administration of the budgeting process will usually be the responsibility of the accounts department. Many organisations set up a budget committee to oversee the process.

The budgetary process is usually governed by a formal budget timetable (see Figure 3.18). This helps to link in the budget with all other aspects of business planning.

The accounts department is involved at all stages of the budgeting process and an effective accounts team will provide a range of advice to managers as the exercise develops. Spreadsheets are effective 'What if?' tools which are often used to help within the budgeting process.

Setting up a system of 'responsibility accounting' such as budgeting involves breaking down an organisation into a

	For year 1 April 2001 to 31 March 2002	
Date	**Narrative**	**Responsibility**
1/9/00	Board of directors to review long-term objectives and strategies and specify short-term goals for the year	Directors
22/9/00	Budget guidelines and standard forms issued to line managers	Accounts
6/10/00	Actual results for year are issued to line management, so that comparisons can be made with current budget and last year's actual results	Accounts
20/10/00	Budget submissions are made to the management accountant	Line management
27/10/00	First draft of the master budget is issued	Accounts
3/11/00	First draft of the budget is reviewed for results and consistency – line managers to justify their submissions	Managing director and individual directors
6/11/00	New assumptions and guidelines issued to line management	Accounts
10/11/00	Budgets revised and resubmitted	Line management
24/11/00	Second draft of master budget issued	Accounts
27/11/00	Final review of the draft budget	Managing director and financial director
	Final amendments	Accounts
1/12/00	Submission to the board for its approval	Financial director

Figure 3.18 A budget timetable

series of 'control centres'. Each individual manager then has the responsibility for managing the budget relating to his or her particular control centre.

Budgetary reports therefore reflect the assigned responsibility in each area of the organisation. As all organisations have a structure of control, it is important that the budgetary system fits around this. The reports should be designed to reflect the different levels within the organisation and the responsibilities of each of the managers concerned.

If the budgeting process reflects the different levels of control, managers will be kept informed not only of their own performance but also that of other budget holders for whom they are responsible. They will also know that managers above them will be assessing their performance (see Figure 3.19). This system can be regularly reviewed at meetings attended by all of the individual managers concerned.

WHAT DO YOU THINK?
Find out more about the budgeting process within your school or college. For example, how are budgets set, what processes take place, and who are the budget holders? What happens if budget holders overspend?

Although it could be claimed that they are mechanistic, budget models formalise the interrelationships between departments and provide a basic understanding of work flows within business organisations.

The overall budget as a plan will only have real value if the performance levels set through the budget are realistic. Budgets that are based upon *ideal* conditions are unlikely to be met and will result in departments failing to meet their targets. For example, the sales department may fail to achieve its sales budget, which may result in goods remaining unsold. Budgets can only be motivating if they are pitched at a realistic level.

There are two approaches to budget setting (see Figure 3.20). The **top-down approach** involves senior managers specifying what the best performance indicators are for the business across all departments and budgeted areas. The **bottom-up approach** builds up the organisational **master budget** on the basis of the submissions of individual line managers and supervisors, based upon their own views of their requirements. In practice, most organisations use a mixture of both methods.

Budget setting should be based upon realistic predictions of future sales and costs. Many organisations base future predictions solely on past figures with adjustments for forecast growth and inflation rates. Although the main advantage of this approach is that budgets are based upon actual data, future conditions may not mirror past ones.

One of the dangers of budgeting is that if actual results are dramatically different from the budgeting ones, the process could lose its credibility as a means of control. Following a budget too rigidly may also restrict a business's activities. For example, if the budget for entertainment has been exceeded and subsequent visiting customers are not treated with the usual hospitality, orders may be lost; on the other hand, if managers realise that towards the end of the year that a department has underspent, they may decide to go on a spending spree.

Budgeting is a routine annual event for many different types of organisations. The process may start in the middle

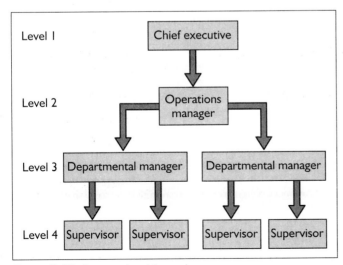

Figure 3.19 A reporting hierarchy

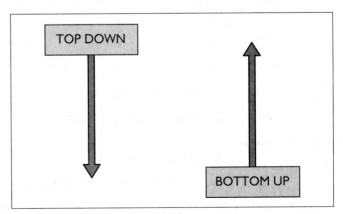

Figure 3.20 Approaches to budget setting

of the financial year, with a revision of the current year's budget and with first drafts of the budget for the coming year. Some organisations plan further ahead with an outline plan for three to five years.

Budgets provide an opportunity for everyone to play a part in either the strategic or tactical development of the organisation. As the activities following the budgetary process unfold, they provide a benchmark against which actual performance can be measured and judged.

As a result, an essential feature of the budgetary control system is the feedback of actual results. The process of measuring the difference between budgeted (intended) and actual outcomes, is known as **variance analysis**. Variance analysis makes it possible to detect problems. Reasons can be sought for variances and speedy action can be taken to improve performance. (Chapter 64 looks at variances in more detail.)

Creating budgets

In practice, budgeting may take place in almost all parts of an organisation. The money values attached to budgets are often linked to quantities such as units, weights and other

forms of measurement. This also helps to link the budgeting process with operational activities so that the budget meets the specific requirements of different parts of the business, such as the number of operating units to produce. There are three key areas of budgetary forecasts:

- **The capital budget**. The term 'capital' refers to the buying of fixed assets. Do we plan now for the money we will need in the future to buy another machine? The capital budget is a simple statement of intent or forecast which specifies the planned purchase of assets, the date of intended purchase and the expected cost of purchase.
- **The cash budget or cash flow forecast**. This forecast looks at the cash coming in to the organisation as well as the cash going out. It is a prediction by a business of how much money it thinks it will receive and how much it thinks it will pay out over a specified time. By forecasting cash flow, managers will know what their future financial requirements will be and will be able to take action beforehand if they need an overdraft or some form of loan.
- **Subsidiary budgets and the master budget.** Functional budgets and budgets for individual balance

CASE STUDY: SPREADWARE BUDGETING

Spreadware Budgeting is designed to help the budget creation process. It is also designed to consolidate a budgeting process and enable multiple budgets to be created easily and quickly.

The great benefit of using this type of software is that revisions of budgets can be made easily and at any time. Budgets can be analysed as soon as actual data become available, which quickly allows variances to be detected and also whether departmental objectives are being met. There is also a forecast option which allows for projected results based upon actual data.

Spreadware Budgeting is interactive which makes it easy to use. It can also be set up within both large and small organisations. The benefits of the system are that:

- an unlimited number of budget periods can be applied to an unlimited number of cost centres

- it is possible to compare the actual versus the budget for the period
- a forecast option allows projections to be developed based upon early actual data
- budgets can be based upon actual numbers, growth rates and previous reporting periods
- there are an unlimited number of budget models.

QUESTIONS FOR DISCUSSION

1 What are the advantages of using computer software for budgeting purposes?
2 How important is it for a manager to be able to: (a) identify variances, and (b) make forecasts?
3 What sort of problems could develop if an organisation became too dependent upon these types of budgeted data?

sheet items are called subsidiary budgets. The exact nature of subsidiary budgets will depend on the organisational structure and the operational processes of an organisation. The term 'master budget' includes the budgeted profit and loss account, balance sheet and cash budget.

The truth is stranger than fiction

Without realising it, we all budget. Our short-term budget might relate to how we are going to get through the next week, not always easy for a student. Our slightly longer-term budget might involve the planning necessary to afford the car tax, MOT and motor insurance, all of which may fall due in the next few months.

Chapter 64 *Variances*

A key feature of the budgeting process is the **feedback** it provides for individuals and groups throughout an organisation. Feedback should reflect the information needs of each level of the organisation, with each level of reporting being interrelated with levels above and below. For example, a budget holder will wish to be informed of his or her own performance, as well as that of the budget holders for whom he or she is responsible.

WHAT DO YOU THINK?

As a manager, how might you want to monitor the budgetary process?

The key benefit of the budgeting process is to analyse how closely actual performance relates to budgeted performance. Wherever actual differs from budgeted performance a **variance** has arisen. The process of analysing the difference between actual performance and budgeted performance is **variance analysis**.

Variances are recorded as being either **adverse** (**A**) or **favourable** (**F**), depending upon whether actual expenditure is more or less than budget. If actual expenditure is *less* than budgeted expenditure, then the variance would be favourable. On the other hand, if actual expenditure is *more* than budgeted expenditure, then the variance is adverse.

Figure 3.21 shows that managers cannot be answerable for cost overruns if these occur in areas where they have no control. For example, whereas expenditure on machine maintenance may be controlled, this is not true of depreciation which is outside the control of the manager.

Understanding variances

Variances may arise for a number of reasons. These include:

1 **random deviations**, which are uncontrollable – as we saw above, these are outside the control of individual managers
2 **an incorrectly set budget** – this may require further research and management action
3 **failure to meet an agreed budget** – this would be because a manager has failed to meet the appropriate figures and deadlines.

Problems of the budgetary process

Budgetary and control systems vary from one organisation to another. They are found both in the private sector and the public sector, and in all sorts of organisations from the very small to the very large. Given the different aims of organisations, budgetary systems reflect the context in which they are put to use. There are, however, certain

Machine shop overhead report for October 2000			
	Budget £	**Actual** £	**Variance** £
Controllable			
Indirect wages	8,000	8,200	200A
Machine maintenance	2,250	1,900	350F
Consumable materials	500	550	50A
Total controllable costs	10,750	10,650	100F
Uncontrollable			
Depreciation	5,700	6,000	300A
Property cost apportionment	8,500	9,000	500A
Total uncontrollable costs	14,200	15,000	800A
Total cost centre overheads	24,950	25,650	700A

A = Adverse
F = Favourable

Figure 3.21 Controllable and uncontrollable costs

problems associated with budgeting processes which have to be recognised.

First, reliance upon budgeting and its processes is no substitute for good management. Budgeting should simply be viewed as one tool among many for managers to use. If forecasting is poor or inadequate allowances are made, the process may create unnecessary pressure upon managers to perform in a particular way. This may be stressful and cause antagonism and resentment within the organisation.

The creation of rigid financial plans which are 'cast in stone' may cause inertia in certain parts of a business and reduce its ability to adapt to change. Budgets may also not reflect the realities of the business environment and may act simply as a straitjacket upon the performance of managers and decision makers. It has also been argued that delays and time lags can make it difficult to compare budgeted and actual results.

> ## WHAT DO YOU THINK?
> Which of the following costs could be controlled by a marketing manager? Give reasons for your answers:
>
> a) Depreciation of furniture.
> b) Insurance of the building.
> c) Wages paid to staff.
> d) Advertising.
> e) Stationery.
> f) Office redecorations.
> g) Training costs.

Standard costing

Standard costing is a key method for budgetary control. Standard costing establishes predetermined estimates of costs and sales and then compares them with actual costs and sales achieved. The predetermined costs are known as **standard costs**. As we have already seen, the difference between standard and actual costs is the variance.

There are a number objectives of standard costing:

- To control costs by establishing a range of standards from which variances can be analysed.
- To assist with the setting of budgets.
- To provide a basis for measuring performance.
- To assist with the process of responsibility accounting.
- To motivate staff and managers.
- To provide a basis for evaluating and improving upon current performances.

According to T. Lucey (1998) in *Management Information Systems*, standard cost may be defined as follows:

> 'A standard expressed in money. It is built up from an assessment of the value of cost elements. Its main uses are providing a basis for performance measurement, control by exception reporting, valuing stock and establishing selling prices.'

Based on this interpretation, a standard must be set at a planned cost per unit from whatever is being costed. A standard cost may include use of materials, the price or other standard upon which cost is based, the planned hours to be worked and the hourly labour rate, as well as the overheads incurred.

Setting standards is the critical part of the standard costing process. Line managers are clearly involved here, assisted by work study staff, engineering specialists, accountants and many other specialists, all of whom can provide an input into the standard-setting process.

> ### The truth is stranger than fiction
> The budgeting process requires good communication between different parts of a business organisation. It can only work if managers take ownership of budgets and use them for control.

Chapter 65 *Cash flow forecasting*

An organisation must ensure that it has sufficient cash to carry out its plans, and ensure that the cash coming in is sufficient to cover the cash going out. At the same time it must take into account any cash surpluses it might have in the bank.

Looking carefully at the availability of liquid funds is essential to the smooth running of any organisation. With cash planning or budgeting it is possible to forecast the flows into and out of an organisation's bank account so that any surpluses or deficits can be highlighted and any necessary action can be taken promptly. For example, overdraft facilities may be arranged in good time so that funds are available when required.

The **cash flow forecast** is an extremely important tool within an organisation and has a number of clear purposes, including the following:

- The forecast can be used to highlight the **timing consequences** of the capital budget and different elements of subsidiary budgets and the master budget. For example, the capital budget may point to when machinery needs to be replaced and this can then be included in the cash flow forecast. Similarly, the trading forecast may have various expenses such as business and water rates, which may be paid quarterly or half-yearly. These can again be included in the cash flow forecast.

- The cash flow forecast is an essential document for the compilation of the **business plan**. It will help to show whether the organisation is capable of achieving the objectives it sets. This is very important if the business applies for finance, where the lender will almost certainly want to know about the ability of the applicant to keep on top of cash flow and meet the proposed payment schedules.

- The cash flow forecast will help to boost the **lender's confidence** and the **owner's confidence.** By looking into the future it will provide them with the reassurance they require that their plans are going according to schedule.

- It will also help with the **monitoring of performance**. The cash-flow forecast sets benchmarks against which the business is expected to perform. If the organisation actually performs differently from these benchmarks, then the cash flow forecast may have highlighted an area of investigation. As we have seen, investigating differences between forecast figures and actual figures is known as variance analysis.

In order to prepare a cash flow forecast you need to know what receipts and payments are likely to take place in the future and exactly when they will occur. It is important to know the length of the lead time between incurring an expense and paying for it, as well as the time lag between

CASE STUDY: PLANWARE

Planware is a trademark property of Invest-Tech Limited. One of its products is a financial planner called Exl-Plan (for Excel), a planning or budgeting tool that enables users to compile three-to-five-year cash flow projections by month for the first year, by quarter for the next two years and annually for the final two years.

This mathematical model helps to prepare cash flow projections which enable organisations to identify their short-term financial projections and banking requirements. The manufacturer claims that there are a number of advantages of using this type of computer-based model. For example:

1 it reduces the tedium of carrying out numerous repetitive calculations

2 it presents a range of results which can be used for estimating banking requirements

3 the computer-based model can assess the consequences of alternative strategies

4 assumptions can be altered to meet different scenarios.

QUESTIONS FOR DISCUSSION

1 How can using computers and spreadsheet packages in particular help with forecasting processes?

2 Who might require this information and how would they use it?

making a sale and collecting the money from debtors. The art of successful forecasting is being able to calculate receipts and expenditures accurately.

Most business transactions take place on credit and, as we have discussed earlier, most payments are made either weeks or months after documentation has been sent. For example, assume goods are paid for three months after a sale. This means that in April the cash will be received for sales in January, in May the cash will be received from February and so on. From the other viewpoint, if you have been given three months' credit you would pay for goods bought in January during April and so on.

When working though a cash flow forecast it is important to look carefully at the timing of every entry.

Example

A cash flow forecast for the six months ended 31 December 2000 can be drafted from the following information:

1 Cash balance 1 July 2000: £4,500.
2 Sales are £15 per unit and cash is received three months after the sale. For the period in question the sale of units is:

2000

Mar	Apr	May	Jun	Jul	Aug
60	60	75	90	55	140

2001

Sep	Oct	Nov	Dec	Jan	Feb
130	150	150	160	170	150

3 Production in units:

2000

Mar	Apr	May	Jun	Jul	Aug
40	50	80	70	80	130

2001

Sep	Oct	Nov	Dec	Jan	Feb
130	150	145	160	170	160

4 Raw materials cost £4 per unit and these are paid for two months *before* being used in production.
5 Wages are £5 per unit and these are paid for in the same month as the unit is produced.
6 Running costs are £4 per unit; 50 per cent of the cost is paid in the same month of production while the other 50 per cent is paid for in the month after production.
7 Sundry expenses of £50 are paid monthly.

Cash flow headings

Cash flow headings may vary according to the nature of the business and the complexity of the exercise as well as the

Receipts from sales				
	£			
July	60 (April)	×	15 =	900
August	75 (May)	×	15 =	1,125
September	90 (June)	×	15 =	1,350
October	55 (July)	×	15 =	825
November	140 (Aug)	×	15 =	2,100
December	130 (Sept)	×	15 =	1,950

Payments per month				
July	£			
Raw materials	130 (Sept)	×	4 =	520
Wages	80 (July)	×	5 =	400
Running costs	80 (July)	×	2 =	160
	70 (June)	×	2 =	140
Sundry expenses			=	50
				£1,270
August	£			
Raw materials	150 (Oct)	×	4 =	600
Wages	130 (Aug)	×	5 =	650
Running costs	130 (Aug)	×	2 =	260
	80 (July)	×	2 =	160
Sundry expenses			=	50
				£1,720
September	£			
Raw materials	145 (Nov)	×	4 =	580
Wages	130 (Sept)	×	5 =	650
Running costs	130 (Sept)	×	2 =	260
	130 (Aug)	×	2 =	260
Sundry expenses			=	50
				£1,800
October	£			
Raw materials	160 (Dec)	×	4 =	640
Wages	150 (Oct)	×	5 =	750
Running costs	150 (Oct)	×	2 =	300
	130 (Sept)	×	2 =	260
Sundry expenses			=	50
				£2,000
November	£			
Raw materials	170 (Jan)	×	4 =	680
Wages	145 (Nov)	×	5 =	725
Running costs	145 (Nov)	×	2 =	290
	150 (Oct)	×	2 =	300
Sundry expenses			=	50
				£2,045
December	£			
Raw materials	160 (Feb)	×	4 =	640
Wages	160 (Dec)	×	5 =	800
Running costs	160 (Dec)	×	2 =	320
	145 (Nov)	×	2 =	290
Sundry expenses			=	50
				£2,100

Figure 3.22 Cash flow chart

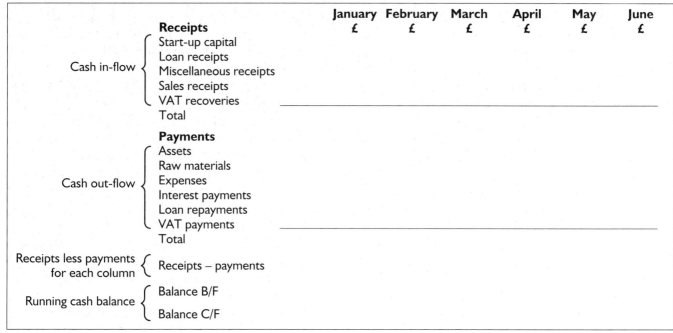

		January £	February £	March £	April £	May £	June £
Cash in-flow	**Receipts**						
	Start-up capital						
	Loan receipts						
	Miscellaneous receipts						
	Sales receipts						
	VAT recoveries						
	Total						
Cash out-flow	**Payments**						
	Assets						
	Raw materials						
	Expenses						
	Interest payments						
	Loan repayments						
	VAT payments						
	Total						
Receipts less payments for each column	Receipts – payments						
Running cash balance	Balance B/F						
	Balance C/F						

Figure 3.23 Outline for a cash-flow forecast

range of possible inflows and outflows which it is possible for a business organisation to have.

Some of the more likely cash inflow headings are as follows:

- **Start-up capital**. This would be the capital put into the business when trading activities begin.
- **Loan receipts**. If a business receives money from a loan it would appear as a receipt.
- **Miscellaneous receipts**. A business organisation may have a number of miscellaneous receipts which could inject finance into the cash flow forecast (for example rent received and income from the sale of an asset).
- **Sales receipts**. The most common form of receipt, this is simply income from sales.
- **VAT recoveries**. If more VAT is paid on purchases than is received on sales, then the VAT recovered from Customs and Excise would be an inflow. (*Note:* this is likely to happen very often.)

Some of the more likely cash outflow headings include the following:

- **Payments for assets**. Asset purchase will be predictable through the capital budget and the amounts used for each purchase will be deducted through the cash flow forecast.
- **Raw materials**. This is likely to be a regular outflow which may relate to a production schedule or the volume of sales.

- **Expenses**. These might include water rates and telephone bills, as well as many other running costs. They will *not* include depreciation as this is not a movement of funds.
- **Interest payments/loan repayments**. Where these appear they are regular payments for the use of capital.
- **VAT payments**. As we have seen, VAT is usually charged for three-monthly periods.

owner anticipates that his receipts over the next six months are likely to be as follows:

Jan	Feb	Mar	Apr	May	June
£1,400	£1,600	£1,500	£1,000	£900	£700

He has also worked out his payments and expects these to be:

Jan	Feb	Mar	Apr	May	June
£1,100	£700	£900	£1,400	£1,000	£900

Prepare S. Todd Ltd's cash flow forecast for the six months.

3 Following their recent fashion revival, Andrew Nut sets up in business as a manufacturer of string vests by putting £28,500 into a business bank account on 1 January. For the first six months of the year he anticipates or budgets for the following situations:

- His forecasts for the purchase of raw materials and sales receipts for finished goods, based upon extensive market research, are as follows:

	Purchases (£)	Sales (£)
January	6,500	5,500
February	7,000	7,100
March	7,300	8,000
April	7,500	14,000
May	6,100	17,000
June	6,500	14,300

- He has arranged one month's credit from suppliers, so raw materials purchased in January will have to be paid for in February.
- He expects one-half of sales to be for cash and the other half on credit. He anticipates two months on average to be taken by credit customers, that is, sales made in January on credit will not be settled until March.
- Wages are expected to be £1,000 per month, paid in the same month.
- Machinery must be purchased for £15,500 on 1 January and must be paid for in the same month.
- Rent for his factory is £6,000 per annum, payable in equal instalments at the start of each month.
- Other costs (overheads) are £1,500 per month, and these are assumed to be paid in the month following that in which they are incurred.
- In April, Andrew Nut expects to receive an inheritance from his Aunt Kitty of £8,000 which he will put straight into the business bank account.

Prepare Andrew Nut's cash-flow forecast for the first six months.

The truth is stranger than fiction

Celtic, the Scottish Premier League club, recently plunged £6 million into the red. Despite high attendance at football games, its achievements have just not managed to meet the aspirations of shareholders and supporters. Despite this, Celtic has continued to buy star players to improve the strength of its squad.

SECTION C *Classification and analysis of costs*

INTRODUCTION   Most managers think about their activities or the activities of their departments within some form of cost structure. The measurement of each activity will be determined by how much expenditure is allocated to the activity, and this will help the decision-maker to think carefully about what alternatives are available and what decisions to take. Over the past twenty years the use of information technology has changed the ways in which information about costs is both generated and made available. Such information ensures that the right decision can be made when required.

Critical thinking

The Channel Tunnel opened one year later than planned at a cost of around £10 billion, which was more than twice the original estimate. As a result banks and shareholders had to help to bail the project out. There were also criticisms that although the French government successfully linked the tunnel to their national railway system, there was inadequate infrastructure on the UK side to do so.

The Channel Tunnel helps to show how difficult large projects are to cost. The most recent example of this is the Millennium Dome. The project designed as a masterpiece for the Millennium ended up as a costly failure. Not only was it heavily criticised by the press; many also felt that the investment should have been made in a project that would have been more worthwhile, less short-term, and of greater benefit to more people.

WHAT DO YOU THINK?
1 Explain why large projects are difficult to cost accurately.
2 What methods might help such projects to meet their financial budgets more accurately?

Chapter 66 *Classification of costs*

Almost all business activities involve some element of **cost** and most managers have to deal with costs on a day-to-day basis. Costs are fundamental – from the early development of business plans through to the controlling and monitoring of expenditure. Costing techniques help managers to work out what they should be doing and to develop measures that help them to control their activities. Information about costs will help to:

- create short-term, medium-term and long-term plans
- control the organisation's activities
- decide between alternative strategies
- appraise performance at strategic, departmental and organisational levels.

Accountants use knowledge of costs to predict future events. In doing so they can anticipate changes in taxation, interest rates, actions of competitors and also of markets. They will also look at past events, in order to guide future decision making.

WHAT DO YOU THINK?
What does the word 'cost' mean to you?

The word 'cost' has several meanings, even in everyday language. The cost of items we purchase is something we think about daily; for us, it is a money sacrifice we have to make for goods or services that we require. Cost also implies some form of measurement as we automatically attach a value to many of the products that we see. It can be an unwelcome word, particularly if we come across hidden costs which we had not anticipated having to pay.

People in organisations frequently talk about calculating the cost of an event, activity or product. Within this context, they are using a knowledge of costs together with a knowledge of revenues and income flows to determine whether or not something they are planning will ultimately reap the rewards they desire.

Nearly all business activities involve some form of cost. A good knowledge of costs and their influences is fundamental in assessing their profitability, as profits are only a reflection of income over these costs. Costs from the past, which have already been incurred, should provide a guide to costs in the future. However, they have to be critically examined, discussed and often adjusted to be of use to the accountant for predicting future profitability. At a later stage, accountants will make informed comparisons between actual events and standards that have been set.

There are two broad approaches to the classification of business costs:

1 One method categorises costs by their type and identifies whether they can be directly related to the final product or service of the business.
2 The other approach is to analyse costs according to whether they remain fixed with changes in output levels. This forms the foundation for decision making as we shall see when we look at contribution and break-even analysis in the next chapter.

Direct and indirect costs

Direct costs

Direct costs are those costs that can be clearly identified with the product or service being provided. Typical examples include the following:

- **Direct labour** – payments made to workers who make products or provide services. An engineering firm may incur direct wages paid to machine operators and an office-cleaning business will pay direct wages to cleaners.
- **Direct materials** – the cost incurred for materials used to make specific products or to provide specific services. An engineering firm may require materials in the form of base metals and ready-made components; the cleaning firm will require chemicals and materials for specific cleaning contracts.
- **Direct expenses** – other costs may be incurred specifically for the final product or service. These may include payments to the product's designer (in the form of royalties), payments made to other businesses for work they have done as subcontractors to help provide the finished product or service for the consumer, and sometimes also power and depreciation, but only if there is a direct link between the cost unit and the use of power or the depreciation taking place.

Indirect costs

Indirect costs are those that cannot be classified as direct costs. Wherever possible, costs incurred by businesses are identified with specific products or services, as this provides them with the most accurate costing of a firm's output.

However, many costs incurred by businesses cannot be easily related to specific units of production or service. For example, it is usually very difficult and time consuming to relate precise amounts of electricity used and property rents incurred to specific units of output. Indirect costs can be classified as follows:

- **Indirect labour** – this would include the cost of management, administration and marketing personnel. Even the cost of many 'blue-collar' workers may need to be classified as indirect labour if they are not doing work that results directly in a product or service. Examples are maintenance workers and stores personnel.

- **Indirect materials** – these include small items which are difficult to relate directly to items of output. In fact, the costs of relating them to specific items of output would outweigh the benefits of slightly more accurate product costs. Examples of indirect costs include lubricating materials, rags for cleaning and small nuts and bolts.

CASE STUDY: TAYLOUR COATS PLC

Taylour Coats manufactures high-class country jackets. Business has developed well over recent years, particularly in the company's main export market, the USA, where English country clothing has become increasingly popular.

The company is managed and owned by Manjit Gill, the Managing Director, and Rosemary Williams, who supervises the operations. They own a factory unit on a trading estate in Gosforth, and employ 20 full-time employees, a foreman, 15 machine operators who cut out the materials for the part-time workers, and four dispatchers. The part-time workers are employed as subcontractors, using their own sewing machines at home to make up the jackets from the cut-out pieces that have been sent to them.

The foreman is paid £400 per week, the machine operators £230 per week and the dispatchers £180 per week. The part-timers are paid £10 for each jacket they make up.

Other business costs include:

- electricity at £100 per week
- rent and rates at £500 per week
- loan repayments, including interest at £200 per week
- other fixed costs of £120 per week
- directors' salaries for Manjit and Rosemary of £600 per week each
- material costs for each jacket of £5.

The existing capacity for Taylour Coats is 400 jackets per week. If it needs to produce more than this, it has to pay higher rates to cover overtime put in by part-time workers, which results in an increase in part-time rates from £10 for each jacket to £15, up to a maximum capacity of 500 jackets. At present jackets are priced at £35 and Taylour Coats has a consistent weekly turnover of 350 jackets.

The company has been approached by two US chain stores which have tested samples and wish to purchase some jackets on a regular basis. Austin Stores Inc. wishes to purchase 100 jackets per week and is willing to pay £28 per jacket. NMAUSA wishes to purchase 50 jackets per week and is willing to pay £32 per jacket. As a personal friend of the directors and an adviser to the business, these figures have been left with you for further analysis.

QUESTIONS FOR DISCUSSION

1. Construct a table to show the fixed, variable and total weekly costs at each 50 units of production up to a maximum of 500 jackets.
2. Present the fixed, variable and total costs for the week in a graphical form.
3. Calculate the profit the company is generating at its present level of sales of 350 jackets per week.
4. Advise the directors as to whether they should accept:
   a) the Austin Stores order
   b) the NMAUSA order
   c) both
   d) neither.
   Support your answer with figures and explanations.

- **Indirect expenses** – these include a wide range of costs such as property rents, power, stationery, rates, telephone and other running expenses, as well as depreciation of fixed assets.

Total indirect costs are called **overheads**.

Fixed and variable costs

Another method of classifying costs, as mentioned above, is according to their relationship with changes in output levels. This identifies costs as either fixed or variable.

Fixed costs

These are costs that do not increase as total output increases. For example, if an organisation has the capacity needed it might increase its production from 25,000 to 30,000 units. Its rent, rates and heating bills will be the same, since they also had to be paid when the organisation was producing 25,000 units (see Figure 3.24).

Variable costs

These are the costs that increase as total output increases because more of these factors need to be employed as inputs in order to increase outputs (see Figure 3.25). For example, if a company produces more items it will need more raw materials.

Total costs

You have been introduced to two different classifications of cost. One describes the nature of costs incurred (direct and indirect costs) and the other how these vary with the level of production (variable and fixed costs). You may find it useful to think of the classifications as follows:

- Direct costs can generally be considered as variable costs
- Indirect costs can generally be considered as fixed costs.

Although this is in some ways a simplification, these statements should help your basic understanding of business costs. Total costs are calculated as follows:

Total costs = Direct costs + Indirect costs

Total costs = Variable costs + Fixed costs

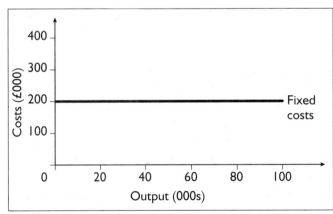

Figure 3.24 Fixed costs

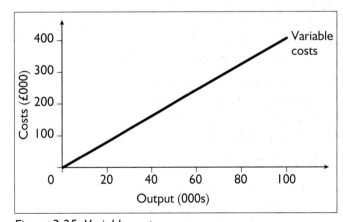

Figure 3.25 Variable costs

The truth is stranger than fiction
Charles Letts, the two centuries old diary-maker, has partially returned to family ownership with the sale by Bemrose, the print business, to a management buyout. The company was bought by Bemrose in 1996. Charles Letts was founded in 1796 and produced the first commercial diary in 1812. It was based in Southwark, South London, until the early 1960s, when it moved to Dalkeith in Scotland.

Chapter 67 Break-even analysis

The **break-even point** is the point at which sales levels are high enough not to make a loss, but not high enough to make a profit.

The concept of break even is a development from the principles of **marginal costing**. Marginal costing is a commonly used technique which uses costs to forecast profits from the production and sales levels expected in future periods. The great benefit of marginal costing over other costing methods is that it overcomes the problem of allocating fixed costs – only variable costs are allocated, as we shall see.

The difference between an item's selling price and the variable costs needed to produce that item is known as its **contribution** (that is, its contribution to the whole profit), calculated as:

Contribution = Selling price per unit – Variable costs per unit.

By producing and selling enough units to produce a total contribution that is in excess of the **fixed costs**, an organisation will make a profit.

For example, Penzance Toys Ltd manufactures plastic train sets for young children. It anticipates that next year it will sell 8,000 units at £12 per unit. Its variable costs are £5 per unit and its fixed costs are £9,000. From the above formula we can deduce that the contribution is £12 minus £5, which is £7 per unit. Therefore – for each unit made – £7 will go towards paying fixed costs. We can also illustrate this using totals to show how much profit will be made if the company sells 8,000 units (see Figure 3.26). The problem can also be looked at by constructing a table as in Table 3.5.

WHAT DO YOU THINK?

Rovers Medallions Ltd produces a standard size trophy for sports shops and clubs. It hopes to sell 2,000 trophies next year at £9 per unit. Its variable costs are £5 per unit and its fixed costs are £4,000. Draw up a profit statement to show how much profit it will make in the year. Also construct a table to show how much profit it will make at each 500 units of production up to 3,000 units.

Marginal costing is particularly useful for making short-term decisions, for example helping to set the selling price of a product, or deciding whether or not to accept an order. It might also help an organisation to decide whether to buy in a component or produce it itself.

Break-even analysis is a concept which is central to the process of marginal costing. Breaking even is the unique point at which an organisation makes neither profit nor loss. If sales go beyond the break-even point, profits are made, and if they are below the break-even point, losses are made. In marginal costing it is the *point at which the contribution equals the fixed costs.*

	(£)
Sales revenue (8000 × £5)	96 000
Less marginal costs (8000 × £5)	40 000
Total contribution	56 000
Less fixed costs	9 000
Net profit	47 000

Figure 3.26 Profit statement for Penzance Toys Ltd

Table 3.5 Profit table for Penzance Toys Ltd

Units of production	Fixed costs (£)	Variable costs (£)	Total costs (£)	Revenue (£)	Profit (loss) (£)
1 000	9 000	5 000	14 000	12 000	(2 000)
2 000	9 000	10 000	19 000	24 000	5 000
3 000	9 000	15 000	24 000	36 000	12 000
4 000	9 000	20 000	29 000	48 000	19 000
5 000	9 000	25 000	34 000	60 000	26 000
6 000	9 000	30 000	39 000	72 000	33 000
7 000	9 000	35 000	44 000	84 000	40 000
8 000	9 000	40 000	49 000	96 000	47 000
9 000	9 000	45 000	54 000	108 000	54 000
10 000	9 000	50 000	59 000	120 000	61 000

To calculate the break-even point there are two stages:

1 Calculate the unit contribution (selling price less variable costs).
2 Divide the fixed costs by the unit contribution.

$$\frac{\text{Fixed costs}}{\text{Break-even point}} = \text{Unit contribution}$$

For example, in the case of Penzance Toys Ltd the contribution per unit is £7 and the fixed costs are £9,000. The break-even point would therefore be:

$$\frac{9,000}{7} = 1,286 \text{ units (to nearest unit).}$$

The **sales value** at the break-even point can be calculated by multiplying the number of units by the selling price per unit. For Penzance Toys this would be:

$$1,286 \times £12 = £15,432.$$

Penzance Toys has covered its costs (fixed and variable) and broken even with a sales value of £15,432. Anything sold in excess of this will provide it with profits.

If an organisation has a **profit target** or selected operating point to aim at, break-even analysis can be used to calculate the number of units that need to be sold and the value of sales required to achieve that target.

For example, consider that Penzance Toys wishes to achieve a target of £15,000 profit. By adding this £15,000 to the fixed costs and dividing by the contribution, the number of units which need to be sold to meet this target can be found. Thus:

$$\frac{£9,000 + £15,000}{£7} = 3,429 \text{ units (to nearest unit).}$$

The difference between the break-even point and the selected level of activity designed to achieve the profit target is known as the **margin of safety**.

A break-even chart can be used to show changes in the relationship between costs, production volumes and various levels of sales activity. The following is the procedure to construct a break-even chart (you may find it useful to look at Figure 3.26 as you read the procedure):

1 Label the horizontal axis for units of production and sales.
2 Label the vertical axis to represent the values of sales and costs.
3 Plot fixed costs. Fixed costs will remain the same over all levels of production, so plot this as a straight line parallel to the horizontal axis.
4 Plot the total costs (variable costs and fixed costs). This will be a line rising from where the fixed cost line touches the vertical axis. It is plotted by calculating the total costs at two or three random levels of production.
5 Sales are plotted by taking two or three random levels of turnover. The line will rise from the intersection of the two axes.

The break-even point will be where the total cost line and the sales line intersect. The area to the left of the break-even point between the sales and total cost lines will represent *losses*, and the area to the *right* of the break-even point between these lines will represent *profit*.

For example, Eddie Bowen plans to set up a small restaurant. In doing so he knows that he will immediately incur annual fixed costs of £10,000. He is concerned about how many meals he will have to sell to break even. Extensive market research indicates that a typical customer will pay £8 for a meal, and Eddie knows that variable costs – such as cooking ingredients and the costs of serving customers – will amount to about £3. Eddie has set himself a profit target of £14,000 for the first year of operation. Our task is to advise Eddie on the number of meals he has to sell and to indicate to him his margin of safety.

Eddie's *unit contribution* is:

$$£8 - £3 \text{ (Selling price – Variable cost)} = £5 \text{ per meal.}$$

His *break-even point* in units will be:

$$\frac{£10,000 \text{ (Fixed costs)}}{£5 \text{ (Unit contribution)}} = 2,000 \text{ meals.}$$

The *sales value* of the meals will be:

$$2,000 \text{ meals} \times £8 \text{ (Selling price)} = £16,000.$$

His *profit target* will be achieved by:

$$\frac{£10,000 \text{ (Fixed costs)} + £14,000 \text{ (Profit target)}}{£5 \text{ (Unit contribution)}} = \frac{4,800}{\text{meals.}}$$

The *margin of safety* will be the difference between the selected level of activity and the break-even point. It will be between 4,800 meals, with a turnover of £38,400, and 2,000 meals, with a turnover of £16,000.

The three random levels of variable costs and sales chosen for the purpose of plotting the break-even chart, at 1,000 meals, 3,000 meals and 5,000 meals, are shown in Table 3.6.

Table 3.6 Random levels of variable costs and sales

	1,000 meals £	3,000 meals £	5,000 meals £
Variable costs (£3 per meal)	3,000	9,000	15,000
Fixed costs	10,000	10,000	10,000
Total costs	13,000	19,000	25,000
Sales	8,000	24,000	40,000

We can now plot the break-even chart which shows graphically the break-even point of 2,000 meals with a sales revenue of £16,000 (see Figure 3.27). The margin of safety can be seen on the chart if we identify the selected level of profit (at 4,800 meals) and the targeted turnover (of £38,400), and compare this point with the break-even point.

The break-even chart is a simple visual tool enabling managers to anticipate the effects of changes in production and sales upon the profitability of an organisation's activities. It emphasises the importance of earning revenue and is particularly helpful for those who are unused to interpreting accounting information.

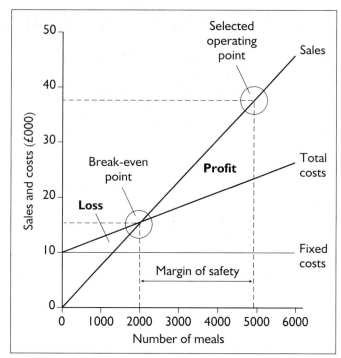

Figure 3.27 Eddie's break-even chart

The break-even chart can be used to explore changes in a number of key variables. These may include the following:

- **Sales volume and value**. By looking at the chart it is possible to predict the effects of any changes in sales trends. For example, a sudden fall in sales may lead to a loss and a sudden increase may improve profitability.
- **Profits or losses at a given level of production**. The break-even chart enables a business to monitor levels of production. By doing this, important decisions can be made if changes take place.
- **Prices**. It is possible to use the break-even chart to analyse different business scenarios. For example, given market research information, what would happen if we reduced the price by £2?
- **Costs**. The effects of any sudden changes in costs can be plotted on the break-even chart.

Any of the above may affect an organisation's ability to achieve its selected operating point and margin of safety. The break-even chart is a useful management technique upon which to base action which enables an organisation to achieve its plans.

CASE STUDY: A GOING CONCERN?

John Smith had a visit from an aged relative who wanted advice. For many years she had run a small hotel in a market town in the Thames valley. After careful consideration she had decided to 'call it a day' and retire, but she was keen to see the business continue and wished to retain her ownership in it.

John is interested in a proposition she has put forward, which involves running the hotel on her behalf. The hotel has been allowed to deteriorate over the years and, in John's opinion, it is obvious that extensive refurbishment is necessary before he could realistically consider her proposal. However, the hotel, which is in a prime spot, was extensively used little more than ten years ago, and John feels that with hard work it has the potential to become successful again.

He has arranged for a number of quotations to be made for the building work. The most favourable received was for £180,000, which involved extensive interior redecoration and refurbishment as well as completely reorganising the reception and kitchen areas.

John's intention is that the finance for the building work should come from a five-year bank loan with a fixed annual interest rate of 10 per cent, payable each calendar month, and based upon the original sum. The loan principal would be paid back in five equal annual instalments.

He has estimated the following fixed and variable costs:

1 *Fixed:*
   - Annual loan repayment £36,000
   - Annual interest on loan £18,000
   - Business rate and water rates £7,000 per annum
   - Insurance £4,500 per annum
   - Electricity £1,300 per quarter
   - Staff salaries £37,000 per annum.
2 *Variable:*
   These include direct labour such as cleaners and bar staff, as well as the cost of food, bar stocks, etc. After careful research John has estimated these to be £2,000 for each 100 customers who visit the hotel.

John has had a local agency conduct an extensive market research survey and feels confident that the hotel will attract about 100 customers per week, who will each spend on average (including accommodation, food and drinks) about £70 in the hotel.

QUESTIONS FOR DISCUSSION

1 Work out the break-even point for the hotel in both numbers of customers and value.
2 Work out the numbers of customers required to make a gross profit of £35,000.
3 Draw a break-even chart showing the break-even point, the profit target and the margin of safety.
4 What other information might John Smith require before deciding to go ahead with the project?

CASE STUDY: THEME HOLIDAYS LTD

Theme Holidays Ltd is a private company that specialises in providing holidays for adults and children alike who require a unique form of entertainment. All of their holidays involve overseas packages based upon a theme. With the opening of Disneyland Paris they are finding that half of the packages they now provide are based on this one resort, while the other half are to theme destinations in the USA.

Theme Holidays is currently reviewing its profitability for 2001. It anticipates that its fixed overheads will be £450,000 for the year. With the Disneyland Paris packages, a quarter of the variable costs go in travel costs, at an average of £30 per package. The company anticipates selling packages at an average of £160 per holiday in 2001.

The US holidays are sold at an average price of £650 per holiday. Travel costs of £200 for the US holidays comprise half of the variable costs of the holiday.

Market research has revealed that, during 2001, Theme Holidays expects to sell 400 holidays.

QUESTIONS FOR DISCUSSION

1 Work out the contribution for both the European and the US holidays.

2 Calculate the company's profit for the year before tax and interest.

3 Market research also revealed that if Theme Holidays reduced its prices by 10 per cent it could sell 300 more holidays per year. Calculate how this would affect profitability and advise accordingly.

4 Theme Holidays is aware of the size of its fixed overheads. How would a 10 per cent reduction in fixed overheads through cost-cutting measures affect both of the above?

The truth is stranger than fiction

Continental Airlines is turning Newark International Airport in New York into the gateway to Europe. Newark today handles more passengers than John F Kennedy and LaGuardia. Continental is investing US$1 billion into developing the airport, with the opening of a monorail link connecting the airport with Manhattan.

Chapter 68 Data for decision making

Every organisation has to make decisions. Often these decisions are influenced by a host of both internal and external factors that can make decision making very difficult. In an uncertain world, organisations require information on which to base their decisions. Statistics and quantitative techniques fulfil this role by providing managers with the ability to make estimates or comparisons of previous or current events, so that decisions about the future can be made.

Much of the information used by organisations on a day-to-day basis is quantitative in nature – that is, it involves figures. Interpreting these figures requires common sense, problem-solving skills and the ability to communicate. The results of decisions are never entirely predictable, but by understanding and using statistics, it is possible to keep the uncertainty to a minimum. Knowledge of statistics is therefore an essential tool of business.

The term 'statistics' contains three fundamental elements:

1 It can be used as a blanket term for describing facts and figures.
2 It enables a mass of information to be presented according to a particular pattern.

3 It provides a method of interpreting business data.

Information for simple problems

The first question any manager in an organisation will ask is 'What information do I need?' Managers at all levels will from time to time have information at their fingertips. It may be derived from the market, or it may relate to their level of output or productivity. The more accurate and complete the information is, the more successful decision taking is likely to be; the more inaccurate or misleading the information, the worse the decision. Information must, wherever possible, be accurate and complete. Where it is vague or lacks reliability, it may mislead managers into making key decisions which turn out badly for the organisation – and for them!

WHAT DO YOU THINK?
To what extent could it be argued today that the amount of information available for managers, and the development of electronic forms of information such as the Internet, have made decision making much more difficult?

CASE STUDY: INFORMATION NEEDS

'Have you ever had the feeling that the information you are giving managers isn't exactly what they wanted? Have you ever tried to find out what they want?

'If you have, then you may well have reached – or at least approached – a state of despair! For years, no matter what variations and improvements I made to the information I gave to managers, I just never seemed to satisfy their exact needs. I even went through the stage of believing it was some kind of plot to make management accountants feel inadequate.

'Then one day I discovered – some people might say stumbled on – a solution to the problem of defining management's information needs. My amazing discovery was that information is the raw

material of decision making and that, in order to know what information managers need, we have to know what decisions they take. This pretty obvious statement led to the development of a process which I have appropriately named "decision information analysis". This requires a careful analysis of the decisions that managers make and then, for each decision, accessing the information needed.'

QUESTIONS FOR DISCUSSION

1 Explain why managers require information.
2 Why is it important to give managers the information they want?
3 What solution is suggested by this case study?

Internal data is information extracted from within an organisation. **External data** is found outside the business in the environment in which it operates. (See Figure 3.28.)

Before gathering information, a number of key questions need to be asked:

1 **What are the precise objectives of the exercise?** It is important to consider the aims of the exercise to ensure that time is not spent collecting unnecessary information.

2 **What units of measurement are to be used?** For example, if you are collecting sales figures, do you require the information to be in pounds sterling, volume or both?

3 **What degree of accuracy is required?** To obtain a high degree of accuracy you will have to spend more time and effort gathering information. However, an investigation of a sample of the total may be just as revealing.

4 **Is the information cost-effective?** If the point of the exercise is to collect information, it must be worth spending the time and money to do so.

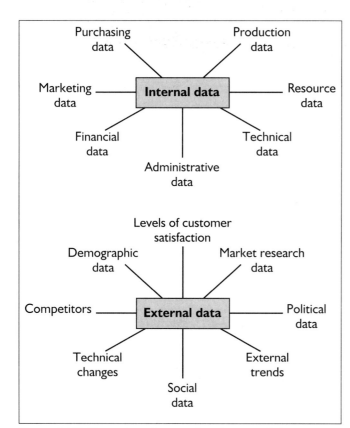

Figure 3.28 Examples of internal and external data

WHAT DO YOU THINK?

Working as a small group, develop a business idea. Discuss and refine the idea, and talk about the sort of information you would need before going ahead with the development of a business plan. Using the four questions above, consider what information you would require to pursue your business idea and also why you would require this information. How difficult would it be to collect this information? What information would you like, but be unable to find?

Each level of management will have different information needs:

1 Strategic level managers deal with policy decisions and matters concerning the future of the organisation. They need to use carefully prepared information, not only from within the business but also from outside.

2 Tactical level managers tend to make decisions based on strategic policy decisions. They are concerned with analysing issues within the organisation and will often require additional information relating to a particular period.

3 Organisational decision makers will need information for grassroots problems associated with the day-to-day running of the organisation. The information required should help to resolve practical operational problems.

As we have seen, **qualitative data** typically consists of attitudes, opinions, reactions, suggestions or subjective descriptions, often given in response to surveys or questionnaires. **Quantitative data** involves amounts, such as the average number of customers who come to a shop during the day. Qualitative data often helps to provide the context within which quantitative facts operate.

Quantitative approaches to decision making are often helpful in that they allow alternatives to be measured in terms of a common denominator. For example, if a company wished to maximise its return on a £10,000 investment over a three-year period, the quantitative comparison in Table 3.7 would show that Project A was the best long-term investment.

Table 3.7 Quantitative comparison of data

Initial investment	Year 1	Year 2	Year 3
£10,000 – Project A	£3,000	£5,000	£8,000
£10,000 – Project B	£2,000	£3,000	£4,000
£10,000 – Project C	£3,000	£4,000	£4,000

Those in favour of quantification argue that without it, resources may be wasted, because decisions tend to be based upon subjective qualitative procedures. But many decisions cannot be reduced to such simple mathematical calculations. Often decisions involve variables which cannot be quantified (except perhaps by dubious 'guestimates').

Different individuals have different styles of decision making and therefore tend to require different types of data. For example, the analytical decision maker may be inclined to use statistical information before arriving at a decision. In contrast, the directive decision maker may prefer to make an intuitive decision based upon what 'feels right'. This decision maker may not consciously weigh up the advantages and disadvantages of the alternatives, but may simply make a decision based upon a 'hunch'.

Research shows that senior managers often have to rely on intuitive judgement when making decisions, simply because there are insufficient data available. Many of the most exciting decisions made by entrepreneurial organisations may be based upon intuition rather than calculated analysis. However, basing managerial decisions solely on intuition is unwise. Organisations operate in complex environments requiring sound judgement. The more that 'chance' can be removed from the equation, the more successful the decision is likely to be.

Managers who say 'I've been in the industry for 30 years' as if that alone provided the basis for making decisions are deluding themselves. But those who have no practical experience on which to base their decisions are equally at a disadvantage. Decision making should be based on a combination of practice, observation and theory.

The truth is stranger than fiction

The replacement tyre market grew by 0.4 per cent in value during 1999, to reach a total value of £711 million. The largest distributor in this market has 783 outlets. The top three types of tyre are Goodyear/Dunlop, Michelin and Pirelli, and these account for 56.2 per cent of market share.

Chapter 69 *Presentation of data*

Imagine that you have been asked to obtain information for a report by your manager. After collecting armfuls of facts and figures from every possible source, you deposit the results of your search on her desk. She complains: 'You cannot expect me to read all of this. I'm busy!'

The fact is that people find it difficult to look at a sea of information. It can be time consuming and it may be difficult to establish what it all means, particularly for those who are not experienced in interpreting figures.

Once statistical data have been obtained, they need to be broken down and presented in a way that reveal their significance. Information can be displayed in the form of a frequency distribution or table, or as a graph or chart. The nature of the data collected and the use to which they are to be put will determine the way in which the data are presented.

Arrays and frequency distributions

When raw data are first assembled, they are unlikely to be in any kind of order. By imposing order on data, it is possible to draw out and interpret the values and concentrations of values contained within them.

An **array** is a simple arrangement of figures into ascending or descending values. For example, suppose that the number of days' credit for 20 customers is varied as follows:

12	21	32	65	18	20	14	51	81	32
31	45	16	51	71	40	24	32	18	33

This could be arranged in ascending order:

12	14	16	18	18	20	21	24	31	32
32	32	33	40	45	51	51	65	71	81

In the past, tally marks were a quick and useful method of counting totals by displaying them in the form of matchsticks. After every four marks, the fifth crossed out the previous four so that the totals could be counted easily. Using tally marks, the average age of a company's employees could be presented in tabular form as shown in Figure 3.29.

Figure 3.29 shows various age bands, but does not show the individual age of each employee. Within each band,

Age range	Tally marks	Number of employees
Under 20	II	2
21–30	卌 卌 I	11
31–40	卌 卌 II	12
41–50	卌 III	8
51–60	卌	5
Over 60	III	3
Total employees		41

Figure 3.29 *Displaying data using tally marks*

some measurements of the 'age variable' appear more than once – for example, the table shows that there are two employees in the 'under 20' age band. Since the table records how many times a value occurs, it can be described as a **frequency distribution**. As groups have been used, it can also be described as a **grouped frequency distribution**.

WHAT DO YOU THINK?

In a factory the following number of machine breakdowns have occurred each hour over a 40-hour week:

8	15	43	12	51	2	4	19
4	18	39	56	12	23	27	28
11	2	5	25	18	51	19	50
12	5	6	29	16	57	19	33
24	37	18	3	12	6	60	39

Construct a grouped frequency distribution from the data using:

- six class intervals of equal width
- class intervals of ten.

Tables

After data have been broken down, they can be organised into a table. A **table** is a matrix of rows and columns demonstrating the relationship between two variables. It summarises information in a form that is clear and easy to read, such as the population forecasts below (see Table 3.8).

Table 3.8 *Displaying data in table format: population forecasts*

Country	Year 2000	2005	2010	2015	2020
UK	59,039	59,599	59,966	60,306	60,674
Austria	8,091	8,162	8,201	8,221	8,172
Greece	10,335	10,448	10,554	10,571	10,594
Spain	39,381	39,333	38,940	38,200	37,231

WHAT DO YOU THINK?

Look at Table 3.8. Explain why a table is a useful method of presenting information and for making comparisons.

Charts

For many people a table is simply a set of figures. They need time to think about it, to analyse the figures and to draw meaningful conclusions. **Charts** are eye-catching and enable information to be presented in a form that can be readily understood. A chart may succeed in making the information more meaningful.

A **pictogram** is a diagrammatic form of display which uses pictures or symbols as well as numbers. The systems used are explained in a key (see Figure 3.30).

One form of statistical representation commonly used in newspapers, articles and other publications is that of the

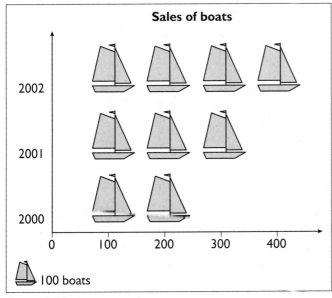

Figure 3.30 A pictogram

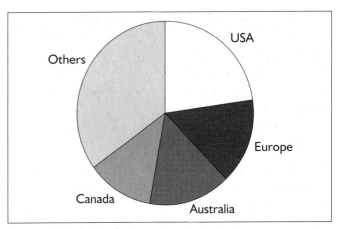

Figure 3.31 A pie chart

pie chart. In a pie chart, each 'slice' represents a component's contribution to the total amount. The 360° of the circle are divided up in proportion to the figures obtained. If you are using a computer spreadsheet such as Excel, it is possible to convert the table into a pie or any other form of chart. If you need to do it by hand, you will need a protractor. The following method can be used to convert each relative proportion to degrees:

$$\frac{\text{Proportion}}{\text{Total}} \times 360°$$

For example, suppose that a company's export figures are as follows:

Exports	Size (£m)
USA	5
Europe	3
Australia	4
Canada	2
Others	6
Total exports	20

$$\text{Exports to the USA} = \frac{5}{20} \times 360° = 90°$$

$$\text{Exports to Europe} = \frac{3}{20} \times 360° = 54°$$

$$\text{Exports to Australia} = \frac{4}{20} \times 360° = 72°$$

$$\text{Exports to Canada} = \frac{2}{20} \times 360° = 36°$$

$$\text{Exports to others} = \frac{6}{20} \times 360° = 108°$$

The pie chart can then be presented as in Figure 3.31.

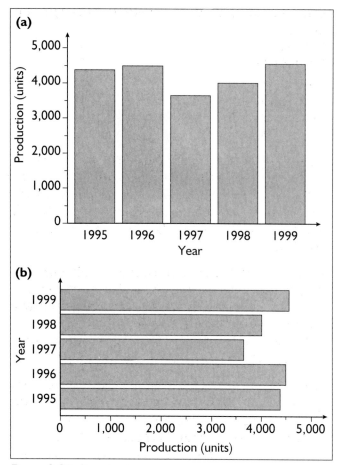

Figure 3.32 Bar charts

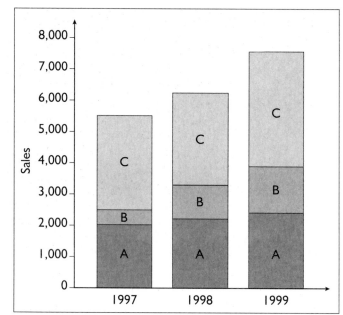

Figure 3.33 A component bar chart

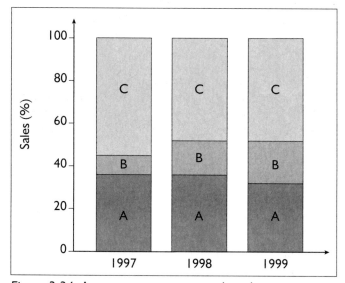

Figure 3.34 A percentage component bar chart

Although pie charts provide a simple form of display, they show only limited information, and it can be difficult to make accurate comparisons of segment sizes.

In **bar charts**, the areas of comparison are represented by bars which can be drawn either vertically or horizontally. The length of the bar is determined by the data. For example, suppose a company's production figures over the past five years are as shown below. The data could be shown in either of the ways depicted in Figure 3.32.

Year	Units produced
1998	4,300
1999	4,500
2000	3,900
2001	4,100
2002	4,600

A **component bar chart** enables component areas to be subdivided. Individual component lengths represent actual figures (see Figure 3.33). With **percentage component** **bar charts** individual component lengths represent the percentages that each component forms of the overall total; all bars will therefore be at the full height of 100 per cent (see Figure 3.34).

Table 3.9 Sales of ASAP plc products				
	(£000)			
	Year 1	**Year 2**	**Year 3**	**Year 4**
Product 1	4,100	4,500	4,400	2,100
Product 2	5,300	5,400	5,700	6,300
Product 3	2,200	4,100	4,300	4,700
Total	11,600	14,000	14,400	13,100

1 Prepare a percentage component bar chart from the figures in Table 3.9.
2 Explain why bar charts are better for making comparisons than pie charts.

A **histogram** is a form of bar chart that has certain unique figures. It represents grouped frequency distributions using bar chart techniques. The key difference between a bar chart and a histogram is that the width of each bar on the histogram relates to a numerical scale, and the width of each block reflects this. The number of observations relating to each variable may now be represented by the *area* covered by the bar on the chart, and not necessarily by the *height* of the bar.

Using the data shown below, the first three bars in a histogram will be normal height; the fourth and fifth bars will need to be twice as high to compensate for the fact that 1,000 is only half the standard class interval (see Figure 3.35).

Sales per salesperson (units)	Number of salespersons
Up to 2,000	2
2,000–4,000	5
4,000–6,000	10
6,000–7,000	10
7,000–8,000	8
8,000–10,000	2

If the class intervals are different, the height of each bar needs to be worked out. In many situations, however, it is likely that the class intervals of each bar will be the same and that this procedure will not be necessary, so that the histogram can be drawn straight from the frequency distribution.

Whereas a histogram is a stepped graph, it might be desirable to show this information in the form of a single curve. Such as curve is known as a **frequency polygon**. It is drawn by constructing a histogram, marking off the mid-point of the top of each rectangle and then joining the mid-points with straight lines (see Figure 3.36).

The curve of a frequency polygon is extended at both ends so that it cuts the axis at points half a class interval beyond the outside limits of the end-classes. The area of the frequency polygon is exactly the same as that of a histogram, since the area lost as each rectangle is cut by the polygon has the same area as the triangle added. If the frequency polygon is smoothed out, it is known as a **frequency curve**.

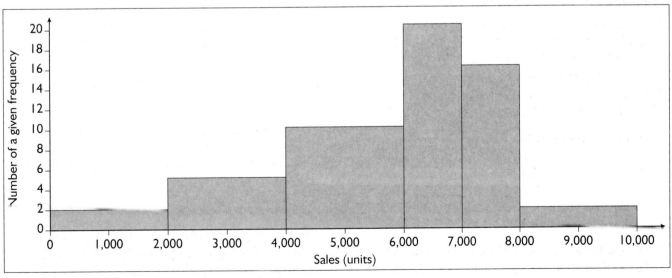

Figure 3.35 A histogram

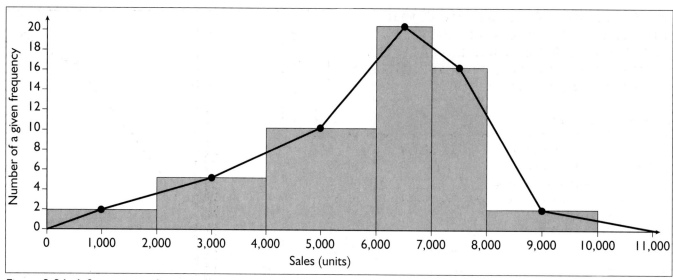

Figure 3.36 A frequency polygon

Gantt charts were named after Henry Gantt, a management scientist who lived during the early years of the twentieth century. They are a useful form of line/bar chart for comparing actual progress with forecast progress and can be used as a visual tool to indicate whether performances are on schedule (see Figure 3.37).

Graphs show the relationships between two variables and can be presented in the form of either a straight line or a curve. Whereas frequency polygons show frequency distributions, **ogive** is the name given to the curve when cumulative frequencies of a distribution are presented in the form of a graph.

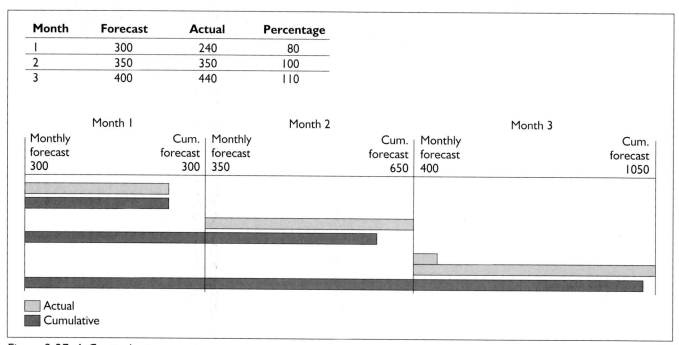

Month	Forecast	Actual	Percentage
1	300	240	80
2	350	350	100
3	400	440	110

Figure 3.37 A Gantt chart

Table 3.10 depicts a firm's sales totals over 40 weeks. Points on the graph will not relate sales achievements directly to output in the same way as an ordinary graph, but will indicate how many times the number of sales units (or less than that number) was achieved.

Table 3.10 Sales totals

Output (units)	Number of times sales realised (weeks)	Cumulative frequency	
0–400	3		3
401–800	9	3+9 =	12
801–1,200	13	3+9+13 =	25
1,201–1,600	11	3+9+13+11 =	36
1,601–2,000	4	3+9+13+11+4 =	40

An example of an ogive is shown in Figure 3.38.

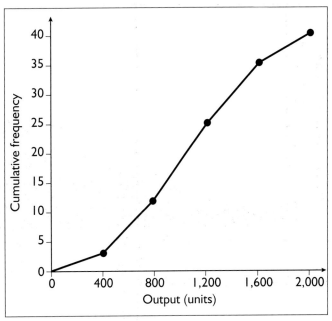

Figure 3.38 An ogive

The truth is stranger than fiction

Henry Gantt's legacy to management is the Gantt chart. Accepted as a commonplace project management tool today, it was an innovation of worldwide importance in the 1920s. But the chart was not Gantt's only legacy; he was also a forerunner of the Human Relations School of Management and an early spokesman for the social responsibility of business.

Chapter 70 *Analysing data*

Simply presenting data is in itself not ideal. When looking at data you have to ask, 'What does this all mean?' or 'How should this be interpreted?' In order to do this, it is necessary to understand the basic principles of data analysis.

Central tendency

Central tendency is sometimes known as the use of averages, and is one good way of making comparisons between one set of data and another. This is then used to represent that data set. There are three methods of calculating an average from a set of data:

1 mean
2 median
3 mode.

Table 3.11 shows the prices of wine cases sold by Red and White Ltd during a particular week. We shall use it to demonstrate the calculation of various statistical measures.

Table 3.11 Red and White Ltd: one week's sales of wine cases (£s)

DAYS		A	B	C	D	E	F	G	H	I	J
						CASES					
	1	41	35	36	48	52	41	60	32	33	34
	2	37	44	53	46	49	29	28	31	30	46
	3	51	42	28	26	27	34	35	26	42	65
	4	46	48	37	39	42	31	30	56	29	54
	5	46	42	81	31	35	34	39	41	35	68
	6	24	90	35	36	43	44	52	46	42	33

Mean

The **mean** is the average of all of the values in Table 3.11, calculated by summing all of the case prices (which in this case equals £2,490), and dividing by the number of cases (60), giving £41.50. The change in average price over time may indicate to Red and White the extent to which people have changed their spending priorities.

Median

The **median** is the middle value in the set of numbers, when they have been placed in ascending order. To find the median manually we have to place all the case prices in order to find the middle value. In this example, as we have two middle values, we would have to average the thirtieth and thirty-first prices. This comes to £40.00.

Mode

The **mode** is the value that occurs most frequently in a set of numbers. In this example, customers buy cases prices at £46 five times – more often than any other value – so the mode is £46. Where there are two values with the same frequency, the set of numbers is said to be **bimodal**.

If Red and White were to analyse its wine sales by country of origin, the mode would indicate which was the most popular (and also the country to which it could justify travelling in search of new wine suppliers).

Dispersion

Although averages are important in providing information about the middle of a **distribution**, they do not tell us how other figures in the distribution are spread. Some data may be tight around the mean, while other values might be well dispersed.

A **range** represents the difference between the highest and lowest values in a set of data. It is easy to find and provides information about a spread of figures. The formula for this is:

Range = Highest value – Lowest value.

The problem with looking at a range is that it can be distorted by one extreme value and it provides no indication of the spread between values. The range for the figures 4, 4, 4, 4, 4 and 20,000 is '4 to 20,000'. This is misleading in terms both of values and of the spread between the extremes. This disadvantage can be overcome and extreme values can be ignored by slicing away the top and bottom quarters and then analysing what is left.

Whereas the median is the middle number of an array of figures and represents 50 per cent, a **quartile** represents a quarter or 25 per cent of a range. The lower or first quartile is the area below which 25 per cent of observations fall, and the upper or fourth quartile is the value above which 25 per cent of observations fall.

From the **interquartile range** conclusions can be drawn about the middle 50 per cent of the data analysed.

Interquartile range = Upper quartile – Lower quartile

For example, the lower quartile, median, upper quartile and interquartile range can be extracted from the array of 20 numbers below as follows:

4	5	8	9	15	18	20	22	24	29
32	35	37	40	44	44	48	52	58	60

- The *lower quartile* will be the bottom 25 per cent of the array. In this case, as 25 per cent of 20 is 5, the lower quartile comprises the 1st–5th numbers.
- The *median* is the central value in the set. As there are 20 numbers, it is the average of the 10th and 11th numbers, which is (29+32)/2, that is 30.5.
- The *upper quartile* will be the top 25 per cent of the array. In this case, as 75 per cent of 20 is 15, the upper quartile comprises the 16th–20th numbers.
- The *range* for this set of numbers is the difference between the last and the first numbers. In this case that is 60–4, which is 56. The *interquartile range* is the difference between the upper and lower quartiles, which is 44–15, that is 29.

Although the interquartile range, or quartile deviation is easy to understand and is unaffected by extreme values, it might not be precise enough for a large sample. In these instances, it could be necessary to use **deciles** or **percentiles**.

A decile represents a tenth of a given distribution. From our example, the first decile will be 10 per cent of 20, that is, the second value, 5; the second decile will be the fourth value, 9; and so on. A percentile represents a hundredth part of a given distribution. The ninety-fifth percentile will be 95 per cent of the 20 values and so will be the nineteenth value of 58.

Mean deviation

A measure of dispersion that further analyses a group of values and makes use of all observations is the **mean deviation**. This simply measures the average *deviation* of all values in a distribution from the actual mean. It averages the differences between the actual values in a distribution and the mean, while at the same time ignoring

the negative signs of differences. For the figures of 5, 6, 13, 20 and 26, the arithmetical mean ($\bar{x}$) is:

$$\bar{X} = \frac{5 + 6 + 13 + 20 + 26}{5} = \frac{70}{5} = 14.$$

The *differences* from the arithmetic mean are:

$$5 - 14, 6 - 14, 13 - 14, 26 - 14$$
$$= -9, -8, -1, 6, 12.$$

If we ignore the negative signs, we can find the mean deviation as follows:

$$\frac{9 + 8 + 1 + 6 + 12}{5} = \frac{36}{5} = 7.2.$$

The mean deviation, or average difference, from the mean is therefore 7.2. It is useful to express this in the following way:

$$\text{Mean deviation} = \frac{\Sigma(\bar{x} - x)^2}{n}.$$

Where $\bar{x} - x$ represents the difference between the mean and the actual value but ignoring the negative signs.

Variance and standard deviation

The major problem of all methods of dispersion looked at so far is that they have limited uses. This is not so in the case of the **variance** and **standard deviation**, which are widely used in statistical analysis and are the most important measures of dispersion.

Instead of ignoring the minuses and differences from the mean, the variance and standard deviation *square* the differences, instantly eliminating the negative signs. When the squared differences have been averaged, a variance is created and the square root of the variance provides the standard deviation.

For example, if the output of a machine over five days was 4, 5, 5, 7 and 9, the arithmetical mean would be 6. The variance measures the extent of the dispersion around the mean by:

1. calculating the difference between the number of units produced each day and the arithmetic mean – shown as $\bar{X} - X$
2. squaring the difference $(\bar{x} - x)^2$
3. finding the average of the total of these squared differences – this is shown as:
$$\frac{\Sigma(\bar{x} - x)^2}{n}$$
where n is the number of values.

For example, in Table 3.12 the variance would be:

$$\frac{16}{5} = 3.2 \text{ units.}$$

Table 3.12

	Outputs	
x	$\bar{X} - X$	$(\bar{X} - X)^2$
4	−2	4
5	−1	1
5	−1	1
7	1	1
9	3	9
	0	16

The standard deviation is the square root of the variance. In our example, this will be:

4 = 1.79 units.

Thus, we have an arithmetic mean of 6 units, a variance of 3.2 and a standard deviation of 1.79 units. By taking into account frequency (f) and denoting standard deviation as s, we can show its formula as follows:

$$s = \sqrt{\frac{\Sigma f(\bar{X} - X)^2}{n}} \text{ or } \sqrt{\frac{\Sigma f(\bar{X} - X)^2}{\Sigma f}}$$

The example given in Table 3.13 takes into consideration frequency and has an arithmetic mean ($\bar{x}$) of 6. The standard deviation will be 1.4 = 1.18.

Table 3.13

Value x	Frequency f	$\bar{x}-x$	$(\bar{x}-x)^2$	$f(\bar{x}-x)^2$
4	4	−2	4	16
5	6	−1	1	6
6	9	0	0	0
7	8	1	1	8
8	3	2	4	12
	30			42

Although it is sometimes difficult to understand the significance of the standard deviation, it can be said that the greater the dispersion, the larger the standard deviation. As all values in the distribution are taken into account, it is a comprehensive measure of dispersion, capable of being developed further.

The truth is stranger than fiction

Various mean temperatures in August around England are:

East Anglia	24.4°C
Midlands	25.1°C
North-east England	22.3°C
North-west England	23.4°C
South-east England	25.3°C
South-west England	23.8°C

End of unit questions

As you have worked through this unit, you will have come across many questions and activities to help you understand the content and internalise your learning. The structure of these does not necessarily reflect the structure of questions you will meet in the exam, however, so the following section provides some exam-type questions by way of example.

Before looking at these questions, you might like to refer back to the 'Examiner speaks' section in the Introduction (see page viii) and to the general advice at the start of the Unit 1 questions.

Note that there is no particular relevance to the total marks allocated to each question, except to illustrate the proportions of the total allocated to each component.

Here is some specific advice on the answering of questions on accounting and finance:

- The **own figure** rule applies to questions involving calculations. In other words, if you make a mistake you are only 'penalised' once. If you feed in an incorrect figure, subsequent calculations will be rewarded on the basis of the figures resulting from your initial mistake. Similarly, if you make a mistake which leads to a wrong answer (for example you end up with a profit whereas the firm is making a loss, or you calculate a ratio incorrectly) and a subsequent question asks you to discuss your results, you will be rewarded for a discussion which is consistent with *your* results, rather than the correct ones.
- Do not be frightened by figures. You can obtain marks for knowledge of accounting techniques, even if your calculations are wrong. Also, approximately 40 per cent marks are still awarded for analysis and evaluation.
- Conversely, if you perform your accounting calculations correctly, your marks will be limited *unless* you can demonstrate the meaning and relevance of your calculations, leading to analysis and evaluation of the firm's position.
- *Always show your working, and also define* the ratio or expression (for example break even, margin of safety) which you are using. A wrong answer with no working cannot be rewarded. A wrong answer with working, or with a demonstration of some understanding of the concept *will* gain some marks.
- Be precise in the terms you use. Terms like *cash, profit, revenue, costs, reserves* all have different meanings.

Reserves are unlikely to be cash so be reluctant to suggest that a firm can use its reserves to finance an investment. Never confuse negative profit (that is, loss) with lack of cash (that is, insolvency).

1 Black and Green plc has published the following balance sheet representing its position at the end of the last financial year:

	£000
Fixed assets at net book value	
Premises	200
Machinery	80
Vehicles	40
Current assets	
Stock	10
Debtors	25
Cash	30
Current liabilities	
Creditors due within one year	75
Total assets minus current liabilities	310
Long-term liabilities	
Loan from Bank	110
Net worth	
Shareholders' funds	200
Capital employed	310

a) Explain the meaning of the term 'Fixed assets at net book value'. **(4 marks)**

b) i) Calculate the value of Black and Green plc's working capital. **(2 marks)**

   ii) From your calculations, suggest reasons for the firm's working capital figure and analyse the possible consequences for Black and Green plc. **(12 marks)**

c) i) Calculate Black and Green plc's gearing ratio. **(2 marks)**

   ii) Black and Green plc is attempting to persuade its bankers to increase the firm's long-term loan by £50,000, in order to invest in new machinery. With reference to the gearing ratio you have calculated, explain whether the bankers might be willing to grant this loan. **(5 marks)**

d) Recommend, with reasons, what information, other than the balance sheet provided, you would wish to see in order to make a full assessment of the financial position of Black and Green plc. **(20 marks)**

2 Morris, Walker and Jackson are partners in a plumbing business. Their business is prospering, with profits after interest and tax rising in the last three years as follows:

1998	£60,000
1999	£80,000
2000	£90,000

They have two vans, but they consider that the increase in business necessitates the purchase of a third one, so have decided to invest in a vehicle costing £15,000. They intend to keep this van for three years and then sell it. Their accountant has told them that she intends to depreciate the vehicle on a declining balance method at 10 per cent per year.

The partners have approached their bankers for the £15,000, as there is no cash in the firm and they are already near to their overdraft limit of £40,000. The bank has asked the partners to produce a cash flow forecast for the next three years before agreeing either to extend the overdraft or grant a three year fixed-term

loan. If the bank does not provide the money, the partners will have to fund the purchase from their own pockets, as the van is essential if they are to meet their increasing orders.

a) Calculate the residual value of the van after three years by depreciating it at 10 per cent per year by:
   i) the declining balance method.
   ii) the straight-line method. **(6 marks)**
b) Analyse the arguments for using the declining balance method for the purpose of depreciating the value of Morris, Walker and Jackson's van. **(10 marks)**
c) Explain how the partnership can be profitable, but have no cash. **(4 marks)**
d) i) Assess the dangers which might exist for Morris, Walker and Jackson of having no cash and a high overdraft. **(12 marks)**
   ii) Recommend whether a three-year loan or an extension of the overdraft might be the better solution for the partnership. **(12 marks)**
e) Evaluate the consequences to Morris, Walker and Jackson of drawing up a cash flow forecast for the next three years. **(16 marks)**

Here, again, is one for you to try for yourself.

3 Primrose Publications plc produces a range of magazines and journals, mainly in the area of fashion, aimed primarily at female readers. Each title is a monthly publication and has its own editor, whose task is to make a profit. If a title fails to break even for three consecutive months, it comes under review, and after six months is likely to be discontinued, even if it is making a positive contribution. Each title is apportioned a share of the firm's fixed costs.

One of the titles produced, called *Style*, is under threat. Its sales have fallen for three consecutive months and are now down to 75,000, from a peak of 100,000. The magazine sells for £3 per copy. The fixed costs attributed to it for a three-month period are £50,00 and the variable costs are calculated at £2.50 per copy.

a) Explain what is meant by a 'positive contribution'. **(4 marks)**

b) Calculate the break-even level of sales and of sales revenue for *Style* and its current margin of safety. **(6 marks)**

c) Evaluate, with reference to alternatives, the appropriateness of using a basis of break even with respect to apportioned fixed costs over three consecutive months in deciding whether Primrose Publications should continue producing each individual title in its portfolio. **(20 marks)**

THE EXAMINER SPEAKS – FOR THE LAST TIME!

And finally . . . a list of ten things to avoid, which annoy examiners (I should know – I am one!) and suggest that you are not thinking about your answers.

- Confusing cash and profit.
- Talking about the 'cost' of a product, when you mean 'price'.
- Thinking that reserves are chests of cash lying around unused in the firm.
- Confusing revenue, turnover and profit.
- Talking about 'making money'. Only the Royal Mint and the firms that print banknotes do that!
- Confusing advertising with promotion.
- Writing pages of theory (especially about motivation or marketing) while ignoring the context of the data or the case.
- Performing calculations either without showing your working or without explaining how they are relevant to solving the problem posed.
- Ignoring the keyword of a question, such as 'assess', 'evaluate', 'recommend' or 'analyse'.
- Ignoring the mark allocation for each part of a question or for each question on an examination paper.

So now you know how to excel in the exam. Go on, please that examiner!

APPENDIX *Information technology and business*

INTRODUCTION It is difficult to imagine a business world without information technology (IT). Businesses both large and small have had to adapt to, and take advantage of, this computerised age.

Critical thinking

The current thinking is that in five years' time a business will have to be electronic or it will not be in business at all.

It is interesting to reflect on how organisations used to operate before the introduction of IT and then to look at how IT has impacted on particular operations. For example, businesses have moved:

- *from* using a typewriter to produce all business correspondence, where the creation of every letter or memo was a separate operation, *to* using a word processor which gives the user the facility to create templates for standard letters and the versatility of presenting documents in different fonts and styles, etc.
- *from* using a calculator, pen and paper to work out lengthy calculations *to* using a computer spreadsheet package where complex calculations can be produced accurately within a fraction of the time
- *from* storing employee and customer records in a tightly packed filing cabinet *to* using a computer database to store, sort and retrieve files efficiently.

Fax machines, modems, laptop computers and mobile phones are further examples of IT which we almost take for granted and would find difficult to imagine life without.

The Internet too offers businesses the opportunity to access huge amounts of information and also allows worldwide communication and trading to take place.

WHAT DO YOU THINK?

1 To what extent do you agree with the statement above, that in five years' time a business will have to be electronic or it will not be in business at all?
2 Investing and keeping up to date with IT can be a very costly exercise. Do you think that the benefits outweigh the costs? Justify your answer with examples.
3 What further advancements do you think might take place in IT in the next 30 years? What impact would your predictions have on organisations?

Application of information technology to business

The application of information technology (IT) in today's business environment is extensive. Organisations have introduced IT at all levels and across all functions. This chapter looks at how IT has been applied to business organisations, initially considering whether IT packages assist business in a presentation capacity or as an aid to decision making. It then discusses the application across different functions of the business, from the strategic level down to the operational level.

An overview

The introduction to this appendix outlined the main IT packages used in business: word processing, spreadsheets and databases. Other software packages commonly used include desktop publishing and project planning. By taking each of the packages in turn it is possible to split them up into two categories – presentation and decision making – and to discuss how they are applied to business. Table 4.1 outlines each of the packages in this way.

Table 4.1 The main IT packages used in business and how they are applied

Package	Application	Examples of application
Word processing	Presentation and decision making	Letters, memos, reports, notices, etc. The presentation of a clear concise report can aid the decision making process
Desktop publishing	Presentation and decision making	As above, for presentation. Often used where more discretion is needed over the layout of a page As above for decision making
Spreadsheets	Decision making	Can be used to assist in any financial decision making scenario such as 'What level of sales do we need to achieve to break-even?' 'How many products do we need to sell to achieve a certain level of profit?' Spreadsheets also offer the facility of using 'What if?' calculations. For example, 'What if the price of raw materials increased by 10 per cent, how would this affect our break-even point?' 'What if the business decided to buy a new machine or take on several extra staff, how would this affect individual budgets and the overall profitability of the business?'
Databases	Decision making	By asking the database a question or a query, it is possible to view just a selection of records. For example, a library might be interested to find out how many books within a section are more than 20 years old. It is possible to access this information through the database. The decision may then be taken to renew certain titles. Similarly, a simple query on the human resource management department's database will enable the organisation to find out the proportion of males to females in a department or across the company
Project planning	Decision making	It is possible to see very quickly how long a project will take using a project planning package. Decisions can then be made with regard to resources, both human and physical, to undertake the project. Various scenarios can then be analysed to ensure efficient completion. For example, what would be the impact on the business if the completion date for the project were brought forward? Or part of the project took longer to complete than anticipated?

Effective decision making can have an impact on the overall competitive advantage of a business. It is important therefore to take a closer look at the application of decision making packages. Table 4.2 outlines four of the main functions within a business – production, marketing, human resources and finance – and states some of the types of decisions that could be made using IT.

It is important to remember that the packages outlined are an *aid* to the decision making process. They should not replace the human judgement required but act as a support mechanism.

The importance of information

Clare Morris in her book *Quantitative Approaches in Business Studies* (1989) summarises just how important information is to an organisation:

> 'A business concern of any kind, even the smallest, today depends to a very large extent on having ready access to large amounts of information, ranging from details of the potential market for its goods and services to estimates of next year's labour requirements, from the attendance record of each employee to the numbers of breakdowns per week for each piece of equipment it owns. The more accurate and complete this information is, the more effective, all other things being equal, the operation of the business can be.'

Organisations rely on IT to provide them with accurate information very quickly. This information is then used to

Figure 4.1 The importance of information

assist businesses in achieving their organisational objectives and hopefully improving their competitive advantage (see Figure 4.1).

How IT helps to achieve organisational objectives

In order to assess how IT helps to achieve organisational objectives, we need to consider how the information provided by the technology supports different levels of decision making in the organisation.

K. M. Bartol and D. C. Martin in their book *Management* (1991) suggest three information levels within the organisation:

Table 4.2 How IT aids decision making in the main functions of business

Function	Decision making packages used	Applications
Production	Spreadsheets Project planning	Calculating the efficiency of different machines The introduction of a new product in the production process
Marketing	Spreadsheets Databases Project planning	Calculating the impact of different pricing strategies Keeping a record of customer profiles Planning the launch of a new product
Human resources	Spreadsheets Databases	Human resource planning for the next five years Calculating pay awards Employee records
Finance	Spreadsheets	Drawing up profit and loss statements Calculating cash flow forecasts Investment appraisal

Table 4.3 The role of IT in achieving organisational objectives

Organisational objective	Information level	Desired outcome to achieve objective	IT to be used to produce information for decision making
1 To improve the time it takes to introduce a new product into the market place	Strategic	Reduce the time it takes to get a product to market by 10 per cent each year for the next five years	Project planning Spreadsheet
	Tactical	Improve production techniques/methods and efficiencies Focus on added value Analyse marketing strategy	Spreadsheet Database
	Operational	Improve training Look at new ways of working	Database Project planning
2 To improve quality	Strategic	Reduce customer complaints by 5 per cent over the next year Reduce wastage by 5 per cent each year for the next five years	Database Spreadsheet
	Tactical	Improve production techniques Buy new machinery Analyse why customers complain	Database Spreadsheet Project planning
	Operational	Monitor customer complaints and wastage Improve training	Spreadsheet Database

- strategic
- tactical
- operational.

The strategic level looks at the information which would be required to make decisions about the business over the next five to ten years, in order to achieve organisational objectives.

The tactical level looks at the information which would be required to make decisions about the business over the next few months to a year, in order to achieve functional objectives which would ultimately support the achievement of organisational objectives.

The operational level looks at the information which would be required to make decisions about the business on a daily or weekly basis. This information would help to achieve personal or departmental objectives, which would assist in achieving functional objectives. This would again assist the fulfilment of organisational objectives.

Figure 4.2 outlines this three-tier information hierarchy.

In order to demonstrate how this process could be applied to business, Table 4.3 looks at two possible organisational objectives and describes the role IT plays in helping to achieve them.

Figure 4.2 The three-tier information hierarchy

Source: Adapted from Bartol and Martin (1991)

CASE STUDY: USING IT EFFECTIVELY

Although there are IT packages available to suit most business applications, it does not always follow that they will be used appropriately or used to their maximum potential. This scenario is true of Organical, a retail company which specialises in supplying a range of organic and environmentally friendly products to the public. With seven retail outlets around the East Midlands, the company recently decided to sell direct by mail order as well.

The mail order department was established seven months ago and comprises a team of six people carefully chosen from within the business to work on the project. After a great deal of hard work and very long hours the team has just launched its first catalogue.

The key stages in developing and launching the catalogue involved:

- selecting a range of products for possible inclusion
- calculating how profitable each product would be
- confirming the range of products to be included based on the profit analysis above
- writing the copy for each product and deciding on which page it should appear
- designing and producing the catalogue using a desktop publishing package
- printing and binding
- marketing and distribution.

Kumaresh is the manager of the mail order department and has the ultimate responsibility for ensuring that the catalogue deadlines were met. He feels that production of the first catalogue was such a demanding task in terms of workload that there must be more effective ways of working to achieve the deadlines more easily. He decides to spend time individually with members of the team discussing their roles and how they can each become more efficient.

He discovers some interesting facts. Although he thought all of his staff were computer literate it seems that their knowledge and skill with some packages is very limited. Everyone seems confident with word processing and uses it effectively. However, his staff's expertise with spreadsheets and databases is very patchy. He feels that they are unaware of how important these packages could be as an aid to decision making, which would ultimately make their jobs easier.

When Kumaresh talks to his team about undertaking some extra training to improve their skill and confidence with spreadsheets and databases he is met with a unanimous feeling that they are all too busy to spend any time away from their desks if they are to meet the deadlines for the next catalogue. Kumaresh feels an obvious tension building up in the department.

1 Refer to the list of key stages involved in developing and launching a catalogue and suggest ways that spreadsheets and databases could be used to aid decision making.

2 Suggest development strategies that Kumaresh could use to improve his team's knowledge, skill and confidence with spreadsheet and database packages. He feels that it is a need which must be addressed before the launch of the next catalogue in six months' time.

The truth is stranger than fiction

Although Europe and the USA have access to similar technology, different lifestyles lead people to use the technology in different ways. Europeans so far have proved to be much more reluctant to buy things over the Internet than Americans. Europeans are more cautious about giving credit card details over the phone or the Internet. In Europe mail order shopping is not considered to be as upmarket as in the USA. However, when we look at mobile telephony, the story is different. In the USA there are gaps in the network and a lot of the phones are still analogue. In Europe, however, the technology is more efficient. In the USA electronic commerce (e-commerce) is based almost entirely on the personal computer. In Europe, it seems likely that it will be delivered more and more via mobile phones.

Information technology packages used in business

This chapter will give you an insight into some of the key features and uses of the main information technology (IT) packages used in business, in particular word processing, spreadsheets and databases.

Word processing

A word processing program allows the user to enter and manipulate text on the computer screen before printing it out. Some packages are also capable of incorporating charts, illustrations and tables.

Why use a word processing package?

- Speed – professionally presented letters, reports, memos, etc. can be produced quickly even if the user is not a trained typist
- Consistency – templates can be created for documents such as standard letters and memos. This not only reduces inputting time but also presents a consistent company image.
- Accuracy – spelling and grammar check facilities should help to improve the accuracy of documents.
- Presentation – the sophistication of word processing packages together with high-quality printers enable the user to present information in a professional manner.

Key features

- Text can be manipulated by copying, cutting, pasting, aligning, etc.
- Text can be formatted by including a border or bullet points, etc.
- Text, tables and drawings can be inputted in a variety of font sizes and styles.
- Illustrations, charts, tables and text, etc. from other files, packages, the Internet or via hardware such as a scanner can be incorporated into documents.

Main uses in business

- Letters
- Memos
- Reports
- Minutes of meetings
- Newsletters
- Notices

Spreadsheets

A spreadsheet is a computer program that enables calculations both simple and complex to be made very quickly. The normal layout for a spreadsheet is a table consisting of a series of rows and columns. The program allows numbers and text to be inputted and manipulated. Spreadsheet packages also include facilities to draw charts and graphs based on the spreadsheet data.

Why use a computerised spreadsheet?

- Speed – manipulating complex numerical data manually can be very time consuming. Once a spreadsheet has been created with the correct numbers, text and formulae, calculations can be worked out within seconds.
- Accuracy – providing all of the data and formulae have been inputted correctly, results should be accurate. This is a particular benefit when carrying out complex calculations. The added advantage is that all the background information to the spreadsheet is displayed on the screen so it is sometimes easier to see where mistakes may have been made.
- Changing data – once a spreadsheet has been created, it is very easy to change the figures or formulae and to see instantly what the results would be. This enables the user to use the spreadsheet to compute a series of 'What if?' scenarios. These have numerous applications in business. For example, a spreadsheet can be used to work out how many items a business needs to sell to make a profit.

Key features

- Both numbers and text can be inputted into a spreadsheet.
- Formulae are used to instruct the computer to carry out a series of calculations.
- Charts and graphs can be drawn from the data contained in the spreadsheet.
- Data can be recalculated using 'What if?' statements.

Main uses in business

- Cash flow forecasting
- Budgeting
- Break-even analysis
- VAT calculations
- Profit and loss statements
- Calculating various functional costings such as production costs, advertising costs, wage and salary costs

Databases

A computerised database is a means of storing information in a structured way so that it can be retrieved easily. For example, a database might be used by a library to keep a computerised record of all its books.

Why use a computerised database?

- Storage capacity – large amounts of data previously stored in several filing cabinets, for example employee records, can be stored on hard, floppy or compact discs.
- Easy and rapid retrieval – a database has the capacity to search through thousands of files very quickly and retrieve particular information, for example about a customer or employee.
- Selection of specific information – instead of searching for just one file or record, the database has the capacity to look for common information. For example, the human resource management department may want to retrieve details of all employees with a particular skill.
- Accurate and efficient analysis of data – the database allows the user to interrogate and analyse data very quickly. For example, a sales manager may be asked to calculate the average spend per customer over a given period. This could be a time consuming manual activity. However, providing the database is asked the right question, accurate calculations can be produced very quickly.

Key features

- Once the file structure of a database has been created it is possible to add, delete, edit and sort records.
- Individual or groups of records may be retrieved, depending on the nature of the query the user has input.

Main uses in business

- Employee records
- Customer records
- Product information
- Stock records

A database can be set up in any situation where large amounts of data need to be organised.

The following example illustrates how much a manual process can be changed as a result of introducing a computerised database. Employers wishing to recruit graduates used to visit universities during the winter months to interview prospective candidates. This process came to be known as 'the graduate milkround'. Today's graduates can take advantage of the huge milkround database on the Internet to seek suitable employment (for more information see www.milkround.co.uk).

CASE STUDY: NEW BEGINNINGS

Alison Chambers thought that Millbury needed a new café-bar style of restaurant. She also knew that she was the right type of person to take on such a venture. Having conducted the relevant market research and thoroughly analysed the viability of the project, the bank agreed to lend her the money. With a background in catering management and some experience of DIY in terms of renovating old properties, Alison felt quite confident of her success.

She soon found the ideal property. Its location near the river was excellent, but it needed major repairs and renovation. She constructed a detailed critical path of the project and employed a team of contractors to carry out the work. Her target was to be open in time for Christmas; it was now the beginning of November.

Alison had decided that there would be enough room for 50 people to sit down and eat. She also wanted a soft seating area where customers could just drink and chat. She wanted to create a relaxed, informal atmosphere.

She started to consider her staffing requirements. She would need a chef and several kitchen assistants, a bar manager and bar staff and several waiting staff.

As part of her catering management background, Alison had received some computer training. She decided to buy a computer, knowing how valuable it would be for her new business. However, she never really had the time to think through how the computer would assist her with her workload.

Christmas was approaching fast and Alison was starting to become concerned that the building

would not be finished in time. Things were not really going according to her critical path. She decided to supervise the day-to-day progress of the building work and help out where she could.

A week before Christmas, Alison was sitting in her office thinking. The building was ready, the staff were employed. The paperwork, however, was very disorganised. Invoices needed to be paid, staff needed their contracts of employment drawing up, delivery notes of stock which had arrived were building up, a handwritten, rough version of the menu needed finishing off – the in-tray seemed endless. Somewhere among all this paper was her computer.

Alison admitted that she needed help and decided to draft in some assistance. She knew you were studying business studies and that therefore you ought to know quite a lot about how computers can assist small businesses. You decide to accept the mission to computerise Alison's café bar.

QUESTIONS FOR DISCUSSION

1 What packages would you recommend Alison to install on her computer and why?
2 How would each of the packages be used in the business? Explain at least three uses for each package.
3 What reporting information would you expect the chef, the bar manager and the head waiter or waitress to provide to Alison on a weekly basis? How could computers assist in the provision of this information?

Other IT packages used in business

Desktop publishing

Desktop publishing packages allow the user to create very high-quality documents which may include graphics and different text styles and fonts. These packages were created in response to the limited application of word processing programs. Today, however, word processing has developed so much that many of the desktop publishing functions can be performed within word processing programs. The main advantage of a desktop publishing package is that it gives the user a greater degree of control over the layout of a page.

Project management

Conducted manually, project management can be a complicated business. However, there are IT packages which can greatly assist the process. The packages range from small scheduling applications to large-scale planning and reporting systems.

The truth is stranger than fiction

All of the computerised applications in this chapter result in manual tasks being completed much quicker. Access to information is quicker, which means decisions can be made more effectively. Businesses that trade online are also feeling the benefits that speed can bring through the Internet. However, businesses have to react very fast when planning on the Internet. The maxim is that an Internet year only lasts for three months. If a business has not got its plan together and launched its product or service online within this time, someone else will beat the business to it.

The costs and benefits of information technology

We have just outlined how important IT is to the survival and growth of the business organisations of today and tomorrow. As with any new investment, however, organisations must try to balance the costs of IT against the benefits. This chapter focuses on these issues and also suggests criteria for judging the effectiveness of IT.

The benefits of IT

Marion Gillie, in an article in the magazine *Personnel Management* (August 1987), categorised the benefits as 'cost displacement, cost elimination and added value':

- Cost displacement refers to any time or expenditure saved as a result of eliminating routine tasks and removal of the duplication of effort. Cost displacement also refers to achieving the same output for less input.

- Cost elimination refers either to the reduction in current costs (for example fewer staff needed or less waste produced) or the saving of future expense (no need for additional staff).
- Added value refers to benefits such as the ability to respond more quickly to requests for information, or to take on tasks which could not (or would not) have been done without the new computer system.

Other benefits

- The introduction of Internet technology means access to a much wider range of information.
- Employees acquire new skills, which may lead to greater job satisfaction.
- New technology allows employees greater flexibility with regard to where and when they work.

Problems, limitations and cost implications of IT

Potential problems and limitations

- The system might break down or be damaged by a virus.
- It is important to keep up to date with changes in technology in order to ensure that the systems being used are the most appropriate. This in itself will require resources and it is also essential that all new investments are evaluated objectively to assess the benefits that they will bring to the business.
- There may be a lack of understanding regarding the capabilities of IT, resulting in the system not being used to its full potential.
- Appropriate security measures need to be implemented to ensure that authorised personnel only have access to restricted information.
- Health and safety may become an issue if the ergonomics of the workplace have not been carefully thought through.

Implementation costs

- Equipment costs – purchasing the appropriate hardware and software.
- Training costs – include the initial cost of training staff and the cost of covering employees' work while they are training.
- Inputting costs – in order to get computer systems operational, additional staff may be required in the early days for inputting data.

Maintenance costs

- Support costs – this could be provided in the form of a help desk.
- On-going maintenance costs of servicing hardware.
- Training – continually investing in education and training to ensure that staff are kept up to date.
- Hardware and software – continually investing in more efficient or more appropriate systems to ensure survival/growth of the business.
- Data protection – ensuring that personal data recorded on computer systems adhere to the principles of Data Protection legislation.

To find out what action an organisation has to take to ensure that it is operating within the law with regards to data protection, visit the government website at www.dataprotection.gov.uk.

Personal costs

- Employees may find themselves with redundant skills or even without a job as a result of the introduction of new technology.
- Employees may feel more isolated and lonely as new technology allows them to work in more remote places rather than just the office environment.

Although it appears by looking at the above lists that the costs seem to outweigh the benefits, the ultimate question that businesses must ask themselves is whether they can afford *not* to introduce new technology. An essential part of the investment in the technology must be to judge its effectiveness. Below are some criteria for judging the effectiveness of IT.

Criteria for judging the effectiveness of IT

IT is an expensive and on-going investment, which means that its contribution to the organisation's success should be evaluated thoroughly. Caroline Daniels, in her book *Information Technology: The Management Challenge* (1994), suggests that the following six factors are the key to effective evaluation:

- Currency – is the information produced by the system up to date, accessible and reliable?
- Content – are the data being inputted into the system accurate?
- Quality – how effectively does the system help a manager do his or her job?
- Flexibility – how easy is the system to use?
- Importance – how dependent is the business on the system?
- Scalability – how appropriate will the current system be for the future of the business?

When should evaluation take place?

- Before implementation. In order to judge how successful an IT system is, you need a benchmark upon which to make a comparison. Before the system is implemented, the users of the potential system should have some idea of how long they are spending on tasks currently, so that a comparison can be made.
- After implementation. Once the system is being used, a detailed evaluation can take place. It is here that the other two questions should be asked: who? and how?

Who should be involved in the evaluation?

- Clerical staff responsible for inputting data into the system.
- Managers using the system on a daily basis for presentation, communication or decision making purposes.
- Technical and maintenance staff involved in providing a support network for the system and its users.

How should evaluation be conducted?

Evaluation can take a variety of forms depending on the time and resources available. The key aim is to make a comparison between the new and the old systems and to make recommendations for the future. Evaluation methods which may be used include:

- questionnaires
- group discussions
- interviews
- observations to assess time, quantity and quality comparisons.

CASE STUDY: TO INVEST OR NOT TO INVEST?

Norman Hill Insurance Services is a small family-run business situated in a small village on the outskirts of Milton. The business operates as a partnership. There are three partners: father, mother, and David, their son. David's wife is the fourth member of the team. The business has built up a very valuable reputation over the past 20 years. It prides itself on providing an excellent service to its customers on all aspects of general insurance. This includes car, house and travel insurance.

During the past five years, the business has been through significant changes as a result of increased competition within the insurance sector. The advancement of companies such as Direct Line, which are able to offer products at a more competitive price over the phone and more recently through the Internet, have forced many small insurance brokers to close. Faced with this aggressive market, the partners took the decision four years ago to introduce information technology into their business, a measure that they felt was necessary if they were going to survive. The IT system is a database of all their customers records. The system not only allows them to retrieve details very quickly, but they are also able to access product information online and print out customers' insurance policies there and then.

Other aspects of the business have not been updated in the same way. An electronic typewriter is still used for all their correspondence. Budgets and cash flow forecasts are worked out using a calculator.

The business is now entering another phase. During the next five years, Norman would like to retire. David does not want to take over, so this would ultimately mean selling the business. With two more brokers in the area closing down, however, their workload over the past 12 months seems to have increased tremendously. Their average working day starts at 9.00 am and finishes at 10.00 pm.

There are two options facing the business:

1. Invest in a more advanced IT system incorporating all aspects of the firm. This would allow it to become more efficient, increase the value of the business and, all being well, take on more customers.
2. Stay the same. With its excellent reputation, the business would with luck retain all of its current customers providing it could compete on price. Although the workload would not be reduced, they are used to working these long hours now, so why change when they are so near retiring?

QUESTIONS FOR DISCUSSION

1. Outline the costs and benefits for both of the above options.
2. If the partners decided to invest, how would they judge the effectiveness of the more advanced system?
3. Which option do you think the partners should decide on? Justify your answer.

The impact of information technology

IT has impacted on many aspects of our lives. From the way we watch television to the way we communicate with our friends and colleagues; from the way we shop to the way we work. This chapter focuses on the impact that IT has had on business organisations.

Organisations are becoming increasingly reliant on the power of IT. Computers, which were once used to aid people in their jobs, are fast becoming an integral part of working life. For example, as decisions have to be made faster and businesses need to be more responsive, IT plays a more vital role. New technology has increased competition not just locally but globally. This has forced many organisations to restructure. Some of the initiatives undertaken are as follows:

- Delayering – making organisations leaner, fitter and flatter, thereby making them more responsive and adaptable to change. With the impact of IT, organisations are able to obtain information much faster and in more detail, therefore reducing the need for lots of layers of management. Where information used to be provided by people, it is now in many cases provided by computers.
- Focusing on 'added value' – eliminating operations which do not add value. This has led to redundancies in some areas, while at the same time other jobs have expanded.
- Empowering employees – giving employees more responsibility in the decision making process. IT has facilitated this initiative.
- Introducing a more flexible workforce – employees do not have to be at their normal place of work in order to

conduct their job. IT has facilitated the expansion of homeworking, hot-desking, etc.

The impact of IT on functional areas of business

The introduction of IT has had an impact on all functional areas of business, through:

- an increase of information online through Intranet facilities
- a reduction in manual operations
- improved decision making
- improved productivity
- improved communication.

Specific examples where IT has had an impact on functional areas

Production function within a textiles company

The scenarios outlined below describe the impact that IT has had on the production function within a textiles company.

A design costing model

Traditionally, designers would begin the process by designing a new garment. They would decide the specifications for the garment, material, design, etc. They would then have to pass that garment to a production manager who would then calculate manufacturing times, material usage, etc. The output from this information would be a manufacturing cost per garment. This would be passed back to the designer who would then talk to the sales executive to establish whether the garment could be sold at a profit. The lead time for the production manager to calculate costings took upwards of two weeks. All the knowledge to make these calculations lay in the hands of the production manager.

In order to reduce the lead time and also eliminate the risk to the business of just one person holding this information, the method of calculating was shared and a spreadsheet was produced to calculate the manufacturing cost per garment. This resulted in the following benefits to the business:

- It reduced the time taken to cost a garment from two weeks to less than one hour.
- The costing of a garment could now be carried out by relatively junior members of staff.

Speeding up the decision making process

Machine efficiencies within the production function used to be calculated manually. This process, using a calculator, pen and paper, took several days to complete. The information regarding how efficient each machine was became available once a week so was effectively out of date before managers received it. Designing a spreadsheet to calculate the information resulted in two distinct improvements:

- Machine efficiencies could be calculated daily and the process of working this out took a few minutes.
- The information could now be used reliably by managers to make effective decisions.

Product function within a mail order business

This scenario looks at how changes in IT have helped to improve efficiencies.

The product team's responsibility within this environment is to select a range of products to go into a mail order catalogue. Historically, product information, cost and selling price, etc. were held on a spreadsheet. Copy for the catalogue was written using a word processing package. The issues with this approach to designing a catalogue were as follows:

- Both documents needed to be kept up to date.
- Only one person could work on each document at any one time.
- Both documents had to be compiled into one catalogue.

During the growth phase of the catalogue, when the number of lines was manageable, this method of producing the catalogue, although not perfect, was adequate.

As the volume of products increased and the catalogue became more complex, a new method of managing the project was required. This new method took the form of a centralised database which allowed product information and product copy to be presented within the same document. This has resulted in:

- a multi-user system which allows several people to access the database at the same time
- only one system to be maintained, so changes to the document need to be made once only
- a reduction in the overall time it takes to compile a catalogue.

The impact of information technology on job design

IT has impacted significantly on many aspects of working life. These can be summarised under the following three headings.

How we work
- IT has enabled employees to develop additional skills.
- IT has facilitated empowerment which has resulted in more employees taking part in the decision making process.
- Many manual operations have been replaced by IT. This has in many cases changed the job content and improved efficiency.

When we work
- IT has assisted the move away from the rigid nine-to-five working day to a working day which could span any time within the 24 hours.

Where we work
- It is no longer essential for all employees to be based at their workplace all of the time. Advancements in IT have led to an increase in homeworking.
- A remote office can be created anywhere providing there is electricity and a phone point. If the laptop you are using has a battery pack, then all you need is a phone point!

The impact of the Internet

Although the technology for the Internet was pioneered in the 1960s, it is only recently that its impact on business organisations has been realised.

Essentially, businesses use the Internet in three ways:

- as an information source
- as a communications tool
- for e-commerce.

The Internet as an information source

David Storey in his book *Effective IT at Work* (1999) describes the power of the Internet as an information source: 'Acquiring and using information faster than the competition is one of the keys to business success. The Internet and the web enable you to acquire better information faster and also communicate it quicker, more effectively and inexpensively.'

The key is knowing what information you want from the Internet and knowing how to search intelligently for that information.

The Internet as a communications tool

Through e-mail, organisations can communicate locally, nationally and internationally with accuracy, reliability, ease and efficiency. Existing and potential customers can be reached at the touch of a button. This leads to obvious gains in speeding up the decision making process and allows organisations to keep up with the competition.

The Internet as e-commerce

Through e-commerce, the Internet offers organisations the facility of promoting and selling products and services to a worldwide audience.

Research recently undertaken by Verdict estimates that by 2004, £2.3 billion worth of groceries will be sold in the UK through the Internet. This compares with an estimated £165 million in 1999.

CASE STUDY: THE CHANGING WORLD OF WORK

During the past 20 years, a significant number of changes have taken place in the world of work. They include the following:

- *From* a reduction in the number of jobs in the primary and secondary industrial sectors *to* a huge increase in jobs created in the services sector. More recently, there has also been a significant increase in the numbers of call-centre jobs and order, collection, distribution and delivery jobs in response to the growth in online shopping.
- *From* markets predominantly made up of local and national customers *to* an increase in competition through the global market place.
- *From* organisations with tall hierarchical structures *to* leaner, flatter, delayered organisations.
- *From* an environment where managers think and workers do *to* a growth in empowerment and staff having a greater involvement in the decision making process.
- *From* employees working at an office in a regular nine-to-five routine *to* an increase in flexible working practices and working from home.
- *From* the security of having a job for life *to* the insecurity of not knowing how long you may be employed by a particular organisation.
- *From* just enjoying one career in a working lifetime *to* enjoying the prospect of building up a portfolio of careers.

QUESTIONS FOR DISCUSSION

1 To what extent do you think that IT has enabled the above changes to take place?
2 How will the above changes impact on you when you are applying for your first job?
3 How important do you think that the Internet is to business organisations? Explain your answer using examples.
4 How do you think the future of IT will shape business thinking?

The truth is stranger than fiction

'Ducati became the first manufacturer to launch a new bike on the Internet and sold all 500 of this year's limited-edition MH900e within hours. In the process, the firm rang up the biggest Internet sales in Italian history. The bike went on sale at 00.01 GMT on January 1 through Ducati's official website ... Initially, the firm planned to build just 1000 of the bikes – 500 this year and 500 in 2001. But since all this year's bikes have been sold and many more have been reserved the firm is considering extending production over further years, but sticking to 500 a year.' (Motor Cycle News, 12 January 2000)

Why not visit Ducati's website to see the bike for yourself? It's at www.ducati.com

SPECIMEN EXAM PAPERS

The following pages contain mock exam papers for Units 1, 2 and 3. The time allowed for each of the papers is as follows.

Unit 1: 1 hour 15 minutes
Unit 2: 1 hour 30 minutes
Unit 3: 1 hour 15 minutes.

When you do the real exams, you will be given an Answer Book which contains boxes in which you will write your answers.

Business Structures, Objectives and External Influences

Specimen Paper Unit 1

Answer all the questions

1 Southern Foods plc is a large company with interests in food processing and the retail trade. Its directors are devising a new mission statement based on a draft submitted by the company's managing director. In its current mission statement the company seeks 'honourably to serve the needs of the community by providing products and services of superior quality at a fair price to all our customers.' The draft of the new mission statement includes references to environmental concerns and to stakeholders other than customers.

(a) Explain what is meant by a mission statement. **2 marks**

(b) Suggest reasons why the directors might be considering a reference to environmental concerns in its revised mission statement. **5 marks**

(c) Suggest and justify amendments to the mission statement which might refer to a stakeholder other than a customer. **9 marks**

(d) Suggest problems of motivation which might arise for assembly line workers employed in the food processing division of this firm. Evaluate methods of maintaining and improving motivation. **10 marks**
Total 26 marks

2 A manufacturer discovers that the demand for its well-known chocolate bar varies with price as shown in the schedule below:

Price in pence	Quantity demanded in million bars per year
35	50
34	52
33	54
32	56
31	58
30	60
29	62
28	64
27	66
26	68
25	70

(a) Calculate and comment upon the price-elasticity of demand when price rises from 30p to 32p. **2 marks**

(b) Assess the possible effects on the firm of a rise in the price of a product which is a close substitute, and evaluate the responses which the firm might make. **9 marks**

(c) Assess the possible effects on the firm of a sharp rise in consumers' disposable income. **6 marks**

(d) Analyse the effects upon this firm of a vigorous 'healthy eating' campaign by the government and evaluate possible responses the firm might make. **11 marks**
Total 28 marks

3 Fizzydrinks plc produces a range of six soft drinks at five different plants throughout the U.K. Two of the products are well-established; the other four have been introduced within the last four years. Two of these new products have produced disappointing results. The Marketing Manager has complained to the Managing Director that the Operations Department, one of whose departments is Research and Development, has not responded to a series of memos outlining consumer dissatisfaction with these products. The Operations Manager has responded that his department is fully stretched trying to co-ordinate production on five different sites.

The board of directors has commissioned a firm of management consultants to advise them on the possible restructuring of the organisation of the company. The preliminary report of the management consultants stated that the span of control seems too narrow.

Here is the current organisational chart of Fizzydrinks plc.

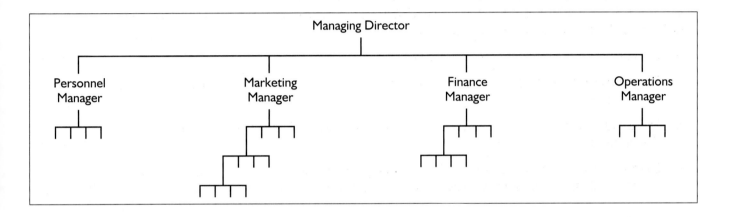

(a) Analyse the problems, resulting from a narrow span of control, which could be created for large-scale manufacturing firms like Fizzydrinks.   **8 marks**

(b) State possible reasons why there is conflict between the Marketing Manager and the Operations Manager and evaluate possible solutions to this problem.   **10 marks**

(c) Discuss alternative structures which a firm producing a range of soft drinks on several sites might introduce, and recommend what you consider to be the most appropriate structure.   **8 marks**

Total 26 marks

Marketing and Production

Specimen Paper Unit 2

Answer all the questions

Harry Ramsden's plc is no mere fish and chip shop. There are 36 restaurants where fresh fish is served in an atmosphere created with glass chandeliers and by smartly dressed staff. The chain has created a distinct theme. More outlets have been franchised for overseas operations as far afield as Australia, Hong Kong and Saudi Arabia. Harry Ramsden's has become an international brand name.

However, losses of £1.9 million in 1998–1999 have forced management to re-think the marketing strategy. The firm, established over 50 years ago, is now operating in an industry where themed restaurants such as Planet Hollywood and Hard Rock Café are common and the competition is getting fiercer. Despite the growth in the market (see Table 1) Harry Ramsden's has failed to maintain its market share. Chairman John Barnes has been quoted as believing the future is in the opening of small scale restaurants rather than the large 200 seater establishments favoured in the past.

Table I

	UK expenditure of eating out £ billion	Fast food sales
1997	22.6	6.0
1998	23.6	6.4
2004 forecast	31.0	8.4

Producing the right meal at the right time in the right place is a critical factor in achieving success in fast food chains. With the rising costs of raw materials, their short shelf life and the pattern of daily and weekly sales, batch production is the preferred method. The development of a large number of small scale units to be supplied by the logistics section of Harry Ramsden's will mean a sophisticated stock control system, particularly as costs per meal are likely to rise.

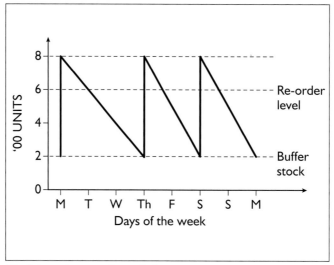

Model stock control graph for small unit restaurant
Source: Adapted from the *Financial Mail on Sunday*

Answer all the questions

1 Assess TWO benefits a franchise operator receives from using the brand name of Harry Ramsden's. **16 marks**

2 Assess the ways in which an understanding of price elasticity of demand could determine the pricing policy of Harry Ramsden's for both takeaway food and restaurant meals. **20 marks**

3 Suggest TWO promotional techniques Harry Ramsden's could use to create awareness of the new outlets. Analyse the factors which will determine the success of these techniques. **20 marks**

4 Using the stock control graph shown state:

    (a) (i)   the re-order quantity; **2 marks**

        (ii) the weekly usage quantity; **2 marks**

        (iii) the number of orders each week. **2 marks**

    (b) Evaluate the factors which would influence Harry Ramsden's when deciding upon the buffer stock level and the reorder quantity. **20 marks**

5 Assess why the average cost of a meal might be higher at one of Harry Ramsden's smaller restaurants and lower in a larger restaurant. **18 marks**

6 Evaluate the case for and against adopting a Just In Time approach to stock holding in the fast food industry. **20 marks**

Total 120 marks

Financial Management

Specimen Paper Unit 3

Answer all the questions

1 (a) Courtmills Ltd makes sports clothing. One product line is sports sweaters, which it sells to retailers at £20 each. The firm's projected output is 80 000 units a year although it has the capacity to make 100 000. The figures below show the relevant costs for the sweaters.

Overhead costs	£300 000
Labour cost/unit	£2
Material cost/unit	£8
Other variable costs	£2

Showing your working in full calculate:

(i) the contribution of each sweater sold **2 marks**

(ii) the break even level of output in respect of quantity and revenue **4 marks**

(iii) the margin of safety at the proposed level of output **2 marks**

(iv) the standard cost of each sweater at the proposed level of output **4 marks**

(b) Courtmills Ltd has been approached by a high street retail chain with an order for 20 000 sweaters at £13 each. The sweaters would be produced under an own brand label and would require the purchase of a new machine costing £20 000.

Assessing the numerical and non-numerical factors together, what advice would you give to Courtmills Limited in accepting or rejecting the order? **20 marks**

(c) Below is an extract from the profit and loss account and balance sheet of Courtmills Ltd for 1998. Some items have not been calculated yet.

	£ million		£ million
Sales revenue	1.4	Fixed assets	2.5
Cost of sales	0.58	Current assets	0.7
Gross profit		Less current liabilities	0.3
Less expenses	0.65	Net assets	
Net profit		Long term liabilities	1.6
		Shareholders funds	1.3
		Capital employed	

Showing your workings in full, calculate the:

(i) gross profit margin; **2 marks**

(ii) net profit margin; **2 marks**

(iii) return on capital employed. **2 marks**

(d) Calculate and comment on the firm's:

    (i) current ratio;   **4 marks**

    (ii) gearing ratio.   **4 marks**

                       Total 46 marks

2 (a) Hilights Ltd makes soft toys for a number of chain stores. The most expensive pieces of production equipment are the two cutting and sewing machines that are computer aided. Each machine costs £70 000 and is expected to have a working life of five years. The company accountant expects to sell the machines at the end of their useful lives for about £3 500 each.

    Assess how the use of an alternative method of depreciation would affect the company's reported profits.   **12 marks**

(b) In August the company accountant prepares a cash flow forecast. Most sales are on credit terms. The chart below shows a summary of the cash flow for Hilights Ltd.

Month	Sept £000	Oct £000	Nov £000	Dec £000	Jan £000	Feb £000	Mar £000	Apr £000
Opening balance	10	(21)	(96)	(252)	(335)			
Sales receipts	18	15	37	92	225	178	24	20
Expenses:								
Purchases	14	20	45	50	8	8	8	10
Wages	15	45	120	90	17	12	18	17
Overheads	20	25	28	35	25	20	20	20
Balance	(21)	(96)	(252)	(335)				

    (i) Use the information above to calculate the projected cash balance of Hilights Limited at the end of January and February.   **2 marks**

    (ii) Evaluate the ways in which a business such as Hilights Limited could overcome its cash flow problems.   **20 marks**

                       Total 34 marks

INDEX